NOTRE DAME FOOTBALL A–Z

Joe Layden

TAYLOR PUBLISHING COMPANY · DALLAS, TEXAS

Published by Taylor Publishing Company, 1550 West Mockingbird Lane, Dallas, Texas 75235.

Library of Congress Cataloging-in-Publication Data
Layden, Joseph, 1959–
    Notre Dame football A-Z / by Joe Layden.
            p. cm.
    ISBN 0–87833–966–3 (pb)
    1. Notre Dame Fighting Irish (Football team) = Encyclopedias. 2. University of Notre
Dame — Football — Encylopedias. I. Title.
GV958.N6L386   1997
796.332'63'0977289 — dc21   97–24660
    CIP

Designed by Mark McGarry
Set in Monotype Dante & Syntax

Published in the United States of America.

10 9 8 7 6 5 4 3 2 1

*For my brother, who once had
the luxury of being a fan*

CONTENTS

PREFACE

It has often been said that no one is neutral on the subject of Notre Dame football. The Fighting Irish, after all, are one of the most visible athletic teams on the planet—and one of the most influential. No school has won more national championships (eight); no school has produced more Heisman Trophy winners (seven); and no school provokes such passion among its followers, such venom among its critics. Love them or hate them, there is no denying the impact of the Fighting Irish.

The phenomenal rise of Notre Dame football can be traced back to November 23, 1887, when the team played its first game against a group of students from the University of Michigan. The Fighting Irish (although that was not yet their nickname) lost that game by a score of 8-0. It would be five months before they scored their first touchdown (in a springtime rematch with the Wolverines), nearly a year before they won their first game, and 37 years before they captured their first national title.

By that time the school had secured the services of a coach named Knute Rockne, an ambitious, competitive man with a keen football mind and a shrewd sense of promotion. Rockne recruited great football players and built Notre Dame into a national power in the 1920s; he was also instrumental in selling the program to fans well beyond the boundaries of South Bend.

Rockne was a great believer in tradition. He understood the benefit of embracing legends, myths, and other half-truths that could inspire players and fans alike. In *Shake Down the Thunder: The Creation of Notre Dame Football*, author Murray Sperber quotes Rockne as writing, "The history or traditions of the school are a great thing to recite to your team, and to keep before them. Exaggerate these as much as you can."

In time, of course, there was no need to exaggerate. Rockne himself became a mythic figure. As did George Gipp, Frank Leahy, Elmer Layden, and other players and coaches of the 1920s, 1930s, and 1940s.

Today, Notre Dame proudly displays a tradition of success unmatched in college football. Rockne's teams, led by the famous Four Horsemen, lost only 12 games in 13 seasons. Leahy's teams won four national titles in the 1940s. Ara Parseghian won championships in 1966 and 1973, Dan Devine in 1977, and Lou Holtz in 1988. The program has produced 29 unanimous first-team All-Americans and 77 consensus All-Americans. Some of the greatest athletes in college football history have played the majority of their games on the famed bluegrass of Notre Dame Stadium: John Lujack, Leon Hart, Paul Hornung, Joe Theismann, Joe Montana, Tim Brown—just to name a few.

Because of this legacy, Notre Dame continues to attract the finest scholastic football talent in the country. And its fan base continues to swell. The fact that Notre Dame has sold out all but one home game in the past 32 years tells only part of the story. The Fighting Irish enjoy extraordinary national—and even international—influence and popularity. This, after all, is the only college football program with a private network television contract: In 1990 NBC paid $30 million for the privilege of broadcasting Notre Dame home games to the rest of the world. The five-year contract has since been extended through the year 2000.

It was with this vast audience in mind that *Notre Dame Football A–Z* was created. Designed for the sports fan in general and the Fighting Irish fan in particular, *Notre Dame Football A–Z* is a comprehensive guide to college football's most famous team. It includes not only biographical sketches of players and coaches but also statistics, prominent awards, memorable games, amusing anecdotes, and assorted bits of trivia.

More than 450 entries, ranging from 50 to 1,000 words, have been assembled in alphabetical order. Although the list is undeniably arbitrary, an effort was made to include relevant historical and statistical data as well as information on the most accomplished athletes and interesting personalities. To that end, *Notre Dame Football A–Z* obviously features individual entries on all of the program's Heisman Trophy winners, consensus All-Americans, and career statistical leaders; and yet, room was also made for some players of only modest ability, such as Daniel Ruettiger, whose life story became the basis for the film *Rudy*.

Each player entry includes a heading with the athlete's name, his position and years on the Notre Dame varsity, his height and weight, and his hometown.

In many cases, career statistics are included at the end of the player's entry (each head coach entry includes the coach's career record). In all entries, accomplishments at Notre Dame are emphasized. So, although a biographical sketch may include information on a person's life both before and after he represented the Fighting Irish, the term "career statistics" refers only to his playing or coaching career at the University of Notre Dame.

ACADEMICS

In 1993, when the NCAA published graduation rates for football players at schools with Division I-A programs, Notre Dame was at the top of the list. Degrees were earned by 98 percent of the scholarship athletes who remained at the institution at least four years.

Notre Dame has won the College Football Association's Academic Achievement award five times since 1980. It has produced 35 first-team Academic All-Americans, including three—quarterback Joe Theismann (Class of 1970), tight end Dave Casper ('73), and kicker Bob Thomas ('73)—who have been inducted into the GTE Academic All-America Hall of Fame.

Notre Dame's First-Team Academic All-Americans

YEAR	NAME	POSITION
1952	Joe Heap	HB
1953	Joe Heap	HB
1954	Joe Heap	HB
1955	Don Schaefer	FB
1958	Bob Wetoska	E
1963	Bob Lehman	OG
1966	Tom Regner	OG
1966	Jim Lynch	LB
1967	Jim Smithberger	DB
1968	George Kunz	OT
1969	Jim Reilly	OT
1970	Joe Theismann	QB
1970	Larry DiNardo	OG
1970	Tom Gatewood	SE
1971	Tom Gatewood	SE
1971	Greg Marx	DT
1972	Greg Marx	DT

1972	Mike Creaney	TE
1973	Dave Casper	TE
1973	Bob Thomas	K
1973	Gary Potempa	LB
1974	Pete Demmerle	SE
1974	Reggie Barnett	CB
1977	Ken MacAfee	TE
1977	Dave Vinson	OG
1977	Joe Restic	FS
1978	Joe Restic	FS
1980	Bob Burger	OG
1980	Tom Gibbons	FS
1981	John Krimm	CB
1985	Greg Dingens	DT
1987	Vince Phelan	P
1987	Ted Gradel	K
1992	Tim Ruddy	C
1993	Tim Ruddy	C

ADAMS, JOHN
Tackle (1942-44) ▪ 6-7, 218 ▪ Charleston, AR

Although there would be nothing terribly unusual about a player of his size in major college football today, John "Tree" Adams was considered a giant in the 1940s. One of 10 children, he was born in Charleston, Arkansas. Until his tenth birthday, he once explained, he was no bigger than the rest of the kids in his neighborhood. "But from 10 until 15, I just shot up like a tree," he said.

Adams played football and basketball at Subiaco Academy, 35 miles from his hometown. He was a two-time all-state tackle in football and an all-state center on the basketball team. He was steered toward South Bend by Reverend George Strassner, a Notre Dame alumnus who taught at Subiaco Academy.

Although Adams is officially listed at 6-7, 218 pounds in Notre Dame media guides, newspaper feature stories of the time frequently reported his height to be closer to 6-8 and his weight to be as high as 250 pounds. He was a bit slow and clumsy when he first arrived on campus, and he was so big that the equipment manager could not find a helmet that would fit him (eventually, the problem was overcome by stitching two helmets together). Adams's sheer size, however, dictated that he receive at least some playing time.

A reserve in 1942, he earned his first monogram as a backup to Ziggy Czarobski on the 1943 national championship team and started at right tackle in 1944. Unlike many of his teammates at the time, Adams did not serve in the military during World War II; he was deemed ineligible because of his size.

The Washington Redskins chose Adams in the second round of the NFL Draft in 1945. He spent his entire professional career—six seasons—with the Redskins.

ADAMSON, KEN

Guard (1957-59) ▪ 6-2, 205 ▪ Atlanta, GA

A prep All-American at Marist High School in Atlanta, Georgia, Ken Adamson was an army brat who also spent time in Germany, Japan, and Arizona while growing up.

At Notre Dame he earned monograms in his sophomore and junior seasons while playing behind All-American guard Al Ecuyer. Adamson was more than just a reserve, though. He led all sophomores in tackles in 1957 with 11; in 1958 he was second among guards in minutes played and second on the team in tackles with 53.

After his junior year Adamson was elected team captain. A few months later, he captured the heavyweight championship at the Bengal Bouts (Notre Dame's on-campus amateur boxing tournament). In the fall of 1959 he had an outstanding year, finishing second on the team in tackles with 84.

After leaving Notre Dame, Adamson played three seasons of professional football with the Denver Broncos.

ALL-AMERICANS

In 1913 quarterback Gus Dorais became the first Notre Dame player to be named first-team All-America. Since that time Fighting Irish athletes have been similarly honored on 171 occasions. Through 1995 the university had also produced 77 consensus All-Americans—more than any other school. Players who receive the majority of votes at their respective positions are designated consensus All-Americans.

Over the years, many combinations of selecting organizations have been utilized in determining consensus All-Americans. Organizations currently used are the Associated Press, United Press International, *Football News*, *The Sporting News*, the Walter Camp Foundation, the Football Writers Association of America, and the American Football Coaches Association.

End Wayne Millner was named a consensus All-American in 1935. After six years with the Boston (and then Washington) Redskins, Millner returned to South Bend as an assistant coach under Frank Leahy.

Notre Dame's consensus All-Americans

PLAYER	POSITION	YEAR
Eddie Anderson	End	1921
Dick Arrington	Guard	1965
Ed Beinor	Tackle	1938
Angelo Bertelli	Quarterback	1943
Art Boeringer	Center	1926
Luther Bradley	Safety	1977
Tom Brown	Flanker	1987
Ross Browner	Defensive End	1976, 1977
Jeff Burris	Safety	1993
Jack Cannon	Guard	1929
Frank Carideo	Quarterback	1929, 1930
Dave Casper	Tight End	1973
George Connor	Tackle	1946, 1947
Bob Crable	Linebacker	1980, 1981
Jim Crowley	Halfback	1924
Pete Demmerle	Split End	1974
Gerry DiNardo	Guard	1974
Larry DiNardo	Guard	1970
Gus Dorais	Quarterback	1913
Bob Dove	End	1941, 1942
Al Ecuyer	Guard	1957
Nick Eddy	Halfback	1966
Clarence Ellis	Cornerback	1971
Vagas Ferguson	Halfback	1979
Pat Filley	Guard	1943
Bill Fischer	Tackle	1947, 1948
Tom Gatewood	Split End	1970
George Gipp	Halfback	1920
Bob Golic	Linebacker	1978
Jerry Groom	Center/Linebacker	1950
Ralph Guglielmi	Quarterback	1954
Terry Hanratty	Quarterback	1968
Leon Hart	End	1948, 1949
Paul Hornung	Quarterback	1955
John Huarte	Quarterback	1962, 1964
Dave Huffman	Center	1978
Art Hunter	Tackle	1953
Raghib Ismail	Flanker	1990
Mirko Jurkovic	Offensive Guard	1991
George Kunz	Offensive Tackle	1968
Joe Kurth	Tackle	1932
John Lattner	Halfback	1952, 1953
Elmer Layden	Fullback	1924
John Lujack	Quarterback	1946, 1947
Todd Lyght	Defensive Back	1989, 1990

Jim Lynch	Linebacker	1966
Ken MacAfee	Tight End	1976, 1977
Greg Marx	Defensive Tackle	1972
Mike McCoy	Defensive Tackle	1969
Creighton Miller	Halfback	1943
Wayne Millner	End	1935
Steve Niehaus	Defensive Tackle	1975
Alan Page	Defensive End	1966
Walt Patulski	Defensive End	1971
Nick Rassas	Defensive Back	1965
Tom Regner	Offensive Guard	1966
Jack Robinson	Center	1934
Frank Rydzewski	Center	1917
Tom Schoen	Defensive Back	1967
Marchy Schwartz	Halfback	1930, 1931
John Scully	Center	1980
Emil Sitko	Fullback	1948, 1949
John Smith	Guard	1927
Jack Snow	Split End	1964
Frank Stams	Defensive End	1988
Monty Stickles	End	1959
Michael Stonebreaker	Linebacker	1988, 1990
Harry Stuhldreher	Quarterback	1924
Chuck Sweeney	End	1937
Aaron Taylor	Offensive Tackle	1992, 1993
Bobby Taylor	Defensive Back	1994
Mike Townsend	Defensive Back	1973
Jim White	Tackle	1943
Bob Williams	Quarterback	1949
Tommy Yarr	Center	1931
John Yonaker	End	1943
Chris Zorich	Nose Tackle	1989, 1990

ALM, JEFF

Defensive Tackle (1986-89) ▪ 6-7, 270 ▪ Orland Park, IL

Although he earned four monograms, it wasn't until his junior year that Jeff Alm broke into the starting lineup. At 6-7, 270 pounds, he was strong enough to be effective against the run, and tall enough to snatch passes out of the air, which, of course, made life miserable for opposing quarterbacks. For example, with his three interceptions in 1988 he became the first defensive lineman since Bernie Crimmins in 1941 to lead the team in that category.

In 1989 Alm was fourth on the team in tackles with 74; he also had one interception. He was named second-team All-America by the Associated Press, Football News and

Gannett News Service. A second-round draft pick in 1990, Alm spent four years in the NFL, all with the Houston Oilers.

ALMA MATER

The alma mater of the University of Notre Dame is "Notre Dame, Our Mother," written by Joseph J. Cassanta (Class of 1923). It was composed specifically to accompany dedication ceremonies for Notre Dame Stadium, which opened on October 11, 1930. The song is a longtime staple of the half-time show of the Band of the Fighting Irish; it is also sung at the end of each Notre Dame pep rally.

Here are the words to "Notre Dame, Our Mother":

> *Notre Dame, Our Mother*
> *Tender, strong, and true,*
> *Proudly in the heavens,*
> *Gleams the Gold and Blue.*
> *Glory's mantle cloaks thee,*
> *Golden is thy fame,*
> *And our hearts forever,*
> *Praise thee, Notre Dame.*
> *And our hearts forever,*
> *Love thee, Notre Dame.*

ANDERSON, EDDIE

End (1918-21) ▪ 5-10, 166 ▪ Mason City, IA

Eddie Anderson was a uniquely talented young man. A consensus All-American during his playing days at Notre Dame, he became one of the most successful coaches in college football history; as if that weren't enough, throughout his career he was also a practicing physician.

Anderson was born in Oskaloosa, Iowa, and went to high school in Mason City. He entered Notre Dame in the fall of 1918 as a 17-year-old, 150-pound freshman. Because of his frail appearance, Anderson was nearly overlooked by first-year coach Knute Rockne. But he had a strength that belied his stature. And he knew how to play football.

A four-year starter, Anderson added a few pounds each year. And each year he improved. He led the Irish with 17 catches for 293 yards and three touchdowns in 1920. In 1921, as a senior, he was named captain. Once again he was the team's leading receiver, this time with 26 catches for 394 yards and two touchdowns. After the season he received first-team All-America honors from *Football World* and second-team honors from the International News Service.

Anderson played professionally for the Rochester Jeffersons in 1922. He also played for the Chicago Cardinals and Chicago Bears before retiring in 1925. Remarkably, playing professional football was one of only three jobs Anderson held at that time. He also coached at Columbia College in Dubuque, Iowa, compiling a record of 16-6-2 in three seasons (1922-24). In 1925 he became head coach at DePaul University in Chicago, where, in seven seasons, his teams won 21 games, lost 22, and tied four. In his spare time Anderson also studied for a degree at Rush Medical College. He graduated in 1929 and began practicing medicine. For the next three decades he balanced the demands of two extraordinarily difficult careers.

In 1933 Anderson was hired by Holy Cross in Worcester, Massachusetts. His record over six seasons was 47-7-4. Holy Cross became a program of national prominence under Anderson, posting undefeated seasons in 1935 and 1937. In 1939 he returned home to accept the head coaching position at the University of Iowa. Anderson inherited a program that had won just a single game the previous season and only 22 games in the previous nine seasons; and yet, in 1939 the Hawkeyes finished second in the Big Ten with a 6-1-1 record, defeating, among others, Notre Dame. The star of that Iowa team was Heisman Trophy-winner Nile Kinnick.

In eight seasons at Iowa, Anderson compiled a record of 35-33-2. His tenure there was interrupted from 1943 through 1945 while he served in the U.S. Army Medical Corps. In 1950 Holy Cross lured Anderson back to Worcester. He remained there until his retirement in 1964. In his 20 years at Holy Cross, the team had just three losing seasons.

Anderson's career record was 201-128-15, a winning percentage of .606. The sixth coach in college football history to win 200 games, he was inducted into the College Football Hall of Fame in 1971. He died in 1976.

ANDERSON, HEARTLY
Guard (1918-21) ▪ Head Coach (1931-33) ▪ 5-11, 170 ▪ Hancock, MI

Heartly "Hunk" Anderson followed high school buddy George Gipp to Notre Dame in 1918. And although his career was not as spectacular as Gipp's and his life not as tragic, he did leave his mark on the school.

Anderson weighed only 168 pounds when he arrived in South Bend; nevertheless, he was named the starting left guard by first-year head coach Knute Rockne. He held that job for the next four seasons, until his graduation in the spring of 1922. After his senior season he received first-team All-America honors from the International News Service and *Football World*.

Anderson played with the Chicago Bears from 1922 through 1925. Professional football was not serious work in those days, however, and even while he was playing, Anderson prepared for a career as a coach. He served as Rockne's assistant from 1922 through 1926 and was head coach at St. Louis University for two years before returning to Notre Dame as an assistant in 1930. After Rockne was killed in a plane crash in 1931, Anderson took over as head coach.

Heartly "Hunk" Anderson was a four-year starter at left guard under Knute Rockne. He took over the head coaching position at Notre Dame after Rockne's tragic death in 1931.

As a head coach, Anderson tried to model himself after Rockne. He stressed fundamentals above all else and believed in thorough preparation. In dealing with players he was firm but accessible. He had success as a coach but nothing like the success he knew as a player. His first team, in 1931, was unbeaten in its first seven games but lost its last two games (to USC and Army) to finish at 6-2-1. In 1932 the Irish went 7-2, and in 1933 they fell to 3-5-1. The following year Anderson was replaced by another former Notre Dame All-American, Elmer Layden, who became head coach and athletic director.

Anderson quickly landed a job as head coach at the University of North Carolina, where he stayed until 1937. He was an assistant coach at the University of Michigan in 1937 and at Cincinnati University in 1938. In 1939 he was named head coach of the Detroit Lions, and in 1940 he joined the Chicago Bears as line coach, a position he held for 11 years. Anderson retired from coaching in 1951 and took a job as an account executive with the Production Steel Company in Detroit.

ANGSMAN, ELMER
Halfback/Fullback (1943-45) ▪ 6-0, 185 ▪ Chicago, IL

A reserve halfback on Notre Dame's 1943 national championship team, Elmer Angsman became the starting fullback in 1944. He carried the ball 58 times for 273 yards (third best on the team) and three touchdowns. In 1945, as a senior, Angsman was the team's top offensive player. He rushed for 616 yards on 87 carries (an average of seven yards per attempt) and also scored 42 points.

Despite those numbers Angsman was overlooked by every All-America team in 1945. He did, however, play in the College All-Star Game in January 1946. And he was a third-round draft choice of the Chicago Cardinals just a few months later. He played with the Cardinals from 1946 through 1952.

ARRINGTON, DICK

Tackle/Guard (1963-65) ▪ 5-11, 232 ▪ Erie, PA

One of Notre Dame's last great two-way players, Dick Arrington grew up in Erie, Pennsylvania. He was captain of the football and wrestling teams and a member of the varsity track team.

Upon arriving in South Bend, Arrington quickly made a name for himself. Like all first-year students, he settled for freshman competition in 1962. Then, as a sophomore, in the final season before the advent of two-platoon football, he stepped into a starting role. As the team's left tackle, he played 310 minutes and had 40 tackles.

In 1964 Arrington changed positions, from tackle to guard; despite playing only offense, he accumulated more than 300 minutes of field time. The next year, as a senior, he was the only Irish player who started on both sides of the ball. Not only did he play right offensive guard, but he also had 36 tackles as a defensive tackle. A consensus first-team All-American in 1965, Arrington was one of Notre Dame's finest all-around athletes in the 1960s. In addition to starring for the football team, he was captain of the wrestling team.

Despite his success as a collegian, Arrington was not drafted until the 18th round in 1965. He did not play in the NFL.

ATHLETIC DIRECTORS

Notre Dame's first director of athletics was Jesse Harper, who took the post in 1913, the same year in which he became the school's football coach. He served as athletic director until 1917 and again from 1931 through 1933, following the death of Knute Rockne.

Only nine people have held the title of athletic director at Notre Dame. Interestingly, each of the first five also served as the school's head football coach at one point in his career.

Gene Corrigan served as Notre Dame's athletic director from 1981-87.

Years	Name
1913-1917	Jesse Harper
1920-1930	Knute Rockne
1931-1933	Jesse Harper
1934-1940	Elmer Layden

NOTRE DAME FOOTBALL A–Z

1945	Hugh Devore
1947-48	Frank Leahy
1949-1981	Edward "Moose" Krause
1981-1987	Gene Corrigan
1987-1995	Dick Rosenthal
1995-present	Mike Wadsworth

B

BACHMAN, CHARLIE
Guard/Fullback (1914-16) ▪ 5-11, 187 ▪ Chicago, IL

A member of the College Football Hall of Fame, Charlie Bachman grew up in Chicago, where he attended Englewood High School, and entered Notre Dame in 1913; by his sophomore year he was the starting right guard on the Irish football team, playing alongside the likes of Knute Rockne, Gus Dorais, and Ray Eichenlaub.

In 1915, as a junior, Bachman switched to fullback, but as a senior he returned to the line. He received All-Western honors in 1916 and was named second-team All-America.

Although his playing career was noteworthy, it was as a coach that Bachman truly left his mark. His first job was at DePauw University, where he was an assistant in 1917. In 1918 he entered the Navy and played football for the Great Lakes service team, which won the U.S. championship. After being discharged in 1919, he accepted the position of head coach at Northwestern University, where, at the tender age of 24, he was known as "The Boy Coach of the Western Conference." He stayed at Northwestern for just one season, leading the Wildcats to a 4-7-1 record.

In 1920 Bachman became head coach at Kansas State. He remained there for eight seasons, compiling a record of 33-23-8, before moving on to the University of Florida in 1928. The Gators were the highest scoring team in the nation that year and swept rivals Georgia and Georgia Tech for the first time in the school's history.

Bachman stayed in Gainesville until 1933 (posting a record of 27-18-3), when he succeeded another Notre Dame alumnus, Jim Crowley, at Michigan State. In 13 seasons with the Spartans he compiled a record of 70-34-10. He resigned in 1946 and entered private business. In 1953, however, he returned to the sideline to coach tiny Hillsdale College in Hillsdale, Michigan.

In addition to his playing and coaching accomplishments, Bachman authored several books on football and became a designer of athletic equipment and apparel.

He was inducted into the College Football Hall of Fame in 1978.

BAGARUS, STEVE
Halfback (1939-40) ▪ 5-11, 160 ▪ South Bend, IN

Born in South Bend on June 19, 1919, Steve Bagarus was a three-sport star at Washington High School. An all-city selection in 1937, he was the only South Bend player named to the Indiana all-state team that year. He also led Washington to a state championship.

Bagarus actually attended Notre Dame on a basketball scholarship and played two seasons for coach George Keogan. He also made the football team as a walk-on. Under coach Elmer Layden, he won his first monogram in 1939 as a third-string halfback. He carried the ball 47 times for 147 yards and caught four passes for 69 yards. He also intercepted three passes as a defensive back.

The next year Bagarus split time at right halfback with Steve Juzwik. His most memorable achievement occurred in the season opener against Army. Before a crowd of more than 75,000 at Yankee Stadium, Bagarus intercepted a pass and ran it back for a touchdown to give the Fighting Irish a 7-0 victory.

Bagarus left school in 1941 when he was drafted into the U.S. Army. Stationed at Camp Callan in San Diego, California, he became the base's premier athlete, playing on championship teams in basketball, baseball, and football. It was during a service all-star game in 1942 that Bagarus caught the attention of Washington Redskins owner George Preston Marshall. Bagarus signed a contract with the Redskins and played two games for the team while on furlough; in 1944, after receiving his discharge from the service, he joined the Redskins full time. In 1945 he was named All-Pro and helped lead the Redskins to the NFL championship with a 28-21 victory over the Chicago Bears.

Bagarus left the Redskins in 1947 and signed with the Los Angeles Rams. He was injured in the second game of the season, though, and his career soon came to an end. A member of the Indiana Football Hall of Fame, Bagarus died in 1981.

BANAS, STEVE
Fullback (1931-33) ▪ 5-11, 185 ▪ East Chicago, IN

Steve Banas was born in Bridgetown, Connecticut, spent several years in Europe as a child, and attended high school in East Chicago, Indiana, where he starred for Catholic Central. An all-state selection in football in his senior year, Banas was a versatile athlete who also played basketball and baseball.

At Notre Dame, Banas earned his first monogram as a sophomore in 1931, as a third-string fullback. He never really owned the fullback position, but he was a consistent contributor during his three years on the varsity. Among his career highlights was a 50-yard touchdown pass to Hugh Devore during a 21-0 victory over Army in 1932.

Banas remained at Notre Dame as an assistant coach after graduating in 1934 and played briefly with the Philadelphia Eagles and Detroit Lions. He later became head coach at St. Mary's College.

BAND OF THE FIGHTING IRISH

As long as there has been football at Notre Dame, there has been a marching band. In fact, the band was actually formed in 1845, some four decades before the Fighting Irish played their first football game. Never has the team taken the field without accompaniment from The Band of the Fighting Irish.

It is the oldest college band in the country and was one of the first to incorporate precision drill marching and picture formations during its performances. The Band of the Fighting Irish, like the school itself, has only recently become a coeducational group. The first women—from nearby St. Mary's College—joined the band in 1970, two years before the university began accepting female students. Four years later, in 1976, the National Music Council declared The Band of the Fighting Irish a "landmark of American music."

Since 1987 the band has been directed by Luther Snavely, who came to Notre Dame from the University of Mississippi.

BANKS, ROBERT
Defensive Tackle/Linebacker (1983-86) ▪ 6-5, 246 ▪ Hampton, VA

Robert Banks became a starter at outside linebacker in his sophomore year and was the team's second-leading tackler with 68. He had 50 tackles the following year but was asked to make the switch to defensive tackle as a senior in 1986 after the graduation of Eric Dorsey. Banks accepted the challenge graciously. And if there were any doubts about his ability to adapt to the new position, they were quickly laid to rest: He had 13 tackles in the season opener against Michigan.

Banks missed two games because of a knee injury but still finished the season with 57 tackles. He played professionally with the Houston Oilers (1988, 1991) and Cleveland Browns (1989-90).

BARNETT, REGGIE
Defensive Back (1972-74) ▪ 5-11, 181 ▪ Flint, MI

Reggie Barnett started at left cornerback in 1973, the year the Fighting Irish won their last national championship under Ara Parseghian. He had 29 tackles and two interceptions, including one in a 24-23 victory over Alabama in the Sugar Bowl. He also broke up six passes.

As a senior Barnett had 37 tackles and one interception. Most impressive of all, he was named first-team Academic All-America. He was drafted by the San Diego Chargers in the 14th round of the 1975 NFL Draft.

Barnett had a strong college career, although not quite as strong as one might have expected based on his high school performance. He earned All-America honors while leading Flint High School to a state championship in 1970 and was named all-state in both football and track (he ran 9.8 seconds for the 100-yard dash).

BARRY, NORMAN
Halfback (1917-20) ▪ 5-10, 170 ▪ Chicago, IL

In 1920 Norman Barry started alongside George Gipp in Notre Dame's backfield and helped lead the Irish to a 9-0 record. He went on to play professionally for the Green Bay Packers and Chicago Cardinals. He later coached DeLaSalle High School to the Chicago city championship. But the highlight of his career came in 1925 when he guided the Cardinals to the NFL championship and was named coach of the year.

Barry later became a practicing attorney and successful politician. He was elected to the Illinois state senate in 1942 and served 10 years before becoming a Cook County circuit judge. He retired in 1978 and returned to private practice. In 1988, just a month before his death, he attended the dedication of the Norman Barry Courtroom at the Notre Dame School of Law.

A member of the Chicago Sports Hall of Fame and the Chicago Catholic League Hall of Fame, Barry received the Distinguished American Award from the National Football Foundation in 1988.

BAUJAN, HARRY
End (1913-16) ▪ 5-8, 167 ▪ Beardstown, IL

A three-year starter on teams coached by Jesse Harper, Harry Baujan began his affiliation with Notre Dame as a teenager. He attended Notre Dame Prep from 1910 through 1913 and then enrolled at the university where he made the football team as a reserve in his freshman year.

At that time the starting left end, and captain of the team, was Knute Rockne. The following year Rockne became an assistant coach, and Baujan began seeing substantial playing time as an end. He started at right end in 1915 and at left end in 1916. Three times he received All-Western and All-Indiana honors.

After graduation Baujan joined the U.S. Army and served in World War I. He played professional football with the Cleveland Indians in 1920 and 1921. In 1922 his playing career came to an end and he accepted a position as an assistant football coach at the University of Dayton. He became head coach in 1923 and athletic director in 1928; he held the latter position for more than 35 years.

Harry Baujan died in 1976 at the age of 86. He was inducted into the College Football Hall of Fame in 1990.

BAVARO, MARK

Tight End (1981-84) ▪ 6-4, 242 ▪ Danvers, MA

Mark Bavaro's greatest fame came as an All-Pro tight end for the Super Bowl champion New York Giants in 1986. But he was also an excellent college football player.

The son of Anthony Bavaro, who played for the San Francisco 49ers in 1960, Mark was a prep All-American at Danvers (Massachusetts) High School. Injuries limited him to a grand total of 3 minutes, 32 seconds in his first two years at Notre Dame; however, in 1983 he succeeded Tony Hunter as the starting tight end and was third on the team in receptions with 23. He also led the Irish with three touchdown receptions. One of his best performances came in a 19-18 Liberty Bowl victory over Boston College in which he led all receivers with five catches for 52 yards.

In 1984 Bavaro had a team-high 32 receptions (for 395 yards and one touchdown) and was named first-team All-America by the Associated Press. A fourth-round NFL draft pick, he played with the Giants (1985-90), Cleveland Browns (1992), and Philadelphia Eagles (1993-94).

After a successful career with the Fighting Irish, Mark Bavaro went on to a nine-year professional career that included a Super Bowl win with the Giants.

BEAMS, BYRON

Tackle (1954-55) ▪ 6-4, 200 ▪ Ada, OK

Byron Beams played for the Fighting Irish in 1954 and 1955 but failed to earn a monogram in either season. A four-sport star at Ada High School in Oklahoma, his college career was interrupted on several occasions by injuries. Nevertheless, Beams was drafted by the Los Angeles Rams in 1957. He played with the Pittsburgh Steelers for two seasons and the Houston Oilers for one season.

BECKER, DOUG
Linebacker (1974-77) ▪ 6-0, 223 ▪ Hamilton, OH

A three-year starter at outside linebacker, Doug Becker was a key member of Notre Dame's 1977 national championship team. He was fifth on the team in tackles with 91 and forced a fumble that led to a touchdown in a 38-10 upset of previously unbeaten Texas in the Cotton Bowl.

Becker earned a monogram in his freshman year after an outstanding career at Badin High School in Hamilton, Ohio. He had 72 tackles in 1975, his first year as a starter, and 89 in 1976. Two of Becker's better performances that season came against Michigan State (six solo tackles) and Georgia Tech (seven solo tackles). In the spring of 1977 he was named Hering Award-winner as the team's outstanding linebacker. He also won the heavyweight division of the university's Bengal Bout boxing tournament, defeating teammate Jim Browner in the final.

The Pittsburgh Steelers drafted Becker in the tenth round in 1978. He played for the Chicago Bears and Buffalo Bills in an NFL career that lasted just one season.

BECTON, LEE
Tailback (1991-94) ▪ 6-0, 191 ▪ Ernul, NC

Lee Becton, one of Notre Dame's all-time rushing leaders, grew up in Ernul, North Carolina. He was a sensational all-around athlete in high school, earning four varsity letters in track and basketball and three letters in football. It was in the latter sport,

One of Notre Dame's all-time rushing leaders, Lee Becton was a member of the "Killer Bee" backfield of the early '90s that also included Jeff Burris, Reggie Brooks, and Jerome Bettis.

however, that he truly excelled. Becton rushed for an astounding 2,011 yards and 32 touchdowns as a senior at West Craven High School. He finished his prep career with 87 touchdowns and more than 5,000 yards rushing. As if that weren't enough, he was also president of his senior class.

As with so many high school superstars, though, Becton needed time to adjust to the academic and athletic rigors of Notre Dame. He played in only five games as a freshman, carrying the ball 15 times for a grand total of 62 yards. The next year he was the team's top reserve at tailback, backing up senior Reggie Brooks. He played in 11 games and became a valuable part of Notre Dame's "Killer Bee" backfield, which included Brooks, Jerome Bettis, and Jeff Burris.

With Brooks lost to graduation, Becton moved into the Irish starting lineup in the fall of 1993. And he wasted little time in proving himself worthy of the promotion, picking up 72 yards on 16 carries in the season opener against

Northwestern. Becton missed the fourth game of the season, a 17-0 victory over Purdue, and carried only six times the following week against Stanford. For the rest of the season, though, he was nearly unstoppable. He rushed for 142 yards against Pittsburgh and 177 yards against USC. By the end of the year he had accumulated 1,044 yards on 164 carries, a feat that placed him in pretty fast company—only four other players in Notre Dame history had broken 1,000 yards rushing in a single season. And no one had ever rushed for more than 100 yards in six consecutive games, as Becton did. He finished the year in fine style, rushing for 138 yards on 26 carries to lead the Fighting Irish to a 24-21 Cotton Bowl victory over Texas A&M; fittingly, he was named the game's Outstanding Offensive Player. After the season Becton was a finalist for the Doak Walker Award and was named honorable mention All-America by United Press International and *Football News*. The Irish finished the season with an 11-1 record and were ranked second in the Associated Press final poll.

Expectations were high for Becton's senior year—*Street & Smith's* named him a pre-season All-American—but injuries prevented him from fulfilling his promise. He pulled his groin muscle in the third game of the year and was sidelined for the better part of five weeks. During that time Becton played only one game—against BYU—and carried the ball just five times. Finally, on November 19, he returned to the starting lineup and led Notre Dame to a 42-30 victory over Air Force. He finished the regular season with a 156-yard performance against USC.

Becton gained 2,029 yards in his career, ninth among Notre Dame's all-time rushing leaders. Passed up in the 1995 NFL Draft, he later signed as a free agent with the Green Bay Packers.

Career Statistics

YEAR	ATT.	YARDS	AVG.	TD
1991	15	62	4.1	0
1992	68	373	5.5	3
1993	164	1,044	6.4	6
1994	100	550	5.5	3
TOTAL	347	2,029	5.8	12

BEINOR, ED
Tackle (1936-38) ▪ 6-2, 207 ▪ Harvey, IL

Two-time All-American Joseph Edward "Beefy" Beinor was one of the most celebrated linemen to come out of Notre Dame in the 1930s. A big, spirited player, he earned his first monogram in 1936 as a second-string tackle behind Bill Steinkemper. In 1937 he started at left tackle and received first-team All-America honors from the Newspaper Enterprise Association and *Newsweek*. The following year, as a senior, he was one of the most decorated collegiate players in the nation. After leading the Irish to an 8-1 record, Beinor was a first-team selection on every major All-America team. He played in the College All-Star Game in 1939.

Beinor was drafted by the Brooklyn Dodgers in 1939 but did not begin his professional career until 1940, when he joined the Chicago Cardinals. He was obtained on waivers by the Washington Redskins late in the 1941 season and retired in 1942 when he entered the U.S. Marine Corps.

In addition to football, Beinor also competed in track and field. As a member of the Lithuanian-American team at the 1938 Lithuanian Olympics, he finished first in the shot put.

BELDEN, BOB
Quarterback (1966-68) ▪ 6-2, 205 ▪ Canton, OH

Bob Belden attempted just 14 passes during his three years on the Notre Dame varsity. He completed eight for a total of 137 yards. Hardly impressive numbers. And yet, unlike many other college quarterbacks with far more extensive experience, Belden found his way to the NFL.

After failing to earn a monogram in his sophomore and junior years, Belden became a third-string quarterback behind Terry Hanratty and Joe Theismann in 1968. He completed all three of the passes he attempted, earned a varsity letter, and so impressed professional scouts that he was drafted by the Dallas Cowboys in the twelfth round in 1969. He spent two seasons with the team.

BELL, GREG
Running Back (1980-83) ▪ 6-0, 210 ▪ Columbus, OH

Injuries limited Greg Bell to just one full season on the Notre Dame varsity, but in that season he offered a glimpse of the form that would carry him through eight NFL seasons.

Bell joined the Fighting Irish in 1980 after starring in basketball, football, and track at South High School in Columbus, Ohio. As a freshman tailback he carried the ball just five times, but as a sophomore wingback, in 1981, he gained 512 yards on 92 carries and was named to *Football News's* Sophomore All-America team. His 5.6-yard rushing average was best on the team, and he caught 11 passes for 135 yards.

Bell returned to tailback in 1982. What was expected to be a great season began with a 95-yard effort on opening day against Michigan but ended the following week when he fractured his leg against Purdue. In 1983 he missed seven games because of injuries and rushed for 169 yards on 37 carries.

Although Bell could have returned for another season, he chose instead to declare himself eligible for the NFL Draft. He was chosen in the first round by the Buffalo Bills, with whom he played from 1984 through 1987. He also played with the Los Angeles Rams (1988-89) and Los Angeles Raiders (1990-91). He rushed for more than 5,000 yards in his professional career and twice led the NFC in touchdowns: 16 in 1988 and 15 in 1989.

Career Statistics (Rushing)

YEAR	NO.	YARDS	AVG.	TD
1980	5	66	13.2	1
1981	92	512	5.6	4
1982	24	123	5.1	1
1983	37	169	4.6	4
TOTAL	158	870	5.5	10

BERCICH, PETE
Linebacker (1990-93) ▪ 6-2, 237 ▪ Mokena, IL

An intense, emotional player, Pete Bercich started at inside linebacker for the Fighting Irish in 1993 and was responsible for calling defensive signals. He was second on the team in tackles with 71, including 11 in a 36-14 victory over Michigan State.

Bercich prepped at Providence High School in New Lenox, Illinois, where he played both football and baseball. He set a school record with 170 tackles in his junior year and had a career total of 392. He received his first varsity letter at Notre Dame in 1991 when, as a sophomore, he started seven games and finished second on the team in tackles with 69. He also received honorable mention All-America honors from *Football News*. A nagging ankle injury limited his playing time in the last two games of the season.

Bercich was a seventh-round pick of the Minnesota Vikings in the 1994 NFL Draft.

BEREZNEY, PETE
Tackle (1943-45) ▪ 6-2, 215 ▪ Northvale, NJ

Although he failed to earn a monogram, Pete Berezney was a member of Notre Dame's national championship team in 1943. A reserve tackle, his playing time was limited by the presence of Ziggy Czarobski, John "Tree" Adams, and All-American Jim White. He saw considerably more action in 1944, however, and by 1945 was a starter at right tackle.

Berezney was a fifth-round draft pick of the Detroit Lions in 1946. He played for the

Los Angeles Dons of the All-America Football Conference in 1947 and the Baltimore Colts in 1948.

BERGMAN, ALFRED
Halfback/Quarterback (1910-14) ▪ 5-9, 160 ▪ Peru, IN

Alfred "Dutch" Bergman started at right halfback in 1911 and at quarterback in 1914. He was a good college football player, though hardly one of Notre Dame's greatest. He is, however, the answer to at least two interesting trivia questions:

1) Who holds the record for the longest kickoff return in Notre Dame history?

Answer: Alfred Bergman, 105 yards, against Loyola of Chicago in 1911. Interestingly enough, Bergman did not even score a touchdown on that play. College football fields at the time were 110 yards long. Bergman took the kick at his own goal line and was tackled at the Loyola five-yard line.

2) Who was Notre Dame's first four-sport athlete?

Answer: Alfred Bergman, who earned varsity letters in football, baseball, basketball, and track between 1911 and 1915.

BERTELLI, ANGELO
Quarterback/Running Back (1941-43) ▪ 6-1, 173 ▪ Springfield, MA

Angelo Bertelli was away at boot camp when he was awarded the Heisman Trophy in 1943. After leaving the Marine Corps, he played professional football with Los Angeles and Chicago.

Heisman Trophy winner Angelo Bertelli came to Notre Dame from Cathedral High School in Springfield, Massachusetts. He was named the most valuable player in Western Massachusetts in his senior year; he also acquired the nickname "The Springfield Rifle," because of his passing ability. Bertelli was also a superb hockey player and thought seriously about attending one of the many eastern colleges that were courting him, such as Dartmouth and Boston College. But the allure of Notre Dame was too great, and eventually Bertelli decided to attend school and play football in South Bend.

He began his college career as a single-wing tailback in 1941. From that position he demonstrated his versatility by passing for 1,027 yards and leading the nation in completion percentage (.569). When Irish coach Frank Leahy decided to switch to the T-formation in 1942, Bertelli moved from tailback to quarterback. That year, as a junior, he threw for

1,039 yards and 10 touchdowns and became one of the college game's biggest stars. One of Bertelli's finest performances came in a 27-10 victory over Stanford, in which he completed 10 consecutive passes and threw for four touchdowns.

Bertelli, who was runner-up for the Heisman Trophy as a sophomore and sixth in the voting as a junior, capped a magnificent career in 1943. In just six games he completed 25 of 36 passes for 512 yards (an average of better than 20 yards per completion). Even more impressive, 10 of those 25 completions were touchdown passes, making Bertelli one of the most efficient college quarterbacks in history. The Fighting Irish rolled up an average of 43.5 points per game in the first six games of the 1943 season. But with four games remaining on the schedule, Bertelli left school to join the U.S. Marine Corps. While he was in boot camp, Notre Dame lost to Great Lakes in the final game of the season. Nevertheless, the Irish won the national title with a 9-1 record. And Angelo Bertelli was the runaway winner of the Heisman Trophy.

Bertelli later played professionally for Los Angeles and Chicago of the All-America Football Conference; unfortunately, a serious knee injury cut his career short after just three seasons. He later became a successful businessman (he operated a beverage distributorship in New Jersey).

In 1972 Angelo Bertelli was elected to the College Football Hall of Fame.

Career Statistics (Passing)

YEAR	ATT.	COMP.	YARDS	TD	PCT.
1941	123	70	1,027	8	.569
1942	159	72	1039	10	.453
1943	36	25	512	10	.694
TOTAL	318	167	2,578	28	.525

BETTIS, JEROME
Fullback (1990-92) ▪ 6-0, 247 ▪ Detroit, MI

With his extraordinary combination of strength and speed, Jerome Bettis was a punishing runner generally regarded as one of Notre Dame's all-time great running backs, despite the fact that he left school one year early.

Born and raised in the Midwest, Bettis came to South Bend after an outstanding career at Mackenzie High School in Detroit. He was a consensus prep All-American who rushed for 1,355 yards and 14 touchdowns as a senior and averaged 15 tackles per game at middle linebacker.

As Rodney Culver's backup at fullback, Bettis played in 11 games as a college freshman. He carried the ball just 15 times, but his 7.7-yard average impressed coaches and teammates alike. The following season Culver was shifted to tailback to make room for Bettis in the starting backfield. If in September it seemed a questionable decision on the part of coach Lou Holtz, by December it seemed a stroke of brilliance: Bettis rushed for 972 yards and 16 touchdowns on 168 carries. He also caught 17 passes for 190 yards and four touchdowns. His 120 points established a single-season scoring record that still stands. In the final game of the season, a 39-28 Sugar Bowl victory over Florida, he rushed for 150 yards and three touchdowns on only 16 carries and was voted the game's MVP. After the season he shared team MVP honors with quarterback Rick Mirer and was named second-team All-America by *Football News, College & Pro Football Newsweekly*, and the Newspaper Enterprise Association.

Jerome Bettis left Notre Dame one year before graduating to play in the NFL and was rewarded with NFC Rookie of the Year honors.

Bettis was bothered by an ankle injury in his junior year but still played in 11 of 12 games. He rushed for 825 yards and 10 touchdowns on 154 carries and caught 15 passes for 239 yards. *Football News* named him honorable mention All-America.

In the spring of 1993 Bettis announced that he would forego his senior year in order to play in the National Football League. In just three seasons—and only two as a starter—he had climbed to fourteenth on Notre Dame's all-time rushing list with 1,912 yards. He was also sixth in career rushing touchdowns with 27. With another season Bettis might have rewritten the Notre Dame record book; but it was hard to argue with his decision. A first-round draft pick of the Los Angeles Rams in 1993, he made an immediate impact as a professional, rushing for 1,429 yards and seven touchdowns and earning NFC Rookie of the Year honors. In his first three seasons in the NFL Bettis rushed for 3,981 yards and 16 touchdowns on 363 carries. He was traded to the Pittsburgh Steelers in 1996.

Career Statistics (Rushing)

YEAR	NO.	YARDS	AVG.	TD
1990	15	115	7.7	1
1991	168	972	5.8	16
1992	154	825	5.4	10
TOTAL	337	1,912	5.7	27

Career Statistics (Receiving)

YEAR	NO.	YARDS	AVG.	TD
1990	0	0	0	0
1991	17	190	1.2	4
1992	15	239	15.9	2
TOTAL	32	429	13.4	6

BEUERLEIN, STEVE

Quarterback (1983-86) ▪ 6-3, 201 ▪ Fullerton, CA

Steven Taylor Beuerlein, Notre Dame's all-time passing leader, was born on March 7, 1965, in Los Angeles. The second oldest of four children, he demonstrated an uncommon aptitude for the sport of football at an early age by reaching the semifinals of the national Punt, Pass, and Kick competition. Despite that early success, and despite what he would later accomplish at Notre Dame, Beuerlein did not start a high school football game until his senior year. A backup behind Doug Butler (who went on to play at Princeton) as a junior, he became a starter in 1982 and led Servite High in Anaheim to a No. 1 ranking in the state of California. Beuerlein passed for 2,244 yards and 12 touchdowns as a senior and was named to several prep All-America teams.

In his freshman year at Notre Dame, Beuerlein supplanted senior Blair Kiel as the starting quarterback in the fourth game of the season. He completed 75 of 145 passes for 1,061 yards and four touchdowns. With a strong, accurate arm and a confident manner, Beuerlein made it clear that he would be the team's quarterback for some time to come.

In 1984, as a sophomore, he passed for 1,920 yards and seven touchdowns and set a record for completion percentage (.603). In 1985 he threw for 1,335 yards and three touchdowns. His best year, though, was 1986, when he completed 151 of 259 passes for 2,211 yards and 13 touchdowns. An Associated Press honorable mention All-American, he was voted outstanding offensive player by his teammates. He

Notre Dame's all-time passing leader, Steve Beuerlein, took the reins early by becoming the starting quarterback his freshman year.

also set Irish career records for pass attempts (850), completions (473), passing yardage (6,527), and total yards of offense (6,459).

Known primarily as a pure, drop-back passer, Beuerlein found a reliable partner in All-American split end Tim Brown, who was the team's leading receiver in 1985 and 1986. Neither player, however, had the good fortune to play on a championship team. In fact, the Fighting Irish were, at best, mediocre in the mid 1980s. During Beuerlein's four years on the varsity, Notre Dame had a combined record of 24-22. In two of those years, the Irish did not even play in a post-season bowl game.

Beuerlein was a fourth-round draft pick in 1987. He played with the Los Angeles Raiders (1987-90), Dallas Cowboys (1991-92), Phoenix/Arizona Cardinals (1993-94), and Jacksonville Jaguars (1995). Through the 1995 season he had completed 752 of 1,425 passes for 10,042 yards and 53 touchdowns.

Career Statistics (Passing)

YEAR	ATT.	COMP.	PCT.	YARDS	TD
1983	145	75	.517	1,061	4

1984	232	140	.603	1,920	7
1985	214	107	.500	1,335	3
1986	259	151	.583	2,211	13
TOTAL	850	473	.556	6,527	27

BISCEGLIA, PAT

Guard (1953-55) ▪ 5-10, 190 ▪ Worcester, MA

One of 13 children, Pasquale George Bisceglia came late to Notre Dame. A baseball, football, and hockey star at Commerce High School in Worcester, Massachusetts, he entered the U.S. Navy after graduation. By the time he enrolled at Notre Dame, in the fall of 1952, he was twenty-two years old.

Bisceglia backed up Ray Lemek in his first two years on the Fighting Irish varsity. Then, in 1955, when Lemek moved to tackle, Bisceglia assumed a spot in the starting lineup. And he did not disappoint. Along with halfback Paul Hornung and fullback Don Schaefer, he was one of the players most responsible for Notre Dame's 8-2 record that season. The Associated Press named Bisceglia first-team All-America; *The Sporting News* named him to its second team and United Press to its third team.

Despite those honors, Bisceglia was not chosen until the 29th round of the 1956 NFL Draft. He did not play professional football.

BLARNEY STONE

The Blarney Stone is, of course, part of Irish folklore. So it should come as no great surprise that it is also part of Fighting Irish folklore.

According to legend, anyone who kisses the Blarney Stone will be rewarded with good luck and skill in the delicate art of flattery. The original Blarney Stone is located in Blarney Castle, near Cork, Ireland. On St. Patrick's Day 1994, a 50-pound chunk of "authentic Blarney Stone" was presented to Notre Dame coach Lou Holtz by Blarney Enterprises, Ltd. Actually, the gift was not cut from the Blarney Stone itself; rather, it was taken from the same quarry that produced the stone used to build Blarney Castle—and the quarry from which the Blarney Stone was removed.

BLEIER, ROCKY

Halfback (1965-67) ▪ 5-11, 195 ▪ Appleton, WI

Robert Patrick "Rocky" Bleier was the starting right halfback on Notre Dame's national championship team in 1966 and captain of the team in 1967. But it wasn't until he reached the NFL, and helped lead the Pittsburgh Steelers to three Super Bowl championships, that he became a household name.

The son of a tavern owner in Appleton, Wisconsin, Bleier became a prep star at Xavier High School. He was a two-time all-state running back, as well as captain of the football, basketball, and track teams, each of which went undefeated during his senior year.

Backing up Bill Wolski at left halfback in 1965, Bleier earned his first Notre Dame monogram and rushed for 145 yards on 26 carries. The following year he was the smallest member of the team's starting backfield. The Fighting Irish were an exceptionally talented group that season, and Bleier's subtle contributions were often overshadowed by the more dramatic exploits of quarterback Terry Hanratty and running backs Larry Conjar and Nick Eddy. Bleier was a tough, versatile player who was third on the team in rushing with 282 yards on 63 carries and second in receiving with 17 catches for 209 yards. He was also the team's leading punter.

Even though he was a starter on Notre Dame's 1966 championship team and the team captain in 1967, Robert "Rocky" Bleier didn't truly gain fame until he helped lead the Pittsburgh Steelers to four Super Bowl championships.

Bleier's leadership abilities were recognized in the spring of 1967 when he was elected captain for the upcoming season. He rushed for 357 yards on 77 carries and caught 16 passes for 171 yards as a senior. With 42 points, he was the team's third-leading scorer. Bleier was overlooked by most All-America teams, and he was nearly overlooked in the NFL Draft. Considered too small and too slow to play professional football, he was not drafted until the 16th round; 416 college football players were taken before the Pittsburgh Steelers finally called his name.

The odds against Bleier making it in the NFL increased substantially in 1968, when after one season with the Steelers, he was drafted into the U.S. Army. He was assigned to combat duty in Vietnam, where on August 20, 1969, he was seriously wounded. Bleier was a private first class carrying a grenade launcher while on patrol in Hiep Douc. He was first hit by small arms fire; then, after crawling 200 yards to what he thought was a safer area, a grenade exploded at his feet, filling both of his legs with shrapnel and nearly severing his foot.

Doctors said Bleier would be lucky to walk without a limp, but he made a miraculous recovery from his wounds and returned to the Steelers in 1971. His playing time increased steadily until, by 1974, he was the team's starting halfback. He helped the Steelers win Super Bowl titles in 1975, 1976, 1979, and 1980.

Bleier's autobiography, *Fighting Back*, was later made into a television movie. He retired from the NFL in 1980 with 3,864 yards rushing on 928 carries; he also caught 136 passes for 675 yards and scored 23 touchdowns.

Career Statistics (Rushing)

YEAR	NO.	YARDS	AVG.	TD
1965	26	145	5.6	2
1966	63	282	4.5	4
1967	77	357	4.4	5
TOTAL	**166**	**784**	**4.7**	**11**

Career Statistics (Receiving)

YEAR	NO.	YARDS	AVG.	TD
1965	3	42	14.0	0
1966	17	209	12.3	1
1967	16	171	10.7	2
TOTAL	**36**	**422**	**11.7**	**3**

BLUE-GOLD GAME

The Blue-Gold game is a springtime tradition at Notre Dame, dating back to 1929. Then it was a rather unsightly—though undeniably popular—contest pitting current players against former players, and it was referred to as the "Varsity vs. Old Timers Game." Not surprisingly, the varsity usually emerged victorious, winning 29 of 36 games. The last three games were embarrassingly one-sided, with the varsity winning by scores of 72-0, 33-0, and 39-0.

In 1968 the parameters of the game were changed. Coach Ara Parseghian decided that a scrimmage between current players—under game conditions—would better serve the interests of the football program, the student body, and the university; it would also permit the "old-timers" to avoid serious damage to their bodies and egos.

The first Blue-Gold game attracted more than 20,000 fans to Notre Dame Stadium, and it has increased in popularity in the years since. The highest recorded attendance for the game was 29,451 in 1990.

BLUEGRASS

In an age when sterile, artificial turf fields seem to be creeping like a blight across the athletic landscape, Notre Dame clings to tradition. The playing surface in Notre Dame Stadium has always been natural Kentucky bluegrass—and there are no plans to convert to a synthetic carpet.

Since 1990, Dale Getz, manager of athletic facilities, has overseen the care of the field. Getz has also served as superintendent of the University of Notre Dame Golf

Course and assistant superintendent of grounds. Prior to Getz, the longtime (26 years) caretaker of Notre Dame Stadium and its bluegrass field was Harold "Benny" Benninghoff.

BOERINGER, ART

Center (1925-26) ▪ 6-1, 186 ▪ St. Paul, MN

A second-string center in 1925, Arthur "Bud" Boeringer became a starter the following season and collected more honors than any other Notre Dame player. He helped lead the Fighting Irish to a 9-1 record and was named first-team All-America by the Associated Press and the International News Service, among others.

Boeringer was an assistant to former Irish quarterback Gus Dorais at the University of Detroit for 16 years. He later took a job as line coach at the University of Iowa, where he worked under another Notre Dame alumnus, Clem Crowe. From 1946 through 1950 he was head coach at Cornell University.

BOLCAR, NED

Linebacker (1986-89) ▪ 6-2, 229 ▪ Phillipsburg, NJ

A two-time captain of the Fighting Irish, Ned Bolcar was one of the team's best linebackers in the 1980s. After playing just 27 minutes as a freshman in 1986, he was promoted to starting inside linebacker in 1987 and logged more playing time (266:59) than any other member of the defense. He also led the team in tackles with 106 and was named second-team All-America by the Associated Press and third-team All-America by *Football News*.

Bolcar lost his starting job to Michael Stonebreaker in 1988, and his playing time was sliced in half. Still, he served as tri-captain and was fourth on the team in tackles with 57. The following year he reclaimed his role as a starter and again led the team in tackles, this time with 109. He was named second-team All-America by United Press International and *The Sporting News*.

A sixth-round NFL draft pick, Bolcar played with the Seattle Seahawks in 1990 and the Miami Dolphins in 1991 and 1992.

BOWL GAMES

Notre Dame played in its first post-season bowl game on January 1, 1925. The Fighting Irish defeated Stanford, 27-10, in the Rose Bowl. Shortly thereafter, university officials, concerned that participation in bowl games interfered with students' academic schedules, adopted a policy that prevented the football team from playing in post-season games for the next 45 years.

It wasn't until Nov. 17, 1969, that executive vice president Reverend Edmund Joyce—expressing a need for the university to raise funds for minority student academic programs and scholarships—announced a change in the long-standing policy. Less than two months later Note Dame lost to Texas, 21-17, in the 1970 Cotton Bowl.

Since that time the Fighting Irish have been a fixture in post-season games—coveted by bowl officials as much for their vast fan following as their ability on the football field. Through the 1995 season, Notre Dame had compiled a record of 13-8 in 21 bowl appearances. Only five schools—Nebraska, Alabama, Penn State, Michigan, and Ohio State—have played in more bowl games.

Notre Dame Bowl Appearances

SEASON	BOWL	DATE	OPPONENT	W/L	SCORE
1924	Rose	Jan. 1, 1925	Stanford	W	27-10
1969	Cotton	Jan. 1, 1970	Texas	L	17-21
1970	Cotton	Jan. 1, 1971	Texas	W	24-11
1972	Orange	Jan. 1, 1973	Nebraska	L	6-40
1973	Sugar	Dec. 31, 1973	Alabama	W	24-23
1974	Orange	Jan. 1, 1975	Alabama	W	13-11
1976	Gator	Dec. 27, 1976	Penn State	W	20-9
1977	Cotton	Jan. 2, 1978	Texas	W	38-10
1978	Cotton	Jan. 1, 1979	Houston	W	35-34
1980	Sugar	Jan. 1, 1981	Georgia	L	10-17
1983	Liberty	Dec. 29, 1983	Boston College	W	19-18
1984	Aloha	Dec. 29, 1984	SMU	L	20-27
1987	Cotton	Jan. 1, 1988	Texas A&M	L	10-35
1988	Fiesta	Jan. 2, 1989	West Virginia	W	34-21
1989	Orange	Jan. 1, 1990	Colorado	W	21-6
1990	Orange	Jan. 1, 1991	Colorado	L	9-10
1991	Sugar	Jan. 1, 1992	Florida	W	39-28
1992	Cotton	Jan. 1, 1993	Texas A&M	W	28-3
1993	Cotton	Jan. 1, 1994	Texas A&M	W	24-21
1994	Fiesta	Jan. 2, 1995	Colorado	L	24-41
1995	Orange	Jan. 1, 1996	Florida State	L	26-31

BRADLEY, LUTHER

Strong Safety (1973, 1975-77) ▪ 6-2, 200 ▪ Muncie, IN

Luther Bradley was one of Notre Dame's finest defensive players in the 1970s. He received All-America honors from several organizations as a sophomore and junior but was then ignored by the wire services until his senior year. In 1977, as a member of Notre Dame's national championship squad, he was named second-team All-America by Associated Press and first-team All-America by United Press International.

Bradley, who also played on Notre Dame's 1973 national championship team, was a hard-hitting defensive back who had 153 career tackles. He holds the Fighting Irish career record for interceptions with 17 (for a total of 218 yards). He also holds the school record for most yards gained by interceptions in a single game. Against Purdue, in 1975, Bradley returned two interceptions for a total of 103 yards. Included in that figure was a 99-yard return for a touchdown, a play that stands as the second-longest return in Notre Dame history.

Bradley was selected to play in the Japan Bowl following his senior season. He was a first-round draft choice of the Detroit Lions in 1978. After four years in the NFL he retired from professional football and accepted a job with Blue Cross-Blue Shield.

Career Statistics (Interceptions)

YEAR	INT.	YARDS	AVG.	TD
1973	6	37	6.2	0
1975	4	135	33.8	1
1976	2	0	0.0	0
1977	5	46	9.2	0
TOTAL	17	218	12.8	1

BRENNAN, MIKE
Offensive Tackle/Guard (1986-89) ▪ 6-5, 260 ▪ Easton, MD

Michael Sean Brennan came to Notre Dame from Mount St. Joseph High School in Baltimore where he was captain of the football and lacrosse teams and a varsity swimmer. Offered lacrosse scholarships from such national powers as Johns Hopkins and North Carolina, he chose instead to attend Notre Dame, where his father had graduated from in 1961.

Brennan was not offered an athletic scholarship but played both football and lacrosse in his freshman year. He concentrated on football in 1987 and in the fall of 1988 was offered a scholarship. He started two games at offensive guard that season before moving to tackle as a senior. In 1989 Brennan was fourth on the team in minutes played (287:42). A fourth-round draft choice of the Cincinnati Bengals in 1990, he spent three years in the NFL.

BRENNAN, TERRY
Halfback (1945-48) ▪ Head Coach (1954-58) ▪ 6-0, 170 ▪ Milwaukee, WI

As an Irish-Catholic kid growing up in Milwaukee, Wisconsin, Terry Brennan faithfully followed the Notre Dame football team. He idolized players such as Creighton Miller (whose jersey number he wore throughout high school and college) and dreamed of playing in South Bend.

Terry Brennan, a devout follower of the Fighting Irish as a young boy in Milwaukee, grew up to earn four monograms as a running back for Notre Dame and went on to coach the Irish from 1954-58.

As it happened, his dream came true. An all-Catholic Conference halfback at Marquette High School, he earned his first monogram at Notre Dame as a freshman running back in 1945. The following year he was the starting left halfback on a team that went 8-0-1 and captured the national championship under Frank Leahy. With 36 points, he shared team scoring honors with Jim Mello; he also led the team in receiving with 10 catches for 154 yards and two touchdowns.

Notre Dame won a second straight national title in 1947, and Brennan was again a key contributor. He led the team in receiving (16 catches for 181 yards and four touchdowns), scoring (66 points), and rushing attempts (87). The highlight of the 1947 season for Brennan was a 27-7 victory over Army in which he returned the opening kickoff 97 yards for a touchdown. Later that year he competed in the pole vault for the track team and won the 165-pound title in the university boxing tournament.

As a senior, in 1948, Brennan, earned his fourth monogram. He rushed for 284 yards on 48 carries and caught five passes for 102 yards. He ended his career with 1,249 yards rushing.

After graduation Brennan coached Mount Carmel High School to three consecutive city championships in Chicago. He returned to South Bend in 1953 to work as an assistant coach and in 1954 succeeded Leahy as the head coach. His career began quite well—his first two teams went 9-1 and 8-2 and finished fourth and ninth, respectively, in the final Associated Press poll—but in 1956 the Irish slipped to 2-8. They went 7-3 in 1957 and 6-4 in 1958.

Brennan resigned after the '58 season and took a job as a conditioning coach for the Cincinnati Reds. He later joined an investment banking firm in Chicago.

Career Coaching Record

YEAR	WON	LOST	TIED
1954	9	1	0
1955	8	2	0
1956	2	8	0

1957	7	3	0
1958	6	4	0
TOTAL	**32**	**18**	**0**

Career Statistics (Rushing)

YEAR	ATT.	YARDS	AVG.	TD
1945	57	232	4.4	2
1946	74	329	4.4	6
1947	87	404	4.6	11
1948	48	284	5.9	2
TOTAL	**266**	**1,249**	**4.7**	**21**

BRILL, MARTY
Halfback (1929-30) ▪ 5-11, 190 ▪ Philadelphia, PA

Marty Brill, the starting right halfback on Notre Dame's national championship teams in 1929 and 1930, was the son of a Philadelphia millionaire. Appropriately enough, he began his college career draped in ivy at the University of Pennsylvania. However, after two frustrating seasons of football, during which his playing time was minimal, he decided to transfer to Notre Dame.

The move proved beneficial to both Brill and the Fighting Irish. He became a starter at right halfback, where his primary obligation was to block for two-time All-American Marchy Schwartz. By the time he left South Bend, Brill was considered one of the finest blocking backs in the program's history. He was also an outstanding defensive back who shared the team lead in interceptions in 1930. And, when given the opportunity, he was a respectable runner.

Brill's best offensive performance came in a 60-20 drubbing of Pennsylvania in Philadelphia. Head coach Knute Rockne allowed Brill a taste of revenge by letting him carry the ball far more often than usual against his former teammates. Brill responded with the game of his life, scoring three touchdowns on runs of 65, 52, and 45 yards. After the season he received All-America honors from several organizations; the All-America Board even placed him on its first team.

Brill went on to become a successful college coach. He was an assistant at Columbia for one year and head coach at LaSalle College in his hometown of Philadelphia for seven years. He later served as head coach at Loyola University in Los Angeles and as an assistant coach at Notre Dame.

BROOKS, REGGIE

Tailback/Defensive Back (1989-92) ▪ 5-8, 200 ▪ Tulsa, OK

Although he was slow to adapt to the rigors of the college game, Reggie Brooks eventually became one of the top football players in the country. He rushed for 1,343 yards as a senior and finished fifth in voting for the Heisman Trophy.

Reggie Brooks followed his older brother, Tony, from Tulsa to South Bend and went on to become one of the top college players in the country. He followed up his outstanding college career by becoming the leading rusher for the Washington Redskins his rookie year.

That performance was precisely what the Fighting Irish expected of Brooks when they recruited him out of Booker T. Washington High School in Tulsa, Oklahoma. An all-state running back and defensive back, he rushed for more than 1,400 yards in his last two seasons, despite being limited to 11 games because of injuries.

In 1989 Brooks followed the lead of his older brother, Tony (a tailback with the Irish from 1987 through 1991), and enrolled at Notre Dame. Although he did see significant time on special teams, Brooks carried the ball just 13 times as a freshman. The following year he started three games at cornerback and performed so well that it seemed unlikely he would ever return to offense. In 1991, however, he was switched back to offense and carried the ball 18 times for 122 yards; he also returned nine kickoffs for 198 yards.

Remarkably, Brooks not only earned a spot in the starting lineup in 1992, but he also developed into one of the best running backs in college football. He became the fourth Notre Dame player to rush for more than 1,000 yards in a single season and the first to do so under coach Lou Holtz. As the most productive member of Notre Dame's "Killer Bee" backfield—which also included Jerome Bettis, Lee Becton, and Jeff Burris—he averaged 8.0 yards per carry, a single-season mark surpassed only by George Gipp in 1920. His career average of 7.6 yards per carry still stands as a school record.

One of three finalists for the 1992 Doak Walker Award (presented to the top junior or senior running back in the nation), Brooks was named second-team All-America by the Associated Press, United Press International, and *The Sporting News*, among others. He was drafted by the Washington Redskins in the second round of the 1993 NFL Draft and led the team in rushing in his rookie season.

Career Statistics (Rushing)

Year	No.	Yards	Avg.	TD
1989	13	43	3.3	0
1990	0	0	0	0
1991	18	122	6.8	2
1992	167	1,343	8.0	13
TOTAL	**198**	**1,508**	**7.6**	**15**

BROOKS, TONY

Tailback (1987-88, 1990-91) ▪ 6-2, 223 ▪ Tulsa, OK

Raymond Anthony Brooks, one of Notre Dame's all-time leading rushers, was born in Tulsa, Oklahoma, the second youngest of four children. At Booker T. Washington High School he led the football team to the 1986 Oklahoma state championship and was named Gatorade national high school player of the year.

Brooks made an immediate impact at Notre Dame, rushing for 262 yards and one touchdown in 1987; the only freshman who logged more time on offense was Ricky Watters, another tailback. In 1988 Brooks was the team's second-leading rusher with 667 yards on 117 carries; he also caught seven passes for 121 yards and two touchdowns.

In the fall of 1989 Brooks left Notre Dame and enrolled at nearby Holy Cross Junior College; he did not play football. After a year of successful course work he returned to Notre Dame in 1990 and started 5 of 10 games while splitting time with Watters. He rushed for 451 yards on 105 carries and caught three passes for 47 yards.

Brooks had his best season in 1991 while sharing the tailback position with Rodney Culver. (The third-string tailback was Reggie Brooks, Tony's younger brother, who would go on to become an All-American in 1992.) Brooks played in 12 games, started four, and gained 894 yards on 147 carries, an average of 6.1 yards per attempt. He played in the 1992 Senior Bowl and was named honorable mention All-America by *Football News*.

Brooks finished his college career with 2,274 yards rushing, sixth on Notre Dame's all-time list. He was a fourth-round draft choice of the Philadelphia Eagles in 1992 but spent only two seasons in the NFL.

Career Statistics (Rushing)

YEAR	NO.	YARDS	AVG.	TD
1987	54	262	4.9	1
1988	117	667	5.7	2
1990	105	451	4.3	4
1991	147	894	6.1	5
TOTAL	**423**	**2,274**	**5.4**	**12**

BROWN, CHRIS

Defensive Back (1980-83) ▪ 6-1, 196 ▪ Owensboro, KY

A high school quarterback, Chris Brown was switched to the secondary at Notre Dame and soon developed a reputation as a fierce hitter. He earned monograms in 1980 and 1981 as a backup to strongside cornerback John Krimm and was promoted to starter at weakside cornerback in 1982. He finished his junior year with 37 tackles two interceptions.

As a senior, Brown had 46 tackles and two interceptions. Drafted by the Pittsburgh Steelers in the sixth round in 1984, he spent two years in the NFL.

BROWN, DEAN
Offensive Tackle/Guard (1986-89) ▪ 6-3, 291 ▪ Canton, OH

An exceptionally strong athlete (his bench press of 455 pounds was best on the team in 1989), Dean Brown grew up in Canton, Ohio, hometown of another Fighting Irish alumnus, Alan Page. Brown was a two-year starter at offensive tackle, though he began his college career as a guard. He played in the Hula Bowl after his senior year and was named honorable mention All-America by *The Sporting News*.

Brown played with the San Diego Chargers in 1990.

BROWN, DEREK
Tight End (1988-91) ▪ 6-6, 252 ▪ Merritt Island, FL

Expectations could not have been higher for Derek Vernon Brown. After a magnificent career at Merritt Island High School he was named prep player of the year by *Parade* magazine; he was a first-team selection on virtually every high school All-America team.

Derek Brown went to Notre Dame after being named prep player of the year by *Parade* magazine. He lived up to expectations as an exceptional receiver and was selected in the first round of the NFL draft in 1992 by the Giants

Brown shouldered the burden of early stardom with unusual grace. He played in 11 games as a college freshman and started in five. He caught 12 passes for 150 yards and three touchdowns; remarkably, the first two receptions of his college career resulted in touchdowns. After the season he was named honorable mention All-America by *The Sporting News*.

As a sophomore Brown led all Fighting Irish receivers in minutes played (236:29) and had 13 receptions for 204 yards. In 1990 he started all 11 games and was second on the team with 15 receptions for 220 yards. For that, he was named honorable mention All-America by *Football News*.

Brown's senior year (1991) was his best. He caught 22 passes for 325 yards and four touchdowns and bolstered his reputation as a premier receiver and blocker. The Newspaper Enterprise Association and the Walter Camp Foundation named him first-team All-America; *Football News* placed him on its third team. Brown was a first-round draft pick (and the fourteenth selection overall) of the New York Giants in 1992. He played with the Giants from 1992 through 1994 and with the Jacksonville Jaguars in 1995 and 1996.

Career Statistics (Receiving)

YEAR	NO.	YARDS	AVG.	TD
1988	12	150	12.5	3
1989	13	204	15.7	0
1990	15	220	14.7	1
1991	22	325	14.8	4
TOTAL	**62**	**899**	**14.5**	**8**

BROWN, EARL

End (1936-38) ▪ 6-0, 178 ▪ Benton Harbor, MI

Earl Melvin Brown Jr. grew up in Benton Harbor, Michigan. A prep star at Benton Harbor High School, he was named all-state in basketball and football. He continued to play both sports at Notre Dame and, in fact, was one of the school's more successful two-sport athletes.

Brown earned his first monogram in 1937 and became a starter as a senior in 1938. He helped lead the Fighting Irish to an 8-1 record and a top-five ranking by the Associated Press. A clever receiver known for redesigning plays on the spur of the moment, Brown had a team-high six catches for 192 yards and four touchdowns in his senior year. He shared team scoring honors with Benny Sheridan (each had 24 points). After the season he received first-team All-America honors from the All-America Board and *Liberty* magazine and second-team honors from the Associated Press.

A few months later Brown was named an All-American guard in basketball for the second consecutive season. As if to demonstrate his versatility, in the middle of the basketball season he took a brief break to participate in the 1939 College Football All-Star Game against the New York Giants.

Rather than play professional football, Brown chose a career in coaching. His first job was at Brown University, where he was head football coach and assistant basketball coach. In 1941 he became end coach at Harvard under Dick Harlow; he was also head basketball coach. Two years later Brown moved to another Ivy League school, Dartmouth College, where he quickly put together one of the better programs in the country. Dartmouth was 6-1 in 1943 and finished sixteenth in the final polls. That same year, Brown coached the Dartmouth basketball team to the Eastern Intercollegiate Basketball Championship.

In March 1944, Brown joined the U.S. Maritime Service. He later became head football coach at the U.S. Merchant Marine Academy.

BROWN, HARVEY

Guard (1921-23) ▪ 5-9, 165 ▪ Youngstown, OH

After playing behind All-American Hunk Anderson in his sophomore year, Harvey Brown moved into the starting lineup in 1922. The following year, as a senior, he served as captain.

Brown was one of the smaller players on the team (in fact, of the starters on the 1923 squad, only quarterback Harry Stuhldreher was smaller), but his size never seemed to be a detriment. He was named second-team All-America by *Collier's* magazine after the 1923 season.

An outstanding student as well as an exceptional athlete, Brown went on to medical school at St. Louis University. He later opened a private practice in Detroit but remained involved in football as a volunteer assistant coach at the University of Detroit.

BROWN, TIM

Flanker/Split End (1984-87) ▪ 6-0, 195 ▪ Dallas, TX

Heisman Trophy winner Timothy Donnell Brown, one of the most explosive players in college football history, was born on July 22, 1966, in Dallas, Texas. The second youngest of six children raised by Josephine and Eugene Brown, he exhibited extraordinary athletic ability at an early age. At Woodrow Wilson High School he accumulated more than 4,000 all-purpose yards and was a prep All-American in football. Despite Brown's best efforts, though, Woodrow Wilson won only four games during his three years on the varsity. Brown also earned three letters in basketball and was one of the fastest high school quarter-milers in the nation.

He began his college career as a split end and was second on the team with 28 receptions for 340 yards in his freshman year. As a sophomore, in 1985, he moved to flanker and led the team with 25 receptions for 397 yards and three touchdowns. He also began to exhibit some of the speed and style that would come to define his career as a kick-return specialist. He returned 14 kickoffs for an average of 24.1 yards; his longest was a 93-yard return for a touchdown against Michigan State.

In 1986 Brown emerged as one of the best offensive players in the college game. He caught 45 passes for 910 yards and five touchdowns; carried 59 times for 254 yards; returned 25 kickoffs for 698 yards and two touchdowns; and returned two punts for 75 yards. His 1,937 all-purpose yards set a school record, and his average of 176.1 yards per game ranked third in the nation. He was named first-team All-America by *The Sporting News, Football News*, United Press International, and the Associated Press.

As impressive as he was as a junior, Brown was even better as a senior. He caught 39 passes for 846 yards, rushed for an additional 144 yards, and returned 23 kickoffs for 456 yards. By returning 34 punts for 401 yards and three touchdowns (including two in one game against Michigan State), he boosted his all-purpose yardage for the season to 1,847. In Notre Dame's 35-10 loss to Texas A&M in the Cotton Bowl, he caught six passes for 105 yards.

Brown was a unanimous first-team All-American in '87 and was named College Player of the Year by the Walter Camp Foundation, *The Sporting News, Football News*, and UPI. He was an easy winner in voting for the Heisman Trophy, outdistancing runner-up Don McPherson of Syracuse University.

By the time he graduated, Brown held several Notre Dame career records, including pass reception yardage (2,493), kickoff return yardage (1,613), combined kick and punt return yardage (2,089), and combined kick and punt returns for touchdowns (six). He was third in pass receptions with 137.

Brown's 4.38 speed in the 40-yard dash made him an immensely appealing pro prospect. A first-round pick of the Los Angeles Raiders, he was the sixth player chosen in the 1988 NFL Draft. His first season was sensational. He led the league in kickoff returns (41 for 1,098 yards), caught 43 passes for 725 yards and five touchdowns, and returned 49 punts for 444 yards. His 2,317 all-purpose yards was an NFL record for a rookie. Although a knee injury limited him to just one game in 1989, Brown returned to the starting lineup in 1990. Through the 1995 season he had caught 405 passes for 6,076 yards and 46 touchdowns. He had also returned 269 punts for 2,811 yards and two touchdowns. He was chosen to play in the Pro Bowl in 1988, 1991, and 1993 through 1995.

Career Statistics (Receiving)

YEAR	NO.	YARDS	AVG.	TD
1984	28	340	12.1	1
1985	25	397	15.9	3
1986	45	910	20.2	5
1987	39	846	21.7	3
TOTAL	137	2,493	18.2	12

Career Statistics (Rushing)

YEAR	NO.	YARDS	AVG.	TD
1984	1	14	14.0	0
1985	4	30	7.5	1
1986	59	254	4.3	2
1987	34	144	4.2	1
TOTAL	98	442	4.5	4

Career Statistics (Kickoff Returns)

YEAR	NO.	YARDS	AVG.	TD
1984	7	121	17.3	0
1985	14	338	24.1	1
1986	25	698	27.9	2
1987	23	456	19.7	0
TOTAL	**69**	**1,613**	**23.4**	**3**

Career Statistics (Punt Returns)

YEAR	NO.	YARDS	AVG.	TD
1984	0	0	0.0	0
1985	0	0	0.0	0
1986	2	75	37.5	0
1987	34	401	11.8	3
TOTAL	**36**	**476**	**13.2**	**3**

BROWNER, JIM

Safety/Fullback (1975-78) ▪ 6-3, 204 ▪ Warren, OH

A three-year starter at strong safety and a defensive stalwart on the 1977 national championship team, Jim Browner was nonetheless overshadowed by his older brother, Ross, who was one of the best defensive linemen in Notre Dame history.

Like his brother, Jim was a high school All-American. He made an immediate impact as a freshman fullback by rushing for 95 yards in the 1975 season opener against Boston College. Despite playing in only nine of 11 games, by the end of the season he had gained 394 yards on 104 carries, third best on the team.

It was an impressive rookie performance, but by 1976 Brown had found a new, and permanent, home at strong safety. He had 80 tackles as a sophomore, 73 as a junior, and 75 as a senior. He was drafted by the Cincinnati Bengals in 1978 and spent two seasons with the team.

BROWNER, ROSS

Defensive End (1973, 1975-77) ▪ 6-3, 247 ▪ Warren, OH

One of the most decorated players in Notre Dame history, Ross Browner grew up in Warren, Ohio. He was a high school All-American who played both offensive and defensive end for Warren Western Reserve, which captured the Ohio State championship.

Great things were expected of Browner from the moment he arrived in South Bend, and he quickly fanned the flames of anticipation by blocking a punt for a safety in a 44-0 victory over Northwestern on Opening Day 1973. He was a starter at defensive end throughout his freshman season and wound up third on the team in tackles with 68. This was particularly impressive in light of the fact that the Irish were an extremely deep, talented team that year—they went undefeated and captured a national championship.

Browner missed the 1974 season with an injury but returned to the starting lineup in 1975. He had 71 tackles and recovered four fumbles.

The following year he became one of the best players in the college game. He had 97 tackles, including a school-record 28 for minus yardage, and four fumble recoveries. A consensus first-team All-American, he was named Lineman of the Year by United Press International and was one of four finalists for the Lombardi Trophy. He also won the Outland Trophy, presented annually to the top interior lineman in college football.

UPI Lineman of the Year, the Outland Trophy, consensus first-team All-America, and the Lombardi Trophy were all honors bestowed upon Ross Browner. The eighth overall player chosen in the 1978 NFL draft, Browner finished his nine-year professional career with the Green Bay Packers.

As impressive as he was in 1976, Browner was even better in 1977. A senior tri-captain, he had 104 tackles and led the Irish to another national championship. For the second consecutive season he was a consensus first-team All-American; he also won the Lombardi Trophy and was fifth in voting for the Heisman Trophy. Browner still holds the Notre Dame career record for tackles by a front-four lineman (post-1956) with 340. He also recovered 12 fumbles, had two safeties, and scored one touchdown.

Browner was the eighth player chosen in the 1978 NFL draft (teammate Ken MacAfee was seventh). He was a starter for the Cincinnati Bengals until the 1985 season when he received a three-month suspension following a positive drug test. He played briefly with the Houston Gamblers of the United States Football League that season but finished the year with the Bengals. He ended his career in 1987 as a member of the Green Bay Packers.

BUDKA, FRANK
Quarterback (1961-63) ▪ 6-0, 190 ▪ Pompano Beach, FL

Frank Budka was an accomplished two-way player who had the misfortune to attend Notre Dame during a comparatively bleak period for the school's football program: The Irish won only 12 games and lost 17 during his time on the varsity. Nevertheless, Budka made a name for himself as a quarterback and defensive back.

As a sophomore, in 1961, while splitting time with Daryle Lamonica, he completed a team-high 40 of 95 passes for 636 yards and three touchdowns; he also had 21 tackles. Lamonica was a decisive winner in the quarterback contest in 1962, so Budka threw only nine passes that season. He did, however, have a fine year on defense, making 51 tackles (fourth on the team) and intercepting one pass.

In 1963, with Lamonica having graduated, Budka, John Huarte, and Sandy Bonvechio shared quarterbacking duties. Budka completed a team-leading 22 of 41 passes for 251 yards and four touchdowns. He also ran for four touchdowns and led the team in scoring with 24 points.

A fourth-round draft choice in 1964, Budka played one season as a defensive back with the Los Angeles Rams.

BULLOCK, WAYNE
Fullback (1972-74) ▪ 6-1, 221 ▪ Newport News, VA

Wayne Bullock was one of the greatest athletes to come out of Newport News, Virginia. At Washington Carver High School he earned 16 varsity letters. Not only was he a two-time all-state running back for the football team, but he also set a state record in the shot put, won the state heavyweight wrestling title, and played two years of varsity baseball and basketball; in his senior year, he was captain of all four teams.

But football was the family sport—his older brother, John, played at Purdue—and Wayne eventually accepted a scholarship from Notre Dame. Although his college career began somewhat slowly—he carried the ball just 27 times as a sophomore—Bullock became one of the program's all-time leading rushers. In 1973, as a junior, he rushed for a team-high 752 yards on 162 carries, helping the Irish to an 11-0 record and a national championship. He was also second on the team in scoring with 66 points. In Notre Dame's dramatic 24-23 victory over Alabama in the Sugar Bowl, Bullock rushed for 79 yards and one touchdown. His best game came against Pittsburgh, when he carried 27 times for 167 yards and four touchdowns. He logged more playing time (259:32) than any other running back.

In 1974 Bullock again led the team in rushing, this time with 855 yards on 203 carries. He was also first in scoring with 72 points. He finished his career with 1,730 yards on 392 carries—at the time, good enough for eighth on the school's all-time list (he's currently in twentieth place). Despite those numbers, Bullock was overlooked by most All-America teams in both 1973 and 1974. He was drafted by the San Francisco 49ers in 1975 but did not play in the NFL.

Career Statistics (Rushing)

YEAR	ATT.	YARDS	AVG.	TD
1972	27	123	4.5	0
1973	162	752	4.6	10
1974	203	855	4.2	12
TOTAL	**392**	**1,730**	**4.4**	**22**

BUMS

In the 1920s, under coach Knute Rockne, the student managers who assisted with the mundane—though undeniably vital—tasks associated with the football program were known as the "Notre Dame Bums." This small (six or seven students) group of volunteers traveled with the football team and helped prepare for games on the road by handling equipment and uniforms and generally doing whatever was asked of them.

Everyone in the football program understood and appreciated the importance of the student managers. There was, however, one problem: the Notre Dame Bums were not, strictly speaking, a part of the program. The university did not know who they were or what their function was. And there was no money in the budget to cover their travel expenses. So when the Fighting Irish went on the road, the Bums became stowaways, hiding beneath the players' berths. Rockne's role in this scheme was to act surprised when the Bums showed up in some far-off town or to feign anger if they were caught by a suspicious train conductor. Really, he valued their contribution and always had plenty of work for them.

Today, the student managers are no longer known as the Notre Dame Bums. And they neither travel nor toil in secrecy. Although their numbers have increased significantly, their duties remain essentially unchanged: to help the Fighting Irish prepare for competition. The student managers organization staffs every athletic practice and game on the campus.

BUONICONTI, NICK

Guard (1959-61) • 5-11, 210 • Springfield, MA

Nick Buoniconti grew up in Springfield, Massachusetts, home of the Basketball Hall of Fame. But it was as a football player that he made his name.

After graduating from Cathedral High School, Buoniconti accepted a scholarship from Notre Dame. Given a chance to play early in his sophomore season when starting left guard Myron Pottios went down with a knee injury, Buoniconti took full advantage of the opportunity and finished third on the team in tackles with 67.

So impressive was Buoniconti's play that he received slightly more playing time than Pottios in 1960—despite the fact that Pottios had been elected team captain. Pottios had a team-high 74 tackles that year; Buoniconti was second with 71.

As a senior, in 1961, it was Buoniconti's turn to be a team leader. As the starting left guard and co-captain, he had a team-high 74 tackles. He was also credited with blocking two kicks. The Fighting Irish were a dismal 12-18 during Buoniconti's three years on the varsity, but his talent and effort were nevertheless recognized. *Football News* named him first-team All-America in 1961, and United Press International and *The Sporting News* each named him second-team All-America.

Although Buoniconti was not drafted until the twelfth round in 1962, he went on to have an outstanding professional career. He played with the American Football League's Boston Patriots from 1962 through 1968, and then joined the Miami Dolphins in 1969. He helped lead the Dolphins to Super Bowl titles in 1973 and 1974. He missed the 1975 season with a broken finger but returned to play one more season with Miami before retiring in 1977.

BURGMEIER, TED
Defensive Back/Split End (1974-77) ▪ 5-11, 186 ▪ East Dubuque, IL

Ted Burgmeier was an All-American defensive back on Notre Dame's 1977 national championship team. He came to South Bend from Wahlert High School in Illinois, where he received all-state honors in football, basketball, and track; he was also a prep All-American in football.

Burgmeier began his college career as a free safety, backing up Randy Harrison in 1974. First-year head coach Dan Devine took advantage of Burgmeier's natural athletic ability in 1975 and moved him to wide receiver. Burgmeier responded with 10 receptions for 185 yards before being sidelined with an injury with two games left in the season.

As a junior Burgmeier went back to defense and became a starter at cornerback. He had 54 tackles and two interceptions and was also the team's leading punt returner with 20 for 138 yards. In 1977 he again had 54 tackles, along with four interceptions. He also returned a team-high 18 punts for 82 yards. He was named second-team All-America by the Football Writers Association of America.

Burgmeier played for the Kansas City Chiefs in 1978.

BURRIS, JEFF

Safety/Running Back (1990-93) ▪ 6-0, 204 ▪ Rock Hill, SC

A consensus All-American in 1993, Jeff Burris was one of the more versatile athletes ever to play in the Notre Dame secondary. He came to South Bend from Northwestern High School in Rock Hill, South Carolina, where he earned four varsity letters and led his team to the state championship. He was twice named South Carolina Player of the Year, and he rushed for a school-record 1,838 yards and 27 touchdowns in his senior year.

One of the most versatile players the Irish have ever seen, Jeff Burris figured prominently on offense, defense, and special teams. In four years, he recorded 89 tackles, 10 interceptions, *and* 10 touchdowns.

Burris grew up in a football family—his older brother, Pat, played at the University of Arkansas in 1989 and 1990. Jeff could have followed in his brother's footsteps; in fact, he could have played just about anywhere. But he chose Notre Dame. And the decision proved to be a good one. Burris played in 10 games as a freshman, handling assignments at cornerback, safety, tailback, and kick return specialist. He did not start a single game, but it was clear that he was going to be an exceptional college football player.

As a sophomore Burris started every game: five at free safety and eight at cornerback. He was fourth on the team in tackles and first in punt returns. As a junior, in 1992, he led the team in interceptions and was third in tackles. *Football News* named him honorable mention All-America for the second consecutive year.

In 1993 Burris was one of the most important players on a team that went 11-1 and finished second in the national rankings. He was also one of the few players in major college football who made substantial contributions on both sides of the ball. Defensively, he had 53 tackles and three interceptions and led the team in minutes played. He also made 204 appearances on special teams—more than any other Irish player. As if that wasn't enough, Burris was consistently called upon by coach Lou Holtz to help the offense, especially in goal-line situations. He rushed for six touchdowns from the tailback position, second best on the team.

In the final game of his college career, Burris had nine tackles to lead the Fighting Irish to a 24-21 victory over Texas A&M in the 1994 Cotton Bowl. In four years he had 89 tackles and 10 interceptions; he also scored 10 touchdowns. After the 1993 season he was named MVP by the National Monogram Club. He received first-team All-America honors from the Associated Press and United Press International, among others.

Burris was a first-round draft pick of the Buffalo Bills in 1994.

Career Statistics (Defense)

YEAR	INT.	YARDS	TACKLES
1991	2	0	63
1992	5	6	73
1993	3	61	53
TOTAL	10	67	189

Career Statistics (Rushing)

YEAR	ATT.	YARDS	AVG.	TD
1990	6	30	5.0	1
1991	0	0	0	0
1992	7	14	2.0	3
1993	16	92	5.8	6
TOTAL	29	136	4.7	44

BUTTON-HOOK

The simple button-hook pass is one of the most common, yet effective, plays in football. It's birth, however, was purely accidental, dating back to a 1913 game between Penn State and Notre Dame. Quarterback Gus Dorais and receiver Knute Rockne were buddies who helped popularize the forward pass during their careers in South Bend. Over the course of this particular game Rockne was assigned the task of running an ordinary pass route; however, he lost his footing and slipped to the ground. As luck would have it, the Penn State defender ran several steps before realizing that the receiver had fallen. Rockne, meanwhile, scrambled to his feet and found himself wide open. Dorais then delivered the pass perfectly.

It wasn't pretty, but it was a completion.

Dorais and Rockne were so intrigued that they decided to incorporate a cleaner version of the play into the Notre Dame offense. Rockne would sprint down the field as hard as he could, carrying his defender along with him, then turn and double back toward the quarterback. Invariably, the defensive player was caught off guard. Dorais and Rockne named their play the "button-hook." And it remains a fundamental part of the game today.

C

CALHOUN, MIKE
Defensive Tackle (1976-78) ▪ 6-5, 237 ▪ Austintown, OH

Mike Calhoun was the only underclassman on Notre Dame's starting defensive line in 1977 when the Irish won the national championship with an 11-1 record. He was seventh on the team in tackles with 72 and second in tackles for minus yardage (13 for negative 63); in Notre Dame's 38-10 Cotton Bowl victory over Texas, he had four tackles.

Calhoun was a three-sport star at Austintown High School, lettering in track and baseball, as well as football. He was named all-state and All-America in his senior year. In his first year on the Notre Dame varsity (1976) he had 92 tackles. As a senior, in 1978, he was third on the team with 99 tackles.

A tenth-round draft pick of the Dallas Cowboys in 1979, Calhoun played with the San Francisco 49ers and Tampa Bay Buccaneers in 1980.

CANNON, JACK
Guard (1927-29) ▪ 5-11, 193 ▪ Columbus, OH

A free-spirited, frequently rebellious man, Jack Cannon is remembered not only as one of the greatest guards in Notre Dame history but also as one of the last to play without a helmet.

He was a star on Notre Dame's 1929 national championship team. Because Notre Dame Stadium was under construction, the Fighting Irish played all of their games on the road that year. If this was an inconvenience to some players, it was an inspiration to Cannon, who enjoyed playing in front of a hostile crowd and loved exploring strange cities in the post-game hours. At times a fiercely competitive player, he was also prone to fits of disinterest when the game was no longer in doubt, a fact that often frustrated coach Knute Rockne.

In the end, though, Cannon was generally regarded as an exceptionally talented

A talented and resilient player under Knute Rockne, Jack Cannon is best known as one of the last Irishmen to play without a helmet.

player. One of his most memorable performances came in a 7-0 victory over Army when he kicked off three times and made a solo tackle each time; he also threw the block that allowed Jack Elder to run 96 yards with an interception for the game's only score. After the 1929 season he was a consensus All-American, earning first-team honors from the Associated Press and United Press among others.

Ever the unconventional sort, Cannon eventually returned to his hometown and became a florist. He was elected to the College Football Hall of Fame in 1965. He died in 1967.

CARBERRY, GLEN

End (1920-22) ▪ 6-0, 180 ▪ Ames, IA

The captain of Notre Dame's 1922 team, Glen "Judge" Carberry grew up in a large, athletic family. He was one of 12 children born to Mr. and Mrs. J.H. Carberry of Ames, Iowa. Several of Glen's six brothers were football players: John Carberry and William Carberry, for example, both starred at the University of Iowa; Richard Carberry played at Columbia College in Dubuque, Iowa.

But Glen was the most accomplished athlete in the family. He entered Notre Dame in 1919 and earned his first monogram in 1920. In 1922 he started at left end and served as team captain, helping the Fighting Irish to an 8-1-1 record.

Carberry played three years of professional football before entering the coaching field. He worked as an assistant to former Notre Dame teammate Jim Crowley at Fordham.

CAREY, TONY

Defensive Back (1964-65) ▪ 6-0, 190 ▪ Chicago, IL

Anthony F. Carey was the second person in his family to attend Notre Dame, following in the footsteps of his older brother, Tom, who was a quarterback for the Fighting Irish in the 1950s.

Tony arrived on campus in 1962 after graduating from Mount Carmel High School in Chicago. He earned his first monogram as a junior, in 1964, when he was one of the top defensive backs in the country. Although he had no varsity experience, Carey became a starter and quickly learned the finer points of his position. In fact, in 269 minutes of playing time he had eight interceptions, which not only led the team but also the entire nation; he also had 46 tackles. After the season he was named second-team All-America by the Newspaper Enterprise Association.

In 1965 Carey had a less spectacular season (three interceptions, 34 tackles), though his play was certainly respectable. A sixth-round draft choice of the Chicago Bears and San Diego Chargers, he did not play in the NFL.

CARIDEO, FRANK
Quarterback (1928-30) ▪ 5-7, 175 ▪ Mount Vernon, NY

As a high school football player at Dean Academy in Mount Vernon, New York, Frank Carideo was a naturally confident and astute quarterback. He was also an exceptional punter, having learned the finer points of kicking into the coffin corner from a man named Leroy Mills, a New York city attorney who had played football at Princeton. Mills was considered an expert on the subject of punting and kicking, and Carideo learned his lessons well. He became one of the finest punters in Notre Dame history.

Of course, he was also a pretty respectable quarterback. In his first year on the varsity (1928), Carideo backed up starting quarterback Jim Brady. In 1929 Carideo became the starter and led the Fighting Irish to a 9-0 record and a national championship under Knute Rockne. An exceptional all-around athlete, he also played defensive back and led the team in interceptions with five for 151 yards. He completed a 10-yard touchdown pass to Jack Elder in a victory over Navy, scored on a 75-yard touchdown run against Georgia Tech, and ran back an interception 85 yards for a touchdown in a 26-6 win over Northwestern. His extra-point kick gave Notre Dame a 13-12 victory over USC, and his 96-yard interception return provided the only touchdown in a season-ending 7-0 victory over Army. Carideo's efforts were widely recognized after the season: He was a first-team selection on every prominent All-America team.

In 1930, as Carideo guided the Fighting Irish to a second straight national title, there were numerous highlights. Against Southern Methodist he set up one touchdown with a 70-yard punt return and a second with a 25-yard completion to end Ed Kosky. He scored a touchdown against Pennsylvania and kicked the game-winning extra point in a 7-6 victory over Army before 110,000 fans at Chicago's Soldier Field. Late in the season, in a 14-0 victory over Western Conference co-champion Northwestern, Carideo nailed four punts inside the one-yard line. He also returned a punt to the Northwestern 28-yard line to set up the winning touchdown. In his final collegiate game, against USC, Carideo caught a 26-yard touchdown pass from Marchy Schwartz as the Irish rolled to a 27-0 victory. After the season, Carideo was again named consensus first-team All-America.

Although he never led the Irish in passing, Carideo is widely regarded as one of the school's best quarterbacks. Feisty and smart, he offset a lack of size with superb on-field leadership and play-calling ability. After graduating in 1931, he became an assistant coach at Purdue. From 1932 through 1934 he was head coach at the University of Missouri. That, however, would be the last time he was in charge of a college football program. Carideo took over the basketball program at Mississippi State in 1936 while also serving as assistant football coach. He coached at Iowa from 1939 to 1942, served as a lieutenant in the U.S. Navy from 1943 through 1945, and returned to Iowa in 1946. In 1950 he retired from coaching and took a job as an insurance executive in Cedar Rapids, Iowa. For many years he provided radio commentary for University of Iowa football games.

Carideo was inducted into the College Football Hall of Fame in 1954. He died in 1992.

CARNEY, JOHN
Kicker (1983-86) ▪ 5-10, 170 ▪ West Palm Beach, FL

Notre Dame's career leader in field goals, John Michael Carney was born in Hartford, Connecticut, and attended high school at Cardinal Newman in West Palm Beach, Florida. He played soccer and football and was named Florida's all-state kicker in 1982. Nevertheless, he was not offered a scholarship by Notre Dame and had to make the team as a freshman walk-on in the fall of 1983. Although he did not attempt a single extra point or field goal that season, he did handle kickoff responsibilities impressively; 43 of his 59 kickoffs reached the opponent's goal line, and only 25 were returned.

Over the next three seasons Carney was one of the best kickers in college football. He made 70 of 75 extra points and 51 of 69 field goals for a total of 223 points. He was not known for his range (he never made a field goal from beyond the 50-yard mark), but he was extremely accurate. In fact, he holds the Notre Dame record for field goal percentage in a season (.895 in 1984) and a career (.739). His 21 field goals in 1984 is a single-season record and his 51 is a career record.

Carney was not drafted in 1987 and did not reach the NFL until 1989 when he signed with the Tampa Bay Buccaneers. Since then, however, he has been one of the league's most consistent and successful kickers. He was traded to the San Diego Chargers in 1990 and led the NFL in scoring in 1994. Carney was also responsible for founding a charitable program in San Diego known as KickStart for Kids, which raises money for children who need reconstructive surgery.

Career Statistics (Kicking)

YEAR	PAT	FG	TP
1983	0-0	0-0	0
1984	25-25	17-19	76

1985	21-24	13-22	60
1986	24-26	21-28	87
TOTAL	**70-75**	**51-69**	**223**

CAROLLO, JOE
Tackle (1959-61) ▪ 6-2, 235 ▪ Wyandotte, MI

Joseph Paul Carollo earned his first monogram in 1959; as a second-string lineman he had 22 tackles. In 1960 he became a starter and led all tackles in playing time with 302 minutes. He also had 30 tackles. His finest season was 1961 when he recorded 40 tackles.

Carollo, who played in the 1962 College All-Star Game, was a second-round draft pick of the Pittsburgh Steelers and Boston Patriots. He played with the Los Angeles Rams (1962-68, 1971), Philadelphia Eagles (1969), and Cleveland Browns (1972-73).

CARROLL, JIM
Guard/Linebacker (1962-64) ▪ 6-1, 225 ▪ Atlanta, GA

Jim Carroll was born in Jonesboro, Arkansas, and grew up in Atlanta. A football and wrestling star during his prep days, he followed another Marist High School graduate, Ken Adamson, to Notre Dame; in fact, both players served as captains of the Fighting Irish—Adamson in 1959, Carroll in 1964,

In his first year on the varsity, 1962, Carroll started at left guard and had 59 tackles; he matched that figure the following year. In 1964, when two-platoon football became the rule in the college game, coach Ara Parseghian elected to use Carroll primarily on defense. It proved to be a wise decision. Carroll set a school record with 140 tackles—52 more than any of his teammates. Notre Dame was the third-ranked team in the nation that year, and Carroll received All-America recognition from numerous organizations, including first-team honors from *The Sporting News*, *Time*, and *Football News* and second-team honors from United Press International.

Drafted by the New York Giants in the twelfth round in 1965, Carroll spent five seasons in the NFL. In addition to the Giants (1965-66), he played with the Washington Redskins (1966-68) and New York Jets (1969).

CARTER, PHIL

Running Back (1979-82) ▪ 5-10, 197 ▪ Tacoma, WA

Phil Carter was overlooked by most All-America teams. And he never made it to the National Football League. Nevertheless, he was an extremely successful college football player who finished his career as one of Notre Dame's all-time leading rushers.

As a third-string halfback in 1979, Carter carried the ball 27 times for 145 yards. He moved into the starting lineup the following year and was second on the team in rushing with 822 yards on 186 carries. He gained 727 yards as a junior in 1981 and 715 yards as a senior in 1982; in each year he was the team's leading ground gainer.

Carter finished his career with 2,409 yards and 14 touchdowns on 557 carries. Through 1985, he was fourth on the school's all-time rushing list.

Career Statistics (Rushing)

YEAR	NO.	YARDS	AVG.	TD
1979	27	145	5.4	0
1980	186	822	4.4	6
1981	165	727	4.4	6
1982	179	715	4.0	2
TOTAL	557	2,409	4.3	14

CARTER, TOM

Defensive Back (1990-92) ▪ 5-11, 184 ▪ St. Petersburg, FL

Had he not elected to forego his senior season, Tom Carter might well have entered the Notre Dame record books in several statistical categories.

A versatile athlete who played quarterback, cornerback, and wide receiver at Lakewood High School in St. Petersburg, Florida, Carter had no trouble adjusting to the college game. He started in six games as a freshman safety. As a sophomore, in 1991, he moved to cornerback and started every game; he had 30 tackles and a team-high five interceptions, including one that he returned 79 yards for a touchdown against Tennessee.

With 4.38 speed in the 40-yard dash, Carter was a quick, aggressive defender as well as a threat on special teams. He had 40 tackles and five interceptions as a senior in 1992 and was named third-team All-America by the Associated Press and *Football News*. Carter needed just three interceptions to move into the top three on Notre Dame's all-time list for interceptions and just seven to tie Luther Bradley's career mark of 17. He chose not to pursue those records, though; instead, he declared himself eligible for the 1993 NFL Draft. He was taken in the first round by the Washington Redskins and led the team in interceptions in his rookie season.

CARTIER FIELD

Prior to the construction of Notre Dame Stadium in 1930, the Fighting Irish played their home football games at Cartier Field, which had a seating capacity of 30,000. Today, the moniker is still in use: The school's practice facility, located near the Joyce Center, goes by the name "Cartier Field."

CASPER, DAVE

Offensive Tackle/Tight End (1971-73) ▪ 6-3, 252 ▪ Chilton, WI

It wasn't until his senior year in college that Dave Casper settled into the position that he would play for more than a decade in the National Football League: tight end. At Chilton High School he had demonstrated unusual versatility by lettering in football, basketball, baseball, and golf (he was an All-American in football and a .446 hitter in baseball, as well as an honors student).

In South Bend, Casper's athletic focus was football, but he was utilized in a variety of ways. In 1970 he played tackle and handled punting duties for the freshman team. In 1971 he earned his first monogram as a second-string offensive tackle, and in 1972, as a junior, he was named honorable mention All-America as a tackle. But he also played defensive tackle, tight end, and wide receiver. In 1973, when the Fighting Irish went undefeated and captured the national championship, Casper started at tight end and served as tri-captain. He was second on the team with 19 receptions for 317 yards and four touchdowns. His 30-yard reception from quarterback Tom Clements set up Bob Thomas's game-winning field goal in a 24-23 Sugar Bowl victory over Alabama.

Casper was a consensus All-American in 1973, earning first-team honors from United Press International and the Newspaper Enterprise Association, among others, and second-team recognition from the Associated Press. He played in the College All-Star Game and the Hula Bowl and was named first-team Academic All-America.

A second-round draft choice of the Oakland Raiders in 1974, Casper spent 11 years in the NFL. He caught 378 passes for 5,216 yards and scored 52 touchdowns. In addition to the Raiders, he played with the Houston Oilers, Minnesota Vikings, and Los Angeles Rams. He is a member of the Academic All-America Hall of Fame.

CASTNER, PAUL

Halfback/Fullback (1920-22) ▪ 6-0, 190 ▪ St. Paul, MN

A two-time All-American on Knute Rockne's great teams of the early 1920s, Paul Castner is perhaps best remembered as the man who suffered a career-ending injury in his senior year, thus opening the barn door for Notre Dame's famed Four Horsemen.

Although he did not play high school football, Castner received a scholarship to attend Notre Dame; a mutual acquaintance had given Rockne a glowing assessment of Castner's athletic ability, and the coach was willing to take a chance. It was a decision he would never regret. Castner was a gifted runner, strong and quick, and by 1920 he was a second-string fullback behind Chet Wynne. He moved to halfback in 1921 and was named second-team All-America by the International News Service.

In 1922 Castner was Notre Dame's starting fullback. He led the team in scoring with 64 points, including a memorable performance against Indiana in which he accounted for all of his team's scoring in a 27–0 victory. Castner scored three touchdowns, kicked three extra points, and drop-kicked two field goals (from 37 and 42 yards) in that game, which turned out to be his last in South Bend.

Late in the season Castner injured his back, prompting Rockne to move Elmer Layden to fullback. Previously, Layden had been splitting time at left halfback with Jim Crowley. With Castner out of the lineup, the Irish played for the first time with Layden at fullback, Crowley and Don Miller at halfback, and Harry Stuhldreher at quarterback. Collectively, of course, this group would come be known as the Four Horsemen, the most famous backfield in football history.

Castner's accomplishments, unfortunately, have often been overlooked. *Collier's* named him second-team All-America in 1923, and he still holds Notre Dame records for kickoff return yards in single game (253) and career kickoff return average (36.5). In addition to his football ability, Castner was an accomplished baseball player who earned three varsity letters and later pitched professionally for the Chicago White Sox. He also founded Notre Dame's hockey program in 1921. In 1975 he co-authored a biography of his former coach entitled *We Remember Rockne*.

Career Statistics (Kickoff Returns)

YEAR	ATT.	YARDS	AVG.	TD
1920	2	55	27.5	0
1921	8	222	27.8	0
1922	11	490	44.5	2
TOTAL	**21**	**767**	**36.5**	**2**

CIFELLI, GUS
Tackle (1946-49) ▪ 6-4, 222 ▪ Philadelphia, PA

August Blaze Cifelli entered Notre Dame after serving two and a half years in the U.S. Marine Corps during World War II. A machine gun operator and boxing instructor in the service, he was a man of modest athletic ability but incomparable toughness. Although he rarely started at Notre Dame, he was a four-year member of the varsity and a winner of three monograms.

The Detroit Lions drafted Cifelli in 1950. He also played for the Green Bay Packers, Philadelphia Eagles, and Pittsburgh Steelers before retiring from the NFL in 1954.

CLARK, WILLIE
Defensive Back/Tailback (1990-93) ▪ 5-10, 185 ▪ Wheatland, CA

The son of a career serviceman, Willie Clark moved several times while growing up. He was born in New Haven, Connecticut, started high school in Madrid, Spain, and graduated from Wheatland High School in Wheatland, California. He rushed for 1,121 yards and 16 touchdowns and was named all-state in his senior year.

At Notre Dame, Clark began each of his first two seasons as a tailback. In the middle of his sophomore season, however, he became a starter at cornerback and free safety. He had one of his best games against Florida, in the 1992 Sugar Bowl, registering six tackles, three pass deflections, and one interception. After the season he showed his speed by qualifying for the NCAA indoor track and field championships at 55 meters.

Despite an injury-riddled collegiate career, Willie Clark was successful not only on the football field but also on the track, qualifying for the NCAA track and field championships at 55 meters.

Clark went back to offense in the fall of 1992 but fractured his wrist just a few days after the season opener and missed the rest of the year. As a senior, in 1993, he bounced back and forth between offense and defense, but injuries again limited his playing time. Clark was drafted by the San Diego Chargers in 1994.

CLASBY, BOB
Defensive Tackle (1979-82) ▪ 6-5, 259 ▪ Milton, MA

Bob Clasby, the son of a former football captain at Harvard, grew up in Milton, Massachusetts, near Boston. A three-sport star (football, lacrosse, and hockey) at Boston College High School, he entered Notre Dame in 1979 and earned his first monogram in 1981. After playing only 17 minutes as a sophomore defensive tackle, he logged more than 184 minutes and made 56 tackles as a junior.

In 1982, as a senior, Clasby was fifth on the team with 65 tackles. A sixth-round NFL draft choice in 1983, he spent two years in the United States Football League before joining the St. Louis Cardinals in 1986. He retired in 1990.

CLASHMORE MIKE

The image of the leprechaun has become synonymous with Notre Dame football. But there was a time when the school had a different mascot. For many years the Fighting

Irish were represented on the field and at pep rallies by an Irish terrier. The first was named Brick Top Shuan-Rhu and was donated to the university on November 8, 1930, by Charles Otis of Cleveland, Ohio. The dog was presented to football coach Knute Rockne before the Notre Dame-Pennsylvania game.

A succession of terriers followed in the pawprints of Brick Top Shuan-Rhu, including one, in 1933, that went by the name Clashmore Mike. So beloved was the mascot that his successors were given the same name. Over the years Clashmore Mike's popularity continued to grow. He had his own column in Notre Dame's football program in the 1930s

Shannon View Mike, one of the incarnations of Fighting Irish mascot Clashmore Mike, is pictured here in the late '40s with team co-captain Jim Martin.

and 1940s; he was even the subject of a book, *Mascot Mike of Notre Dame*, that was published by Dunne Press in 1949.

Alas, Clashmore Mike's career came to an end in 1966, when the leprechaun–a more traditional symbol of Irish good fortune–was adopted as the school's official mascot.

CLATT, CORWIN

Fullback (1942, 1946-47) ▪ 6-0, 200 ▪ Peoria, IL

After starring at East Peoria High School, Corwin Clatt enrolled at Notre Dame. He was the team's leading rusher in 1942 with 698 yards on 138 carries. He also shared team scoring honors (30 points) with halfback Creighton Miller.

Clatt left Notre Dame in 1943 to serve in the armed forces but returned to the team after World War II and earned monograms in 1946 and 1947. He played with the NFL's Chicago Cardinals in 1948 and 1949.

CLEMENTS, TOM

Quarterback (1972-74) ▪ 6-0, 189 ▪ McKees Rock, PA

Although he graduated more than two decades ago and has spent long periods of time away from South Bend, Tom Clements remains a part of the Fighting Irish family.

He came to Notre Dame from McKees Rock, Pennsylvania, in the fall of 1971. One year later he became the starting quarterback. It was a job he held for three years.

Clements threw for more than 1,100 yards as a sophomore and led Notre Dame to an 8-3 record. As a junior his statistics were less impressive (60 of 113 for 882 yards), but that season was his most memorable. The Fighting Irish went undefeated, capping an 11-0 year with a 24-23 victory over Alabama in the Sugar Bowl. Clements led a dramatic 79-yard scoring drive late in the fourth quarter, and Bob Thomas's 19-yard field goal with 4:26 remaining sealed the victory and gave the Fighting Irish their second national championship under coach Ara Parseghian. Clements was named the game's MVP.

As a senior Clements passed for 1,549 yards and 8 touchdowns as he led Notre Dame to a 10-2 record. Through 1995 he was ranked seventh on the school's career passing list.

After leaving Notre Dame Clements began a long and successful career in the Canadian Football League. In 1975, as a member of the Ottawa Rough Riders, he received the Schenley Award as the CFL's Most Outstanding Rookie; he was an Eastern Conference All-Star in both 1976 and 1977. He also led Ottawa to victory in the 1976 Grey Cup with a game-winning touchdown pass with 19 seconds remaining. In 1981 Clements received the Jeff Russel Trophy, given annually to the CFL Eastern Conference MVP. In 1984 he led Winnipeg to the Grey Cup championship and was voted the game's MVP. Finally, in 1987, he capped a brilliant pro career by throwing for more than 4,600 yards and 35 touchdowns and winning the CFL's Most Outstanding Player award.

During his CFL career Clements also attended law school at the University of Notre Dame, from which he graduated magna cum laude in 1986. He spent five years with a Chicago law firm before the lure of football drew him back to South Bend. From 1992 through 1996 Clements was an assistant under Notre Dame coach Lou Holtz. He was also an adjunct associate professor of law.

Clements was inducted into the Canadian Football Hall of Fame in 1994

Tom Clements has been a part of Fighting Irish history since he went to South Bend as a freshman in 1971. After a memorable football career, he excelled in the Canadian Football League while also attending Notre Dame's law school. After practicing law for several years, he returned once again to serve as an assistant under Lou Holtz.

Career Statistics

YEAR	ATT.	COMP.	YARDS	TD	PCT.
1972	162	83	1,163	8	.512
1973	113	60	882	8	.531
1974	215	122	1,549	8	.567
TOTAL	490	265	3,594	24	.541

COFALL, STAN

Halfback (1914-16) ▪ 5-11, 180 ▪ Cleveland, OH

Stanley Cofall was a three-year starter at left halfback. During his time on the varsity Notre Dame (under coach Jesse Harper) won 21 games and lost just 4. A first-team All-American in 1916, Cofall went on to play professionally for the Cleveland Browns (1920) and New York Giants (1921). He rushed for 30 touchdowns in his career at Notre Dame, fourth on the school's all-time list.

COLEMAN, HERB

Center (1942-43) ▪ 6-1, 198 ▪ Chester, WV

A native of Chester, West Virginia, Herb Coleman was captain of his high school basketball and football teams, as well as a four-year star in baseball. After earning All-Ohio Valley honors in his senior year, he entered Notre Dame.

Coleman was a backup center in 1942 and a starter on the 1943 national championship team coached by Frank Leahy. A member of the Navy's V-5 program, he received a medical discharge from the service because of back and knee injuries incurred while playing football. Although he did not rejoin the Fighting Irish after his discharge, Coleman did eventually resume his football career. He played professionally for the Chicago Rockets in 1946 and 1947 and the Baltimore Colts in 1948.

COLLEGE FOOTBALL HALL OF FAME

The College Football Hall of Fame was established in 1951 by the National Football Foundation. For the first 40 years of its existence it was located in Kings Island, Ohio. In the fall of 1995, however, a new 58,000-square-foot Hall of Fame was opened in downtown South Bend, Indiana.

The $14 million museum, which is designed to resemble a football stadium, includes a 360-degree theater that recreates the sights and sounds of the game-day experience; the Hall of Champions, where all enshrinees are honored; the Training Room, an interactive display in which visitors can test themselves against some of the greatest players in college football history; and the Hall of Honor, which recognizes college football's most significant contributors.

More than 500 players and coaches have been inducted into the College Football Hall of Fame, including 35 former Notre Dame players and five former coaches; no other school is so well represented.

Notre Dame Hall of Fame Inductees

PLAYERS

YEAR	NAME	POSITION	YEARS PLAYED
1951	George Gipp	HB	1952
1951	Elmer Layden	FB	1922-24
1954	Frank Carideo	QB	1928-30
1958	Harry Stuhldreher	QB	1922-24
1960	John Lujack	QB	1943, 1946-47
1963	George Connor	OT	1946-47
1965	Jack Cannon	G	1927-29
1966	Edgar Miller	OT	1922-24
1968	Adam Walsh	C	1922-24
1970	Don Miller	HB	1922-24
1971	Louis Salmon	FB	1900-03
1972	Angelo Bertelli	QB	1941-43
1972	Ray Eichenlaub	FB	1911-14
1973	Leon Hart	TE	1946-49
1974	Marchmont Schwartz	HB	1929-31
1974	Heartley Anderson	OG	1918-21
1975	John Smith	OG	1925-27
1976	Creighton Miller	HB	1941-43
1977	Ziggy Czarobski	OT	1942-43, 1946-47
1978	Frank Hoffmann	OG	1930-31
1979	John Lattner	HB	1951-53
1982	Bert Metzger	OG	1928-30
1983	Bill Fischer	OG	1945-48
1983	Bill Shakespeare	HB	1933-35
1984	Emil Sitko	HB	1946-49
1985	Paul Hornung	QB	1954-56
1985	Fred Miller	T	1926-28

Tailback Fred Miller, who played for the Irish in the late 1920s, was inducted into the College Football Hall of Fame in 1985.

1987	Tommy Yarr	C	1929-31
1988	Bob Williams	QB	1948-50
1990	Wayne Millner	E	1933-35
1992	Jim Lynch	LB	1964-66
1993	Alan Page	DE	1964-66
1994	Jerry Groom	C/LB	1948-50
1995	Jim Martin	E/T	1946-49
1996	Ken MacAfee	TE	1974-77

Coaches

YEAR	NAME	RECORD	YEARS COACHED
1951	Knute Rockne	105-12-5	1918-30
1970	Frank Leahy	87-11-9	1941-43, 1946-53
1971	Jesse Harper	34-5-1	1913-17
1980	Ara Parseghian	95-17-4	1964-74
1985	Dan Devine	53-16-1	1975-80

COLLINS, GREG

Linebacker (1972-74) ▪ 6-3, 228 ▪ Troy, MI

Greg Collins was the leading tackler on the 1973 national championship team. An all-state linebacker at Brother Rice High School in Troy, Michigan, he won his first monogram at Notre Dame in 1972 as a second-string outside linebacker. The following year he was credited with 133 tackles and 11 sacks in anchoring a defense that allowed just 66 points all season. The highlight of his season came in a 45-23 victory over the

An important player in Notre Dame football off the field is public address announcer Mike Collins. He has held that position since 1981.

University of Southern California when he had 18 tackles, forced one fumble, and recovered another. He was also credited with 16 solo tackles in the team's Sugar Bowl victory over Alabama. He led all defensive players with 225 minutes played.

In 1974 Collins was elected captain and again led the Irish in tackles (144). After the season he received second-team All-America honors from the Associated Press and *Football News*. Collins played for the San Francisco 49ers in 1975, the Seattle Seahawks in 1976, and the Buffalo Bills in 1977.

COLLINS, MIKE

Mike Collins, a former news anchor at WNDU-TV in South Bend, is the public address announcer at Notre Dame

Stadium. A 1967 graduate of the University of Notre Dame, Collins has held this position since 1981, when he succeeded longtime (34 years) announcer Frank Crosiar. During the regular work week, Collins is managing editor at WSBT, a South Bend television station.

CONJAR, LARRY

Fullback (1965-66) ▪ 6-0, 212 ▪ Oxon Hill, MD

Larry Conjar did not play his first season of varsity football until 1965, in the fall of his junior year. He surprised most Notre Dame followers by not only earning a monogram but also by winning the starting fullback job and rushing for more than 500 yards. He was, in fact, the team's third-leading scorer with 42 points. And in one game, a 28-7 victory over USC, he played like an All-American, rushing for 116 yards and four touchdowns on 25 carries.

The next season, as the Fighting Irish marched toward a national championship, Conjar was one of the most reliable and productive players on an offense that was nothing short of spectacular. Notre Dame was ranked third in the NCAA in total offense in 1966, and Conjar contributed significantly to that effort. He rushed for 521 yards on 112 carries (second on the team behind consensus All-American Nick Eddy), caught four passes for 62 yards, and scored seven touchdowns. After the season he was named first-team All-America by *Football News* and third-team All-America by United Press International and Associated Press.

A second-round draft choice of the Cleveland Browns in 1967, Conjar spent four years in the NFL. In addition to the Browns, he played with the Philadelphia Eagles and the Baltimore Colts. He carried the ball 30 times in his professional career for a total of 102 yards.

CONLEY, TOM

End (1928-30) ▪ 5-11, 175 ▪ Philadelphia, PA

After graduating from Roman Catholic High School in Philadelphia, where he was an all-city end, Tom Conley came to Notre Dame. He earned his first monogram as a sophomore in 1928. The following year, when starting right end Manny Vezie went down with an injury, Conley stepped in and helped the Irish capture a national championship. His performance under pressure so impressed his teammates that he was elected captain in his senior year.

Conley was named second-team All-America by the Associated Press, United Press, and the Newspaper Enterprise Association after the 1930 season.

CONNOR, GEORGE
Tackle (1946-47) • 6-3, 225 • Chicago, IL

George Connor, one of college football's most accomplished linemen, grew up in Chicago. As a tackle for the De La Salle Institute football team, he was a star in the city's Catholic League. He was recruited by just about every major college football program in the country and soon narrowed his choices to two: Holy Cross College in Worcester, Massachusetts, and the University of Notre Dame. It wasn't an easy decision, for Connor had ties to both schools. His high school coach, Joe Gleason, had been a halfback for the Fighting Irish in the 1930s; and his uncle, George S.L. Connor, was a monsignor at Holy Cross. In the end, family loyalty prevailed, and Connor accepted a scholarship from Holy Cross, even though he really wanted to attend Notre Dame.

George Connor originally enrolled in Holy Cross, but found himself face to face with Fighting Irish Head Coach Frank Leahy when both were stationed at Pearl Harbor. Upon Connor's discharge from the Navy, he enrolled in Notre Dame.

The transition from high school to college football was unusually smooth. Although he was merely a 17-year-old freshman, Connor earned a spot in the starting lineup in the first game of the 1942 season. He remained at Holy Cross the following year and was elected team captain. When the season ended he won the George Bulger Lowe Award as the outstanding college football player in New England and was named to several All-America teams.

Connor, a member of the Navy's V-12 program, was called to active duty in 1944 and found himself based in Pearl Harbor. One day, rather unexpectedly, he was summoned by Commander Frank Leahy, the Notre Dame coach, who had also joined the Navy during World War II. Leahy had recruited Connor in high school, and he wanted the young ensign to understand that he was still impressed by his character and athletic ability. If Connor was interested in transferring, there would be a place for him at Notre Dame when the war ended. When Connor was discharged, he accepted Leahy's offer, in part because he wanted to be closer to his father, who had fallen ill.

There were few restrictions on transfers in 1946; servicemen returning to school—or transferring to new schools—were immediately declared eligible to play. Connor, a strong but agile player, became a starting tackle. He played on two of the finest teams in Notre Dame history: the 1946 and 1947 national championship teams. In 1946 he won the Outland Trophy as the outstanding interior lineman in college football. He was captain of the team in 1947 and played in the East-West Shrine Game in 1948. In each of his two seasons in South Bend, Connor was a consensus All-American.

The New York Giants selected Connor in the first round of the 1948 National Football League Draft, but he spent his entire eight-year professional career with the

Chicago Bears. As a two-way tackle he was named All-Pro in 1949 and 1950. In 1951 he continued to play offense and defense, even though the NFL had by then adopted the two-platoon system; in fact, he received All-Pro honors as an offensive tackle and defensive tackle. In 1952 Connor moved to outside linebacker and was again named All-Pro. He retired from the NFL in 1955 and began a career in private business.

George Connor was inducted into the College Football Hall of Fame in 1963 and the Pro Football Hall of Fame in 1975.

COOK, ED
Guard (1953-54) ▪ 6-1, 210 ▪ Philadelphia, PA

Ed Cook earned only one monogram at Notre Dame—as a senior in 1954, when he was a third-string guard. He turned out to be something of a late bloomer, though. Although he was not drafted by any NFL team, Cook signed with the Chicago Cardinals in 1958. He played with the Cardinals for eight years and the Atlanta Falcons for two years, before retiring in 1967.

COSTA, PAUL
Halfback/Defensive End (1961, 1963-64) ▪ 6-4, 230 ▪ Port Chester, NY

Paul Costa earned his first monogram in 1961. As a sophomore running back he carried the ball 32 times for 188 yards and was among the team leaders in kickoff return yardage. After missing the 1962 season, he had 82 yards on 21 carries in 1963. In 1964 he was a reserve defensive end.

Costa's professional career was markedly better than his college career. Drafted in the fourth round by the Green Bay Packers and Kansas City Chiefs in 1964, he spent eight seasons with the Buffalo Bills. In that time he caught 102 passes for 1,699 yards and six touchdowns.

COTTON, FOREST
Tackle (1920-22) ▪ 6-1, 182 ▪ Elgin, IL

Forest G. "Fod" Cotton played for the Fighting Irish during the early years of Knute Rockne's tenure. During his three seasons on the varsity, the team had a combined record of 27-2-1. Cotton's contribution to that mark was not insignificant. He was a reserve guard in 1920 and earned his first monogram in 1921 as a second-string tackle behind All-American Hunk Anderson. In 1922, he became a starter.

After graduating from Notre Dame in 1923, Cotton played professional football with the Rock Island Independents. He later held coaching positions at St. Ambrose College in Davenport, Iowa, and Catholic University in Washington, D.C.

COUTRE, LARRY

Halfback (1946-49) ▪ 5-9, 170 ▪ Chicago, IL

During his first three years on the Notre Dame varsity, Larry Coutre played behind All-American Emil Sitko, one of the greatest running backs in Notre Dame history. He won the Hering Award as "most improved back" in 1948, when he rushed for 152 yards on 27 carries, but his big break came in 1949 when Sitko was moved from right halfback to fullback. That created an opening for Coutre, who stepped into the starting lineup and gave the Fighting Irish one of the strongest running attacks in college football.

Coutre rushed for 645 yards on 102 carries that season. He was second on the team (behind Sitko) in yards gained, but his average per carry (6.3 yards) was a team high. He was also fourth in scoring with 42 points and second in receiving with 13 catches for 271 yards.

Despite those impressive numbers, and despite his obvious contributions to Notre Dame's 10-0 record, Coutre was overlooked when post-season honors were handed out. Four of his teammates—Sitko, Leon Hart, Bob Williams, and Jim Martin—were named All-Americans. But Coutre settled for an invitation to compete in the College All-Star Game.

In the spring of 1950 Coutre was drafted in the fourth round by the Green Bay Packers. He also played for the Baltimore Colts before leaving the NFL in 1953.

COVINGTON, JOHN

Safety/Linebacker/Defensive End (1990-93) ▪ 6-1, 211 ▪ Winter Haven, FL

One of 20 children in a highly athletic family (one sister was a college track star; a brother played football at Central Florida), John Covington was captain of the basketball and football teams at Winter Haven High School.

He began his college career impressively, playing in all 12 games, primarily as a free safety, in his freshman year. As a sophomore, he alternated between free safety, strong safety, and linebacker, and as a junior, in 1992, he also played defensive end. Covington started every game at strong safety in 1993. He was fourth on the team in tackles with 58.

The Indianapolis Colts drafted Covington in the fourth round of the 1994 NFL Draft.

COWHIG, GERRY
Fullback/Halfback (1942, 1946) ▪ 6-3, 211 ▪ Dorchester, MA

Gerry Cowhig scored 18 points while playing behind starting fullback Corwin Clatt in 1942. His college career was interrupted while he served in World War II, but he returned to Notre Dame in the fall of 1946. Cowhig was the second-string left halfback in a backfield loaded with talent (Terry Brennan and Emil Sitko were the starting halfbacks; Jim Mello was the fullback). He contributed to the team's national championship by scoring two touchdowns and rushing for 199 yards. He was named captain of the Fighting Irish for one game—a 0-0 tie against Army played in front of 74,000 fans at Yankee Stadium. The tie ended Army's 25-game winning streak and spoiled the Cadets' chances for a third-consecutive national title.

Cowhig played fullback for the Los Angeles Rams (1947-49), Chicago Cardinals (1950), and Philadelphia Eagles (1951). He retired in 1952 and spent the next three decades working as a sales manager for a freight company in Los Angeles.

CRABLE, BOB
Linebacker (1978-81) ▪ 6-3, 225 ▪ Cincinnati, OH

Two-time consensus All-American Bob Crable played football for Gerry Faust at Moeller High School in Cincinnati. He helped lead Moeller to three consecutive Ohio state championships before coming to Notre Dame. By the time he left South Bend, he was widely acknowledged as the finest linebacker ever to wear the uniform of the Fighting Irish.

A backup in his freshman year, Crable had only 13 tackles. However, as a sophomore, in 1979, he was the team's most accomplished defensive player. He led the Irish in tackles in 9 of 11 games and finished the season with a school-record 187 tackles (a single-season mark that still stands today). The Associated Press and *Football News* each named him third-team All-America.

Crable had a team-high 154 tackles in 1980—including 10 tackles in a 17-10 loss to Georgia in the Sugar Bowl—and was named first-team All-America by *Football News*, *The Sporting News*, United Press International, the American Football Coaches Association, the Newspaper Enterprise Association, and the Walter Camp Foundation; AP placed him on its second team.

As a senior captain in 1981, Crable was reunited with his high school coach, Faust, who took over for Dan Devine. Crable capped a remarkable career by making 167 tackles and intercepting two passes. As in 1980, he was a near-unanimous first-team All-American; and, for the second consecutive year, he was named MVP by the Notre Dame National Monogram Club.

In addition to the single-season mark for tackles, Crable holds the Notre Dame record for career tackles (521); he also shares (with Bob Golic) the record for tackles in a single game (26). A first-round draft pick of the New York Jets in 1982, he suffered several injuries and played only three years in the NFL. He is currently a coach and teacher at his alma mater, Moeller High School.

CRIMMINS, BERNIE
Guard (1939-41) ▪ 5-11, 185 ▪ Louisville, KY

Bernie Crimmins was a three-sport star at St. Xavier's High School in Louisville, Kentucky. He was heavily recruited by the University of Kentucky, as well as several schools in the Big Ten. Notre Dame, too, was interested. Crimmins visited several schools, liked them all, and eventually sought the advice of his father, who strongly recommended Notre Dame.

In South Bend Crimmins was a backup fullback for two years under coach Elmer Layden. When Frank Leahy arrived in 1941, Crimmins was moved to the line; despite his relative lack of size, he became a starter at right guard and helped lead the Fighting Irish to an 8-0-1 record. He was named first-team All-America by *Collier's* magazine and second-team All-America by United Press International.

In the spring of his senior year, Crimmins served as captain of the Notre Dame baseball team. He spent one season with the Green Bay Packers before returning to South Bend to work as an assistant coach under Leahy. He was a part of the Irish coaching staff, working primarily with running backs, through 1951 when he became head football coach at Indiana University (where his record was 13-32). Crimmins came back to Notre Dame in 1957 and spent two more seasons as an assistant coach.

CROTTY, JIM
Running Back (1957-59) ▪ 5-10, 185 ▪ Seattle, WA

Jim Crotty was Notre Dame's starting right halfback in 1958, his second year on the varsity. A solid all-around player, he rushed for 315 yards on 67 carries, caught 13 passes for 137 yards, and returned a team-high nine kickoffs for 228 yards; he also had 38 tackles.

As a senior Crotty was moved to fullback, to help fill in the gap left by the graduation of Nick Pietrosante. His numbers dipped slightly, but he still had a good season: 62 carries for 184 yards; eight receptions for 104 yards; three touchdowns.

Crotty was a twelfth-round draft pick of the Washington Redskins, with whom he spent parts of two seasons. He also played for the Buffalo Bills.

CROWLEY, JIM
Halfback (1922-24) ▪ 5-11, 162 ▪ Green Bay, WI

Jim Crowley, a running back in Notre Dame's famous Four Horsemen backfield of the 1920s, was raised in Green Bay, Wisconsin. His mentor was Earl "Curly" Lambeau, the founder and long-time coach of the Green Bay Packers and a former Notre Dame football player. It was Lambeau who recommended Crowley to Notre Dame coach Knute Rockne. Crowley was a working-class kid and could not afford the cost of an education at a private school such as Notre Dame; since Notre Dame did not award athletic scholarships at the time, Crowley (like most athletes of his era) settled for an arrangement that permitted him to take a part-time job on campus in exchange for room, board, and tuition. The deal, in essence, was brokered by Lambeau.

Crowley split time with Elmer Layden at left halfback in his sophomore season. The following year Layden, despite his lack of size (6-0, 162), was moved to fullback. In 1923 and 1924, Crowley had the left halfback position all to himself. He made the most of the opportunity, rushing for 536 yards and four touchdowns as a junior and 739 yards and six touchdowns as a senior.

It was in that same year that Crowley and his teammates were immortalized, thanks to the dramatic prose of sportswriter Grantland Rice. After watching Notre Dame's 13-7 victory over Army on October 18, 1924, Rice dubbed the Fighting Irish backfield (which also included right halfback Don Miller and quarterback Harry Stuhldreher) "The Four Horsemen" in a story that appeared in the *New York Herald-Tribune*. The passage would eventually become one of the most famous in the history of sports journalism. And the fame and popularity of the Four Horsemen would transcend the boundaries of college football.

The Fighting Irish did not lose a game in the fall of 1924. Their 10-0 record included a 27-10 victory over Stanford in the Rose Bowl that clinched the national championship. After the season Crowley, a deceptively quick and clever ball carrier, was named a consensus All-American. During his three years on the Notre Dame varsity, he scored 15 touchdowns and rushed for 1,841 yards.

Crowley's appearance belied a quick and biting wit. Nicknamed "Sleepy Jim" by Rockne because of his heavy eyelids, Crowley was actually a smart and funny man who on more than one occasion had the audacity to banter with the legendary coach. Rockne, for example, once chastised Crowley for blowing an assignment during practice. "What's dumber than a dumb Irishman?" he yelled. Crowley smiled and responded, "A smart Norwegian."

When his college career was over Crowley played briefly with the Green Bay Packers and the Providence Steamroller. He returned to the college game in 1926 as an assistant coach at the University of Georgia. In 1929 he became the head coach at Michigan State, where he compiled a record of 22-8-3 in four seasons. In 1933 he moved on to Fordham where one of his players was Vince Lombardi, who would, of course, become one of the greatest coaches in NFL history. In the Bronx, Crowley maintained a standard of excellence that had been established by Frank Cavanaugh. His 1937 team, for example, went 7-0-1 and was ranked third in the nation in the final Associated Press poll. In 1941 the sixth-ranked Rams won seven games and lost just one; they defeated Missouri, 2-0, in the 1942 Sugar Bowl.

Crowley left college coaching in 1942 with a career mark of 78-21-10. He received a commission as a lieutenant commander in the Navy Reserve and was assigned to the Naval Preflight Training School in Chapel Hill, North Carolina, where he also coached the service football team.

Three years later Crowley became the first commissioner of the All-America Football Conference. He left that position in 1947 to become owner and coach of the Chicago Rockets. The Rockets won only one game in Crowley's first season, though, prompting him to resign. He later went into private business, working in insurance in Wilkes-Barre, Pennsylvania. He also tried his hand at broadcasting, serving as station manager and sports director of station WTVU in Scranton, Pennsylvania. He later did color commentary on Canadian Football League games for NBC.

Jim Crowley was inducted into the College Football Hall of Fame in 1966. He died on January 15, 1986.

Career Statistics (Rushing)

YEAR	ATT.	YARDS	AVG.	TD
1922	75	566	7.5	5
1923	88	536	6.1	4
1924	131	739	5.6	6
TOTAL	294	1,841	6.3	15

CULVER, RODNEY
Running Back (1988-91) ▪ 5-10, 226 ▪ Detroit, MI

Rodney Culver was captain of the 1991 Fighting Irish and a consistent performer at tailback throughout his four seasons on the varsity. He came to Notre Dame from St. Martin dePorres High School in Detroit, where he scored 20 touchdowns and rushed for more than 1,500 yards in his senior year.

With 4.38 speed in the 40-yard dash and a strong, compact body, Culver proved to be a versatile addition to the Notre Dame offense, although he began his freshman season in the defensive backfield. He carried the ball 30 times for 195 yards in 1988 and 59 times for 242 yards in 1989. When he was a junior, in 1990, he succeeded Anthony Johnson as the starting fullback and rushed for 710 yards on 150 carries. The first fullback to lead the team in rushing since Jerome Heavens in 1977, he was named honorable mention All-America by *Football News*.

Culver was switched to tailback in 1991, largely because of the emergence of Jerome Bettis as a potential superstar at fullback. He started in 8 of 11 games as a senior and rushed for 550 yards on 101 carries. He finished his career with 1,697 yards rushing, nineteenth on Notre Dame's all-time list.

Culver played with the Indianapolis Colts in 1992 and 1993 and with the San Diego Chargers in 1994 and 1995.

Career Statistics (Rushing)

YEAR	NO.	YARDS	AVG.	TD
1988	30	195	6.5	3
1989	59	242	4.1	5
1990	150	710	4.7	5
1991	101	550	5.4	2
TOTAL	**340**	**1,697**	**5.0**	**15**

CZAROBSKI, ZYGMONT
Tackle (1942-47) ▪ 6-0, 213 ▪ Chicago, IL

Zygmont "Ziggy" Czarobski was a boisterous, fun-loving young man from Chicago's South Side. As a starting tackle for the Mt. Carmel High School football team, he earned all-city and all-state honors in his senior year. A talented athlete with a vibrant personality, Czarobski was, throughout his high school and college careers, the most well-liked player on his team. He had a wonderful sense of humor that could break the tension in any locker room; later in life, that gift would make him a popular speaker on the banquet circuit.

Czarobski arrived in South Bend in the fall of 1941. He played on the freshman team for one year before moving into the starting lineup at right tackle as a sophomore in 1942. In 1943 he helped the Irish capture their first consensus national championship under coach Frank Leahy. He missed the 1944 and 1945 seasons while serving in World War II, but returned to Notre Dame in 1946. He reclaimed his job as the starting right tackle and became a pivotal member of two of the best college football teams in history: the Fighting Irish of 1946 and 1947, both of which captured national championships.

A penchant for self-deprecating humor notwithstanding, Czarobski was a strong, smart player. He could, and often did, beat his man with brute force. But he was just as likely to use the considerable knowledge he had accrued to outwit his opponent.

The Chicago Cardinals of the All-America Football Conference drafted Czarobski in 1945 with the hope that he would forego his final two years of college eligibility. Ziggy did not leave school until 1948, at which time he signed with the Chicago Rockets. He spent two years in Chicago before retiring from professional football.

Ziggy Czarobski, one of the most popular players ever to wear a Notre Dame uniform, was inducted into the College Football Hall of Fame in 1977. He died in 1984.

D

DABIERO, ANGELO
Halfback (1959-61) ▪ 5-8, 170 ▪ Donora, PA

Angelo Dabiero was Notre Dame's leading rusher in 1960 and 1961. A tough, compact player who grew up in Donora, Pennsylvania, he earned his first monogram as a sophomore, in 1959, when he gained 118 yards on 36 carries; he also caught six passes for 64 yards.

The next season Dabiero moved into the starting lineup and rushed for a team-high 325 yards on 80 carries. In 1961, as a senior, he had his finest season: first on the team in rushing (92 carries for 637 yards); second in receiving (10 catches for 201 yards); second in scoring (24 points); first in punt returns (11 for 97 yards); second in kickoff returns (eight for 200 yards); first in interceptions (five for 78 yards); and third in tackles (47). He also logged a team-high 464:34 of playing time.

Dabiero's numbers were impressive, but he had the misfortune of playing for some of Notre Dame's weakest teams, and his individual accomplishments were largely overlooked. Most All-America teams failed to recognize him, and he was not chosen in the 1961 NFL Draft.

DAHL, BOB
Defensive Tackle (1988-90) ▪ 6-5, 261 ▪ Chagrin Falls, OH

Bob Dahl was a two-year starter at defensive tackle whose work ethic was admired by coaches and teammates alike. An all-state tight end and defensive lineman at Chagrin Falls High School, he did not make the Notre Dame varsity until his sophomore year—and he appeared in only three games that season.

As a junior, though, Dahl was forced into a starting role when incumbent George Williams was lost for the season because of academic problems. Dahl responded admirably, playing more than 209 minutes and making 52 tackles. Williams returned in

1990, but Dahl had played so well that coach Lou Holtz was compelled to find room for both men. Williams wound up starting at left tackle, while Dahl moved to right tackle. He started all 12 games, had 35 tackles, and was named honorable mention All-America by *Football News*.

A third-round NFL draft choice, Dahl played with the Cincinnati Bengals from 1992 through 1995 and with the Washington Redskins in 1996.

DAMPEER, JOHN

Offensive Tackle (1970-72) ▪ 6-3, 237 ▪ Kermit, TX

John Dampeer was a freshman at Notre Dame in the fall of 1968. In 1969, the first year he was eligible for varsity competition, he fractured an ankle and missed the entire season. So it wasn't until 1970, his third year on campus, that he finally had a chance to play varsity football. He made the most of the opportunity, though. Dampeer not only started every game at right tackle, but he also logged more field time (300:19) than any other Irish player.

Dampeer started again in 1971 and was elected co-captain in 1972. An aggressive but agile lineman, he was named first-team All-America by *Football News*. He was drafted by the Cincinnati Bengals in 1973 but did not play in the NFL.

DANCEWICZ, FRANK

Quarterback (1943-45) ▪ 5-10, 180 ▪ Lynn, MA

The Fighting Irish of 1943 featured two of the college game's greatest quarterbacks: Angelo Bertelli and John Lujack. Bertelli, a senior, had a spectacular, albeit short, year (he was called to active duty in the Marine Corps after six games) and was duly rewarded with the Heisman Trophy after leading Notre Dame to the national title. Lujack, in his first year on the varsity, was Bertelli's backup. That, of course, left little room for Frank Dancewicz.

By 1944, though, Bertelli had graduated and Lujack, too, had joined the armed forces. That left Dancewicz as the quarterback, and although he wasn't the most accurate of quarterbacks (he completed just 68 of 163 passes), he did have nine touchdown passes and threw for nearly 1,000 yards. The following season, as team captain, he completed 30 of 90 passes for 489 yards and five touchdowns. He also had a team-high three interceptions.

Dancewicz was named second-team All-America by several organizations, including United Press, the International News Service, and the American Football Coaches Association. He was a first-round draft choice of the Boston Yanks in 1946.

After a three-year professional career, Dancewicz became head coach at Salem High School, in Salem, Massachusetts. He later coached at a number of schools in the Boston area, including his alma mater, Lynn Classical, as well as at Boston University and Lafayette College. He was also supervisor of physical education and health for the Lynn school system. At the time of his death in 1985, he was a physical education instructor at Lynn Classical.

DAVIE, BOB

Head Coach (1996-present) ▪ Sewickley, PA

On November 24, 1996, 42-year-old Bob Davie was formally introduced as the twenty-eighth head football coach at the University of Notre Dame. He succeeded Lou Holtz, who resigned after 11 seasons at the helm of the most visible program in college football.

Upon Lou Holtz's resignation at the end of the 1996 season, Bob Davie was named as the twenty-eighth head football coach at the University of Notre Dame.

A relatively obscure figure outside coaching circles, Davie graduated from Youngstown State College in Youngstown, Ohio, in 1976 with a degree in education. He immediately jumped on the coaching treadmill, starting with a job as a graduate assistant at the University of Pittsburgh. From there he moved on to the University of Arizona, where he coached linebackers in 1978 and 1979 before returning to Pittsburgh in 1980. He helped the Panthers rank first in the nation in total defense in 1980 and 1981 and second in 1982.

In 1983 Davie began a two-year stint as defensive coordinator at Tulane. In 1985 he moved to Texas A&M where he spent four years coaching linebackers before being named defensive coordinator in 1989; in 1993 he was also named assistant head coach. At Texas A&M Davie produced some of the best defensive teams in college football. The Aggies led the nation in pass efficiency defense in 1993 and were first in the Southwest Conference in total defense for three consecutive seasons. From 1991 through 1993 Texas A&M won three consecutive conference titles and compiled a record of 32-5.

Davie's success at A&M led to an invitation to join the coaching staff at Notre Dame. He came to South Bend in 1994 as defensive coordinator, and although he loved the job, he was terribly homesick. He detested the cold weather, and he missed his wife and two children, who were still in Texas. Eventually, though, Davie adapted to the weather, his new home, and the rigors of his job. His family moved to South Bend, and together they embraced the Notre Dame culture. Less than three years later, just one day after the final game of the 1996 regular season, Davie was named head coach of the Fighting Irish.

Although other names were tossed about—the most prominent being Northwestern coach Gary Barnett—Notre Dame athletic director Mike Wadsworth said that Davie was the school's first choice. Davie had clearly demonstrated his proficiency as a defensive strategist; more importantly, he had filled in as head coach in 1995 when Holtz underwent neck surgery and had handled the assignment impressively. Well liked by both the coaching staff and the players, Davie seemed the logical choice. Still, there were odds to overcome: Not since Terry Brennan replaced Frank Leahy in 1954 had an assistant coach been promoted to head football coach at the University of Notre Dame.

"Obviously it's a great day for me personally, and it's a great day for my family," Davie said at a press conference announcing his promotion. "I promise to the Notre Dame family that I'm going to do everything in my power so that hopefully, one day, people will look back on this and say it was a great day for Notre Dame football."

DAVIS, TRAVIS

Free Safety/Tailback (1991-94) ▪ 6-0, 197 ▪ Carson, CA

Travis Davis was named honorable mention All-America by *USA Today* after his senior year at Banning High School in Wilmington, California. As the team's starting tailback, he rushed for more than 1,600 yards and scored 19 touchdowns. A gifted athlete with exceptional speed, he was also captain of his high school track team.

Despite those credentials, Davis had a difficult time making the transition from high school to college: He played in only two games as a freshman defensive back. As a sophomore, though, he played in eight games and earned his first monogram, and by the time he was a senior he had become Notre Dame's starting strong safety. Davis finished sixth on the team in tackles in 1994 with 56 and was a standout on special teams. His most memorable performance came against USC, when he had nine tackles. He also had six solo tackles in a 21-20 victory over Michigan State.

Davis was drafted by the New Orleans Saints in the seventh round of the 1995 National Football League Draft.

DAWSON, LAKE

Flanker/Split End (1990-93) ▪ 6-1, 202 ▪ Federal Way, WA

Notre Dame's leading receiver in both 1992 and 1993 was a former prep star from Federal Way, Washington, named Lake Dawson. A split end and safety in high school,

Lake Dawson was the leading receiver in 1992 and 1993 for Notre Dame. Upon graduation, he joined fellow Irishmen Joe Montana and Tim Grunhard on the Kansas City Chiefs.

he earned all-state honors at both positions and was named Gatorade Circle of Champions Player of the Year in the state of Washington. He was also captain of the basketball team and a district champion in track and field (his specialty was the hurdles).

Dawson was a second-string split end behind Tony Smith in his freshman year at Notre Dame. He switched to flanker as a sophomore and not only became a starter but also finished the year as the team's second-leading receiver with 24 catches (including a career-high six for 81 yards in a 45-21 victory over Purdue). Among his season highlights was a 40-yard touchdown reception (from Rick Mirer) in Notre Dame's 39-28 upset of third-ranked Florida in the Sugar Bowl.

In 1992 Dawson went back to split end, led the Fighting Irish with 25 receptions for 462 yards, and was named honorable mention All-America by *Football News*. In 1993 he rotated back to flanker, but the shift didn't seem to faze him in the least. Once again he led the team in receptions (25 for 395 yards) and was an honorable mention All-American.

Dawson was a third-round pick of the Kansas City Chiefs in the 1994 NFL Draft.

Career Statistics (Receiving)

YEAR	REC	YARDS	AVG.	TD
1990	6	107	17.8	0
1991	24	433	18.0	1
1992	25	462	18.5	1
1993	25	395	15.8	2
TOTAL	80	1,197	14.9	4

DEMMERLE, PETE
End (1972-74) ▪ 6-1, 190 ▪ New Canaan, CT

Pete Demmerle, a consensus All-American wide receiver, came to Notre Dame from New Canaan High School, which he led to the Connecticut state championship in 1969 (he scored four touchdowns in a span of 4:26 in the title game). A prep All-American in football, he also was captain of the baseball team.

There was never any real doubt about where Demmerle would go to college—his father, uncle, and cousin all graduated from Notre Dame. Demmerle followed suit in 1971, and though it wasn't until 1973 that he saw any significant playing time, he blossomed once inserted into the starting lineup. An excellent blocker, he was also the team's leading receiver in 1973, catching 23 passes for 404 yards and five touchdowns. He was the favorite target of quarterback Tom Clements, and together they were the focus of an offense that scored 358 points. Notre Dame won the national championship that season, and Demmerle played a vital role. He caught three passes for 59 yards in a 24-23 Sugar Bowl victory over Alabama and was also on the receiving end of what proved to be a crucial two-point conversion.

Demmerle's senior year was even more impressive. He caught 43 passes for 667 yards and six touchdowns and was a consensus first-team All-American. He was no slouch in the classroom, either, as demonstrated by his selection as a first-team Academic All-American and a recipient of post-graduate scholarships from the NCAA and the National Football Foundation.

A thirteenth-round draft pick of the San Diego Chargers in 1975, Demmerle did not play professional football. He chose instead to pursue a career in law; he is currently a practicing attorney.

Career Statistics (Receiving)

YEAR	ATT.	YARDS	AVG.	TD
1972	0	0	0	0
1973	26	404	15.5	5
1974	43	667	15.5	6
TOTAL	69	1,071	15.5	11

DEVINE, DAN

Head Coach (1975-80) ▪ Augusta, WI

Daniel J. Devine, who coached Notre Dame to a national championship in 1977, was born in Augusta, Wisconsin, and raised in Proctor, Minnesota, near Duluth. One of nine children, he displayed an early interest in sports and went on to captain his high school football team. Later, at the University of Minnesota-Duluth, he served as captain of both the basketball and football teams and president of the student body.

A two-and-a-half year tour of duty as a bombardier in the Army Air Corps interrupted Devine's college career, but he eventually graduated in 1948 with a degree in Social Studies. His first coaching job was at East Jordan High School in Michigan where his teams went undefeated in 1948 and 1949. The following year he joined the staff at Michigan State University, first as a freshman coach and later as a varsity assistant in charge of the offensive backfield.

Devine accepted his first head coaching assignment in 1955 at Arizona State University. In three years his teams won 27 games, lost three, and tied one. Included in that record was the school's first undefeated team, which was ranked twelfth in the final Associated Press poll. Devine's success at ASU led to an offer from the University of Missouri where, in 13 seasons, he compiled a record of 92-38-7. The Tigers reached

the Orange Bowl in Devine's second season; the following year, 1960, they won 10 of 11 games, including a 21-14 victory over Navy in the Orange Bowl, and were ranked fifth in the country.

Devine's Missouri teams never lost more than three games in a single season. He also served as athletic director from 1966 until 1971 when he left to become head coach of the Green Bay Packers. He guided the Packers to a 10-4 record and a divisional title in 1972 and was named NFC Coach of the Year by United Press International and the Pro Football Writers Association of America; *Football News* even named him its man of the year. Overall, though, Devine was only moderately successful in Green Bay. He left in 1974, with an overall record of 25-28-4, to return to the college game.

In 1955 Dan Devine began his career as a head coach at Arizona State. He went on to lead the Missouri Tigers to an Orange Bowl victory in 1960 and the Green Bay Packers to a division title in 1972 before taking on the position at Notre Dame in 1974.

On December 17, 1974, Devine officially became Notre Dame's twenty-fourth head football coach. Although he had the unenviable task of succeeding Ara Parseghian, he withstood the pressure. His first Irish team went 8-3, his second went 9-3, and his third, in 1977, won 11 of 12 games and finished first in *every* final poll—the first time in history that a Fighting Irish team had been named unanimous national champion. The season ended with a surprisingly one-sided 38-10 victory over top-ranked Texas in the Cotton Bowl.

In six years at Notre Dame, Devine had a record of 53-16-1. Citing the poor health of his wife as a primary reason, he retired after the 1980 season with a career record of 126-42-7, a winning percentage of .742. He later came out of retirement to become the executive director of the Arizona State Sun Angel Foundation in Phoenix. In 1992 he returned to Missouri to serve as athletic director. He retired again in 1994.

Devine was elected to the College Football Hall of Fame in 1985.

Career Coaching Record

YEAR	WON	LOST	TIED
1975	8	3	0
1976	9	3	0
1977	11	1	0
1978	9	3	0
1979	7	4	0
1980	9	2	1
TOTAL	53	16	1

DEVORE, HUGH

End (1931-33) ▪ Head Coach (1945, 1963) ▪ 6-0, 170 ▪ Newark, NJ

The youngest of nine children, Hugh Devore was born in Newark, New Jersey, in 1910. He attended St. Benedict's Prep where he is remembered as one of the best all-around athletes in school history. As captain of the football team, he earned all-state honors for two consecutive years; he was also captain of the baseball and basketball teams.

Devore played on the freshman basketball and football teams at Notre Dame in 1930. Freshman were not eligible for varsity competition at the time, but Devore made his presence known on the football field during daily scrimmages against the varsity. He received his first monogram in 1931 and became a starter in 1932. As a senior, in 1933, he served as co-captain of the football team; the following spring he started in left field for the Irish baseball team.

Devore graduated with honors in the spring of 1934 and immediately accepted a job offer from first-year coach Elmer Layden. One year later he moved to Fordham where he was named line coach by another member of the Four Horsemen backfield: Jim Crowley. Devore stayed at Fordham for three seasons, until he received his first head coaching opportunity, at Providence College. He transformed the Friars into one of the better small-college programs in the country.

Hugh Devore devoted himself to Notre Dame as both a player (in the 1930s) and as a head coach (in 1945 and 1963).

In 1942 Devore left Providence to become an assistant coach at Holy Cross in Worcester, Massachusetts. His time there was brief, though; just one year later he returned to South Bend as an assistant to Frank Leahy. In 1945, while Leahy was serving in the military, Devore was named interim head coach and guided the Irish to a 7-2-1 record. Upon Leahy's return in 1946, Devore took to the road again, this time to become head coach at St. Bonaventure University. In 1949 he left St. Bonaventure to take over the football program at New York University, and in 1952 he became an assistant coach with the Green Bay Packers.

Devore was nothing if not restless, and soon he was back in the college game. He was named head coach at the University of Dayton in 1954 but stayed only two seasons before leaving to become coach of the Philadelphia Eagles. In 1958 he returned to Notre Dame, this time as freshman coach under Terry Brennan; he was also named assistant athletic director.

Devore served as interim coach a second time in 1963, after the departure of Joe Kuharich. He suffered through a 2-7 season before turning the program over to Ara Parseghian.

DiNARDO, GERRY

Offensive Guard (1972-74) ▪ 6-1, 237 ▪ Howard Beach, NY

Just a few short months after the graduation of All-American guard Larry DiNardo, another member of the family arrived on the campus of Notre Dame. And he proved to be more than capable of walking in his big brother's footsteps.

Gerry DiNardo became a three-year starter at right guard. He was a member of the 1973 national championship team and helped the Irish rank fourth in the nation in total offense. With DiNardo anchoring an extraordinary offensive line, Notre Dame rushed for a school-record 3,502 yards.

In 1974, after leading the team to a 10-2 record, DiNardo, like his brother before him, became a consensus first-team All-American. Rather than play professionally, he went into coaching. His resume includes stints as head coach at Vanderbilt and, most recently, Louisiana State University.

DiNARDO, LARRY

Offensive Guard (1968-70) ▪ 6-1, 235 ▪ Queens, NY

Two-time All-American guard Larry DiNardo was one of Notre Dame's most consistent performers in the late 1960s. He led the team in minutes played (283:41) in 1969 and was a Dean's List student. United Press International and the Walter Camp Foundation each named DiNardo first-team All-America.

As a senior, in 1970, he was elected co-captain and helped the Fighting Irish set a school record for total offense with 510.5 yards per game. A consensus All-American, he received first-team recognition from UPI, the Associated Press, *The Sporting News*, and many others. Coach Ara Parseghian once said of DiNardo, "He has that certain football smartness and leadership quality that makes him a top-notch performer both on and off the field." Apparently so, because he was also a first-team Academic All-American in his senior year.

DiNardo, whose younger brother, Gerry, also became an All-American at Notre Dame, was a seventh-round draft pick of the New Orleans Saints. He chose a career in law, however, and today works as an attorney in Chicago.

DINGENS, GREG

Defensive Tackle (1982-85) ▪ 6-5, 257 ▪ Bloomfield Hills, MI

Greg Dingens earned four monograms as a defensive tackle and started five games as a senior in 1985. But he was truly distinguished by his ability to excel both on the field and in the classroom. Dingens was a second-team Academic All-American in 1983 and

1984, as well as a first-team Academic All-American in 1985. He was awarded post-graduate scholarships by the NCAA and the National Football Foundation and was a Rhodes Scholar candidate.

Athletically, Dingens was having his best season (15 tackles and more than 111 minutes of playing time) in 1985 when he suffered a serious knee injury in the fifth game. He missed the second half of the season and enrolled in medical school the following year.

DORAIS, CHARLES
Quarterback (1910-13) ▪ 5-7, 145 ▪ Chippewa Falls, WI

Notre Dame's first—and, for seven decades, only—four-year starter at quarterback, Charles Emile "Gus" Dorais is often credited with popularizing the forward pass. In the summer of 1913, prior to his senior year, Dorais and teammate Knute Rockne were working as lifeguards at the Cedar Point Resort in Sandusky, Ohio. During their free time, the two young men practiced throwing the ball to each other. They devised various pass patterns and worked on plays that they thought might be valuable in the coming months.

If that seems typical enough, well, it really wasn't. Not at the time, anyway. Although the forward pass had been legal since 1906, it was not until 1913, when Notre Dame began using it on a regular basis, that the play was considered anything more than a novelty.

The Irish outscored their first three opponents that season by a combined score of 169-7. Then on November 1, they routed perennial national power Army, 35-13, behind the passing of Gus Dorais and the receiving of Knute Rockne. Dorais completed his first 12 passes, including three for touchdowns, as the Irish stunned the Cadets. In the wake of that victory, Notre Dame became a program of national prominence, and the forward pass enjoyed widespread acceptance for the first time.

Quarterback Charles "Gus" Dorais was made famous when he (with the help of receiver Knute Rockne) popularized the forward pass in a 1913 game against Army. Dorais completed his first twelve passes of the game, three of them for touchdowns.

Dorais led Notre Dame to three consecutive undefeated seasons. A gifted all-around athlete, he still holds the school record for most field goals attempted in a single game (he made three of seven in a 30-7 victory over Texas in 1913). After leaving Notre Dame he played professionally for several teams, including the Massillon Tigers, before settling into a long career as a coach. He started out at Columbus College in Iowa (1914 through 1917) and worked briefly as an assistant at Notre Dame following World War I, but he spent the bulk of his career (1925 through

1942) at Detroit University. His overall college coaching record was 150-70-13. He also had a record of 20-31-2 as head coach of the NFL's Detroit Lions from 1943 through 1947. In 1954 he was inducted into the College Football Hall of Fame.

Incidentally, Dorais was not known as "Gus" until he arrived in South Bend. He was given the nickname while taking a freshman literature course. During a discussion of Dante's *The Inferno*, a professor pointed out that the book's illustrator was a French artist named Gustave Dore and that his last name, while spelled differently, took the same pronunciation as Dorais's name: *dor-RAY*. Classmates began calling Dorais "Gustave," which was soon shortened to "Gus."

DORSEY, ERIC

Defensive Tackle (1982-85) ▪ 6-5, 270 ▪ McLean, VA

Eric Dorsey and his cousin, Allen Pinkett, both came to Notre Dame in 1982. And although Pinkett went on to greater fame as a collegian, Dorsey had a respectable career in his own right. He became a starting defensive tackle as a sophomore in 1983 but was limited to only 53 minutes of playing time the following year because of a nagging ankle injury.

As a senior, in 1985, he started every game and led all Irish linemen with 87 tackles; he also led all linemen in playing time (261:25). Dorsey was named honorable mention All-America by the Associated Press and was a first-round draft choice of the New York Giants in 1986. He played with the Giants from 1986 through 1992.

DOVE, BOB

Left End (1940-42) ▪ 6-2, 195 ▪ Youngstown, OH

Bob Dove came to Notre Dame from South High School in Youngstown, Ohio, where he received all-city honors as an end. He chose Notre Dame in part because of a pleasant recruiting trip, during which he mistakenly got the impression that freshman football players were housed in the newly-completed—and comparatively lavish—Breen-Phillips Hall. As Dove discovered the following August, when he arrived for pre-season workouts and was assigned a single bed and locker in Spartan Bronson Hall, a freshman was a freshman at Notre Dame—regardless of his athletic prowess.

And, for all freshman, there was an indoctrination period, which included a session with legendary equipment manager John "Mac" McAllister. On the first day of practice in the fall of 1939, Dove tried to explain to McAllister that he had not been given any socks. McAllister chided the rookie for "losing" his gear and refused to give him another pair. Dove sheepishly pulled on his cleats—sans socks—and jogged out onto the field. Within an hour he had to stop practicing because of blisters, a fact that did not please head coach Elmer Layden.

From that rather inauspicious start, Dove rose to become one of the finest ends Notre Dame has ever produced. An eager, aggressive young man, he became a starter in his sophomore year—after failing to earn a letter as a freshman—and was one of the finest athletes on coach Frank Leahy's first two squads (in 1941 and 1942).

Dove was a consensus All-American in both 1941 and 1942. He also won the Knute Rockne Trophy as the nation's outstanding college lineman in 1942, as the Irish went 7-2-2 and set the stage for a national title the following year. He played in the East-West Shrine Game following his senior year and was selected by the Washington Redskins in the third round of the 1943 National Football League Draft. Dove played for the Chicago Rockets and Chicago Cardinals during his eight-year professional football career and then became an assistant coach with the Detroit Lions.

He later returned to his hometown and became assistant athletic director at Youngstown State University.

DRAFT PICKS

The National Football League has been drafting college athletes since 1936. Since that time 410 players from the University of Notre Dame have been selected. Included in that figure are 55 first-round draft picks, beginning with running back Bill Shakespeare in '36. Five Notre Dame players (more than any other school) have been taken with the first pick in the entire draft: Angelo Bertelli (1944), Frank Dancewicz (1946), Leon Hart (1950), Paul Hornung (1957), and Walt Patulski (1972).

Following is a list of all Fighting Irish players drafted in the first round:

YEAR	PLAYER	POSITION	TEAM
1936	Bill Shakespeare	HB	Pittsburgh
1944	Angelo Bertelli	QB	Boston
1945	Frank Szymanski	HB	Detroit
1945	John Yonaker	E	Philadelphia
1946	Frank Dancewicz	QB	Boston
1946	John Lujack	QB	Chicago
1946	Emil Sitko	HB	LA Dons
1946	George Connor	T	NY Giants
1949	Frank Tripucka	QB	Philadelphia
1949	Bill Fischer	G	Phoenix
1950	Leon Hart	E	Detroit
1951	Bob Williams	QB	Chicago
1951	Jerry Groom	C	Phoenix
1954	Art Hunter	T	Green Bay
1954	John Lattner	HB	Pittsburgh

1954	Neil Worden	FB	Philadelphia
1955	Joe Heap	HB	NY Giants
1955	Ralph Guglielmi	QB	Washington
1955	Frank Varrichione	T	Pittsburgh
1957	Paul Hornung	QB	Green Bay
1959	Nick Pietrosante	FB	Detroit
1960	George Izo	QB	Phoenix, NY Jets
1960	Monty Stickles	E	SF, San Diego
1965	Jack Snow	WR	Minnesota
1967	Tom Regner	G	Houston
1967	Alan Page	DT	Minnesota
1967	Tom Seiler	G	NY Jets
1968	Kevin Hardy	DE	New Orleans
1969	George Kunz	T	Atlanta
1969	Jim Seymour	E	LA Rams
1970	Mike McCoy	DT	Green Bay
1972	Clarence Ellis	DB	Atlanta
1972	Walt Patulski	DE	Buffalo
1972	Mike Kadish	DT	Miami
1975	Mike Fanning	DT	LA Rams
1976	Steve Niehaus	DT	Seattle
1978	Ross Browner	DE	Cincinnati
1978	Luther Bradley	DB	Detroit
1978	Ken MacAfee	TE	San Francisco
1980	Vagas Ferguson	RB	New England
1982	Bob Crable	LB	NY Jets
1983	Tony Hunter	TE	Buffalo
1984	Greg Bell	RB	Buffalo
1986	Eric Dorsey	DT	NY Giants
1988	Tim Brown	WR	LA Raiders
1989	Andy Heck	OT	Seattle
1991	Todd Lyght	DB	LA Rams
1992	Derek Brown	TE	NY Giants
1993	Rick Mirer	QB	Seattle
1993	Jerome Bettis	FB	LA Rams
1993	Tom Carter	DB	Washington
1993	Irv Smith	TE	New Orleans
1994	Bryant Young	DT	San Francisco
1994	Aaron Taylor	OG	Green Bay
1994	Jeff Burris	FS	Buffalo

DuBOSE, DEMETRIUS

Linebacker (1989-92) ▪ 6-2, 234 ▪ Seattle, WA

Adolphus Demetrius DuBose, who led the Fighting Irish in tackles for two consecutive years, was a prep All-American at Bishop O'Dea High School in Seattle. He was also captain of the basketball team and runner-up in the shot put at the Washington state track and field championships.

DuBose was promoted into a starting role late in his sophomore year at Notre Dame. The following season, as a junior, he started 11 games at inside linebacker and had a team-high 127 tackles. He was named first-team All-America by *Football News* and was one of 10 semifinalists for the 1991 Butkus Award, which is presented annually to the best linebacker in the country.

As a senior captain in 1992, DuBose again led the team in tackles with 87, despite missing two games with injuries. A smart, agile linebacker known for his ability to make plays anywhere on the field, he was named honorable mention All-America by United Press International and *Football News*. He also received the Nick Pietrosante Award from his teammates.

An outstanding student, DuBose graduated in just three and a half years with a degree in government. He was a second-round draft pick of the Tampa Bay Buccaneers in 1993.

DUERSON, DAVE

Defensive Back (1979-82) ▪ 6-3, 202 ▪ Muncie, IN

Two-time All-American Dave Duerson grew up in Muncie, Indiana, and graduated from Muncie Northside High School, the same school that produced Luther Bradley, Notre Dame's career leader in interceptions.

Duerson arrived in South Bend two years after Bradley's departure and quickly made a name for himself. As a freshman cornerback in 1979, he had 24 tackles, two interceptions, and led all first-year players in minutes played; he was also the team's top punt returner with an average of 17.4 yards.

Duerson's performance improved with each successive season. He had 34 tackles while playing strong safety in his sophomore year and 55 tackles as a junior free safety. In 1982 he remained at free safety and assumed the role of captain. He had 63 tackles and a team-high seven interceptions. He also returned 34 punts for 245 yards, an average of 7.2 yards per return.

Football News named Duerson third-team All-America in 1981 and first-team All-America in 1982. The Football Writers Association of America also named him first-team All-America in '82. He is Notre Dame's career leader in punt returns with 103. He is also second in punt return yardage with 869.

Duerson was drafted by the Chicago Bears in the third round in 1983 and spent 11 years in the NFL. In addition to the Bears (1983-89), he played for the New York Giants (1990) and Arizona Cardinals (1991-93). He won Super Bowl rings with the Bears in '86 and the Giants in '91.

Career Statistics (Punt Returns)

YEAR	NO.	YARDS	AVG.
1979	12	209	17.4
1980	25	194	7.8
1981	32	221	6.9
1982	34	245	7.2
TOTAL	**103**	**869**	**8.4**

DURANKO, PETE
Defensive Tackle/Fullback/Linebacker (1963-66) ▪ 6-2, 235 ▪ Johnstown, PA

In 1963, the last year before the advent of two-platoon football, Pete Duranko rushed for 93 yards on 26 carries as a sophomore fullback. In 1964 he began the year at inside linebacker but broke his wrist in the first game and missed the rest of the season.

The next year, however, he was healthy, and he finally found a permanent home. As a starting defensive tackle, Duranko played 267 minutes and had 95 tackles, second on the team behind Jim Lynch.

Given an extra year of eligibility because of his injury in '64, Duranko returned in the fall of 1966. With 73 tackles he helped the Irish post a 9-0-1 record and capture a national championship. He was named first-team All-America by United Press International and the American Football Coaches Association, second-team All-America by *The Sporting News*, and third-team by Associated Press. He also played in the 1967 College All-Star Game. Duranko played defensive end and linebacker with the Denver Broncos from 1967 through 1970.

E

EBLI, RAY
End/Tackle (1940-41) ▪ 6-2, 197 ▪ Ironwood, MI

Because St. Ambrose High, in Ironwood, Michigan, did not have a football program, Ray Ebli competed only in basketball and track during his high school years. Nicknamed "Lil Abner" because of his striking physical resemblance to the popular comic strip character of the time, Ebli did not let a lack of experience interfere with his plans. He made the freshman football team at Notre Dame as a walk-on in 1938 and won his first monogram as a third-string end in 1940. In 1941 head coach Frank Leahy shifted Ebli to left tackle, where he split time with Jim Brutz.

Ebli played for the Chicago Cardinals in 1942. After serving in World War II, he returned to professional football in 1946 as an end for the Buffalo Bills. He also played for the Chicago Rockets.

ECUYER, AL
Guard (1956-58) ▪ 5-10, 205 ▪ New Orleans, LA

A New Orleans parochial league all-star and a high school All-American, Al Ecuyer adjusted quickly to the college game. In his first year on the varsity he led all guards in minutes played with 324, despite suffering from an assortment of injuries, including a broken thumb, a sprained ankle, and a pinched nerve in his shoulder.

In 1957 he increased his playing time to 374 minutes and shared the team lead in tackles with Jim Schaaf (both players had 88). His best performance came in a 21-13 loss to Iowa, in which he registered a team-high 18 tackles. Ecuyer was a consensus All-American in 1957, earning first-team honors from United Press, *The Sporting News*, and the International News Service and second-team honors from the Associated Press.

Ecuyer led the Irish in tackles again in 1958, with 78, and was named first-team All-America by United Press and *The Sporting News*. He was drafted by the New York

Giants in the eighteenth round of the 1959 NFL draft but did not play in the NFL. He opted instead for a career in private business and eventually became a vice president with Prudential Securities.

EDDY, NICK

Halfback (1964-66) ▪ 6-0, 195 ▪ Lafayette, CA

A unanimous All-American, Nick Eddy was the leading rusher on Notre Dame's national championship team in 1966. Throughout his college career he was a steady, productive player adept at both carrying and receiving the ball.

In his first year on the varsity, 1964, Eddy was the youngest starter in a backfield that included halfback Bill Wolski, fullback Joe Farrell, and quarterback John Huarte. The Heisman Trophy that year went to Huarte, who had a sensational season. Overshadowed was an impressive debut by Eddy, who was second on the team in rushing (98 carries for 490 yards) and third in receiving (16 catches for 320 yards) and scoring (44 points), as well as first in kickoff returns.

The next year Eddy rushed for 582 yards on 115 carries and caught 13 passes for 233 yards—both team highs; he was fourth in scoring with 36 points. By the end of the season he had already cracked the school's top-20 in career rushing yardage.

As it was for many of his teammates, 1966 was the highlight of Eddy's career. A terrific all-purpose running back, he rushed for 553 yards on just 78 carries (an average of 7.1 yards per attempt) and caught 15 passes for 123 yards. On a team that led the NCAA in scoring with 362 points, he was the leading scorer (60 points). If there was a regrettable moment in that season for Eddy, it came when he arrived in East Lansing, Michigan, the day before top-ranked Notre Dame's showdown with No. 2 Michigan State. Eddy, already nursing a sore shoulder, slipped while stepping off a train and aggravated the injury. He did not play at all. With Eddy on the sideline, the Fighting Irish were fortunate to come away with a 10-10 tie. It was the only stain on an otherwise perfect season.

Appropriately enough, Eddy was a consensus first-team All-American in 1966. He also finished third in voting for the Heisman Trophy (Florida quarterback Steve Spurrier won the award) and was invited to play in the College All-Star Game. He graduated with 1,625 yards rushing, at the time good enough for eighth place on the school's all-time list.

A second-round draft pick in 1967, Eddy played with the Detroit Lions from 1967 through 1970, sat out the 1971 season with a knee injury, and returned in 1972. He carried the ball 152 times for 523 yards in his professional career. After retiring in 1973, Eddy went into private business. Today he works for All-State Insurance.

Career Statistics (Rushing)

YEAR	NO.	YARDS	AVG.	TD
1964	98	490	4.8	5
1965	115	582	5.1	4
1966	78	553	7.1	8
TOTAL	291	1,625	5.6	17

Career Statistics (Passing)

YEAR	NO.	YARDS	AVG.	TD
1964	16	352	22.0	2
1965	13	233	18.0	2
1966	15	123	8.2	0
TOTAL	44	708	16.1	4

EDWARDS, GENE

Quarterback (1924-26) ▪ 6-1, 165 ▪ Weston, WV

Eugene "Red" Edwards was Harry Stuhldreher's backup at quarterback on Notre Dame's 1924 national championship team. He became a starter the following season, after Stuhldreher's graduation, and held the job for two years, during which the Irish posted a combined record of 16-3-1. Although he played quarterback, Edwards never led the team in passing; however, in 1925 he was the leading receiver with four catches for 28 yards.

Just one year after leaving Notre Dame, Edwards became an assistant coach at St. Vincent College in Latrobe, Pennsylvania. He left after two years to take a job in private business in his hometown of Weston, West Virginia, but within a year, had returned to the sidelines as head coach at St. Vincent.

EICHENLAUB, RAY

Fullback (1911-14) ▪ 6-0, 210 ▪ Columbus, OH

A four-year starter at fullback, Ray Eichenlaub was a pioneer of Fighting Irish football. Along with quarterback Gus Dorais and end Knute Rockne, he was one of the star players on the team that stunned Army, 35-13, in November of 1913. That victory gave Notre Dame its first true taste of national exposure, largely because Dorais and Rockne utilized the forward pass to an extent not previously seen in college football; but Eichenlaub was equally important, scoring two touchdowns and anchoring a running game that provided balance to the offense.

In Eichenlaub's four years in South Bend, the Fighting Irish compiled a record of 25-2-2. He scored 176 career points, including 12 touchdowns in just seven games during the 1913 season; that same season he was named second-team All-America. But statistics do not tell the entire story. Eichenlaub's spirit and reputation are probably best reflected in one of the many stories (perhaps true, perhaps not) involving the legendary Rockne.

In the fall of 1917 Rockne was an assistant coach at Notre Dame. While trying to persuade a talented young athlete named George Gipp to come out for the football team, he said, "I've got just the pair of cleats for you."

Gipp looked at the coach, wide-eyed.

"A special pair?"

"Yeah," Rockne said. "They belonged to Ray Eichenlaub."

Big shoes to fill, indeed.

EILERS, PAT
Split End/Flanker (1987-89) ▪ 5-11, 193 ▪ St. Paul, MN

After one year at Yale University, Pat Eilers transferred to Notre Dame in 1986 and earned his first monogram as a walk-on in 1987. In 1988, with the graduation of Heisman Trophy winner Tim Brown, he started six games at flanker and caught six passes for 70 yards. He moved to split end in 1989 and started all 13 games. Although his numbers were modest (five receptions for 53 yards, zero touchdowns), Eilers was considered a vital member of the Notre Dame offense. He was a smart, aggressive player with good hands and exceptional blocking skills.

Ignored in the 1990 NFL Draft, Eilers signed as a free agent with the Los Angeles Rams. He proved to be a productive NFL player in stints with the Minnesota Vikings (1990-91), Phoenix Cardinals (1992), Washington Redskins (1993-94), and Chicago Bears (1995-96).

ELLIS, CLARENCE
Defensive Back (1969-71) ▪ 6-0, 178 ▪ Grand Rapids, MI

Clarence Ellis, a two-time All-American, was one of Notre Dame's most accomplished defensive backs. He became a starter in 1969, his first year on the varsity, and held the job for three seasons. Along the way he intercepted 13 passes, scored one touchdown, and received praise and recognition from every corner of the college football world.

Ellis had 31 tackles and three interceptions as a sophomore; he also broke up 13 passes, which still stands as a school record. The following year he intercepted seven passes, had 27 tackles, and logged more playing time (269:49) than any other defensive player. In Notre Dame's 24-11 victory over Texas in the 1971 Cotton Bowl, he made six tackles, broke up three passes, and was named Most Valuable Defensive Player. United Press International and the Newspaper Enterprise Association each named Ellis first-team All-America.

As a senior, in 1971, Ellis had his finest season. He had 35 tackles and three interceptions and was a consensus first-team all-American. He was also invited to play in the College All-Star Game and the Senior Bowl.

Ellis, who is tied for third place on Notre Dame's list for career interceptions, was a first-round draft choice of the Atlanta Falcons in 1972; however, his NFL career lasted just three seasons. He later became a computer systems analyst.

Career Statistics (Interceptions)

YEAR	NO.	YDS.	AVG.	TD
1969	3	98	32.6	1
1970	7	25	3.6	0
1971	3	34	11.3	0
TOTAL	13	157	12.1	1

ENRIGHT, REX
Fullback (1923, 1925) ▪ 5-10, 172 ▪ Rockford, IL

Rex Enright, a prep star from Rockford, Illinois, earned his first monogram in 1923 as a reserve fullback. He was the starting fullback in 1925, a year the Irish went 7-2-1.

Enright graduated from Notre Dame with a law degree but opted instead for a career in football. He played professionally with the Green Bay Packers before becoming an assistant coach at the University of North Carolina. He later became athletic director at the University of South Carolina, a position he held until his death in 1960 at the age of 59.

EVANS, FRED
Fullback/Halfback (1940-42) ▪ 5-11, 178 ▪ South Bend, IN

South Bend native Fred "Dippy" Evans entered Notre Dame in 1939 after an outstanding prep career at Riley High School, where he was an all-city and all-state running back and most valuable player in the Northern Indiana Conference. A superb all-around athlete, Evans earned varsity letters in football, track, baseball, and basketball at Riley; in his senior year he captured the sprint title at the Indiana high school track and field championship.

Evans was a second-string halfback in his sophomore year. As a junior, in 1941, he was switched to fullback by first-year coach Frank Leahy and became not only a starter but also the team's leading rusher. Evans gained 480 yards on 141 carries; he also scored a team-high 11 touchdowns and 67 points.

Although he was expected to start in 1942, Evans was injured in preseason practice and played only one minute during the regular season. A member of the Army Air Corps Reserve, he resumed his football career on the professional level after World War II, playing for the Cleveland Browns, Buffalo Bills, Chicago Bears, and Chicago Rockets.

F

FANNING, MIKE
Defensive Tackle (1972-74) ▪ 6-6, 250 ▪ Tulsa, OK

All-American tackle Mike Fanning actually began his career as a defensive end. He was captain of the football and wrestling teams at Tulsa's Edison High School, where he earned all-state and All-America honors and was named Tulsa's lineman of the year in his senior year. In the winter of 1972 he was one of only two freshmen named to *Amateur Wrestling News'* freshman-sophomore All-America team after posting a 25-1-1 record.

Fanning earned his first football monogram as a second-string defensive end in the fall of 1972. The next year, on a team that won the national championship, he started at tackle and led all defensive linemen in playing time. He had 61 tackles, fourth best on the team, and was named Midwest Linemen of the Week after recording three quarterback sacks in an opening-day victory over Northwestern. That winter he qualified for the heavyweight finals of the NCAA wrestling tournament after winning all 18 of his matches.

In 1974, as a senior, Fanning was again fourth on the team in tackles (85). The Associated Press named him second-team All-America; the Newspaper Enterprise Association, *Sporting News*, *Time*, and the Walter Camp Foundation all named him first-team All-America. Fanning was a first-round draft choice of the Los Angeles Rams in 1975. He also played with the Detroit Lions and Seattle Seahawks before retiring in 1984.

FAUST, GERRY
Head Coach (1981-85) ▪ Dayton, OH

On November 24, 1980, Gerard Anthony Faust became the twenty-fourth head football coach at the University of Notre Dame. His appointment came as something of a surprise, for although Faust was a charismatic coach and teacher with a proven record of success, he lacked experience at the college level. For nearly two decades he had been one of the premier prep coaches in the country, leading Moeller High School in Cincinnati to a record of 174-17-2. But he had *never* coached a college football team.

After two successful decades as a prep coach, Gerry Faust was named head coach at Notre Dame in 1980. His five years in that position were impressive for a man with no collegiate experience—but not impressive enough for the Fighting Irish. He submitted his resignation at the end of the 1985 season.

It was an extraordinarily difficult move, and though Faust handled it with a degree of grace and dignity, there is no denying that his tenure at Notre Dame was one of the least successful the school has known. In five seasons under Faust, the Fighting Irish won 30 games, lost 26, and tied one. Only two other coaches—Hugh Devore and Joe Kuharich—have had lower career winning percentages.

Faust grew up in Dayton, Ohio, and graduated from Chaminade High School. A two-year starter at quarterback, he was coached by his father, Gerry Sr., who directed the football program at Chaminade for 49 years. Faust played college football at the University of Dayton where one of his coaches was Hugh Devore. After graduating in 1958 he returned to Chaminade to work as an assistant coach. In 1963 he took over as head coach at Moeller and led the team to a 9-1 record.

Over the next 18 years Faust's teams won 12 city championships and five state championships; on four occasions they ended the season as the top-ranked team in the nation. In that same time period more than 250 Moeller athletes received college football scholarships; 20 players, including All-Americans Bob Crable and Steve Niehaus, went to Notre Dame. Faust coached 22 high school All-Americans at Moeller and was named prep coach of the year in 1979.

Still, he could not possibly have been prepared for the overwhelming pressure he would experience at Notre Dame. In his first season the Fighting Irish lost four of their first six games and finished 5-6. They improved to 6-4-1 in 1982 and 7-5 in 1983 and 1984. But there were only minor bowl appearances (the Liberty Bowl in '83 and the Aloha Bowl in '84), and by 1985 the heat was on Faust. After another losing season (5-6), he submitted his resignation.

Faust was not out of work long, though. He became head coach at the University of Akron in 1986 and compiled a record of 43-53-3 in nine years. After resigning in 1994 he accepted a position in the school's development office.

Coaching Record

YEAR	WINS	LOSSES	TIES
1981	5	6	0

1982	6	4	1
1983	7	5	0
1984	7	5	0
1985	5	6	0
TOTAL	30	26	1

FEENEY, AL

Center (1910-13) ▪ 5-11, 180 ▪ Indianapolis, IN

A native of Indianapolis, Al Feeney entered Notre Dame in the fall of 1910. He was a backup center and failed to earn a monogram in his freshman year. As a sophomore, however, he stepped into a starting role, and he did not relinquish it for the next three years. In Feeney's three seasons as a starter, the Irish had 20 victories and two ties. They did not lose a game.

After leaving Notre Dame, Feeney played professional football with the Canton Bulldogs. He later became head of the Indiana state police. In 1947 he was elected mayor of Indianapolis. He died in 1950.

FERGUSON, VAGAS

Running Back (1976-79) ▪ 6-1, 194 ▪ Richmond, IN

A strong, explosive running back, Vagas Ferguson gained 3,472 yards during his four seasons at Notre Dame. When he left in 1979, he was the school's all-time leading rusher. Ferguson's mark would later be eclipsed by Allen Pinkett, but his career remains one of the brightest in Notre Dame history.

In 1977, as a sophomore, Ferguson gained 493 yards on 80 carries. He was clearly the third offensive option in a powerhouse backfield that also included quarterback Joe Montana and fullback Jerome Heavens (who rushed for nearly 1,000 yards that season). In the 1978 Cotton Bowl, however, Ferguson gained 100 yards and scored three touchdowns and was named the game's Outstanding Offensive Player as the Fighting Irish defeated top-ranked Texas 38-10 to capture the national championship.

By his junior year Ferguson had become Notre Dame's premier running back, although he was surely helped by the presence of Heavens, a senior who was as adept at opening holes as he was at running through them. Ferguson set a Notre Dame record for yardage in a single game when he rushed for 255 yards against Georgia Tech. He finished the year with 1,192 yards and seven touchdowns. Heavens gained 728 yards, giving the Fighting Irish one of the most potent running attacks in college football.

Heavens and Montana were gone by 1979, leaving Ferguson to shoulder most of the offensive burden. As it turned out, he was more than up to the challenge. In an 11-game season Ferguson carried the ball 301 times, an average of 27.4 carries per contest. Both numbers are Notre Dame single-season records, as is the 1,437 yards he accumulated on the ground. For one so prolific, Ferguson's college career ended rather quietly. He carried the ball just 10 times for 19 yards in the 1979 Cotton Bowl as the Fighting Irish fell behind 34-12 and were forced to resort to an exclusively aerial attack. Ferguson did go out a winner, as Notre Dame rallied for a 35-34 victory over Houston.

A consensus All-American in 1979, Ferguson was a first-round draft choice of the New England Patriots in 1980. During his modest four-year NFL career he played with the Patriots, Oilers, and Browns. He rushed for 1,163 yards on 290 carries and scored five touchdowns. Ferguson later returned to his hometown and became athletic director at Richmond High School.

Career Statistics (Rushing)

YEAR	ATT.	YARDS	AVG.	TD
1976	81	350	4.3	2
1977	80	493	6.2	6
1978	211	1,192	5.6	7
1979	301	1,437	4.8	17
TOTAL	673	3,472	5.2	32

FIGARO, CEDRIC

Linebacker (1984-87) ▪ 6-2, 246 ▪ Lafayette, LA

The third of four children in a sports-minded family (brother Kevin and sister Stephanie both played basketball at Southwestern Louisiana), Cedric Figaro was a two-time All-American at linebacker for the Fighting Irish.

His influence was felt almost immediately: In 1984 he played more minutes than any other freshman defensive player. By 1985 he had moved into the starting lineup. Figaro had 62 tackles that season and was a second-team pick on *Football News*'s sophomore All-America team. In 1986 and 1987 he was named third-team All-America by that same publication. He had 59 tackles as a junior and 53 as a senior.

Figaro was a sixth-round draft pick of the San Diego Chargers in 1988. He played with the Chargers (1988-90), Cleveland Browns (1991-92), and St. Louis Rams (1995-96).

FIGHTING IRISH

It wasn't until 1927 that University of Notre Dame president Matthew Walsh officially adopted "Fighting Irish" as the school's nickname. Prior to the turn of the century the university's athletic teams often competed under the moniker "Catholics." And in the 1920s, when the Four Horsemen were running roughshod over the opposition, Notre Dame was commonly referred to as the "Ramblers."

Now, of course, the term "Fighting Irish" is known by football fans around the globe. But the precise origin of the nickname remains somewhat vague. The media is generally credited with popularizing the term "Fighting Irish" as a way of capturing the spirit and tenacity of the teams that often represented the University of Notre Dame on the playing field. For example, Francis Wallace, a Notre Dame graduate who wrote for the *New York Daily News*, frequently used the expression in his stories in the 1920s. And others soon followed suit, since it seemed a rather harmless, colorful expression.

However, historians also acknowledge that "Fighting Irish" was probably not originally a term of endearment; rather, it may have begun as a derisive expression favored by Notre Dame's opponents; a way of taunting representatives of a small, private, Catholic institution. There are, in fact, numerous tales of the birth of the "Fighting Irish."

As one story goes, Notre Dame was trailing Michigan at half-time of a 1909 encounter. Then, as now, athletes with surnames such as Kelly and Ryan were common in South Bend. And there was a certain pride in that heritage. One Notre Dame player supposedly became so angry with his teammates' lackluster performance that he shouted, "What's the matter with you guys? You're all Irish and you're not fighting worth a lick!" Notre Dame rallied to win the game, and the player's remarks soon made their way to the press box. The next day, newspapers around the country reported details of a stirring victory by the University of Notre Dame "Fighting Irish."

That is one story. Another dates back to 1899 when Notre Dame was playing Northwestern in Evanston, Illinois. At half-time the Northwestern fans began chanting "Kill the Fighting Irish!"

Whatever its origins, there is no question that the nickname is now embraced by Notre Dame fans and alumni. As a writer for the *Notre Dame Scholastic* wrote in 1929, "The unkind appellation became symbolic of the struggle for supremacy of the field. The term, while given in irony, has become our heritage. So truly does it represent us that we are unwilling to part with it."

FILLEY, PAT

Guard (1941-44) ▪ 5-8, 175 ▪ South Bend, IN

The first two-time captain in the history of Notre Dame football, Patrick Joseph "Peanut" Filley was a native of South Bend. He received all-city and all-state honors in football at Central High School and was a three-time state champion in wrestling.

A four-year member of the Fighting Irish varsity, he earned his first monogram in

1942 as a second-string guard behind Bob McBride. In 1943 Notre Dame went 9-1 and captured its first national title in 13 years. On a team so rich with talent that it included four future Hall of Famers—quarterbacks Angelo Bertelli and John Lujack, halfback Creighton Miller, and tackle Ziggy Czarobski—diminutive Pat Filley was the emotional leader. The smallest player in the starting lineup, he was admired for both his spirit and talent, as reflected by the fact that he was elected captain while only in his junior year. After the season he was one of six Irish players to receive All-America recognition; United Press and *The Sporting News* both named him to their first teams.

In 1944 Filley again served as captain, and again he was named an All-American. Although he was a tenth-round draft pick of the Cleveland Browns, Filley never played professional football. Instead, he became an assistant coach at Cornell in 1945 (working for former Notre Dame coach Ed McKeever). Ten years later he was forced to give up coaching because of an arthritic condition. He settled into a long career (more than three decades) as an athletic administrator, holding such titles as assistant director, ticket manager, director of operations, and finally, associate director in charge of scheduling.

FISCHER, BILL
Tackle (1945-48) ▪ 6-2, 230 ▪ Chicago, IL

Bill "Moose" Fischer played high school football at Lane Tech in the Chicago Public League. He led his team to an appearance in the city championship game and was named all-state in his senior year. As part of his reward, Fischer—like all members of the all-state team—was honored at a banquet at the University of Illinois in Champaign. There he received an enthusiastic sales pitch from Fighting Illini head coach Ray Eliot.

Fischer liked everything about Illinois. He liked the program. He liked the coach. He liked the players. He liked the idea of representing his state university. So he decided to accept Illinois's offer.

Meanwhile, Notre Dame coach Hugh Devore continued the recruiting process, albeit quietly. Athletes in the 1940s did not sign letters of intent, so they were not contractually bound to a school. The entire business was conducted on the honor system. If a player agreed to attend a particular school, coaches from competing programs generally backed away.

Most of the time, anyway.

In the summer of 1945, just days before he was scheduled to begin preseason practice at Illinois, Fischer accompanied Notre Dame assistant coach Gene Ronzani on what was supposed to be a brief trip to South Bend. As it turned out, the trip lasted four years. Fischer enrolled in classes at Notre Dame and began practicing with the football team. He saw considerable playing time as a reserve tackle in his freshman year and then moved into the starting lineup as a guard in his sophomore year. In three seasons as a starter he did not experience a loss. The Fighting Irish went 26-0-2 and won two national championships (1946 and '47). In 1947 Fischer was a true iron man, leading the team in playing time with 300 minutes. He was a two-time consensus All-American and won the Outland Trophy as college football's outstanding interior lineman in 1948.

Fischer was a first-round draft choice of the Chicago Cardinals in 1949. During his five years in the NFL he was twice named All-Pro. He returned to South Bend in 1954 and spent five years working as an assistant coach under Terry Brennan. He later went into private business.

Bill Fischer was inducted into the College Football Hall of Fame in 1983.

FLANAGAN, CHRISTIE
Halfback (1925-27) ▪ 6-0, 170 ▪ Port Arthur, TX

When freshman running back Christie Flanagan suited up for his first practice session at Notre Dame, he took one look at his uniform and realized that it was going to be a long year. The pads were worn, the jersey and pants were too big. Worst of all, one shoe was a size 9, the other a size 10. When Flanagan asked Knute Rockne for a different pair of cleats, the legendary coach just laughed. This, as Flanagan came to discover, was his initiation period.

A few weeks later, though, after Flanagan performed impressively in a drill against the varsity, he was given a brand new pair of shoes. And by the time he was a sophomore, in 1925, he was a starting halfback. In fact, he led the Fighting Irish in rushing with 556 yards on 99 carries. He was also the team's scoring leader with 45 points. In 1926 he gained 535 yards on 68 carries (an average of 7.9 yards per carry) and was named second-team All-America in leading the Irish to a 9-1 record.

It was in that season that Flanagan was immortalized by famed sportswriter Grantland Rice. Two years earlier, during Notre Dame's drive to a national championship, Rice had christened Notre Dame's brilliant backfield "The Four Horsemen." Now it was Flanagan's turn. After watching Flanagan score the game's only touchdown on a 70-yard run from scrimmage in a 7-0 victory over Army, Rice called him "The Lone Horseman." He also wrote that Flanagan was "harder to hold than a Broadway bankroll."

Flanagan shouldered the burden of comparison for the rest of the season and throughout his senior year. And he did so with uncommon grace and poise. In 1927 he rushed for a career-best 731 yards on 118 carries as Notre Dame went 7-1-1. United Press and the Newspaper Enterprise Association each named Flanagan first-team All-America.

By the time he left Notre Dame Flanagan was fourth on the school's all-time rushing list. Heading into the 1996 season, he was in seventeenth place overall and seventh among three-year players. Flanagan chose a career in private business after graduation. He did not play professional football.

Career Statistics (Rushing)

YEAR	ATT.	YARDS	AVG.	TD
1925	99	556	5.6	7
1926	68	535	7.9	4
1927	118	731	6.2	4
TOTAL	285	1,822	6.4	15

FLANIGAN, JIM

Defensive Tackle/Linebacker (1990-93) ▪ 6-2, 276 ▪ Sturgeon Bay, WI

A reserve linebacker in his first two years, Jim Flanigan switched to defensive tackle as a junior and became one of Notre Dame's best linemen. He started the final 23 games of his college career and had his most memorable game against Purdue in 1993, recording 10 tackles. He also had eight tackles in a 31-24 upset of top-ranked Florida State, a performance that helped him land on the cover of *Sports Illustrated*.

Flanigan, who was named Wisconsin Player of the Year in high school, was drafted by the Chicago Bears in the third round of the 1994 NFL Draft.

FOLEY, TIM

Offensive Tackle/Center (1976-79) ▪ 6-5, 265 ▪ Cincinnati, OH

Tim Foley was a starting tackle on Notre Dame's national championship team in 1977 and a first-team All-American in 1979. He was a teammate of Irish linebacker Steve Heimkreiter at Roger Bacon High School in Cincinnati and a backup behind Harry Woebkenberg at left tackle in his freshman year at Notre Dame. He moved into the starting lineup the following season and remained there for three years.

Foley was named honorable mention All-America by the Associated Press in 1978. In 1979 he was chosen first-team All-America by United Press International, the Newspaper Enterprise Association, and *The Sporting News*; AP named him to its second team. Foley played with the Baltimore Colts in 1981.

FORWARD PASS

In the early part of the twentieth century, football, even at Notre Dame, was a muscular, conservative sport. Offensive schemes were simple: block well and open holes for the running backs. There was little tolerance for creativity or innovation. That all changed on November 1, 1913, at West Point, New York.

The forward pass had been a legal play since 1906, but it was largely ignored by coaches, fans, and players. When Notre Dame stunned an exceptionally talented team from Army by a score of 35-13, however, the sport was forever altered. In that game quarterback Gus Dorais and end Knute Rockne (who were also roommates) took the forward pass—previously restricted to sideshow status—to a national stage.

Army was the premier college football program of the time; Notre Dame, despite its success (the team had not lost a game in three years), was merely a small, Midwestern school toiling in comparative obscurity. But the Fighting Irish had a few surprises planned for the Cadets, and chief among them was the forward pass. Dorais and Rockne had practiced the play repeatedly during the previous summer when they worked together as lifeguards. Now they had an opportunity to show what they could do.

Notre Dame's offensive attack on that November day revolved around the passing game. And Army had never seen anything like it. The Cadets, like most teams of that era, considered the pass to be a play born of desperation; it was a weapon to be used only when all else failed. The sight of Dorais dropping back to pass on first down utterly befuddled the Army defense. Predictably, the Cadets began to overcompensate for Notre Dame's aerial attack, which naturally allowed the Fighting Irish to develop their running game. Never before had a college football team been armed with such a daring, yet logical, offensive game plan.

By the end of the day Dorais had completed 14 of 17 passes for 243 yards (including a record 40-yard completion to Rockne), and Notre Dame had thoroughly outplayed college football's marquee program. The attendant publicity not only gave Notre Dame a much-needed dose of national recognition but also lifted the forward pass to a level of respectability it had not previously known.

FOUR HORSEMEN

On October 19, 1924, one day after Notre Dame's 13-7 victory over Army, famed sportswriter Grantland Rice offered readers of the *New York Herald Tribune* the following bit of lyricism:

Outlined against a blue, gray October sky the Four Horsemen rode again. In dramatic lore they are known as famine, pestilence, destruction and death. These are only aliases. Their real names are Stuhldreher, Miller, Crowley and Layden. They formed the crest of the South Bend cyclone before which another fighting Army football team was swept over the precipice at the Polo Grounds yesterday afternoon as 55,000 spectators peered down on the bewildering panorama spread on the green plain below.

Poetic as it was, Rice's story might well have been little more than fish wrapping if not for the energetic work of George Strickler, who served as student publicity aide to

The famous Four Horsemen, as sportswriter Grantland Rice dubbed them, led Notre Dame to their first national championship in 1925. Shown here from left to right: Don Miller, Elmer Layden, Jim Crowley, and Harry Stuhldreher.

Notre Dame head coach Knute Rockne. Strickler, who would later become sports editor of the *Chicago Tribune*, recognized an opportunity to immortalize both the writer and his subject. And so he devised an elaborate publicity stunt. When the team returned to South Bend after the Army game, Strickler convinced the Four Horsemen— quarterback Harry Stuhldreher, left halfback Jim Crowley, right halfback Don Miller, and fullback Elmer Layden—to pose for a photograph. The players, in uniform, sat on the backs of four horses borrowed from a local livery stable. Strickler then made sure the photos were distributed on the wire services, and the legend of the Four Horsemen was born.

Fortunately, Notre Dame had a football team worthy of the hype that soon enveloped the Four Horsemen. The Fighting Irish went 10-0 and captured their first national championship. The season ended with a 27-10 victory over Stanford in the 1925 Rose Bowl.

Though physically unimposing (not one of the players weighed more than 162 pounds), the Four Horsemen achieved something close to mythic stature. They were perhaps the greatest backfield in the history of college football, a contention supported by the fact that during their time in South Bend, the Fighting Irish won 29 games and lost just one.

FRY, WILLIE

Defensive End (1973, 1975-77) ▪ 6-3, 242 ▪ Memphis, TN

At Northside High School in Memphis, Tennessee, Willie Fry was the embodiment of the student-athlete. An all-state and All-America football player in his senior year, he also led his team to the state finals in basketball and competed for the varsity track team. Not only that, he was also a member of the National Honor Society, senior class president, and recipient of the Outstanding American High School Student award.

Fry's reputation preceded him at Notre Dame, but he seemed unfazed by the pressure. In his freshman year, as a second-string defensive end, he appeared in every game for a team that captured the 1973 national championship. He missed the 1974 season with injuries, but became a starter in 1975 and was fifth on the team in tackles with 78.

In 1976 Fry became Notre Dame's first junior captain since Bob Olson eight years earlier. He had 77 tackles and was named second-team All-America by *Football News* and honorable mention All-America by the Associated Press. As a senior, in 1977, he had 47 tackles and helped lead the Irish to another national title. After the season Fry received second-team All-America honors from United Press International.

FURJANIC, TONY
Linebacker (1982-85) ▪ 6-2, 228 ▪ Chicago, IL

Anthony Joseph Furjanic was one of Notre Dame's best defensive players in the mid 1980s. He earned his first monogram through his play on special teams as a freshman in 1982 and then became a starter at middle linebacker in his sophomore year. He had a remarkable 142 tackles—more than twice the amount recorded by any other Irish player—and logged a team-high 318 minutes of playing time.

As a junior, in 1984, Furjanic suffered a torn knee ligament and played in only six games. By the fall of 1985, though, he had obviously recovered. He led the team in tackles (147) and minutes played (327) and was named honorable mention All-America by the Associated Press and United Press International.

An eighth-round NFL draft pick in 1986, Furjanic played with the Buffalo Bills (1986-88) and the Miami Dolphins (1988).

G

GANN, MIKE

Defensive Tackle (1981-84) ▪ 6-5, 256 ▪ Orlando, FL

Mike Gann was born in Stillwater, Oklahoma, and attended high school in Lakewood, Colorado. (His family moved to Orlando, Florida, while he was in college.) A *Parade* prep All-American, he earned his first Notre Dame monogram as a freshman in 1981 and became a starter at defensive tackle in 1982. A knee injury, which required surgery, cut his sophomore year short, but he returned to the starting lineup in 1983 and had 52 tackles in 274 minutes of playing time.

Gann was third on the team in tackles with 60 in 1984 and was named second-team All-America by the Newspaper Enterprise Association. He spent nine seasons with the Atlanta Falcons.

GASPARELLA, JOE

Quarterback (1944-45) ▪ 6-3, 210 ▪ Pittsburgh, PA

A highly touted high school prospect, Joe Gasparella came to Notre Dame as a freshman in 1944. According to preseason press releases, he was considered by the coaching staff to be "as good if not better than Angelo Bertelli or Johnny Lujack at the same time." High praise indeed; unfortunately, Gasparella never came close to living up to that billing.

With Lujack serving in the military, the Irish needed a new quarterback in the fall of '44. The job was Gasparella's for the taking, but he was beaten out by sophomore Frank Dancewicz, who had backed up Bertelli and Lujack the previous season. Gasparella played reasonably well when given the opportunity, but he attempted just 28 passes (completing 13). Dancewicz retained the starting job in 1945, and Gasparella played even less. He completed one of four passes for 50 yards, and carried the ball just twice the entire season.

With the return of several armed services veterans in 1946—including Lujack, who would win the Heisman Trophy in 1947—came major changes in the Fighting Irish line-up. A number of players who had been on the roster the previous two years were suddenly squeezed out. One of those was Gasparella. He was, however, selected by the Pittsburgh Steelers in the fourth round of the 1948 NFL Draft. He spent three seasons with the Steelers and one season with the Chicago Cardinals.

GATEWOOD, TOM
Split End (1969-71) ▪ 6-2, 208 ▪ Baltimore, MD

Tom Gatewood, Notre Dame's all-time leading receiver, arrived in South Bend in the fall of 1968. By the time he graduated in 1972, he owned the majority of the school's receiving records and had twice been named All-America. He caught 157 passes for 2,283 yards, an impressive enough figure but one that surely would have been much higher if not for the fact that he played in era when freshmen were not eligible for varsity competition.

As it happened, Gatewood broke into the starting lineup as a sophomore, in 1969, and quickly proved himself to be not only the best wide receiver on the team but also one of the best in the country. He had 47 catches for 743 yards and eight touchdowns in more than 277 minutes of playing time.

In 1970, as a junior, he was the second leading receiver in college football with 77 catches for 1,123 yards and seven touchdowns. He also set school records for receptions and yardage in a single season—both marks still stand. He was also third in the team in scoring with 48 points. In Notre Dame's 24-11 victory over Texas in the Cotton Bowl, he caught a 26-yard touchdown pass in the first quarter but had to leave the game early with a pulled hamstring. After the season, he was a consensus All-American, with first-team honors from United Press International, the Newspaper Enterprise Association, and the Walter Camp Foundation, among others.

A team captain in 1971, Gatewood had another outstanding year, though statistically not as impressive as his junior year (a fact that can be partially attributed to the graduation of quarterback Joe Theismann). He finished the season with 33 receptions for 417 yards and four touchdowns and was named first-team All-America by *Time* and second-team All-America by UPI. For the second consecutive year he was also named first-team Academic All-America; his success in the classroom was further rewarded with scholarships from the NCAA and the National Football Foundation.

The New York Giants selected Gatewood in the fifth round of the 1972 NFL Draft, but he spent only two seasons in the league and saw little playing time. He later went into private business.

Career Statistics (Receiving)

YEAR	NO.	YARDS	AVG.	TD
1969	47	743	15.8	8
1970	77	1,123	14.6	7
1971	33	417	12.6	4
TOTAL	157	2,283	14.5	19

GIBBONS, TOM

Safety/Cornerback (1977-80) ▪ 6-1, 181 ▪ Alexandria, VA

A three-year starter in the defensive backfield, Tom Gibbons was also a scholar who earned first-team Academic All-America honors as a senior in 1980. He was a consistent player who had 46 tackles as a sophomore, 48 as a junior, and 41 as a senior. He also intercepted nine passes.

A second-team Academic All-American in his sophomore and junior years, Gibbons graduated in 1981 with a degree in engineering.

Career Statistics

YEAR	TACKLES	INT.	YARDS
1977	5	1	38
1978	46	3	48
1979	48	3	74
1980	41	2	55
TOTAL	140	9	215

GIBSON, OLIVER

Defensive Tackle/Nose Guard (1990-94) ▪ 6-3, 275 ▪ Romeoville, IL

After his senior year at Romeoville High School, Oliver Gibson was named national prep defensive player of the year by *USA Today*. He was an outstanding high school athlete who served as captain of both the football and basketball teams. He went to Notre Dame on a football scholarship but played only three games in 1990 because of an injury; Gibson later applied for and received a medical redshirt, which gave him a fifth year of eligibility.

In the winter of 1991 he made the Fighting Irish basketball team as a walk-on but by the following summer had once again turned his full attention to football. Playing in 11 games at tackle and defensive end, he began to look like a player who would soon make an impact at Notre Dame. Gibson's playing time increased over the course of the next two seasons; by the time he was a senior he had become the starting nose guard. Gibson was fourth on the team (and first among linemen) with 59 tackles in 1994. He was one of five defensive players to start every game. When the season ended, Gibson was named Lineman of the Year by the Moose Krause Chapter of the National Football Foundation and Hall of Fame; he also was co-winner of the Nick Pietrosante Award, given annually to the player who best exemplifies the courage and spirit displayed by the late Notre Dame All-American fullback, who died of cancer in 1988.

Gibson ended his college career with one of his best games, recording seven tackles in a Fiesta Bowl loss to Colorado. He was selected by the Pittsburgh Steelers in the fourth round of the 1995 National Football League Draft.

GIPP, GEORGE

Halfback (1917-20) ▪ 6-0, 180 ▪ Laurium, MI

The story of George Gipp—perhaps the most famous college football player in history—has passed into legend. He was a small-town boy from Laurium, Michigan, who came to Notre Dame in 1916 with the hope of getting an education and perhaps playing a little baseball. Football was not on his agenda.

As it happened, though, Fighting Irish assistant football coach Knute Rockne spotted Gipp fooling around with a football one afternoon. Gipp was drop-kicking the ball with stunning distance and accuracy. Rockne, never one to miss an opportunity, encouraged the kid to give football a try. Gipp agreed, and soon he was making a name for himself on the football field.

In four years Gipp proved to be one of the most talented and versatile players ever to wear a Notre Dame uniform. As a starting halfback, he led the team in rushing and passing for three consecutive seasons. He rushed for 2,341 yards in his career, a Notre Dame record that stood for 50 years. He also passed for 1,769 yards. On defense Gipp was no less formidable. He was a fierce tackler and pass defender who, reportedly, did not allow a single completion. Gipp was a consensus All-American in 1920. In addition to individual awards, his influence can be seen in Notre Dame's record (27-2-3) during his time in South Bend.

The real Gipper was not quite the man immortalized by the handsome and clean-cut Ronald Reagan. George Gipp, whose death at age 25 was certainly tragic, was more at home in a pool hall than a classroom. Twice he tried to transfer out of Notre Dame, and once he was nearly expelled (only Rockne saved him) for skipping classes.

Still, George Gipp's status as an icon stems less from his accomplishments on the field than from his tragic death at the age of 25. Gipp was a senior at Notre Dame when he came down with streptococcic throat. Two weeks after he was named Notre Dame's first All-American, he passed away, but not before offering this deathbed farewell to Rockne:

"I've got to go, Rock. It's all right. I'm not afraid. Some time, Rock, when the team is up against it, when things are wrong and the breaks are beating the boys—tell them to go in there with all they've got and win just one for the Gipper. I don't know where I'll be then, Rock. But I'll know about it, and I'll be happy."

That, at least, is the story that was later dramatized in the unabashedly sentimental motion picture *Knute Rockne, All-American*, in which Ronald Reagan played a clean-cut George Gipp. (Historians would later reveal that Gipp was, in fact, an undisciplined young man who was far more comfortable in a pool hall than he was in a classroom; he twice tried to transfer out of Notre Dame and once was nearly expelled for skipping classes—only Rockne's intervention saved him.)

Rockne did not share George Gipp's words with a Notre Dame team until November 10, 1928. The Fighting Irish were 4-2, decimated by injuries, and about to face a very talented Army team at Yankee Stadium. According to a story that appeared in the *New York News*, Rockne told his players, "The day before he died, George Gipp asked me to wait until the situation seemed hopeless—then ask a Notre Dame team to go out and beat Army for him. This is the day, and you are the team."

Notre Dame, of course, went on to beat Army that day, by a score of 12-6. After scoring a touchdown, halfback Jack Chevigny reportedly shouted, "That's one for the Gipper!"

Gipp, who also started in centerfield for the Notre Dame baseball team, was inducted into the College Football Hall of Fame in 1951.

Career Statistics (Rushing)

YEAR	ATT.	YARDS	AVG.	TD
1917	63	244	3.9	0
1918	98	541	5.5	6
1919	106	729	6.9	7
1920	102	827	8.1	8
TOTAL	369	2,341	6.3	21

Career Statistics (Passing)

YEAR	ATT.	COMP.	YARDS	TD	PCT.
1917	8	3	40	1	.375
1918	45	19	293	1	.422
1919	72	41	727	3	.569
1920	62	30	709	3	.484
TOTAL	187	93	1,769	8	.497

GLADIEUX, BOB
Halfback (1966-68) ▪ 5-11, 185 ▪ Louisville, OH

During his three-year high school career, Bob Gladieux led Louisville High to a 28-1-1 record; he was the state's leading scorer in 1964. At Notre Dame his career was significantly less sensational, although he did eventually find a measure of stardom.

Gladieux's playing time increased each season. He carried the ball 27 times for 111 yards as a sophomore and 84 times for 384 yards as a junior (he also caught 23 passes for 297 yards). In 1968, as a senior, he became the focus of the team's offense. He rushed for a team-high 713 yards on 152 carries and caught 37 passes for 442 yards (second on the team). He also scored 84 points, tying Bob Kelly's single-season record.

Despite those numbers, Gladieux was overlooked by most All-America teams. An eighth-round draft pick of the Boston Patriots, he spent four seasons in the NFL. He rushed for 239 yards on 65 attempts and caught 25 passes for 252 yards; he did not score a touchdown.

Career Statistics (Rushing)

YEAR	NO.	YARDS	AVG.	TD
1966	27	111	4.1	3
1967	84	384	4.6	5
1968	152	713	4.7	12
TOTAL	263	1,208	4.6	20

Career Statistics (Receiving)

YEAR	NO.	YARDS	AVG.	TD
1966	12	208	17.3	2
1967	23	297	12.9	2
1968	37	442	11.9	2
TOTAL	72	947	13.2	6

GOEDDEKE, GEORGE
Center (1964-66) ▪ 6-3, 228 ▪ Detroit, MI

George Goeddeke came to South Bend in 1963 after graduating from St. David's High School in Detroit, where he was captain of the football and basketball teams. He made the Irish varsity in 1964 as a backup to starting center Norm Nicola; however, he did not officially earn his first monogram until 1965 when he was promoted to a starting role. He played 206 minutes that season, despite missing two full games after having his appendix removed.

In 1966 Goeddeke was the starting center on a team that did not lose a game and brought Notre Dame its first consensus national championship since 1949. One of 12 Irish players to receive All-America honors that year, he was a second-team choice by United Press International; the Associated Press named him to its third team.

The Denver Broncos drafted Goeddeke in the third round in 1967. He spent six years in the NFL, all with the Broncos.

GOLDEN DOME

The Golden Dome, which tops the Administration Building, is the most recognizable symbol of the University of Notre Dame. The original was destroyed by fire in 1879, but it was rebuilt in only a few months.

The Golden Dome that sits atop the University of Notre Dame Administration Building is perhaps the most recognizable symbol of the university itself. Students and alumni are sometimes even referred to as "Domers." The Administration Building once represented the entire university campus. In 1879 it was destroyed by fire, but it was rebuilt in a matter of months. Today the building houses many of the university's administrative offices, including that of Rev. Edward A. Malloy, Notre Dame's sixteenth president.

The Golden Dome has a long, symbolic link to Fighting Irish football: the color of the team's helmets, of course, is gold; moreover, the paint for the helmets is mixed on campus by student-managers and contains bits of real gold dust. The paint is applied to each player's helmet the night before each home game.

GOLIC, BOB
Linebacker (1975-78) ▪ 6-3, 244 ▪ Willowick, OH

Notre Dame's first two-sport All-American since Moose Krause, Bob Golic was a four-year starter on the football team and a national champion in wrestling. He came to South Bend in 1975 after an exceptional prep career at St. Joseph's High School, where he was an all-state football player and a state heavyweight wrestling champion. His career record as a high school wrestler was 67-4-2, including a 28-0-1 mark as a senior.

Golic became a starter at middle linebacker midway through his freshman year. He finished the season with 82 tackles, fourth best on the team. In 1976 he was third with 99 tackles, and in 1977, while playing middle guard, he set a single-season record with 146 tackles. He was named defensive MVP of the 1978 Cotton Bowl, in which the Irish defeated Texas 38-10 to secure a national championship. Golic had 17 tackles that afternoon to help keep Heisman Trophy winner Earl Campbell in check. If that was his finest game, though, it wasn't particularly unusual; Golic had at least 10 tackles in every game in 1977 (his personal high was 18 against Michigan State). After the season he was named second-team All-America by United Press International and the Associated Press.

In 1978, as a senior tri-captain, Golic had 152 tackles and was a consensus All-American, earning first-team honors from both AP and UPI. He finished his career with 479 tackles (through 1995 he stood second, behind Bob Crable, on the school's all-time list), six interceptions, and two fumble recoveries.

In addition to his achievements on the football field, Golic continued to excel as a wrestler in college. He had a three-year record of 54-4-1, including a fourth-place finish at the 1977 NCAA tournament and a third-place finish in 1978.

Golic was a second-round draft pick of the New England Patriots in 1979. He also played with the Cleveland Browns and Los Angeles Raiders in an NFL career that spanned 14 years.

Bob Golic was an exceptional athlete and one of the great contributors to Notre Dame football success in the late 1970s. In addition to being a national wrestling champion, Golic was a four-year starter in football. His best season was 1977 when he had at least 10 tackles in every game and as many as 18 in a game against Michigan State.

GOLIC, MIKE
Linebacker/End (1981-84) ▪ 6-5, 257 ▪ Willowick, OH

Like his brother, All-American Bob Golic, Mike Golic wore number 55 and played linebacker for the Fighting Irish. He was not as accomplished a player as his brother, who was nothing less than one of the greatest linebackers in Notre Dame history; he was, however, a very good football player.

Mike Golic broke into the starting lineup as a junior defensive end in 1983. He was fourth on the team with 59 tackles, third in sacks with four for 35 yards, and was named honorable mention All-America by the Associated Press and defensive MVP by his teammates. The following year, as a senior captain, he missed two games because of injuries and wound up with only 25 tackles.

A tenth-round NFL draft choice, Golic played for the Houston Oilers (1985-87), Philadelphia Eagles (1988-92), and Miami Dolphins (1992).

GOMPERS, BILL

Halfback (1945-47) ▪ 6-1, 175 ▪ Bridgeville, PA

A reliable ball carrier and blocker throughout his college career, William George Gompers had the misfortune to attend Notre Dame at the same time as one of the school's all-time great running backs: Emil Sitko, who led the Irish in rushing for four consecutive years (1946-1949).

Gompers was an all-city halfback at Catholic Central High School in Wheeling, West Virginia. He earned his first monogram at Notre Dame in 1945 as a second-string halfback behind Elmer Angsman. Angsman led the team in rushing with 616 yards on 87 carries; Gompers had 185 yards and three touchdowns on 36 carries. By 1946 Angsman was gone, but Sitko had arrived. Still, Gompers received considerable playing time. He carried the ball 51 times for 279 yards and three touchdowns and played an important role in Notre Dame's drive to a national title.

In his senior year, Gompers carried the ball 20 times for 136 yards (an average of 6.8 yards) and one touchdown. He played for the Buffalo Bills of the All-America Football Conference in 1949.

GRASMANIS, PAUL

Nose Guard/Defensive End (1992-95) ▪ 6-2, 279 ▪ Jenison, MI

Paul Ryan Grasmanis, a Fighting Irish captain in 1995, was an all-state guard at Jenison High School in Michigan. He was one of seven freshmen who won monograms in

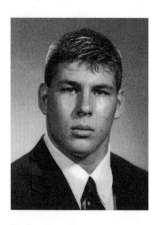

Starting his college career at nose guard, Paul Grasmanis was moved to defensive end in 1994 but was back at nose guard his senior year. He recorded 69 tackles that year, including 13 in a game against Navy.

1992; after missing three games because of an ankle injury early in the 1993 season, he saw time at nose guard in the last seven games and established himself as a contender for a starting job the following year.

Grasmanis did start as a junior, but not at guard; instead, after being moved by coach Lou Holtz to defensive end, he started 10 games and made 49 tackles. As a senior, in 1995, Grasmanis went back to nose guard and started every game. He had 69 tackles in 243:40 of playing time and was named honorable mention All-America by *Football News*. The best performance of his career came in a 35-17 win over Navy, in which he had 13 tackles, including 10 solo tackles.

An emotional, hard-working player, Grasmanis was drafted by the Chicago Bears in the fourth round of the 1996 NFL Draft.

GREEN, MARK

Tailback (1985-88) ▪ 6-0, 184 ▪ Riverside, CA

One of Notre Dame's all-time leading rushers, Mark Green grew up in Riverside, California, and attended Poly High School, the same school that produced National Basketball Association all-star Reggie Miller. A consensus prep All-American who rushed for nearly 1,400 yards and had 10 interceptions as a senior, Green came to Notre Dame in the fall of 1985. Coach Gerry Faust played him at flanker that season, and Green responded with nine receptions for 116 yards.

In 1986, under first-year head coach Lou Holtz, Green was shifted to tailback. Again, the transition was smooth: He rushed for a team-high 406 yards on 96 carries and was third in receiving with 25 catches for 242 yards. In 1987 Green again led the team in rushing with 861 yards on 146 carries. He caught 13 passes for 98 yards and scored six touchdowns. *Football News* named him honorable mention All-America.

As a senior captain in 1988, Green was named honorable mention All-America by *The Sporting News* and *Football News*. He led all running backs in minutes played and was third in rushing with 646 yards on 135 carries. In four seasons he rushed for 1,977 yards, good enough for eleventh place on the school's career rushing chart. A fifth-round draft choice of the Chicago Bears in 1989, he spent four seasons in the NFL.

Career Statistics (Rushing)

YEAR	NO.	YARDS	AVG.	TD
1985	5	64	12.8	0
1986	96	406	4.2	2
1987	146	861	5.9	6
1988	135	646	4.8	7
TOTAL	382	1,977	5.2	15

Career Statistics (Receiving)

YEAR	NO.	YARDS	AVG.	TD
1985	9	116	12.9	0
1986	25	242	9.7	0
1987	13	98	7.5	0
1988	14	155	11.1	0
TOTAL	61	611	10.0	0

GREENEY, NORM

Guard (1930-32) ▪ 5-11, 190 ▪ Cleveland, OH

A third-string guard on Notre Dame's national championship team in 1930, Norm Greeney moved up to second-string in 1931 and became a starter in 1932. He was, at year's end, an extremely capable athlete overlooked on a line that included All-Americans Joe Kurth and Moose Krause.

Greeney played for the Green Bay Packers in 1933 and the Pittsburgh Steelers in 1934 and 1935. He later went into coaching.

GROOM, JERRY

Center/Linebacker (1948-50) ▪ 6-3, 215 ▪ Des Moines, IA

Jerry Groom was a backup center as a sophomore in 1948. With the advent of the two-platoon system in 1949, however, he became a starting linebacker and soon developed into one of the finest defensive players in the history of Notre Dame football.

At Dowling High School in Des Moines, Iowa, Groom had been a standout on both sides of the ball. He played center and linebacker and was named all-state as a junior

Jerry Groom was inducted into the College Football Hall of Fame in 1994. As a center and linebacker for the Irish, he helped the team win its third consensus national championship in four years in 1949.

and senior. Groom was leaning strongly toward attending the University of Iowa until he had an opportunity to chat with Notre Dame coach Frank Leahy, who was the guest speaker at Groom's senior banquet. Leahy, of course, knew all about Groom, and though he was not the greatest sales-man in the world, he knew how to pull the right strings when recruiting a 17-year-old kid. Notre Dame, after all, sold itself; for the coach, it was often simply a matter of reading the record book and arranging a nice campus visit.

Groom promised Leahy he would take a trip to South Bend before committing to play football at any other school. And, once there, he fell in love. This, after all, was 1947, and Notre Dame was the most successful and famous football program in the world. The Fighting Irish had just won a national championship; another loomed on the horizon. And Groom wanted to be a part of it.

In the post-war years, freshmen were once again ruled ineligible for varsity competition, so Groom played on the freshman team in 1947. He backed up Bill Walsh at center in 1948 and became the starting middle linebacker in 1949 as the Irish went 10-0 and captured their third consensus national championship in four years. The team slipped to 4-4-1 in 1950, but Groom, as captain, had another fine season. Playing both linebacker and center, he was named a consensus All-American and was invited to play in the 1951 East-West Shrine Game.

The Chicago Cardinals selected Groom in the first round of the 1951 NFL Draft. After a five-year professional career, he took a job in the private sector and eventually became an executive with Levi-Strauss. He was inducted into the College Football Hall of Fame in 1994.

GRUNHARD, TIM

Offensive Guard/Center (1986-89) ▪ 6-3, 292 ▪ Chicago, IL

After playing nearly 300 minutes and helping the Fighting Irish average 287.7 yards rushing in 1989, Tim Grunhard was named second-team All-America by the Newspaper Enterprise Association. A tough, combative offensive lineman who was considered a throwback to a different era by coach Lou Holtz, Grunhard earned four monograms and started 24 games in his career. He was an honorable mention All-American in his junior year.

The Kansas City Chiefs chose Grunhard in the second round of the 1990 NFL Draft. He played with the Chiefs from 1990 through 1996.

A tough offensive lineman, Tim Grunhard was instrumental in Notre Dame's running game in the late 1980s. He went on to play professionally with the Kansas City Chiefs.

GUGLIELMI, RALPH

Quarterback (1951-54) ▪ 6-0, 185 ▪ Columbus, OH

An all-city selection in football and basketball, Ralph Guglielmi led Grandview High School to the Central Ohio football championship before going to Notre Dame, where he became one of the school's all-time passing leaders.

Guglielmi was a backup to starting quarterback John Mazur in his freshman year but was elevated to starter as a sophomore. He completed 61 of 142 passes for 683 yards and four touchdowns that season. He also helped the Irish to a No. 3 ranking in the final Associated Press poll. He threw for 792 yards and eight touchdowns as a junior, in 1953, and in 1954 was a unanimous first-team All-American. Guglielmi completed 68 of 127 passes for 1,162 yards and six touchdowns as Notre Dame won nine of 10 games under first-year coach Terry Brennan. He played in the East-West Shrine Game and was named MVP of the 1955 College All-Star Game.

Heading into the 1996 season, Guglielmi was ranked ninth among the school's all-time passing leaders. He completed 209 of 436 passes for 3,117 yards and 18 touchdowns; he also rushed for 200 yards and 12 touchdowns and had 10 career interceptions. He is tied with Rick Mirer for most consecutive games with a pass completion (34).

Guglielmi was the No. 1 pick of the Washington Redskins in the 1955 NFL draft. He also played with the St. Louis Cardinals, New York Giants, and Philadelphia Eagles in a professional career that spanned nine years. He later went into private business.

Career Statistics

YEAR	ATT.	COMP.	YARDS	TD	PCT.
1951	53	27	438	0	.509
1952	142	61	683	4	.429
1953	113	52	792	8	.460
1954	127	68	1,160	6	.535
TOTAL	436	209	3,117	18	.479

H

HAINES, KRIS
Split End (1975-78) ▪ 6-0, 181 ▪ Sidney, OH

Kris Haines, a starter on the 1977 national championship team and Notre Dame's leading receiver in 1978, grew up in Sidney, Ohio. Coached by his father at Sidney High School, he played running back and set school records for rushing in a single game (307 yards) and a season (1,407 yards).

At Notre Dame Haines was switched to split end. He earned his first monogram in 1975 under first-year head coach Dan Devine, although he failed to catch a single pass. The next year he worked his way up the depth chart, saw a modest increase in playing time, and by 1977 was in the starting lineup. He had 28 catches for 587 yards, an average of 21 yards per reception, and demonstrated a knack for performing well under pressure. For example, he caught a 27-yard pass from Rusty Lisch to set up the winning touchdown in a season-opening victory over Pittsburgh; and he caught five passes for 120 yards as the Irish rallied for a 31-24 victory over Purdue.

As a senior Haines had a team-high 32 receptions for 699 yards; he was fourth in scoring with 30 points. A ninth-round draft pick of the Washington Redskins in 1979, Haines spent three seasons in the NFL.

HANRATTY, TERRY
Quarterback (1966-68) ▪ 6-1, 200 ▪ Butler, PA

Terry Hanratty was only a sophomore in 1966 when he led the Fighting Irish to a national championship. He beat out classmate Coley O'Brien in preseason camp and went on to have one of the finest debut seasons by a Notre Dame quarterback. In just eight games (he missed the last two games because of a shoulder injury) Hanratty completed 78 of 147 passes for 1,247 yards and eight touchdowns; he also rushed for 124 yards and five touchdowns. In voting for the Heisman Trophy, he finished sixth.

Notre Dame fans expected a lot from Hanratty—he had been a prep All-American at Butler High School in Pennsylvania—but he exceeded even their lofty expectations; rarely had a first-year quarterback exhibited such poise and confidence. And it was clearly no fluke. In 1967 he returned to the starting lineup, healthy and strong, and led the Irish to an 8-2 record. He completed 110 of 206 passes for 1,439 yards and nine touchdowns; he also scored seven touchdowns on the ground. An honorable mention All-American, he finished ninth in voting for the Heisman.

A sophomore in 1966 who was having one of the finest debut seasons of a Notre Dame quarterback, Terry Hanratty led the Fighting Irish to a national championship and found himself in the running for the Heisman, which he never won despite three nominations.

Hanratty's senior season was his best. He completed 59 percent of his passes (116 of 197) for 1,466 yards and 10 touchdowns; he also rushed for 279 yards and four touchdowns. After the season he was showered with honors: consensus All-American (including first-team honors from United Press International, Associated Press, and many others); Monogram Club MVP; third-place finisher in voting for the Heisman Trophy.

In his career, Hanratty completed 304 of 550 passes for 4,152 yards and 27 touchdowns (his favorite target for three years was Jim Seymour, the school's second-leading all-time receiver); he also rushed for 586 yards and 16 touchdowns. Through 1995 he held school records for pass attempts in a single game (63); pass attempts per game in a season (28.1); pass completions per game in a season (16.6); pass completions per game in a career (11.7); and passing yards per game in a career (159.7). When he graduated he was the school's all-time leader in pass completions; through the 1995 season he was third on that list.

Hanratty was selected by the Pittsburgh Steelers in the second round of the 1969 NFL Draft. He played seven seasons with the Steelers and helped the team win a Super Bowl title in 1975; he also played for the Tampa Bay Bucaneers in 1976. In his eight-year NFL career, he completed 165 of 431 passes for 2,510 yards and 24 touchdowns. After retiring from professional football he became a stockbroker.

Career Statistics (Passing)

YEAR	ATT.	COMP.	PCT.	YARDS	TD
1966	147	78	.531	1,247	8
1967	206	110	.534	1,439	9
1968	197	116	.588	1,466	10
TOTAL	550	304	.533	4,152	27

HARDY, KEVIN

Defensive Tackle (1964-67) ▪ 6-5, 270 ▪ Oakland, CA

Kevin Hardy was one of the best all-around athletes ever to attend the University of Notre Dame. A starter at right tackle in his freshman year, he missed most of his sophomore season with an injury but returned to the starting lineup as a junior and earned All-America honors; in his senior year he played both defensive tackle and defensive end and was once again named All-America.

But Hardy was more than just a football player. As a freshman, in 1964-65, he became the first Notre Dame athlete in 19 years to receive varsity letters in three different sports. Hardy averaged 2.3 points a game for the Fighting Irish basketball team (which qualified for the NCAA Tournament); he also played on the varsity baseball team. In fact, Hardy was quite an accomplished baseball player: As a junior he played right field and led the team in hitting with an impressive .398 average.

Interestingly enough, Hardy's best sport was the one he embraced last. He did not even begin playing organized football until his junior year in high school. By the time he left South Bend, however, he was one of the best players in the country. Hardy was taken in the first round of the 1968 NFL Draft by the New Orleans Saints. He later played for the San Francisco 49ers, Green Bay Packers, and San Diego Chargers in a five-year NFL career.

HARPER, JESSE

Head Coach (1913-17) ▪ Papaw, IL

The son of a Midwestern cattle rancher, Jesse Harper played college football for coach Amos Alonzo Stagg at the University of Chicago. His choice of schools was a matter of practicality: "We lived in Iowa," he once told a reporter. "I could always get a free ride into Chicago on a cattle train. For that reason I went to Morgan Park Academy, a Chicago prep school, and then to the University."

Injuries prevented Harper, a 5-10, 155-pound halfback, from playing much during his sophomore and junior years at Chicago, but as a senior, in 1905, he helped the Maroons win the Western Conference title with a 7-0 record.

After graduating in 1906, Harper (with help from Stagg) landed a job as head football coach at Alma College in Alma, Michigan. In three years he compiled a record of 10-4-4. That performance, at such a young age, allowed Harper to move on to Wabash College in Indiana. Over the course of the next four years he went 15-9-2, including a

Jesse Harper had an amazing 34-5-1 record as Notre Dame's head football coach in addition to coaching basketball, baseball, and track. He is most remembered as the coach who oversaw the Dorais-Rockne combination that revolutionized football by making the most of the forward pass.

remarkable campaign in 1910 when Wabash went 4-0 and outscored its opponents 118-0. (The rest of the team's games were canceled after a player was killed during a game against St. Louis.)

In 1911 Wabash came within three points of upsetting Notre Dame. Two years later Harper was given an opportunity to coach the Fighting Irish. He was only 29 years old, but he demonstrated quickly that he could handle the job.

In fact, it was during his first year in South Bend that Harper coached his most memorable game. On November 1, 1913, Notre Dame—then a little-known Catholic school from the Midwest—accepted $1,000 to travel to West Point for a game against perennial East Coast power Army. The Fighting Irish upset the Cadets, 35-13, on the strength of a brash and innovative passing attack led by quarterback Gus Dorais and end Knute Rockne.

The forward pass had been legal for several years, but most teams considered it nothing more than a novelty. Football was a simple game of brute strength. As Dorais filled the air with passes, though, it became apparent that football could also be a game of speed and style, a game of finesse.

Notre Dame's dramatic and entertaining victory over Army helped popularize the sport of college football and forever altered the way the game was played. For that, Harper deserves considerable credit. Along with Rockne, by then an assistant coach, he was also the man who developed the famous "Notre Dame shift" in 1914. The Irish would line up in a standard T formation, then shift into one of three different formations just before the ball was snapped, thereby keeping the defense off balance.

It was also under Harper that the Fighting Irish adopted a less provincial attitude toward intercollegiate athletics, adding such opponents as Texas, Yale, Princeton, and Army to the football schedule.

Harper's record in five seasons at Notre Dame was 34-5-1. He also coached baseball, basketball, and track, and served as director of athletics. He retired in 1918 and entered the family cattle ranching business, allowing Rockne to take over the football program. In 1931, after Rockne was killed in a plane crash, Harper returned to his position as athletic director for two years.

Jesse Harper died on July 31, 1961. He was inducted into the College Football of Fame in 1970.

Career Coaching Record

YEAR	WON	LOST	TIED
1913	7	0	0
1914	6	2	0
1915	7	1	0
1916	8	1	0
1917	6	1	1
TOTAL	34	5	1

HARRISON, RANDY

Free Safety (1974-78) ▪ 6-1, 207 ▪ Hammond, IN

Randy Harrison had the distinction of being the first player in the modern era of Notre Dame football to earn five monograms. A starter at free safety in his freshman year, he had 57 tackles and seemed to be destined for stardom. The next year he had 54 tackles.

But in 1976, as a junior, he broke his forearm in the second game and sat out the rest of the season. Because he started two games (logging a total of 32 minutes), Harrison earned a monogram; however, the NCAA determined that he would still have two seasons of eligibility remaining. So he returned in 1977. Unfortunately, a fractured rib caused him to miss four games that season, as well.

Harrison was healthy in 1978, his fifth year on the varsity, but by then he had lost his starting job to Joe Restic. He had 22 tackles and one interception.

HART, LEON

Right End (1946-49) ▪ 6-4, 245 ▪ Turtle Creek, PA

Leon Hart was among the last of college football's great two-way players—and one of only two linemen ever to win the Heisman Trophy. He came to South Bend from Turtle Creek High School where he was an outstanding athlete who earned 10 varsity letters in football, baseball, basketball, and track. Hart was recruited by many schools, most notably the University of Pittsburgh, but wound up playing for Frank Leahy at Notre Dame.

For the 1940s, Hart was an enormous college football player, and his size has been the subject of many humorous anecdotes. There is the story, for example, of Hart reporting to practice in August of his freshman year and telling equipment manager John MacAllister that he needed a pair of size-14 shoes. MacAllister handed him a pair of size 13 shoes; when Hart complained, MacAllister gruffly told the freshman, "Nobody that wore size 14s was ever any good—so you're wearing 13s." So, until he reached the NFL, Leon Hart wore cleats that were one size too small.

One of only two linemen ever to win the Heisman Trophy, Leon Hart was an all-around athlete and academic. After leaving Notre Dame with a degree in mechanical engineering, he went on to play with the Detroit Lions as they won three national championships.

Although his offensive skills were solid (as a fullback, he was a fine blocker; as a wide receiver, he had sure hands), it was on defense that Hart made his reputation. He was big and strong, with good speed and a nose for the football. And, perhaps most importantly, he was a winner. During his four years in South Bend, Hart never tasted defeat. The

Fighting Irish compiled a record of 36-0-2 and won three national titles. Hart played a major role during that extraordinary period of dominance, and his exploits were duly noted. He was a three-time first-team All-American (1947-1949); in his junior and senior years, he was a consensus All-American. In 1949 he not only won the Heisman Trophy (the only other lineman to win the award was Yale's Larry Kelly in 1936), but he also received the Maxwell Award as the nation's top college player. And, most impressive of all, in a year when baseball star Jackie Robinson was the National League MVP and golfer Sam Snead won both the Masters and PGA Championship, Leon Hart was named Male Athlete of the Year by the Associated Press.

Hart graduated from Notre Dame with a degree in mechanical engineering, but it would be several years before he was ready to stop playing football. He won three NFL championships with the Detroit Lions and was named All-Pro on offense and defense in 1951; this at a time when two-platoon football was the norm in the NFL and few players went both ways. Hart retired from professional football in 1957 and went into private business. He was elected to the College Football Hall of Fame in 1973.

HAYES, DAVE
End (1917, 1919-20) ▪ 5-8, 160 ▪ Hartford, CT

Dave Hayes worked his way through Phillips Exeter Academy, graduating in the spring of 1916, and showed up in South Bend a few months later with no money and no athletic pedigree. He knocked on the door of university president Father Matthew J. Walsh and said, quite naively, that he wanted to attend Notre Dame and play football for Knute Rockne, who was then an assistant under Jesse Harper. Walsh, impressed by the kid's spunk, offered Hayes a scholarship.

Of course, in those days a scholarship was not exactly a free ride. Hayes helped pay for his education by waiting tables in a local restaurant, and he lived in a room above the restaurant. At 5-8, 160 pounds, he was physically unimposing, but he made a quick and lasting impression on his coaches in the first few days of football practice.

Hayes made the freshman team as a walk-on and became a starting end in 1917. While serving in the U.S. Army during World War I, he was seriously wounded. A bullet shattered his left leg and doctors questioned whether he would ever walk again, let alone play football. Miraculously, he returned to Notre Dame in the fall of 1919 and was back in the starting lineup by the second game of the season. He also played on the 1920 team—the first undefeated squad coached by Rockne.

Hayes played two seasons of professional football with the Green Bay Packers before entering private business.

HEAD COACHES

Notre Dame began playing football in 1887, but it wasn't until 1894 that J.L. Morrison became the program's first head coach. Embracing the sport with varying degrees of seriousness, the school went through 12 coaches over the next 18 years. With the arrival of Jesse Harper as coach and athletic director in 1913, though, Notre Dame football began a long, steady climb toward national prominence.

Twenty-eight men have held the title of head football coach at the University of Notre Dame. It is widely regarded as the most difficult and demanding job in college football.

YEAR	COACH	RECORD
1894	J.L. Morrison	7-4-1
1895	H.G. Hadden	3-1-0
1896-1898	Frank Hering	12-6-1
1899	James McWeeney	6-3-1
1900-1901	Patrick O'Dea	14-4-2
1902-1903	James Faragher	14-2-2
1904	Louis Salmon	5-3-0
1905	Henry J. McGlew	5-4-0
1906-1907	Thomas Barry	12-1-1
1908	Victor M. Place	8-1-0
1909-1910	Frank C. Longman	11-1-2
1911-1912	John L. Marks	13-0-2
1913-1917	Jesse Harper	34-5-1
1918-1930	Knute Rockne	105-12-5
1931-1933	Heartly Anderson	16-9-2
1934-1940	Elmer Layden	47-13-3
1941-43, 1946-53	Frank Leahy	87-11-9
1944	Ed McKeever	8-2-0
1945, 1963	Hugh Devore	9-9-1
1954-1958	Terry Brennan	32-18-0
1959-1962	Joe Kuharich	17-23-0
1964-1974	Ara Parseghian	95-17-4
1975-1980	Dan Devine	53-16-1
1981-1985	Gerry Faust	30-26-1
1986-1996	Lou Holtz	100-29-2
1997-present	Bob Davie	0-0-0

HEAP, JOE

Halfback (1951-54) ▪ 5-11, 180 ▪ Abita Springs, LA

Joseph Lawrence Heap grew up in a family of 10 children. A football and track star in high school, he led Holy Cross High to the New Orleans city football championship in 1949 and 1950 and was named all-state in his senior year.

Heap earned four monograms at Notre Dame and was a three-year starter at left halfback. In his senior year he was second on the team in rushing with 594 yards on 110 carries. He was first in scoring (48 points), receiving (18 receptions for 369 yards), and kickoff returns (7 for 143 yards).

A three-time Academic All-American, Heap was a first-round draft choice of the New York Giants in 1955. He played just one year in the NFL.

HEARDEN, TOM

Running Back (1924-26) ▪ 5-9, 160 ▪ Green Bay, WI

Thomas "Red" Hearden was a reserve fullback on Notre Dame's national championship team in 1924. He started at right halfback in 1925 and was co-captain of the 1926 team. He graduated with a law degree in 1927.

Hearden played with the Green Bay Packers and Chicago Bears before entering the practice of law. He later returned to the football field as a coach, starting at St. Norbert's High School in West DePere, Wisconsin. He later served as an assistant on the coaching staffs of Marquette University, the University of Wisconsin, and the Green Bay Packers. Poor health forced his retirement in 1957.

HECK, ANDY

Offensive Tackle/Tight End (1985-88) ▪ 6-7, 258 ▪ Annandale, VA

When Notre Dame went undefeated and captured a national championship in 1988, Andy Heck was one of only two senior starters on the team. In his first three seasons he played tight end; however, during spring drills coach Lou Holtz decided to take advantage of Heck's blocking ability by moving him to offensive tackle. Notre Dame's offensive line had been depleted by graduation, and Holtz reasoned that Heck could help in the rebuilding process.

But no one expected the move to be such a resounding success. Heck started all 12 games in '88 and shared the team lead in playing time with 256:16. Presented by his teammates with the Nick Pietrosante Award for his spirit and courage, Heck was a consensus All-American. He earned first-team honors from the Associated Press, *Football News*, *The Sporting News*, and the Newspaper Enterprise Association.

Heck was drafted in the first round by the Seattle Seahawks in 1989 and played with the team through the 1993 season. He played for the Chicago Bears from 1994 through 1996.

HEENAN, PAT
End (1959) ▪ 6-2, 190 ▪ Detroit, MI

Walk-ons are rare at Notre Dame; rarer still is the walk-on who makes an impact. Pat Heenan was clearly the exception to the rule.

While a high school student in Michigan, he worked as an assistant to trainer Hugh Burns of the Detroit Lions. During his first three years in South Bend he was an all-campus end as a member of a championship intramural team. But he never played a minute of intercollegiate football.

In his senior year, however, Heenan tried out for the Fighting Irish varsity. He didn't just make the team—he became the starting right end. Heenan was the team's second-leading receiver with 12 receptions for 198 yards and one touchdown. He also had 28 tackles. He later played one season with the Washington Redskins.

HEIMKREITER, STEVE
Linebacker (1975-78) ▪ 6-2, 228 ▪ Cincinnati, OH

If not for injuries in his freshman and junior seasons, Steve Heimkreiter might have become Notre Dame's career leader in tackles. He played only 42 minutes in 1975 but earned a spot in the starting lineup as an outside linebacker in 1976. That season he had a team-high 118 tackles and more than 219 minutes of playing time.

In 1977 Heimkreiter missed three full games because of injuries, yet still wound up with 98 tackles, third best on a team that went 11-1 and captured a national championship. In his senior year he had a remarkable 160 tackles to break Bob Golic's year-old single-season record. Heimkreiter finished his career with 398 tackles, third on the all-time list (behind Golic and Bob Crable). He played with the Baltimore Colts in 1980.

HEISMAN TROPHY

The John W. Heisman Memorial Trophy is presented annually by the Downtown Athletic Club of New York to the outstanding college football player in the nation. Voting is done by members of the national media and former winners of the Heisman. The award was originally called the DAC Trophy. It was renamed in 1936 following the death of John W. Heisman, who played football at Penn and Brown and had a distinguished 36-year coaching career that included stops at Auburn, Oberlin, Clemson, Akron, Penn, Rice, Washington and Jefferson, and Georgia Tech. He was also the Downtown Athletic Club's first athletic director.

The trophy itself, which depicts a ball carrier preparing to ward off a tackler, is made of bronze and was created by a New York sculptor named Frank Eliscu. Jim Crowley, one of Notre Dame's famous Four Horsemen in the 1920s, assisted Eliscu by providing models from his Fordham University football team.

The Heisman was first presented in 1935 to halfback Jay Berwanger of the University of Chicago. Notre Dame halfback Bill Shakespeare finished third in the voting that year. Since then seven Fighting Irish players have won the award, starting with quarterback Angelo Bertelli in 1943. Moreover, Notre Dame has had three players finish second in the voting: Bertelli (1941), Joe Theismann (1970), and Raghib Ismail (1990). No other university has been so well represented.

Here are Notre Dame's Heisman Trophy winners, along with voting results:

1943

1) Angelo Bertelli, Quarterback, Notre Dame (648)
2) Bob O'Dell, Pennsylvania (177)
3) Otto Graham, Northwestern (140)
4) Creighton Miller, Notre Dame (134)
5) Eddie Prokop, Georgia Tech (85)
6) Hal Hamburg, Navy (73)
7) Bill Daley, Michigan (71)
8) Tony Butkovich, Purdue (65)
9) Jim White, Notre Dame (52)

1947

1) John Lujack, Quarterback, Notre Dame (742)
2) Bob Chappuis, Michigan (555)
3) Doak Walker, SMU (196)
4) Charley Conerly, Mississippi (186)
5) Harry Gilmer, Alabama (115)
6) Bobby Layne, Texas (74)
7) Chuck Bednarik, Penn (65)
8) Bill Swiacki, Columbia (61)

1949

1) Leon Hart, End, Notre Dame (995)
2) Charlie Justice, North Carolina (272)
3) Doak Walker, SMU (229)
4) Arnold Galiffa, Army (196)
5) Bob Williams, Notre Dame (189)
6) Eddie LeBaron, Pacific (122)

7) Clayton Tonnemaker, Minnesota (81)

8) Emil Sitko, Notre Dame (79)

1953

1) John Lattner, Right Halfback, Notre Dame (1,850)

2) Paul Giel, Minnesota (1,794)

3) Paul Cameron, UCLA (444)

4) Bernie Faloney, Maryland (258)

5) Bob Garrett, Stanford (231)

6) Alan Ameche, Wisconsin (211)

7) J.C. Caroline, Illinois (193)

8) J.D. Roberts, Oklahoma (108)

9) Lamar McHan, Arkansas (78)

1956

1) Paul Hornung, Quarterback, Notre Dame (1,066)

2) John Majors, Tennessee (994)

3) Tom McDonald, Oklahoma (973)

4) Gerry Tubbs, Oklahoma (724)

5) Jim Brown, Syracuse (561)

6) Ron Kramer, Michigan (518)

7) John Brodie, Stanford (281)

8) Jim Parker, Ohio State (248)

9) Kenny Ploen, Iowa (150)

10) Joe Walton, Pittsburgh (97)

1964

1) John Huarte, Quarterback, Notre Dame (1,026)

2) Jerry Rhome, Tulsa (952)

3) Dick Butkus, Illinois (505)

4) Bob Timberlake, Michigan (361)

5) Craig Morton, California (181)

6) Steve DeLong, Tennessee (176)

7) Cosmo Iacavazzi, Princeton (165)

8) Brian Piccolo, Wake Forest (124)

1987

1) Tim Brown, Flanker, Notre Dame (1,442)

2) Don McPherson, Syracuse (831)

3) Gordie Lockbaum, Holy Cross (657)

4) Lorenzo White, Michigan State (632)

5) Craig Heyward, Pittsburgh (170)

6) Chris Spielman, Ohio State (110)

7) Thurman Thomas, Oklahoma State (99)

8) Gaston Green, UCLA (73)

9) Emmitt Smith, Florida (70)
10) Bobby Humphrey, Alabama (63)

HELDT, MIKE

Center (1987-90) • 6-4, 267 • Tampa, FL

A three-year starter at center and a captain in his senior year, Mike Heldt was one of the most consistent—and consistently overlooked—players in the Notre Dame lineup in the late 1980s.

He went to South Bend in the fall of 1987 after an outstanding career at Leto High School in Tampa, Florida. A backup to Chuck Lanza in his freshman year, Heldt became the starting center in 1988; in fact, he shared the team lead in playing time with 256:16. He started all 13 games in 1989 and was named honorable mention All-America by *The Sporting News* and *Football News.*

In 1990 Heldt again started every game, running his streak of consecutive starts to 37. He logged 298:27 of playing time, more than any other offensive player except quarterback Rick Mirer. By the end of the season Heldt had become a bit more familiar to College football fans, thanks largely to being named to several All-America teams.

The San Diego Chargers drafted Heldt in the tenth round in 1991. He played with the Indianapolis Colts in 1992 and 1993.

HELWIG, JOHN

Guard/Linebacker (1948-50) • 6-2, 194 • Los Angeles, CA

At Mt. Carmel High School in Los Angeles, John Helwig was a superior all-around athlete who set a national scholastic record in the shot put. He earned his first monogram at Notre Dame in 1948 as a backup guard. With the temporary switch to two-platoon football, Helwig became a starting linebacker on one of the best teams in Fighting Irish history: the 1949 national championship squad.

He started again at linebacker in his senior year and also set indoor and outdoor school records in the shot put. Helwig was drafted by the Chicago Bears in the eleventh round of the 1950 NFL Draft. He played with the Bears from 1953 through 1956.

HENTRICH, CRAIG

Kicker/Punter (1989-92) • 6-1, 197 • Godfrey, IL

Craig Anthony Hentrich was arguably the best all-around kicker who ever wore a Fighting Irish uniform. A *USA Today* first-team All-American in his senior year at

Marquette High School in Alton, Illinois, he played safety and quarterback in addition to handling place-kicking and punting duties.

Hentrich made a smooth transition from high school to college. As a freshman in 1989 he set a single-season school record by averaging 44.6 yards per punt. He also kicked eight field goals and 44 extra points for a total of 68 points. The following year he was even better, hitting all 41 of his extra-point attempts and 16 of 20 field goals for a team-high 89 points (a school record for kickers). He also broke his own school record with an average of 44.9 yards per punt. After the season, he was named honorable mention All-America by *Football News*.

Although he missed two games because of a knee injury and kicked only five field goals in 1991, Hentrich still managed to set a school record for most extra points in a season (48). He underwent knee surgery to repair torn ligaments after the 1991 season but was fully recovered by the fall of 1992. In his senior year he averaged 43.8 yards per punt; he also made 10 of 13 field goals and 44 of 46 extra points for a total of 74 points. *Football News* named him honorable mention All-America as both a place-kicker and punter.

Hentrich holds Notre Dame career records for punting average (44.1), extra points (177), and extra point percentage (.983). He is the school's second-leading all-time scorer (behind fellow kicker John Carney) with 294 points. An eighth-round draft pick of the New York Jets in 1993, he played with the Green Bay Packers in 1994 and 1995.

Career Statistics (Kicking)

YEAR	FG	PAT	POINTS
1989	8/15	44/45	68
1990	16/20	41/41	89
1991	5/8	48/48	63
1992	10/13	44/46	74
TOTAL	39/56	177/180	294

Career Statistics (Punting)

YEAR	NO.	YARDS	AVG.	LONG
1989	26	1,159	44.6	66
1990	34	1,526	44.9	63
1991	23	986	42.9	61
1992	35	1,534	43.8	62
TOTAL	118	5,205	44.1	66

HERING AWARD

At the conclusion of spring practice each year, the Notre Dame coaching staff honors the outstanding and most improved players at each position. Initiated by Knute Rockne as a way to encourage players to participate in spring training sessions, the awards are named after Frank Hering, the school's first paid football coach. Hering coached at Notre Dame from 1896 through 1898 and had a record of 12-6-1. He was also the school's first basketball coach.

HIGGINS, LUKE

Tackle (1942) ▪ 6-0, 210 ▪ Edgewater, NJ

Luke Higgins, a two-time all-state tackle from Cliffside High School in Edgewater, New Jersey, played just one season of varsity football at Notre Dame. He was a member of the freshman team in 1941 and earned a monogram in 1942 as a backup behind Bob Neff and Ziggy Czarobski.

Higgins served in the U.S. Marine Corps during World War II and did not play again at Notre Dame. He did, however, play with the Baltimore Colts in 1947.

HO, REGGIE

Kicker (1987-88) ▪ 5-5, 135 ▪ Kaneohe, HI

Reginald Thomas Ho made the Fighting Irish varsity as a walk-on in his junior year. A soccer player and place-kicker at St. Louis High School in Honolulu, he spent his first two years at Notre Dame concentrating exclusively on academics.

Ho kicked only one extra point (and no field goals) in 1987 but was the team's leading scorer the following year with 59 points. He made 9 of 12 field goal attempts and 32 of 36 extra points. In the 1989 Fiesta Bowl, he had two extra points and a 32-yard field goal as the Irish defeated West Virginia to clinch the national championship.

A second-team Academic All-American in 1988, Ho graduated with a grade point average of 3.7. He declined an additional year of eligibility in order to attend medical school.

HOFFMAN, FRANK

Guard/Tackle (1930-31) ▪ 6-2, 224 ▪ Seattle, WA

Frank "Nordy" Hoffmann did not play football at St. Martin's High School in Seattle, Washington. In fact, he wasn't formally introduced to the game until his sophomore year at Notre Dame when he succeeded in making the squad as a walk-on. He earned a monogram as a reserve tackle in his junior year, helping the Fighting Irish win a national championship with a 10-0 record.

In 1931, first-year head coach Hunk Anderson shifted Hoffmann to right guard, where he not only became a starter but also one of the best linemen in the country. He was a fiercely competitive player who developed a reputation for toughness by repeatedly playing while injured. The Associated Press named him to its All-America first team when the 1931 season ended.

Hoffman was a versatile young man whose talents also included music (he played the piano) and track and field (he was, at the time, one of the finest shot-putters the school had ever produced). But it was football that was his greatest gift. He was inducted into the College Football Hall of Fame in 1978. Hoffman held a variety of jobs in his lifetime. He was head of the United Steel Workers legislative office, executive director of the Democratic Senatorial Campaign Committee, and Sergeant at Arms of the U.S. Senate.

HOLOHAN, PETE
Flanker (1978-80) ▪ 6-5, 228 ▪ Liverpool, NY

As a senior at Liverpool High School (near Syracuse), Pete Holohan became the first athlete in New York state history to be named first-team all-state in both football and basketball. He also earned prep All-America honors in football.

Originally recruited to play quarterback, Holohan spent a year on the Notre Dame junior varsity. He was moved to flanker as a sophomore, in 1978, and became a starter when Tom Domin went down with an injury during preseason practice. Over the next three seasons Holohan caught 63 passes for 983 yards and two touchdowns.

Although he was not drafted until the seventh round in 1981, Holohan enjoyed a long and productive career as a professional football player. In 12 years with the San Diego Chargers (1981-87), Los Angeles Rams (1988-90), Kansas City Chiefs (1991), and Cleveland Browns (1992), he caught 363 passes for 3,981 yards and 16 touchdowns.

Career Statistics (Receiving)

YEAR	NO.	YARDS	AVG.	TD
1978	20	301	15.1	1
1979	22	386	17.5	0
1980	21	296	13.2	1
TOTAL	63	983	15.6	2

HOLTZ, LOU

Head Coach (1986-96) ▪ Follansbee, WV

Lou Holtz, one of only a handful of coaches in the history of college football to win more than 200 games, was born in Follansbee, West Virginia, and grew up in East Liverpool, Ohio. His childhood was decidedly unspectacular. In fact, Holtz was a small child with a slight speech impediment who lacked confidence. He was not much of an athlete; nor was he much of a student. Remarkably enough, he would one day become the head football coach at a university renowned for producing exceptional student-athletes.

Lou Holtz was brought in as head football coach in 1986 to revitalize the Fighting Irish. When he left the program ten years later, he had an impressive 100-30-2 record.

Holtz always felt a link to the Fighting Irish. As a child growing up in the 1940s, he was taught by the Sisters of Notre Dame at St. Aloysius grade school. When classes were interrupted for lunch, recess, and dismissal, the students walked out to the strains of the Notre Dame Victory March. At the same time Holtz began to read newspaper accounts of Notre Dame's exploits on the football field; sometimes he listened to live radio broadcasts. Frank Leahy was the coach then, and the Fighting Irish rarely lost a game. To a 10-year-old boy attending Catholic school in the Midwest, Notre Dame seemed like just about the greatest place in the world.

Despite his lack of size (5-10, 150 pounds), Holtz played college football at Kent State University, where he was a backup linebacker. He had the heart and desire for the game, if not the talent. When his playing career was over, there was no internal debate about what he would do. Lou Holtz loved football; if he could not be a player, then he would be a coach.

The first stop was a position as an assistant coach at the University of Iowa. He stayed there precisely one year, long enough to earn a masters degree in education. From 1961 through 1963 he served as an assistant at the College of William & Mary, and from 1964 through 1965 he was an assistant at the University of Connecticut. He paid his final dues as an assistant in 1968, at Ohio State University, before landing his first head coaching assignment, at William & Mary, in 1969. Holtz inherited a weak program, but within two years he led William & Mary to the Southern Conference title and its first post-season appearance (in the Tangerine Bowl).

It was at William & Mary that Holtz began to build a reputation for being a "fixer," someone who could turn around a struggling program. At his next job, as head coach at North Carolina State, he compiled a record of 33-12-3-the best four-year record in the history of the school. Under Holtz, the Wolfpack went to four consecutive bowl games and finished in the Associated Press Top 20 three times. That led to an offer from the New York Jets. But professional football did not agree with Holtz, and his year in New

York was one of the most unpleasant of his life. The Jets won only three of their first 13 games and Holtz resigned in the final week of the regular season.

He didn't take long to recover from that stumble, though. In 1977 Holtz accepted an offer to become head coach at the University of Arkansas, and he attacked the job with renewed vigor. The Razorbacks went 11-1 in his first season, defeated Oklahoma in the Orange Bowl, and finished as the third-ranked team in the country. In seven seasons in Fayetteville, Holtz compiled a record of 60-21-2 (a winning percentage of .735) and led the Razorbacks to six consecutive bowl appearances. By the end of 1983 he had a career record of 106-53-5—a life's work for many coaches. But Lou Holtz was just getting warmed up. He spent two seasons at the University of Minnesota before finally getting the job he'd always wanted: head coach at the University of Notre Dame.

Holtz came to South Bend in 1986 at a time when the Fighting Irish program had fallen to a level of mediocrity not seen in more than two decades. Gerry Faust's teams won 30 games and lost 26 between 1981 and 1985. Holtz was assigned the formidable task of restoring the program to its previous glory. It was the hardest job in college football—perhaps the hardest job in all of sports—but Holtz, armed with just the right combination of enthusiasm, skill, blind ambition, and naiveté, accepted it. In his first season Notre Dame was a deceptive 5-6 (the five losses were by a total of just 14 points). In 1987, with a team that included Heisman Trophy winner Tim Brown, the Irish improved to 8-4. Included in that mark were impressive victories over USC and Michigan State (teams that would later meet in the Rose Bowl). After the season Holtz was one of four finalists for the Football Writers Association of America Coach of the Year Award.

The renovation project was complete one year later, as Notre Dame went 12-0 in 1988 and captured its eleventh consensus national championship. The season's highlights included a dramatic 31-30 victory over top-ranked Miami in the sixth game of the season and a 34-21 victory over West Virginia in the Fiesta Bowl. Holtz was named Coach of the Year by the FWAA, *The Sporting News*, and *Football News*, as well as several other organizations.

Expectations, of course, were high the following year. The Irish opened the season atop the Associated Press poll and stayed there throughout the regular season. They won 12 consecutive games, defeating, among others, Big Ten champion Michigan and Pac 10 champion USC. The Irish lost to Miami in the final game of the regular season, though, and despite a 21-6 victory over Colorado in the Orange Bowl, they had to settle for second in the final AP poll. Once again, Holtz was a finalist for the FWAA Coach of the Year Award.

Notre Dame did not win another consensus national championship under Holtz, but the program nonetheless flourished. He never had a losing season in South Bend and took each of his teams to a post-season bowl game. On April 27, 1990, Holtz became only the ninth person to be named an honorary alumnus of the University of Notre Dame. Among the previous honorees are former football coaches Ara

Parseghian and Gerry Faust and former basketball coach Richard "Digger" Phelps. In 1993 the Fighting Irish won 11 of 12 games and were ranked second in the country. They fell to 6-5-1 in 1994 but rebounded the following year, winning nine games and losing three.

Still, 1995 was one of the most difficult for Holtz. It began with an upset at the hands of perennial Big Ten doormat Northwestern (though the Huskies later proved that the victory was not merely a fluke by winning the conference title). Holtz missed one game when he underwent surgery to correct a nagging neck injury; to avoid aggravating the problem, he coached another game from a box above the stadium, joining his players on the sideline only in the final minutes.

Through 10 seasons at Notre Dame, Holtz had 92 victories, 27 losses, and 2 ties. No other Fighting Irish coach—not Rockne, Leahy, or Parseghian—won that many games in his first 10 years. A small, unassuming man whose appearance belied a fiercely competitive nature, Holtz was an immensely successful public speaker whose passion and self-deprecating wit played well with corporate audiences. Although he was in South Bend for more than a decade and was clearly one of the most successful coaches in the history of college football (with a career record of 216-95-8 through 1996), Holtz always spoke of Notre Dame with a degree of reverence.

"I'm not the owner of the company here," he was quoted as saying. "I'm just the caretaker. At most places the football coach feels like a czar. It's *his* team. Not at Notre Dame. I'm just here to keep an eye on things for a while."

On November 19, 1996, Holtz announced that he would no longer be keeping an eye on things. Offering no specific explanation—other than to say, "it just feels right"—Holtz resigned as head coach. Less than one week later he was succeeded by defensive coordinator Bob Davie.

Career Coaching Record

YEAR	WON	LOST	TIED
1986	5	6	0
1987	8	4	0
1988	12	0	0
1989	12	1	0
1990	9	3	0
1991	10	3	0
1992	10	1	1
1993	11	1	0
1994	6	5	1
1995	9	3	0
1996	8	3	0
TOTAL	100	30	2

HORNUNG, PAUL
Quarterback (1954-56) ▪ 6-2, 205 ▪ Louisville, KY

When Paul Hornung arrived at Notre Dame, football wasn't even his best sport. Basketball was. As a sophomore he averaged 6.1 points a game for the Fighting Irish. On the football field he was merely a backup fullback who rarely got a chance to carry the ball.

But things began to change in Hornung's junior year. He played quarterback for most of the season, and his athletic ability served him well. He completed 46 of 103 passes for 743 yards and nine touchdowns, as well as rushing for 472 yards. Hornung also knew how to play defense—he intercepted five passes as a junior, including two in a 21-7 victory over fourth-ranked Navy. He also ran for one touchdown and passed for another in that game. Such exploits became commonplace for the remarkably versatile Hornung. He threw a game-tying touchdown pass and kicked the game-winning field goal in a 17-14 victory over Iowa. He also passed for 354 yards in a season-ending loss to USC.

A high school basketball star, Paul Hornung found his talent for football at Notre Dame. He won the Heisman Trophy in 1956, becoming the only player from a losing team to do so.

As a senior Hornung ranked second in the nation in total offense with 1,337 yards. He rushed for seven touchdowns, passed for three, and kicked 14 extra points. By the end of the year he was personally responsible for more than half of Notre Dame's offensive output. The Fighting Irish had one of their worst seasons in 1956, losing eight games and winning just two. Nevertheless, Hornung was named the winner of the Heisman Trophy. He is the only player from a losing team to win the award.

Hornung went on to star as a running back with the Green Bay Packers, although it wasn't until Vince Lombardi took over as head coach that he really began to thrive. In his first two years in the NFL Hornung had played quarterback, halfback, fullback, and tight end; he was an immense physical talent, but the Packers really didn't know how best to utilize his ability. Lombardi arrived in 1959, took one look at Hornung, and made him the starting left halfback; he would also continue to serve as the team's place-kicker. Once he was able to focus on a single offensive position, Hornung became one of the league's most productive players. He scored an NFL record 176 points on 15 touchdowns, 15 field goals, and 41 extra points in 1960. He also rushed for 671 yards.

Although he served in the U.S. Army in 1961, Hornung received permission to play on Sundays. Remarkably enough, he once again led the league in scoring with 146 points—including 19 points in the Packers' 37-0 victory over the New York Giants in the NFL championship game. He was named Player of the Year at the conclusion of the 1961 season.

Injuries forced Hornung to miss most of the 1962 season, and accusations of gambling led NFL Commissioner Pete Rozelle to suspend him for one season in 1963. Hornung returned to the Packers in 1964 and scored 107 points. A series of recurring injuries prompted his retirement in 1966. A tough, intelligent player who was also a deceptively strong blocker, Hornung gained 3,711 yards on 893 carries in nine NFL seasons. He also caught 130 passes for 1,480 yards. He scored 760 points on 62 touchdowns, 190 extra points, and 66 field goals.

In 1985 Paul Hornung was inducted into the College Football Hall of Fame. One year later he entered the Pro Football Hall of Fame. He is currently a private businessman who also does color commentary for televised college football games.

Career Statistics (Passing)

YEAR	ATT.	COMP.	YARDS	TD	PCT.
1954	19	5	36	0	.263
1955	103	46	743	9	.447
1956	111	59	917	3	.531
TOTAL	233	110	1,696	12	.472

Career Statistics (Rushing)

YEAR	ATT.	YARDS	AVG.	TD
1954	23	59	6.9	2
1955	92	472	5.1	6
1956	94	420	4.5	7
TOTAL	209	1,051	5.0	15

HOWARD, JOE
Split End (1981-84) ▪ 5-9, 171 ▪ Clinton, MD

A diminutive but determined athlete, Joe Howard played both basketball and football at Notre Dame. As a freshman wide receiver he caught 17 passes for 463 yards—an average of 27.2 yards per reception. He also scored three touchdowns, including one on a 96-yard pass from quarterback Blair Kiel in a 35-3 victory over Georgia Tech.

As a sophomore he caught 28 passes for 524 yards, and as a junior he caught 27 passes for 464 yards; he also led the team in punt returns with 28 for 202 yards. Just days after Notre Dame's victory over Boston College in the 1984 Liberty Bowl, Howard accepted an invitation from coach Digger Phelps to join the Fighting Irish basketball team as a point guard. He started 11 games, averaged 5.5 points, and was voted most inspirational player by his teammates.

In the fall of 1984 Howard was slowed by injuries in the first half of the season but still caught 13 passes for 212 yards. He also averaged 7.5 yards on punt returns. His career average of 19.6 yards per reception is fourth on Notre Dame's all-time list. Although he was overlooked in the draft because of his size, Howard spent six years in the NFL. He played with the Buffalo Bills from 1986 through 1988 and the Washington Redskins from 1989 through 1991.

Career Statistics (Receiving)

YEAR	NO.	YARDS	AVG.	TD
1981	17	463	27.2	3
1982	28	524	18.7	2
1983	27	464	17.2	2
1984	13	212	16.3	0
TOTAL	**85**	**1,663**	**19.6**	**7**

HUARTE, JOHN

Quarterback (1962-64) ▪ 6-0, 180 ▪ Santa Ana, CA

John Huarte was a prep star at Mater Dei High School who went on to win the Heisman Trophy at Notre Dame. The journey, however, was not nearly as smooth as it might sound. In fact, injuries kept Huarte on the sideline for much of his sophomore and junior seasons. He attempted only eight passes in the 1962 season and 42 the following year. Virtually no one expected him to step in as a senior and suddenly become the best college football player in the country. But that is precisely what happened.

The Fighting Irish went 2-7 in 1963. When new head coach Ara Parseghian arrived the next fall, he began the task of rebuilding. And he placed Huarte at the center of the project. Huarte responded magnificently. He completed 114 of 205 passes for 2,062 yards and 16 touchdowns. Together, Huarte and wide receiver Jack Snow led a spectacular reversal of fortune. The Fighting Irish won nine games and lost just one. If not for a 20-17 upset at the hands of USC in the final game of the season, Notre Dame would have captured the national championship in Parseghian's rookie year.

Huarte set a dozen school records as a senior. In addition to winning the Heisman by a narrow margin over Tulsa's Jerry Rhome, he was named United Press International

When Ara Parseghian arrived at Notre Dame in 1963, he took relatively unknown and previously injury-ridden John Huarte and made him the center of Fighting Irish football. Huarte responded by completing 114 of 205 passes and scoring 16 touchdowns.

Player of the Year. After graduation Huarte was drafted by the Philadelphia Eagles but chose instead to play for the New York Jets of the American Football League. Unfortunately, Huarte ran into more than a little competition in training camp. The Jets had also signed a rookie quarterback out of Alabama: Joe Namath. The Jets offered Namath a $400,000 contract, twice what they offered Huarte. That was a fair indication of the team's opinion of the quarterbacks' comparative skills. Indeed, Namath became the Jets' starter and eventually the AFL Rookie of the Year.

Huarte, meanwhile, spent most of his rookie season on the taxi squad. His professional career never measured up to the promise of the fall of 1964. After being released by the Jets in 1966, he bounced around the NFL and AFL for eight seasons, with stops in Boston, Philadelphia, Kansas City, Chicago, and Minnesota. He also played for Memphis in the World Football League. In his entire professional career he completed just 19 of 48 passes for 230 yards. He threw one touchdown.

Huarte retired from professional football in 1975 and entered private business.

Career Statistics

YEAR	ATT.	COMP.	YARDS	TD	INT.	PCT.
1962	8	4	38	0	0	.500
1963	42	20	243	1	0	.467
1964	205	114	2,062	16	11	.556
TOTAL	255	138	2,543	17	11	.541

HUFF, ANDY

Running Back (1969, 1971-72) ▪ 5-11, 212 ▪ Toledo, OH

A dependable blocker and ball carrier during his two years as a starting fullback, Andy Huff grew up in a family devoted to the game of football. His father, Ralph, played at Indiana in the 1930s, and his three brothers all played for schools with major Division I programs in the 1960s and 1970s.

Huff rushed for 304 yards as a second-string halfback in his sophomore year but needed surgery to correct a shoulder injury the following spring. After sitting out the entire 1970 season, he returned in the fall of 1971 as a starting fullback. That year he rushed for 295 yards and two touchdowns on 68 carries. As a senior, in 1972, he was the team's second-leading rusher with 567 yards on 124 carries; he also had a team-high 60 points and was named offensive MVP by the National Monogram Club.

HUFFMAN, DAVE

Center (1975-78) ▪ 6-5, 245 ▪ Dallas, TX

In 1977 Notre Dame scored 382 points and accumulated 4,840 yards of total offense. Predictably, the headlines that year went to quarterback Joe Montana, running back Jerome Heavens, and tight end Ken MacAfee. But an equally important role was played by center Dave Huffman, an exceptional blocker and on-field leader.

A prep All-American at Dallas's Thomas Jefferson High School, Huffman came to Notre Dame as a tackle. He was converted to center in his sophomore year by coach Dan Devine, quickly worked his way into the starting lineup, and held the job for nearly three full seasons.

After helping the Fighting Irish win a national championship in 1977, Huffman was named to virtually every preseason All-America team in 1978. He didn't disappoint. Led by Huffman, Montana, and linebacker Bob Golic, Notre Dame went 9-3 and finished seventh in the final Associated Press rankings. Huffman was a consensus All-American, earning second-team honors from the Associated Press and first-team honors from United Press International and *The Sporting News*, among others.

A second-round draft choice in 1979, Huffman spent his entire 12-year NFL career with the Minnesota Vikings. After retiring in 1992, he went into broadcasting.

HUFFMAN, TIM

Offensive Guard/Tackle (1977-80) ▪ 6-5, 165 ▪ Dallas, TX

The younger brother of All-American Dave Huffman, who played for the Fighting Irish from 1975 through 1978, Tim Huffman was a three-year starter on the offensive line. The brothers played only a few minutes together in 1977 when Tim was a freshman, but the following year, they lined up next to each other every week, with Dave at center and Tim at guard.

Tim Huffman started 10 games as a junior. Injuries, however, kept him on the sideline for much of his senior year. A ninth-round draft pick in 1981, Huffman played with the Green Bay Packers until his retirement in 1985.

HUGHES, ERNIE

Offensive Guard/Defensive End (1974-77) ▪ 6-3, 248 ▪ Boise, ID

Ernie Hughes was an All-American guard on Notre Dame's national championship team in 1977. A versatile athlete, he played fullback and defensive end in high school (he also set a school record in the shot put) and began his college career as a second-string defensive lineman. Coach Dan Devine, however, moved Hughes to offense in

1975, and he became a three-year starter. Nicknamed "The Enforcer" because of his fiercely competitive nature, Hughes was recognized as offensive player of the game after a 31-30 victory over Air Force in 1975. The Associated Press and United Press International each named him second-team All-America in 1977.

Hughes was drafted in the third round by the San Francisco 49ers in 1978. He also played with the New York Giants before retiring in 1983.

HUNTER, AL
Halfback (1973, 1975-76) ▪ 5-11, 190 ▪ Greenville, NC

One of Notre Dame's all-time leading rushers, Al Hunter grew up in Greenville, North Carolina. A two-year captain at J.H. Rose High School, he was a prep All-American in 1971. Most national programs expressed an interest in Hunter, whose tremendous speed was evident on the track as well as the football field: He set school records in the 100-yard dash (9.3) and 220-yard dash (21.4).

In his first year on the Fighting Irish varsity, Hunter was a second-string halfback. He rushed for 150 yards and three touchdowns for a team that went undefeated and captured the 1973 national championship; his 93-yard kickoff return for a touchdown helped the Irish defeat Alabama, 24-23, in the Sugar Bowl.

After missing the 1974 season, Hunter returned in 1975 and became a starter at left halfback. He was second on the team in rushing (558 yards on 117 carries) and scoring (48 points). His best effort came in a 24-17 loss to USC when he rushed for 82 yards and one touchdown and passed for a two-point conversion.

In 1976 Hunter continued to improve. He rushed for a team-high 1,058 yards and 12 touchdowns on 233 carries. He led the team in scoring with 78 points and was third in receiving with 15 catches. He also returned 12 kickoffs for 241 yards. Despite those impressive numbers, Hunter received no more than honorable mention recognition from the major All-America teams. A fourth-round draft choice of the Seattle Seahawks in 1977, he played four seasons in the NFL, all with the Seahawks. Through the 1995 season, Hunter was nineteenth on Notre Dame's career rushing list.

Career Statistics (Rushing)

YEAR	ATT.	YARDS	AVG.	TD
1973	32	150	4.7	3
1975	117	558	4.8	8
1976	233	1,058	4.5	12
TOTAL	382	1,766	4.6	23

HUNTER, ART

Tackle/Center (1951-53) ▪ 6-3, 226 ▪ Akron, OH

Art Hunter played three positions in three years and handled each assignment gracefully.

He earned his first monogram as a starting center in his sophomore year (1951). As a junior he played right end and was the team's third-leading receiver with 16 receptions for 246 yards and one touchdown. Finally, in 1953, he was moved to tackle, and again he adapted smoothly. Hunter led the team in minutes played (423) and recovered three fumbles, including one for a touchdown. He was invited to play in the East-West Shrine Game and was a consensus All-American, earning first-team honors from United Press, the International News Service, and *The Sporting News*, among others.

Hunter was a first-round draft pick of the Green Bay Packers in 1954. He also played for the Cleveland Browns, Los Angeles Rams, and Pittsburgh Steelers before retiring in 1965.

HUNTER, TONY

Tight End/Split End (1979-82) ▪ 6-5, 226 ▪ Cincinnati, OH

Tony Hunter was the first three-sport captain in the history of Cincinnati's Moeller High School. Not only was he Ohio's player of the year in football in 1978, but he was also a prep All-American in basketball and an outstanding sprinter in track. He was recruited by Dan Devine but wound up playing two years under Gerry Faust, who had been his coach at Moeller.

With his combination of speed and size, Hunter was a favorite target of Notre Dame quarterbacks throughout his career; in fact, he led the team in receiving for three consecutive seasons (1980-82).

As a freshman, in 1979, Hunter started seven games at split end and finished with 27 receptions for 690 yards and two touchdowns. He had 23 receptions in 1980; in 1981 he played tight end and wingback, as well as split end, and finished with 28 receptions and two touchdowns. By the time he was a senior he had developed into an outstanding blocker as well as a receiver, and he spent the entire season at tight end. The team's top receiver with 42 catches for 507 yards, he was named first-team All-America by the Newspaper Enterprise Association.

Hunter caught 120 passes for 1,897 yards in his career. Through 1995 he was sixth on the school's all-time list for receptions. His 25.6-yard average per reception in 1979 was a single-season record.

A first-round draft choice in 1983 (and the twelfth player selected overall), Hunter played with the Buffalo Bills in 1983 and 1984 and the Los Angeles Rams from 1985 through 1987. He caught 134 passes for 1,501 yards and 9 touchdowns.

Career Statistics (Receiving)

YEAR	NO.	YARDS	AVG.	TD
1979	27	690	25.6	2
1980	23	303	13.2	1
1981	28	397	14.2	2
1982	42	507	12.1	0
TOTAL	**120**	**1,897**	**15.8**	**5**

I

IRELAND

On November 2, 1996, The Fighting Irish of Notre Dame played their first football game in Ireland. They defeated Navy, 54-27, in the Shamrock Classic at historic Croke Park in Dublin before a crowd of 38,651.

Two other college football games had been played in Dublin—Boston College beat Army in 1988, and Pittsburgh beat Rutgers in 1989—but neither game was played at Croke Park. In fact, this was the first time that a non-Gaelic sporting event of any kind had ever been held at Croke. Previously, only Gaelic football and hurling had been allowed; not even soccer or rugby, considered to be "British" games, were permitted in the ancient park.

American college football, however, was acceptable—as long as it featured the Irish and as long as it promised to bring a good deal of tourist money to the city and its environs during the teams' four-day visit. Presumably, no one was disappointed. An estimated 15,000 Americans made the transatlantic trip to Ireland; an additional 10,000 U.S. citizens living abroad in Europe were in attendance. That sort of interest allowed Notre Dame and Navy to share a $1.7 million appearance fee.

With the victory, the Fighting Irish improved to 2-0 in international contests; they had previously defeated Miami, 40-15, in a game played on November 24, 1979, in Tokyo, Japan.

IRISH EYES

While many college athletic programs offer free information on the Internet, demand for news about the University of Notre Dame football team is so strong that it prompted the birth of Irish Eyes, an on-line service that charges a fee. Although Irish Eyes also includes information on the university's other athletic teams, the emphasis is on football coverage, which is provided throughout the year. It is the first computer on-line service dedicated to covering a specific collegiate sports program.

Information is updated on a daily basis.

IRISH GUARD

When The Band of the Fighting Irish takes the field for pregame ceremonies, it is escorted by Notre Dame's Irish Guard. Members of the Irish Guard are dressed in the traditional Irish kilt. The color of the kilt is Notre Dame plaid: blue, gold, and green.

ISMAIL, RAGHIB

Flanker/Split End (1988-90) ▪ 5-10, 175 ▪ Wilkes-Barre, PA

Raghib Ramadan "Rocket" Ismail was born in Newark, New Jersey, on November 18, 1969. His family moved to Wilkes-Barre, Pennsylvania, after the death of his father,

The most highly recruited high school athlete in 1988, Raghib "Rocket" Ismail truly lived up to expectations when he joined the Fighting Irish. He kicked off his college career by averaging 27.6 yards per reception, earned MVP honors in the 1989 Orange Bowl, and was a consensus first-team All-American his junior year. He left Notre Dame a year early to play professionally in the CFL and is currently playing in the NFL.

Ibrahim. Ismail grew up to become one of the best all-around athletes in Pennsylvania state history. (His brother, Quadry, was also a talented athlete who played collegiately at Syracuse University.) At Meyers High School he rushed for 4,494 yards and 62 touchdowns in three years as a varsity football player; won state track championships in the 100 meters, long jump, and 400-meter relay; and earned two letters as a guard on the varsity basketball team.

A *Parade* and *USA Today* prep All-American, Ismail was among the most coveted high school players in the nation. Notre Dame won the recruiting war, and he enrolled in the fall of 1988. At 5-10 and less than 175 pounds, Ismail appeared to be too small to play tailback. But with 4.33 speed in the 40-yard dash, he was quick enough to play split end. Coach Lou Holtz immediately moved Ismail, and he responded impressively. While starting in six games and playing in all 12 as a freshman, he caught 12 passes for 331 yards—an incredible average of 27.6 yards per reception. He also averaged 36.1 yards per kickoff return and scored a total of four touchdowns. After the season he was named honorable mention All-America by *The Sporting News*.

To better utilize Ismail's athletic gifts, Holtz moved him to flanker in 1989. And indeed, Ismail, who proved to be resilient as well as versatile, made the coach look like a genius. He caught 27 passes for 535 yards, rushed for 478 yards, and scored three touchdowns on punt and kickoff returns. The Associated Press, *The Sporting News*, *Football News*, the Newspaper Enterprise Association, and the Football Writers Association of America all named him first-team All-America. In Notre Dame's 21-6 victory over top-ranked Colorado in the Orange Bowl, Ismail was voted MVP.

As a junior, in 1990, Ismail was a unanimous first-team All-American. He had a sensational year, despite groin and ankle injuries that prevented him from starting three games. He caught 32 passes for 699 yards and two touchdowns, rushed for 537 yards on 67 carries, and again led the team in kickoff and punt returns. After his team beat Notre Dame, 24-21, Penn State coach Joe Paterno went so far as to call Ismail "one of the three or four best players ever to play college football." *The Sporting News* and the Walter Camp Foundation each named him Player of the Year in 1990, and he was runner-up (behind Brigham Young University quarterback Ty Detmer) in voting for the Heisman Trophy.

Ismail finished his career with 4,187 all-purpose yards. He is Notre Dame's career leader in yards per reception (22.0). Through 1995, he was second in punt return average (13.4 yards) and fifth in kickoff return yardage (27.6). He shares (with Tim Brown) the record for touchdowns on kickoff returns (five).

During his career at Notre Dame, Ismail lowered his time in the 40-yard dash to 4.28 seconds and was an occasional competitor in national and international track and field events. But it was football that dictated his future. Ismail left school after his junior year to play for the Toronto Argonauts of the Canadian Football League. In 1993, after two seasons in the CFL, he signed with the NFL's Los Angeles Raiders. Through the 1995 season he had caught 88 passes for 1,357 yards and nine touchdowns. He had also returned 104 kickoffs for 2,234 yards.

Career Statistics (Receiving)

YEAR	NO.	YARDS	AVG.	TD
1988	12	331	27.6	2
1989	27	535	19.8	0
1990	32	699	21.8	2
TOTAL	71	1,565	22.0	4

Career Statistics (Rushing)

YEAR	NO.	YARDS	AVG.	TD
1988	0	0	0.0	0
1989	64	478	7.5	2
1990	67	537	8.0	3
TOTAL	131	1,015	7.7	5

Career Statistics (Kickoff Returns)

YEAR	NO.	YARDS	AVG.	TD
1988	12	433	36.1	2
1989	20	502	25.1	2
1990	14	336	24.0	1
TOTAL	46	1,271	27.6	5

Career Statistics (Punt Returns)

YEAR	NO.	YARDS	AVG.	TD
1988	5	72	14.4	0
1989	7	113	16.1	1
1990	13	151	11.6	0
TOTAL	25	336	13.4	1

IZO, GEORGE

Quarterback (1957-59) ▪ 6-2, 210 ▪ Barberton, OH

After coming off the bench to spark a 29-22 victory over Purdue midway through the 1958 season, George Izo became Notre Dame's starting quarterback. He led the team in passing with 60 completions for 1,067 yards and nine touchdowns. He was also a defensive standout, with 21 tackles and a team-leading four interceptions.

As a senior, in 1959, Izo split time at quarterback with Don White. He completed 44 of 95 passes for 661 yards and six touchdowns. Izo was a first-round draft pick of the NFL's Chicago Cardinals and the New York Titans of the American Football League. Over six seasons he played with the Cardinals, Washington Redskins, Detroit Lions, and Pittsburgh Steelers.

J

JOHNSON, ANTHONY
Fullback (1986-89) ▪ 6-0, 220 ▪ South Bend, IN

Playing alongside the likes of Tony Rice, Ricky Watters, Tim Brown, and Raghib Ismail, it's no great surprise that Anthony Johnson was often overlooked. In truth, though, he was one of the most dependable players to wear a Notre Dame uniform in the late 1980s.

An exceptional prep athlete who played both soccer and football at John Adams High School in South Bend, Johnson entered Notre Dame in the fall of 1986. He started in five games as a freshman and rushed for 349 yards. The next year he rushed for 366 yards and a team-high 11 touchdowns. As a junior he gained 282 yards on 69 carries, and as a senior he had his finest season: 515 yards and 11 touchdowns on 131 carries. He was named honorable mention All-America by *The Sporting News* and was presented with the Nick Pietrosante Award for his courage, dedication, and spirit.

Johnson finished his college career with 1,512 yards rushing. His 32 rushing touchdowns is third on the all-time list, behind only Allen Pinkett (49) and Louis "Red" Salmon (36). A second-round NFL draft choice, he played for the Indianapolis Colts (1990-93), New York Jets (1994), Chicago Bears (1995), and Carolina Panthers (1996).

Career Statistics (Rushing)

YEAR	NO.	YARDS	AVG.	TD
1986	80	349	4.4	5
1987	78	366	4.7	11
1988	69	282	4.1	5
1989	131	515	3.9	11
TOTAL	**358**	**1,512**	**4.2**	**32**

JOHNSTON, MIKE

Kicker (1980-83) ▪ 5-11, 185 ▪ Rochester, NY

At Cardinal Mooney High School in Rochester, New York, Mike Johnston kicked only two field goals in his career. So it's no shock that he wasn't offered a college scholarship. Instead, he made the team at Notre Dame as a walk-on in 1980 after getting a recommendation from another Rochester native and Notre Dame alumnus, kicker Bob Thomas of the Chicago Bears.

Johnston handled kickoffs in his first two seasons. After the graduation of Harry Oliver in 1982, Johnston was awarded a scholarship and assigned to field-goal duty as well. He responded admirably, kicking 13 consecutive field goals to start the season and setting a school record with 19 field goals in 22 attempts. (The previous record was 18, set by Oliver in 1980.) In addition, he made all 19 of his extra point attempts for a total of 76 points, also a Notre Dame record for a kicker. *Football News* named Johnston third-team All-America; *The Sporting News* and the Associated Press named him honorable mention.

In 1983 Johnston was far less spectacular. Although he made all 33 of his extra point attempts, he connected on just 12 of 21 field goals attempts. He was not selected in the 1984 NFL Draft and did not play in the NFL.

JONES, ANDRE

Linebacker (1987-90) ▪ 6-4, 225 ▪ Hyattsville, MD

A two-year starter at outside linebacker, Andre Jones's most memorable performance came in a 1989 game against Stanford: He had a career-high 12 tackles to help lead the Fighting Irish to a 27-17 victory. Jones finished the season with 49 tackles, seventh best on the team.

In 1990, as a senior, he was second on the team in tackles with 58, despite missing two games because of a thigh injury. Jones was a seventh-round draft pick of the Pittsburgh Steelers in 1991.

JOYCE, EDMUND

The Reverend Edmund P. Joyce was Notre Dame's longtime executive vice president and chairman of the Faculty Board on Athletics. He worked happily and diligently for more than three decades in the long shadow of university president Reverend Theodore Hesburgh, overseeing the financial interests of one of the most successful private universities in the world.

Born January 26, 1917, in Honduras, where his father worked for the United Fruit

Company, Joyce attended high school in Spartanburg, South Carolina. He enrolled at Notre Dame in the fall of 1933 and graduated in 1937. An intense fan of sports who was drawn to Notre Dame in part because of his fascination with Knute Rockne's football program, he tried out for the varsity basketball team in his freshman year but was unceremoniously cut. Many years later Joyce would still refer to that incident as one of the great disappointments of his life. In truth, though, it was one of the few failures he experienced.

After leaving Notre Dame, Joyce took an accounting job in his hometown. Two years later, in 1939, he became a certified public accountant. But he soon experienced a degree of restlessness. He sought a commission in the Navy but was turned down because of color blindness. Then he applied to the FBI. The Bureau took more than a year to respond to Joyce's application, and by the time he received notification of acceptance, he had settled on a dramatically different pursuit: the priesthood.

Joyce entered Holy Cross College in Washington, D.C., in 1945, and was ordained on June 3, 1949, in Sacred Heart Church on the campus of Notre Dame. He was immediately named assistant vice president for business affairs and within a year became acting vice president. In 1952, after a year of study at Oxford University, he was promoted to executive vice president. For the next 35 years he was, in effect, Notre Dame's chief executive officer. He balanced the books, presided over the construction of more than 40 new buildings, and helped increase endowment from

For more than three decades Reverend Edmund P. Joyce served Notre Dame as its executive vice president and chairman of the Faculty Board on Athletics. He was instrumental in maintaining the highest academic standard for Fighting Irish athletes.

approximately $9 million to $400 million. By the time he retired in 1987, Joyce was in charge of an annual operating budget in excess of $175 million. And under that umbrella was the university's athletic program.

Joyce was an unabashed fan of the Fighting Irish football team. In the late 1950s and early 1960s, when the team had stumbled a bit, he gently but convincingly reassured fans and alumni that Notre Dame would not be "de-emphasizing" varsity sports; athletic programs were vital to the school's financial and emotional well-being. At the same time, Joyce had to police the programs he so vigorously defended. To that end, in 1962, he appointed a mechanical engineering professor and fencing instructor named Mike DeCicco to the position of full-time academic advisor. DeCicco reported directly to Joyce, rather than to coaches or other athletic department personnel. And he had clout—the power to suspend a player from a game or practice if he failed to meet certain academic requirements.

In sum, Joyce made it clear that he would hold Notre Dame to a higher standard. He expected the school's athletic teams to succeed on the playing field; and he expected the athletes to succeed in the classroom. There would be no compromises. It was under Joyce that Notre Dame set rigorous standards for academic and athletic achievement that have been matched by few universities with Division I-A football programs. For many years Joyce was an outspoken advocate of academic integrity within the NCAA. He served as secretary-treasurer of the College Football Association and received the Distinguished American Award from the National Football Foundation. He holds numerous honorary degrees, including one from Notre Dame.

On May 8, 1987, the university's double-domed athletic facility—which houses the basketball and hockey programs—was renamed the Edmund P. Joyce Athletic and Convocation Center. Father Joyce retired on May 31, 1987.

JURKOVIC, MIRKO
Offensive Guard/Defensive Tackle (1988-91) • 6-4, 289 • Calumet City, IL

A consensus first-team All-American as an offensive guard in 1991, Mirko Jurkovic actually began his college career on defense.

He was a two-way star at Thornton Fractional North High School in Calumet City, Illinois, and became one of only two freshmen to earn Notre Dame monograms in the fall of 1988. Jurkovic played 48 minutes at defensive tackle that season and helped the Fighting Irish win a national championship. The next year he made a smooth transition to offensive guard, playing 69 minutes as a backup to senior Tim Grunhard.

Jurkovic was promoted into a starting role in 1990 and by 1991 had become one of the top offensive linemen in college football. He played more minutes than any other Notre Dame offensive player and helped the Fighting Irish rank eleventh nationally in total offense. After the season he received first-team All-America honors from the Walter Camp Foundation, the Newspaper Enterprise Association, United Press International, *The Sporting News*, *Football News*, and *College and Pro Football Newsweekly*. He was also named Notre Dame Lineman of the Year by the Moose Krause Chapter of the National Football Foundation and Hall of Fame.

Jurkovic played with the Chicago Bears in 1992.

K

KADISH, MIKE

Defensive Tackle (1969-71) ▪ 6-5, 249 ▪ Grand Rapids, MI

Mike Kadish overcame serious knee problems to become one of college football's top defensive linemen in 1971. He began his college career in 1969 as an offensive lineman but was switched to defensive tackle less than a week before the season opener. Playing next to All-American Mike McCoy, he adapted quickly to the defensive game; he seemed to have unlimited potential.

During preseason practices in 1970, however, Kadish injured his knee and was forced to miss the first four games of the regular season. He started the final seven games and finished the season with a respectable 47 tackles. Shortly after the team's Cotton Bowl victory over Texas, he underwent surgery to repair his damaged knee.

Kadish recovered quickly and was at nearly full strength by the start of the 1971 season. That year he had a team-high 97 tackles and was named first-team All-America by *The Sporting News*. Drafted in the first round by the Miami Dolphins in 1972, Kadish spent nine years in the NFL—all with the Buffalo Bills.

KANTOR, JOE

Fullback (1961, 1963-64) ▪ 6-1, 212 ▪ Cleveland, OH

A graduate of St. Ignatius High School in Cleveland, Joe Kantor made the Notre Dame varsity in 1961 as a reserve fullback, rushing for 29 yards on five carries. A knee injury kept him on the sideline in 1962, but in 1963 he led the team in rushing with 330 yards on 88 carries. He also scored two touchdowns.

Kantor reinjured his knee prior to the 1964 season, and although he was not completely healthy, he did see significant time as a second-string fullback behind Joe Farrell. He rushed for 158 yards on 47 carries and caught two passes for 43 yards.

Kantor played with the Washington Redskins in 1966.

KELL, PAUL

Tackle (1936-38) ▪ 6-2, 209 ▪ Princeton, IL

Paul Ernest Kell was born in Princeton, Illinois, but graduated from Niles High School in Michigan, where he was an all-state tackle in 1934. One of Niles's high school opponents was Benton Harbor High, which featured an end named Earl Brown. Brown had already declared his intention to attend Notre Dame, and he later convinced Kell to do the same. "After one game against Earl, I decided we should be wearing the same colors," Kell later explained.

Of the two, Brown went on to greater fame as a collegian (he was an All-American in 1938), but Kell had a good deal of success himself. He earned his first monogram in 1936 and was a starter at right tackle in 1938. After graduating in 1939 with a degree in physical education, Kell played two seasons with the Green Bay Packers.

KELLEY, MIKE

Offensive Tackle/Center (1981-84) ▪ 6-5, 266 ▪ Westfield, MA

Mike Kelley's college career did not begin impressively. He injured his back in preseason workouts and sat out the entire 1980 season. Then, in 1981, a knee injury kept him on the sideline for much of the first half of the season.

By 1982, however, Kelley was healthy. He started 11 games at offensive tackle that season and 12 games at center the following year. He was named offensive MVP by his teammates in 1983 and honorable mention All-America by the Associated Press. As a senior, in 1984, the Football Writers Association of America named him second-team All-America.

Kelley was drafted in the third round by the Houston Oilers in 1985. He spent three seasons with the Oilers and one with the Philadelphia Eagles.

KELLY, BOB

Halfback (1943-44) ▪ 5-10, 182 ▪ Chicago, IL

Bob Kelly was one of several young players who helped Notre Dame maintain a level of excellence on the football field during World War II.

The son of U.S. Congressman Edward A. Kelly, he was an all-state running back at Chicago's Leo High School in 1942. Like many talented high school seniors that year, he was heavily recruited. Because so many college athletes had left school to serve in the armed services, the NCAA altered its eligibility rules to allow freshmen to participate in varsity sports; it was the only way most schools could field a complete team.

Kelly very nearly accepted an appointment to West Point but changed his mind at the last minute and opted for Notre Dame. This did not sit well with Army's football coach, Earl "Red" Blaik, who placed a call to the Notre Dame athletic department and threatened to end the Army-Notre Dame football series if Kelly was allowed to enroll in South Bend. When Congressman Kelly got wind of the situation, he intervened, and by the fall of 1943 Bob Kelly was a member of the Fighting Irish varsity.

He served as a backup to starting right halfback Julie Rykovich on a team that went on to win the national championship with a 9-1 record. Notre Dame's backfield that season included Heisman Trophy winner Angelo Bertelli at quarterback and consensus All-American Creighton Miller at left halfback.

In 1944, Notre Dame's starting lineup averaged 19 years of age. The head coach was Ed McKeever, who stepped in while Frank Leahy served in the U.S. Navy. Despite their youth, the Irish won eight of 10 games and finished ninth in the Associated Press final rankings. Bob Kelly led the team in rushing (681 yards on 136 carries), scoring (84 points), punt return average (10.8 yards), and kickoff return average (26.6 yards).

A member of the U.S. Navy's V-12 program during his first two years at Notre Dame, Kelly was called to active duty in 1945. He returned to South Bend in 1946 but, like many athletes in those first post-war years, found himself caught in a numbers game. The Fighting Irish fielded one of their most talented teams that season—a team that included numerous returning servicemen, some of whom had played as far back as 1941. Bob Kelly had been the team's MVP in 1944, but he did not earn a letter in 1946. Nevertheless, he was drafted by the Green Bay Packers in the eighth round of the 1947 NFL Draft. He spent two years (1947-48) with the Los Angeles Dons of the All-America Football Conference and one year (1949) with the Baltimore Colts.

KELLY, JIM
End (1961-63) ▪ 6-2, 215 ▪ Clairton, PA

A high school All-American from Clairton, Pennsylvania, split end Jim Kelly teamed up with two of Notre Dame's most well-known quarterbacks during his three years on the varsity: Daryle Lamonica and John Huarte.

In 1961 Kelly, playing in a backup role, caught nine passes for 138 yards and scored two touchdowns. He also had 26 tackles as a defensive end. The following year, as a starter, he caught a school-record 41 passes for 523 yards and four touchdowns. To say he was the quarterback's favorite target would be a gross understatement. Lamonica completed 64 of 128 passes that season; incredibly, Kelly was on the receiving end of 64 percent of those completions. Of Kelly's 41 receptions, 11 came in a single, spectacular performance against Pittsburgh. He shared team scoring honors (24 points) with Lamonica and halfback Joe Farrell; and, with 21 tackles, he was obviously no slouch on defense.

By the time the season ended, Kelly had 349 minutes of field time, fifth highest on the team. He was named first-team All-America by *Football News*.

As a senior, in 1963, Kelly was compelled to adjust to a new quarterback—actually, he adjusted to several new quarterbacks since Huarte, who would go on to win the Heisman Trophy in 1964, split time that year with Frank Budka and Sandy Bonvechio. The Fighting Irish suffered through a 2-7 season under coach Hugh Devore, and Kelly caught a modest 18 passes for 264 yards and two touchdowns. Still, he again led the team in receiving and was third in scoring with 12 points. He also had 21 tackles.

United Press International, *Football News*, and the American Football Coaches Association all named Kelly first-team All-America in 1963. He played professionally with the Pittsburgh Steelers (1964) and Philadelphia Eagles (1965, 1967).

Career Statistics (Receiving)

YEAR	NO.	YARDS	AVG.	TD
1961	9	138	15.3	2
1962	41	523	12.8	4
1963	18	264	14.7	2
TOTAL	68	925	13.6	8

KELLY, TIM
Linebacker (1968-70) ▪ 6-1, 225 ▪ Springfield, OH

Tim Kelly was an all-state linebacker at Springfield Catholic Central High School. He came to Notre Dame in the fall of 1967 and broke into the starting lineup the next year as a sophomore. He was second on the team in tackles in 1968 with 80 and third in 1969 with 71. He also led all linebackers in playing time as a junior with more than 225 minutes.

As a senior co-captain, in 1970, Kelly had 99 tackles, second best on the team, and was named defensive MVP by the National Monogram Club. He played in the College All-Star Game in 1971 and was a fifth-round draft choice of the Boston Patriots.

KERR, BUD
End (1937-39) ▪ 6-1, 194 ▪ Newburgh, NY

William Howard "Bud" Kerr was born in Tarrytown, New York, and grew up in Newburgh. A marginal high school athlete, he earned just one varsity letter in football at Newburgh Free Academy; in fact, he spent more of his time playing trumpet in the school band.

Kerr worked for four years after high school so that he could save money to attend college. At the same time, he began to take more of an interest in football. As a running back for the Newburgh town team, he attracted the attention of a handful of college scouts. On the advice of friends, he decided to attend Notre Dame.

In the fall of 1936 Kerr arrived in South Bend. He made the varsity in his sophomore year but failed to earn a monogram. As a junior, in 1938, he was a second-string end behind All-American Earl Brown. Kerr succeeded Brown as the starting left end in 1939, and despite the fact that he did not catch a single touchdown pass, he was included on virtually every major All-America team.

KIEL, BLAIR
Quarterback (1980-82) ▪ 6-1, 206 ▪ Columbus, IN

When Blair Kiel began his senior year at Notre Dame, he seemed poised to rewrite the team's record books. He was about to become the first Irish quarterback since Gus Dorais to start four consecutive seasons. And he needed just 72 completions to break Terry Hanratty's career record. Kiel's final season in South Bend, however, coincided with Steve Beuerlein's first season. By the time November rolled around, Kiel was spending most of his time on the bench.

Still, there is no denying Kiel's accomplishments. He came to Notre Dame in 1980 after earning consensus prep All-America honors at East High School in Columbus, Indiana, and beat out Tim Koegel for the starting quarterback job. He completed 48 of 124 passes for 531 yards and played more minutes than any freshman quarterback since Dorais in 1910. The next year he completed 67 of 151 passes for 936 yards and seven touchdowns.

In 1982, as a junior, Kiel had his finest season, completing 118 of 219 passes for 1,273 yards and three touchdowns. A smart, agile quarterback who performed best when throwing short, high-percentage passes, he opened the season by completing 15 of 22 passes for 141 yards in a 23-17 victory over Michigan and ended it with an 11-for-19 (for 151 yards) performance in a 19-18 Liberty Bowl win over Boston College.

But 1983 marked the arrival of Beuerlein, who represented immediate competition for Kiel. After consecutive early-season losses to Michigan State and Miami, in which Kiel threw a total of five interceptions, Beuerlein became the starter. Kiel finished his Notre Dame career with 297 completions in 609 attempts. He passed for 3,650 yards and 17 touchdowns. Through 1995, he was fourth on the school's career passing list, behind Beuerlein, Rick Mirer, and Hanratty. He was also fourth on the career punting list with an average of 40.67 yards per kick. His 10,534 yards was a career record.

Kiel was drafted in the eleventh round by the Tampa Bay Buccaneers in 1984. He also played with the Indianapolis Colts and Green Bay Packers before retiring in 1991.

Career Statistics (Passing)

YEAR	ATT.	COMP.	PCT.	YARDS	TD
1980	124	48	.387	531	0
1981	151	67	.444	936	7

1982	219	118	.539	1,273	3
1983	115	64	.557	910	7
TOTAL	**609**	**297**	**.488**	**3,650**	**17**

Career Statistics (Punting)

YEAR	NO.	YARDS	AVG.
1980	66	2,649	40.1
1981	73	2,914	39.9
1982	77	3,267	42.4
1983	43	1,704	39.6
TOTAL	**259**	**10,534**	**40.67**

KILEY, ROGER

End (1919-21) ▪ 6-0, 180 ▪ Chicago, IL

After backing up Bernie Kirk, the team's leading receiver, in 1919, Roger Kiley became a starter at left end in 1920. He started again in his senior year and was named first-team All-America by the Newspaper Enterprise Association and the International News Service; he also received second-team honors from Walter Camp and *Football World*.

Kiley had a brief professional career (he played for the Chicago Cardinals in 1923) but soon turned his attention to the practice of law. He eventually became an appellate court judge in Illinois.

KINDER, RANDY

Running Back (1993-96) ▪ 6-1, 204 ▪ East Lansing, MI

Randolph Samuel Kinder, one of Notre Dame's career rushing leaders, was born on April 4, 1975, in Washington, D.C. He attended high school in Michigan, where he set a state record for rushing (2,464 yards) in his senior year and won state track titles in the 200 and 400 meters.

Kinder had an immediate impact as a collegian, rushing for 94 yards on 12 carries in a 36-14 win over Michigan State in the third game of his freshman season. Although primarily a backup to starting tailback Lee Becton, he finished the year with 537 yards rushing on 89 attempts—an average of 6.0 yards per carry. As a sophomore Kinder started in five games and rushed for a team-high 702 yards. Unfortunately, his season ended just days before the Irish were to play in the 1995 Fiesta Bowl when he tore a ligament in his right knee.

In the fall, though, Kinder was healthy. He played in 10 games in 1995 and rushed for a team-high 809 yards on 143 carries. He also caught eight passes for 75 yards and scored

10 touchdowns. In 1996, as a senior, he appeared in seven games and rushed for 254 yards on 53 carries. He finished his career with 2,302 yards, good enough for sixth place on Notre Dame's all-time list. Kinder also earned All-America honors in track and field.

Career Statistics (Rushing)

YEAR	NO.	YARDS	AVG.	TD
1993	89	537	6.0	2
1994	119	702	5.9	4
1995	143	809	5.6	9
1996	53	254	4.7	3
TOTAL	404	2,302	5.55	18

KLEINE, WALLY
Defensive Tackle (1983-86) ▪ 6-9, 274 ▪ Midland, TX

William Walter Kleine was blessed with good genes. His older cousin, Joe Kleine, grew to be nearly seven feet tall and played basketball at Notre Dame and the University of Arkansas before embarking on a career in the National Basketball Association. Wally, meanwhile, concentrated on football.

A tight end at Midland High School, Kleine was switched to defensive tackle in college. He sat out the 1982 season after undergoing arthroscopic surgery on both knees and played only 25 minutes in 1983. In 1984, however, he started all 12 games and had 48 tackles in 230 minutes of playing time. A few months later, during spring practice, he won the Hering Award as most improved player.

A second date with the arthroscope forced Kleine to miss nearly half of his junior year. But as a senior in 1986, he led all defensive linemen in minutes played (224:34) and tackles (74). Named second-team All-America by *Football News*, Kleine was drafted by the Washington Redskins in the second round of the 1987 NFL Draft.

KNAFELC, GREG
Quarterback (1977-79) ▪ 6-5, 209 ▪ Green Bay, WI

Greg Knafelc was introduced to the game of football by his father, Gary, a wide receiver with the Green Bay Packers in the 1950s. Greg was a basketball and football star at Green Bay's Premontre High School but was never more than a backup at Notre Dame. He completed just two of three passes for 13 yards and one touchdown in his college career. Despite those meager numbers, Knafelc made it to the NFL; he played one season with the New Orleans Saints in 1983.

KNAPP, LINDSAY

Offensive Tackle (1989-92) ▪ 6-6, 271 ▪ Deerfield, IL

High school All-American Lindsay Knapp earned his first Notre Dame monogram as a freshman in 1989 when he played in six games at offensive tackle. By his junior year he was one of the most consistent players on the offensive line, starting in all 12 games and helping the Irish rank among the most productive offenses in college football.

Knapp started all 12 games again as a senior in 1992. He was named first-team All-America by *College and Pro Football Newsweekly*, as well as Notre Dame Lineman of the Year by the Moose Krause Chapter of the National Football Foundation and Hall of Fame. Knapp also excelled in the classroom: He won the State Farm/Mutual Broadcasting Student-Athlete of the Year Award in 1992 and, as an economics major, graduated with a 3.249 grade point average. He was a fifth-round draft pick of the Kansas City Chiefs in 1993.

KOKEN, MIKE

Halfback (1930-32) ▪ 5-9, 168 ▪ Youngstown, OH

Mike Koken was a reserve halfback on Notre Dame's 1930 national championship team—the last squad to be coached by Knute Rockne. He became a starter in his senior year, leading the Fighting Irish to a 7-2 record.

After graduation Koken played one season of professional football with the Chicago Cardinals. He later became vice president and sales manager of a freight trucking company near South Bend.

KOSIKOWSKI, FRANK

End (1946-47) ▪ 6-0, 202 ▪ Milwaukee, WI

Frank Kosikowski entered Notre Dame in the fall of 1946 after serving in the U.S. Navy. A member of the Fleet City Navy team that captured the Armed Service Championship in 1945, he was a backup end behind Jack Zilly and Leon Hart during his first year in South Bend. He earned a second monogram in 1947, helping the Fighting Irish to a second straight national title.

An athletic player who had both size and speed (he shared the Wisconsin state 200-yard dash record in high school), Kosikowski left Notre Dame in 1948 to pursue a career in professional football. He played with the Buffalo Bills and Cleveland Browns of the All-America Football Conference in 1948.

KOVATCH, JOHN
End (1939-41) ▪ 6-3, 181 ▪ South Bend, IN

John Kovatch distinguished himself in the city of South Bend well before he came to Notre Dame. A star basketball and football player at Washington High School, he was also senior class president and valedictorian.

Although he was a fierce tackler and blocker, Kovatch's pass-catching ability was suspect. He was a starting end at Washington yet had just one reception in his senior year. He developed into a capable receiver for the Fighting Irish, but it was his defensive ability that allowed him to finally break into the starting lineup with three games remaining in his career.

Kovatch played professionally with the Washington Redskins (1942, 1946) and Green Bay Packers (1947).

KOWALKOWSKI, SCOTT
Linebacker/Defensive End (1987-90) ▪ 6-2, 230 ▪ Farmington Hills, MI

Scott Thomas Kowalkowski, the son of former Detroit Lion and Green Bay Packer Bob Kowalkowski, was a two-year starter on defense. He earned honorable mention All-America honors as a defensive end in 1989 and as an outside linebacker in 1990.

Kowalkowski had 107 tackles in his career and was invited to play in the 1991 Senior Bowl. Perhaps his greatest attribute was his durability: From 1987 through 1990 he appeared in every Notre Dame football game. He is the only player who can make that claim.

Kowalkowski played with the Philadelphia Eagles from 1991 through 1993 and with the Detroit Lions from 1994 through 1996.

KRAUSE, MOOSE
Tackle (1931-33) ▪ 6-3, 217 ▪ Chicago, IL

Edward Walter Krauciunas, the son of Lithuanian immigrants, was raised on Chicago's south side near the Union Stockyards. He began working in the family butcher shop when he was just a boy. Theresa Krauciunas hoped that her son would develop a taste for music and the arts; she even arranged for him to take violin lessons. By the time he entered high school, though, Edward was six feet tall and weighed 175 pounds, and suddenly people were calling him "Moose." It was a nickname that would last a lifetime, through stellar basketball and football careers at Notre Dame and through 32 years as the university's much-admired athletic director.

It was while he was in high school that Moose's surname was altered. His football coach at DeLaSalle Institute, Norm Barry, could neither pronounce nor spell

Krauciunas, so he shortened it to Krause. The change didn't seem to bother Moose, who became one of the city's finest all-around athletes. He was captain of the baseball, basketball, and football teams; in the latter two he received all-state honors. With Moose leading the way, the DeLaSalle Meteors captured two national catholic basketball championships.

Edward "Moose" Krause excelled in many sports at Notre Dame, including football, basketball, baseball, and track. After a several years of enjoying a variety of careers in sports and a short stint in the Navy, Krause returned to his alma mater as athletic director, a position he held for 32 years.

After he graduated, Krause planned to work in the stockyards. But Barry stepped in and arranged a meeting with Notre Dame football coach Knute Rockne. Impressed by Krause's size and demeanor, Rockne offered the boy a scholarship. In return, Krause agreed to work in the university dining hall. For him, it was a dream come true; a way to escape from the backbreaking labor of the stockyards.

Krause earned Rockne's respect in his freshman year when he decked the varsity's starting quarterback during a practice scrimmage. One year later he was in the starting lineup. He played tackle for three years under Heartly "Hunk" Anderson and was named All-America in his senior year. Along the way he gained a well-deserved reputation for toughness. For example, Krause played 521 out of a possible 540 minutes in his junior year. And as a senior he broke his jaw on the first play of an all-star game yet played all but four minutes.

It was on the basketball court, however, that Krause had his greatest success. As the team's starting center, he earned All-America honors three times (from 1932 through 1934). He was so big and strong that he was virtually immovable; in fact, he is often held responsible for the creation of one of basketball's fundamental rules: the three-second violation, which stipulates that a player cannot stand in the foul lane for more than three seconds. During Krause's time in South Bend the Fighting Irish won 54 basketball games and lost just 12. He scored 547 points in his career, a school record at the time.

Krause also played baseball and threw the javelin and discus for the Fighting Irish track team. He was a smart man, too, graduating cum laude from Notre Dame with a degree in journalism. After leaving college Krause had a tryout with the Chicago Cubs; he was also offered a job with the Chicago Bears of the NFL. But professional sports were not in his future. Instead, he became basketball coach and athletic director at St. Mary's College in Minnesota. While there Krause picked up a little extra money by assembling a barnstorming semipro basketball team. Among his team's opponents were the Harlem Globetrotters.

After six years at St. Mary's, Krause moved on to Holy Cross College in Worcester, Massachusetts. And he continued to play semipro basketball, which, in the days before the formation of the National Basketball Association, was quite a competitive endeavor.

In 1942 Krause accepted an offer from Frank Leahy to return to South Bend and work as an assistant football coach. The next year he also assumed the role of head basketball coach. Like so many others, Krause put his career on hold during World War II. He joined the U.S. Marine Corps in February 1944 and became an air-combat intelligence officer. He was discharged two years later, in January 1946, and immediately returned to his positions at Notre Dame. The demands of working under Leahy while trying to run a basketball program proved overwhelming, however, and by 1947 Krause was devoting all of his energy to basketball. Then, in 1949, he was offered the job he really wanted: athletic director. He resigned as basketball coach with a career mark of 98-48.

For the next 32 years, until 1980, Krause ran Notre Dame's athletic programs with a firm but loving hand. Considered a bright, energetic man with a gift for diplomacy and fundraising, he was chiefly responsible for the hiring of scores of coaches and the construction of such facilities as the Joyce Athletic and Convocation Center. In 1976 he was inducted into the Basketball Hall of Fame in Springfield, Massachusetts.

Moose Krause died on December 10, 1992. Since 1986, the Moose Krause Chapter of the National Football Foundation and Hall of Fame has paid tribute to him by presenting the Moose Krause Lineman of the Year Award to Notre Dame's outstanding lineman. Below are the honorees.

YEAR	PLAYER	POSITION
1986	Robert Banks	Defensive End
1987	Chuck Lanza	Center
1988	Frank Stams	Defensive End
1989	Jeff Alm	Defensive Tackle
1990	Chris Zorich	Nose Tackle
1991	Mirko Jurkovic	Offensive Tackle
1992	Lindsay Knapp	Offensive Tackle
1993	Aaron Taylor	Offensive Tackle
1994	Oliver Gibson	Nose Guard
1995	Ryan Leahy	Offensive Guard

KRIMM, JOHN
Defensive Back (1978-81) ▪ 6-2, 190 ▪ Columbus, OH

John Krimm was born in Philadelphia and grew up in Columbus, Ohio, where he was an all-state selection in football and track. At Notre Dame he was a three-year starter at cornerback. A solid hitter with a good speed and range, he finished his career with 116 tackles and four interceptions. The New Orleans Saints drafted Krimm in the third round of the 1982 NFL Draft, but his professional career lasted just two seasons.

KUCHTA, FRANK

Center (1956-57) ▪ 6-1, 205 ▪ Cleveland, OH

In 1956 Frank Kuchta was a backup center behind Ed Sullivan. The following year both Kuchta and Sullivan were forced to step aside for Bob Scholtz, a talented sophomore who would become a three-year starter. Kuchta did, however, see a significant amount of playing time; he finished the season with 23 tackles and so impressed NFL scouts that he was drafted in the ninth round by the Washington Redskins. His professional career lasted three seasons.

KUECHENBERG, BOB

Offensive Tackle/Defensive End (1966-68) ▪ 6-2, 245 ▪ Hobart, IN

Bob Kuechenberg was a starting offensive tackle on Notre Dame's national championship team in 1966. In the third game of the 1967 season, however, he was switched by coach Ara Parseghian to defensive end; the Irish had some obvious weaknesses on defense that season, and Parseghian felt that Kuechenberg, one of the team's biggest and most athletic players (he also played third base on the Fighting Irish baseball team), could be of help. And he was. He had 32 tackles and deflected four passes in that abbreviated first season on defense.

As a senior in 1968, Kuechenberg had 44 tackles and was named defensive MVP by the National Monogram Club. A fourth-round draft pick of the Philadelphia Eagles in 1969, he played 14 seasons in the NFL, all with the Miami Dolphins. He played in four Super Bowls and won two championship rings.

KUHARICH, JOE

Guard (1935-37) Head Coach (1959-62) ▪ 6-0, 193 ▪ South Bend, IN

When Joe Kuharich was a boy growing up in South Bend, he used to walk by Cartier Field and dream of playing for the Fighting Irish. On one particularly memorable day, Knute Rockne took him by the hand and invited him inside to watch the team practice. He decided then that someday he would be more than a spectator.

At Riley High School Kuharich was an intense but small (150-pound) lineman. He was so slight that Fighting Irish coach Elmer Layden doubted whether he could play college football. Initially, in fact, Kuharich wasn't even offered a scholarship; he had to earn it on the field.

He arrived at Notre Dame in 1934 along with several other fine athletes from South Bend, including guard Joe Ruetz, end Johnny Murphy, and a young seminarian named Theodore Hesburgh, who would later become the president of the university. Kuharich, as it turned out, fit in well. He gained 25 pounds in his freshman year and another 20 by the time he graduated. He earned three monograms and was a two-year starter at right guard.

After graduating in 1938, Kuharich worked as a graduate assistant at Notre Dame. In 1939 he coached at Vincention Institute in Albany, New York. He played professionally with the Chicago Cardinals in 1940 and 1941, and then served four years in the U.S. Navy during World War II. He received his discharge in the fall of 1945 and immediately rejoined the Cardinals. But Kuharich's playing days were nearly over. He took a job as an assistant with the Pittsburgh Steelers in 1946, moved on to the University of San Francisco in 1947, and was promoted to head coach at USF in 1948. He won 26 games and lost 14 in four years with the Dons, and in 1951 he led the team to a 9-0 record.

That performance helped Kuharich get an offer to coach the Chicago Cardinals in 1952, but he stayed just one year before becoming an independent scout. In 1954 he signed on as an assistant with the Washington Redskins, and in 1955 he was promoted to head coach. After guiding the Redskins to an 8-4 record (they had won only three games the previous season), he was named NFL Coach of the Year. He stayed with the Redskins until December 22, 1958, when he was offered a chance to come home . . . back to South Bend . . . to coach at Notre Dame.

South Bend native Joe Kuharich grew up watching the Irish and dreamed of playing under Knute Rockne. He made his dream come true in 1935 as a small but quick freshman. He returned to his hometown in 1959 after a successful professional coaching career to take the head coaching position at Notre Dame.

Unfortunately, Kuharich was not nearly as successful at Notre Dame as he had been in Washington. The Fighting Irish won 17 games and lost 23 during his four seasons. His winning percentage of .425 is the lowest of any coach in the program's history. Kuharich left Notre Dame after the 1962 season. He then served as supervisor of officials for the National Football League for two years. From 1964 through 1969 he was head coach and general manager of the Philadelphia Eagles.

Career Coaching Record

YEAR	WON	LOST	TIED
1959	5	5	0
1960	2	8	0
1961	5	5	0
1962	5	5	0
TOTAL	17	23	0

KULBITSKI, VIC
Fullback (1943) ▪ 5-11, 203 ▪ St. Paul, MN

After starting at fullback for the University of Minnesota for two years, Vic Kulbitski received a military transfer to Notre Dame in 1943. Although he could not crack the starting lineup (Jim Mello was the first-string fullback), he was a strong, capable football player who was a valuable addition to the Fighting Irish during their drive to a national title.

Kulbitski later played three years of professional football with the Buffalo Bills of the All-America Football Conference.

KUNZ, GEORGE
Offensive Tackle/Tight End (1966-68) ▪ 6-5, 240 ▪ Arcadia, CA

For the first two games of his varsity career, George Kunz was Notre Dame's starting right defensive tackle. He was just a sophomore then and clearly a player with great potential; unfortunately, an injury forced him to the sideline for the rest of the year.

As a junior Kunz was shifted to tight end. He started the first two games of the season and did a respectable job, catching seven passes for 101 yards. As the season wore on, however, coach Ara Parseghian began to juggle his lineup. When Bob Kuechenberg was moved from offensive tackle to defensive end, Kunz was asked to plug the hole at tackle. He made the adjustment with ease and remained at tackle for the rest of his collegiate career.

As co-captain of the 1968 team, Kunz was a consensus All-American, earning second-team honors from the Associated Press and first-team honors from every other prominent selection committee. He was also a first-team Academic All-American and a recipient of post-graduate scholarships from the NCAA and the National Football Foundation.

A first-round draft pick in 1969, he spent 10 years in the NFL—six with the Atlanta Falcons and four with the Baltimore Colts.

KURTH, JOE
Tackle (1930-32) ▪ 6-2, 197 ▪ Madison, WI

Two-time All-American Joe Kurth transferred to Notre Dame from the University of Wisconsin. The youngest of 12 children, he was born in Madison, Wisconsin, and later moved to Los Angeles. In 1930 he became the first sophomore to start on a Notre Dame championship team.

By 1931 Kurth had become one of the best linemen in college football. He was a smart player with a well-deserved reputation for toughness, as evidenced by his performance in a 19-0 victory over Carnegie Tech. Kurth had been injured the previous week against Pittsburgh and spent three days in the hospital but returned to the starting lineup against Carnegie. After the season Kurth was named first-team All-America by United Press International and second-team All-America by the Associated Press.

In 1932 his performance was even more impressive: He was a unanimous first-team All-American and a participant in the East-West Shrine Game. After leaving Notre Dame, Kurth played two years of professional football with the Green Bay Packers.

L

LAMBEAU, CURLY
Fullback (1918) ▪ 5-10, 188 ▪ Green Bay, WI

Earl "Curly" Lambeau played only one season of football at Notre Dame, but his contributions to the sport were as notable as those of any Fighting Irish alumnus.

As a freshman Lambeau was the starting fullback on coach Knute Rockne's first team, which compiled a record of 3-1-2. Lambeau was a reliable performer on that team; in fact, although he was overshadowed by the exploits of sophomore halfback George Gipp, Lambeau was the only freshman to earn a letter in 1918. Unfortunately, a promising college career was interrupted when he contracted a case of tonsillitis and had to withdraw from school.

To support himself, Lambeau took a job with the Indian Packing Corporation in his hometown of Green Bay, Wisconsin. His competitive juices were still flowing, however, and he soon convinced his employers to bankroll his dream of starting a professional football team. With $500 from the Indian Packing Corporation, Lambeau purchased equipment and uniforms and went about the business of recruiting players. By 1921 the Green Bay Packers had joined the American Professional Football Association; one year later the APFA became the National Football League.

Lambeau served as both player and coach for the early Packers teams. He is remembered as one of the NFL's pioneers, a man who embraced the comparative recklessness of the forward pass at a time when the professional game was slow and conservative. Considering Lambeau's background, this is not terribly surprising. After all, it was Notre Dame, in 1913, that revolutionized college football by fully incorporating the forward pass into its offensive attack. And Rockne was a receiver on that team. Even though Lambeau played only one season under Rockne, he could not help but be influenced by the coach's innovative approach to the sport.

In 1929 Lambeau put away his cleats and turned his full attention to coaching. A keen judge of talent, he soon assembled the finest collection of players available at the time. The 1929 Packers featured linemen Mike Michalske and Cal Hubbard and running back Johnny McNally. All three players eventually found their way into the Pro Football Hall of Fame. They were the foundation of a Green Bay team that captured NFL championships in 1929, 1930, and 1931. In a four-year period—from 1929 through 1931—the Packers won 34 of 41 games. Lambeau also led them to NFL championships in 1936, 1939, and 1944.

The franchise's fortunes turned in the post-World War II years, however, and by 1951 Lambeau had resigned. He later coached the Chicago Cardinals and Washington Redskins before retiring in 1955. His career winning percentage of .623 (229-134-22) is seventh on the NFL's all-time list.

Curly Lambeau was inducted into the Pro Football Hall of Fame in 1963; he died on June 1, 1965.

LAMONICA, DARYLE
Quarterback (1960-62) ▪ 6-2, 205 ▪ Fresno, CA

A gifted quarterback with a tremendous arm, Daryle Lamonica played on nothing but mediocre teams in college (Notre was 12-18 during his three years on the varsity); thus, his talent was not truly acknowledged until he became a professional.

Lamonica came to Notre Dame from Clovis High School in California, where he

When Daryle Lamonica played at Notre Dame in the early 1960s, the team was not at the height of its success, and his career was good but not great. It wasn't until four years into his professional career, when he was traded to Oakland, that he found his niche. In his first season with the Raiders he was named AFL Player of the Year.

was a four-sport star who received all-state honors in football in his senior year. Although he succeeded George Izo as Notre Dame's starting quarterback in 1960, he was not the team's leading passer; George Haffner completed 30 of 108 passes, while Lamonica completed 15 of 31. Lamonica proved to be a versatile athlete, though: He was the team's second-leading scorer with 18 points; he averaged 37.4 yards per punt; and he had 33 tackles as a defensive back.

In 1961, while splitting time with Frank Budka, Lamonica completed 20 of 52 passes for 300 yards and two touchdowns. He scored 18 points, was the team's leading punter, and had 29 tackles.

As a senior Lamonica was clearly the number one quarterback, and his statistics reflected that status. He completed 64 of 128 passes (41 of those completions were to All-America wide receiver Jim Kelly); threw for six touchdowns and rushed for four more; and averaged 36.5 yards per punt. He played only sparingly on defense.

After the season Lamonica was named third-team All-America by the Associated Press. In the 1963 draft, he was not selected until the twelfth round. He spent the first four years of his professional career with the American Football League's Buffalo Bills, but it wasn't until he was traded to the Oakland Raiders in 1967 that he became one of the league's biggest stars.

In his first season with the team, Lamonica led the Raiders to the AFL championship and was named AFL Player of the Year. He completed 220 of 425 passes for 3,228 yards and 30 touchdowns in guiding the Raiders to a Super Bowl appearance against the Green Bay Packers. He led the Raiders to the AFL title game in 1969 and was again named AFL Player of the Year after completing 221 of 426 passes for 3,302 yards and 32 touchdowns.

Lamonica remained with the Raiders until his retirement following the 1974 season. In his 12-year career, he completed 1,288 of 2,601 passes for 19,154 yards and 164 touchdowns.

Career Statistics (Passing)

YEAR	ATT.	COMP.	YARDS	PCT.	TD
1960	15	31	242	.484	0
1961	20	52	300	.384	0
1962	64	128	821	.500	6
TOTAL	99	211	1,363	.426	6

LANZA, CHUCK
Center (1984-87) ▪ 6-2, 270 ▪ Germantown, TN

Born in Pittsburgh and raised in Tennessee, Charles Louis Lanza was a two-year starter at center and a participant in every Fighting Irish football game from 1984 through 1987.

He enrolled at Notre Dame in the fall of 1983 but sat out the season with injuries. In 1984 he earned his first monogram, and in 1985 he played 80 minutes as a second-string center. Lanza became the team's starting center in 1986 and was named honorable mention All-America by the Associated Press. As a senior captain, in 1987, he continued to improve, earning first-team All-America honors from *Football News* and second-team honors from AP and United Press International. He was also named Lineman of the Year by the Moose Krause Chapter of the National Football Foundation and Hall of Fame.

Lanza played with the Pittsburgh Steelers from 1988 through 1990.

LATTNER, JOHN

Right Halfback (1951-1953) ▪ 6-1, 190 ▪ Chicago, IL

Heisman Trophy winner John Lattner was one of the most versatile players on the Notre Dame roster in the early 1950s.

He first made his mark in 1951, as a sophomore, when he rushed for 341 yards and six touchdowns in helping the Irish to a 7-2-1 record. As a junior Lattner continued to

John Lattner was the most consistent player the Fighting Irish had in the early 1950s. He was a strong rusher, punter, kick returner, and defenseman, and he was awarded the Heisman Trophy in 1953.

improve. He rushed for 732 yards and five touchdowns and caught 17 passes for 252 yards. After the season he was named the Maxwell Award winner as the outstanding college player in the nation. He also was fifth in voting for the Heisman Trophy.

Lattner's senior season was one for the record books. Even though he did not lead the fighting Irish in any of the most visible statistical categories (passing, rushing, receiving, scoring), he still won the Heisman Trophy. Lattner's contributions were measurable—he rushed for 651 yards and scored nine touchdowns—but it was his ability to contribute in so many areas that made him the most valuable member of the Irish football team. He served as the team's punter; he ran back punts and kickoffs; he excelled in the defensive secondary, where he had 13 career interceptions. Indeed, John Lattner was a tireless competitor who was rarely spotted on the sideline.

After the 1953 season Lattner was named a consensus All-American and Maxwell Award winner for the second consecutive season. In one of the closest races in history, he edged Paul Giel of the University of Minnesota for the Heisman. Lattner's exploits helped Notre Dame compile a 9-0-1 record in coach Frank Leahy's final season. Several organizations named Notre Dame the No. 1 team in the nation; but the wire services opted for the University of Maryland.

Lattner's professional career was brief and unspectacular. He played one season with the Pittsburgh Steelers before joining the armed services. While playing in a military game he suffered a serious knee injury and never played professionally again. Lattner later opened a restaurant in Chicago and became an executive with a company that produced business forms. He was inducted into the College Football Hall of Fame in 1979.

Career Statistics

YEAR	ATT.	YARDS	AVG.	TD	REC.	YARDS	AVG.
1951	68	341	5.0	6	8	157	19.6
1952	148	732	4.9	5	17	252	14.8

| 1953 | 134 | 651 | 4.9 | 9 | 14 | 204 | 14.6 |
| TOTAL | 350 | 1,724 | 4.9 | 20 | 39 | 613 | 15.7 |

LAUTAR, JOHN

Guard (1934-36) ▪ 6-1, 184 ▪ Moundsville, WV

The son of a West Virginia coal miner, John Lautar did not play organized football until his senior year at Moundsville High School. He graduated at the age of 16 and went to work in the engineering department of a glass manufacturing company in Ohio. After saving some money for school, he arrived in South Bend and enrolled in the university's engineering department. He also joined the football team.

Lautar played guard on the freshman team in 1933, moved up to the varsity in 1934, and became a starter in 1935. As a senior, in 1936, he assumed the responsibilities of team captain when Bill Smith relinquished the role. (Smith had been elected captain but missed the entire season while recuperating from surgery.) Lautar performed admirably as a stand-in, leading the Fighting Irish to a 6-2-1 record and earning first-team All-America honors from United Press International.

LAW, JOHN

Guard (1926-29) ▪ 5-9, 163 ▪ Yonkers, NY

John Law was the captain of Notre Dame's 1929 national championship team, which was coached by Knute Rockne. He played on the varsity for four years and won three varsity letters. As a junior and senior he was the starting right guard, despite his diminutive stature. In fact, at 5-9, 163 pounds, Law was not only the smallest player on the Fighting Irish line, he was also the smallest player in the entire starting lineup.

Law played one year of professional football with the Newark Bears of the first American Football League. He stayed involved in football as a coach for many years, first at Manhattan College and later at Sing Sing prison in Ossining, New York. In 1961 he was appointed to the New York State Commission of Correction by Governor Nelson Rockefeller. He died in 1962.

LAWRENCE, DON

Tackle (1956-58) ▪ 6-1, 220 ▪ Cleveland, OH

A three-time monogram winner, Don Lawrence was a consistently productive lineman for the Fighting Irish in the late 1950s. He had 48 tackles as a junior in 1957 and 43 tackles as a senior in 1958. A seventh-round draft choice of the Washington Redskins in 1959, he played three seasons of professional football.

LAYDEN, ELMER
Running Back/Quarterback (1922-24) ▪ Head Coach (1934-40) ▪ 5-11, 162 ▪ Davenport, IA

As a member of the famed Four Horsemen in the 1920s and a highly successful coach in the 1930s, Elmer Layden was one of the most influential and important members of the Notre Dame community.

Yet another outstanding Notre Dame player who went on to become the team's head coach, Elmer Layden will be best remembered as one of the Four Horsemen. He also served five years as commissioner of the NFL.

He came to South Bend from Davenport, Iowa, after a dazzling prep career. A star guard in basketball, he helped Davenport High School win two state championships; he also finished first in six events at the Iowa state track and field championship in his junior year.

Layden entered Notre Dame in 1921, at the age of 18. The next year, as a sophomore, he played quarterback and left halfback on a team that went 8-1-1. In 1923 head coach Knute Rockne moved Layden to fullback, despite the fact that he weighed only 162 pounds. Layden had surprisingly little trouble adjusting to the demands of the new position; he gained 420 yards on 102 carries and caught six passes for 78 yards. He also scored seven touchdowns to help the Fighting Irish post a 9-1 record.

But it was in 1924 that Layden had his most memorable season. Individually, his statistics were no more impressive than they had been the previous two years: 423 yards rushing on 111 carries. As a team, though, Notre Dame experienced a spectacular season. The Fighting Irish went 10-0 and captured their first consensus national championship. Along the way they outscored their opponents 285-54.

In the third game of the year, against Army, the Four Horsemen were born. They were brought vividly to life by sportswriter Grantland Rice in the October 19 edition of the *New York Herald-Tribune*. In describing Notre Dame's 13-7 victory over Army at the Polo Grounds in New York, he compared Layden and the rest of the Irish backfield—Jim Crowley, Don Miller, and Harry Stuhldreher—to the Four Horsemen of dramatic lore. The nickname, of course, stuck, and the attendant national publicity helped promote the career of each player, as well as the health of the Notre Dame program.

Layden was the was the fastest of the Four Horsemen—he could run the 100-yard dash in 10 seconds flat—but that was not his only skill. He was also the team's best defensive player and punter. In the 1925 Rose Bowl, Layden ran back two interceptions for touchdowns and also scored on a seven-yard run as the Fighting Irish clinched the national title with a 27-10 victory over Stanford. After the season he was named a consensus All-American.

After graduating in 1925 Layden returned to Iowa to practice law and coach football at tiny Columbia College in Dubuque. In two seasons he compiled a record of 8-5-2 before moving on to Duquesne University in Pittsburgh. The school had meager resources, but Layden, who also served as athletic director, made the best of the situation. Duquesne had a record of 48-16-6 during Layden's seven-year tenure. In 1933 the school beat Miami, 33-7, in a post-season game known as the Festival of Palms, a precursor of the Orange Bowl. Perhaps even more impressive was a 7-0 loss to powerful cross-town rival Pittsburgh that same season.

Layden's accomplishments at Duquesne prompted interest from his alma mater. He was considered not only a fine football coach but also a skilled administrator and polished public speaker. And a staunch Catholic. In short, he was everything Notre Dame wanted in a football coach. So late in the fall of 1933—before the season was even over, in fact—Elmer Layden became Notre Dame's sixteenth football coach. He would succeed Hunk Anderson, whose team was struggling through a 3-5-1 season. He also was named athletic director, replacing Jesse Harper.

Although Layden did not bring a consensus national title to South Bend, his teams were all successful. His worst year was his first, when the Irish went 6-3. Overall, he won 47 games, lost 13, and tied 3. On November 12, 1938, he led Notre Dame to its 300th victory—19-0 over Minnesota. That same year, the Irish finished 11-0 and were named national champions by several organizations, although not by the Associated Press.

When his contract expired after the 1940 season, Layden was offered a one-year extension (his previous contract had been for five years). He found the terms unacceptable and refused to sign. Instead, he accepted a lucrative position as the commissioner of the National Football League. Five years later he resigned from that post and moved into private business in Chicago.

Elmer Layden was inducted into the College Football Hall of Fame in 1951. He died June 30, 1973.

Career Statistic (Rushing)

YEAR	ATT.	YARDS	AVG.	TD
1922	80	453	5.7	0
1923	102	420	4.1	5
1924	111	423	3.8	5
TOTAL	294	1,841	6.3	10

Career Coaching Record

YEAR	WON	LOST	TIED
1934	6	3	0
1935	7	1	1
1936	6	2	1
1937	6	2	1
1938	8	1	0
1939	7	2	0
1940	7	2	0
TOTAL	**47**	**13**	**3**

LEAHY, BERNIE

Halfback/Fullback (1929-31) ▪ 5-10, 175 ▪ Chicago, IL

Bernie Leahy was not related to Notre Dame coaching legend Frank Leahy, although the two were teammates at Notre Dame in 1929 when the Fighting Irish went 9-0 and won the national championship under coach Knute Rockne.

Leahy was a reserve on the 1929 team, won his first varsity letter as a halfback in 1930, and saw considerable playing time at fullback in 1931 under first-year coach Hunk Anderson. He played professionally with the Chicago Bears in 1932.

LEAHY, FRANK

Tackle (1928-30) ▪ Head Coach (1941-43, 1946-53) ▪ 5-11, 183 ▪ Winner, SD

Frank Leahy's winning percentage as a head coach at Notre Dame was .855, the second best in NCAA history behind only Knute Rockne. In 11 seasons he accumulated 87 wins, 11 losses, and 9 ties. But his attachment to South Bend actually reaches farther into the past.

Leahy was a three-sport star at Winner High School in Winner, South Dakota, before his family moved to Omaha, Nebraska, after his junior year. If the move was traumatic, Leahy didn't let on; in fact, despite being the new kid in town, he was named captain of the baseball, football, and basketball teams at Central High School. If he adapted to his new surroundings with surprising ease, it was probably because he was an exceptionally strong-willed and competitive young man. Leahy even briefly considered becoming a professional boxer while he was still in high school, but after hearing a motivational speech by Knute Rockne, he was sold on the idea of attending Notre Dame.

Leahy played three years for the Fighting Irish and was a tackle on Rockne's 1929 national championship team. His playing career came to an end prior to the 1930 season when he tore cartilage in his knee. That injury, although devastating at the time, may have been a blessing. Leahy spent the season on the sideline, often right next to Rockne. He absorbed the coach's wisdom and became fascinated with the idea of one day becoming a coach himself. As for the coach, well, he was more than happy to encourage Leahy's new passion. When the season ended Rockne had to travel to the Mayo Clinic in Rochester, Minnesota, for treatment of phlebitis. He invited Leahy to come along so that doctors could examine his knee. The two men shared a hospital room for a week, during which Rockne talked endlessly about football strategy and philosophy . . . and Leahy listened.

"In the week I was confined to a hospital bed, I learned more about football and the technique of coaching than in all my previous college playing," Leahy would later say. "Right then I decided to become a coach."

After graduating in 1931, Leahy jumped on the coaching treadmill. He accepted a position as a line coach at Georgetown University then moved to Michigan State the following year to work under another Notre Dame alumnus, Jim Crowley. In 1933 Crowley accepted the head coaching job at Fordham and took his assistant with him. Leahy remained at Fordham for six years. From 1935 through 1938 he coached the legendary "Seven Blocks of Granite," the linemen who helped Fordham become one of the best college teams in the country (one of those players was Vince Lombardi). The Rams lost only two games during that period.

After coaching the Irish for over a decade, Frank Leahy had the second-best winning percentage in the NCAA, .855—second to his own college coach, Knute Rockne.

Leahy became a head coach for the first time in 1939 at Boston College. If he was a neophyte, though, it didn't show. A smart, demanding coach who always referred to his players as his "lads," he led the Eagles to a 20-2 record over two years. The last of those victories was a stunning 19-13 victory over Tennessee in the 1941 Sugar Bowl, a performance that earned Leahy an invitation to return to South Bend as head football coach of his alma mater. He accepted, of course, and once again the transition was smooth. In Leahy's first season the Fighting Irish went 8-0-1. Two years later, in 1943, the team won nine of 10 games and captured its first wire-service national championship.

Leahy's coaching career was interrupted by a two-year stint in the Navy. But when he returned, Notre Dame quickly found its way back to the top of the rankings. In 1946 the Fighting Irish went 8-0-1, outscored their opponents 271-24, and won another consensus national championship. But that was merely the beginning of a remarkable four-year run during which the team did not lose a game. Notre Dame won consensus national championships in 1947 and 1949. By the end of the '49 season, Leahy had compiled a post-World War II record of 36-0-2. And he wasn't through yet. After suffering through a .500 season (4-4-1) in 1950, the Fighting Irish improved to 7-2-1 in 1951. They were third in the Associated Press poll in 1952 and second in 1953.

Poor health—he collapsed because of an inflamed pancreas at half-time of the Georgia Tech game—prompted Leahy to retire after the 1953 season. He was only 45 years old when he coached his last game. Despite his relatively short career, his resumé is one of the most impressive in the history of college football: His teams were undefeated in six of his 11 years at Notre Dame; 36 of his players were named All-Americans, and 12 have been inducted into the College Football Hall of Fame. He was an innovative coach who introduced the audible and the pro-type zone defense to college football. In addition to his on-field accomplishments, Leahy was honored by Pope Pius XII as a Knight of Malta in 1951, and he seconded the nomination of General Dwight D. Eisenhower at the 1956 Republican National Convention. Leahy nearly accepted an offer to coach football at Texas A&M in 1958, but a physical examination indicated that the stress might very well kill him. So he declined the invitation

Frank Leahy was inducted into the College Football Hall of Fame in 1970. He died of leukemia on June 21, 1973.

Career Coaching Record

YEAR	WON	LOST	TIED
1941	8	0	1
1942	7	2	2
1943	9	1	0
1946	8	0	1
1947	9	0	0
1948	9	0	1
1949	10	0	0
1950	4	1	1
1951	7	2	1
1952	7	2	1
1953	9	0	1
TOTAL	**87**	**11**	**9**

LEHMANN, BOB
Guard (1961-63) ▪ 6-0, 215 ▪ Louisville, KY

Joseph Robert Lehmann graduated from Flaget High School in Louisville, Kentucky, the alma mater of Paul Hornung, who starred for both the Fighting Irish and the NFL's Green Bay Packers. After playing behind Nick Buoniconti as a sophomore, Lehmann became a starter and one of Notre Dame's top linemen in 1962. A tireless two-way player, he had 61 tackles (second on the team) and logged more than 367 minutes of field time, a figure exceeded only by guard Jim Carroll and center Ed Hoerster.

In the spring of 1963 Lehmann was elected team captain. In the fall he was one of the few bright spots in an otherwise dreary 2-7 season. He was second on the team in tackles with 95 and first in minutes played with 361. The Associated Press named Lehmann second-team All-America, and the American Football Coaches Association named him to its third team. He was also a first-team Academic All-American.

Despite his success at the college level, Lehmann was not drafted until the seventeenth round in 1965. He did not play professional football.

LEMEK, RAY
Guard/Tackle (1953-55) ▪ 6-1, 205 ▪ Sioux City, IA

At Heelan High School in Sioux City, Iowa, Ray Lemek was a four-sport star who captained the basketball and football teams in his senior year. His high school coach was Ed Simonich, a Fighting Irish fullback in the late 1930s, so it was no surprise that Lemek chose to attend Notre Dame.

He adapted quickly to the college game; in fact, he started at left guard and played all but nine minutes in the first game of his sophomore season. He remained a starter at guard until the penultimate game of his junior year when a severe knee injury forced him to the sideline.

Lemek missed spring practice in 1955 but came back to start at right tackle in his senior year; he was also team captain. As a professional, Lemek spent five seasons with the Washington Redskins and three with the Pittsburgh Steelers.

LEONARD, JIM
Guard/Fullback (1931-33) ▪ 6-0, 187 ▪ Pedricktown, NJ

When James "Big Jim" Leonard entered St. Joseph's Prep, he had never played football. By the time he graduated, though, he was one of the most highly acclaimed players in Philadelphia. He led St. Joseph's to the city championship and was named first-team all-city in 1929.

Leonard played freshman football in 1930, Knute Rockne's final year as head coach. The following season, under Hunk Anderson, he was a reserve fullback. He remained in the backfield in his junior year but switched to guard as a senior, in 1933. He was something of an iron man that year, playing in six full games without sitting out a single play.

After graduating in 1934 Leonard joined the Philadelphia Eagles as a quarterback. He stayed with the club until his retirement in 1937. When his playing career ended, Leonard went into coaching. He was an assistant with the Eagles before accepting an invitation to resurrect the football program at tiny St. Francis College in Loretto, Pennsylvania.

LEOPOLD, BOBBY

Safety/Linebacker (1976-79) ▪ 6-2, 217 ▪ Port Arthur, TX

A two-year starter at linebacker and strong safety, Bobby Leopold set a Notre Dame record by returning three interceptions for touchdowns. Remarkably enough, he had only six interceptions in his entire career.

An aggressive, hard-hitting player who was equally adept at pass coverage and defending against the run, Leopold had 180 career tackles, including 66 in his senior year. Although bothered by knee and ankle injuries throughout his college career, he went on to play four seasons with the San Francisco 49ers.

LIND, MIKE

Fullback (1960-62) ▪ 6-0, 195 ▪ Chicago, IL

Harry Norman "Mike" Lind was a four-sport athlete at Chicago's Calumet High School in the late 1950s. He competed for the wrestling, baseball, and swimming teams, but it was football that brought him his greatest notoriety. He helped lead Calumet to the Chicago city title in 1956 and was an all-city running back in 1957.

Two years later Lind was the starting fullback at Notre Dame. Although only a sophomore, he was one of the better players on a team that struggled throughout the season and won only two of 10 games. He rushed for 167 yards on 53 carries and had 17 tackles on defense. The next year Lind was the team's second-leading rusher with 450 yards on 87 carries; he was also second in scoring with 24 points and sixth in receiving with four catches. Defensively, he had 31 tackles.

Lind was elected captain of the 1962 team, but injuries limited him to just 21 minutes of playing time the entire season. He played professionally with the San Francisco 49ers (1963-64) and Pittsburgh Steelers (1965-68). In his six-year NFL career he rushed for 661 yards and eight touchdowns on 221 carries.

LISCH, RUSTY

Quarterback (1976-77, 1979) ▪ 6-4, 210 ▪ Belleville, IL

After backing up Rick Slager as a freshman, Rusty Lisch beat out Joe Montana in the summer of 1977 and was pronounced starting quarterback by coach Dan Devine. By the end of the season, though, it was Montana directing the Fighting Irish to a national championship. Lisch completed a respectable 51 of 94 passes for 568 yards and six touchdowns. But he was not nearly as impressive as Montana, who completed 99 of 189 passes for more than 1,600 yards.

Montana was even better in 1978; Lisch, meanwhile, sat out the season. He returned in 1979 and finally got a chance to start for an entire season. In 10 games he completed 108 of 208 passes for 1,781 yards and four touchdowns. He also threw 10 interceptions.

A good all-around athlete who led his team to two consecutive championships in the Campus Bookstore Basketball Tournament, Lisch was drafted by the St. Louis Cardinals in the fourth round in 1980. He played with the Cardinals from 1980 through 1983 and with the Chicago Bears in 1984. In five NFL seasons he completed 55 of 115 passes for 547 yards and one touchdown. He was intercepted 11 times.

A solid quarterback in his own right, Rusty Lisch had the misfortune to play the position for Notre Dame at the same time as Joe Montana. He survived the Montana years, however, and went on to play professional football.

Career Statistics (Passing)

YEAR	ATT.	COMP.	PCT.	YARDS	TD
1976	41	16	.381	267	2
1977	94	51	.543	568	2
1979	208	108	.519	1,437	4
TOTAL	**343**	**175**	**.510**	**2,272**	**8**

LIVINGSTONE, BOB
Halfback (1942, 1946-47) ▪ 6-0, 168 ▪ Hammond, IN

Robert Edward Livingstone was a starter at left halfback in 1942. World War II rather dramatically interrupted his career, but after a three-year stint in the U.S. Army he returned to South Bend. He rushed for 191 yards on 40 carries as a backup behind Terry Brennan at left halfback on Notre Dame's national championship squad in 1946. In 1947 he helped the Irish win a second consecutive national title by rushing for 242 yards and four touchdowns on 45 carries. He also caught four passes for 78 yards.

Before coming to South Bend, Livingstone played high school football at Hammond High in Indiana, where he received all-state honors in 1940. After leaving South Bend, he had a brief but hectic professional career, playing for the Chicago Rockets (1948), Chicago Hornets (1949), and Buffalo Bills (1950) of the All-America Football Conference, as well as the Baltimore Colts (1951) of the NFL.

LOFTUS SPORTS CENTER

The Loftus Sports Center, built in 1987 and 1988, is one of the most impressive all-purpose college sports facilities in the nation. Constructed at a cost of $6.3 million, the Loftus Center also houses the Haggar Fitness Complex and Meyo Field in a building that is 614 feet long and 210 feet wide.

The Loftus Center includes locker room facilities, classrooms, and a 154-seat auditorium that is used for academic lectures and football team meetings. The Haggar Fitness Complex houses more than 40,000 pounds of free weights and a wide assortment of cardiovascular equipment. Perhaps the most unique area of the Loftus Center, though, is Meyo Field, which features a 100-yard Astro Turf football field and a six-lane indoor track. The field, of course, is ideal for indoor workouts for the Irish football team, particularly when preparing for road games on artificial turf. And it obviously serves as a warm and comfortable home for athletes who wish to work out during the harsh South Bend winter. The facility is not, however, the exclusive domain of the football team. The field is also marked for soccer and lacrosse; and a netting system allows the golf, tennis, and softball teams to practice indoors.

The Loftus Sports Center was donated by John R. Loftus, who played basketball for the fighting Irish in the 1940s.

LOMBARDI AWARD

The Lombardi Award is presented each year to the outstanding lineman in college football. Sponsored by the Rotary Club of Houston and voted on by a panel of coaches and media representatives, it honors the player whose performance and character best illustrate the ideals set forth by the legendary Vince Lombardi.

Since its inception in 1970, four Notre Dame players have been named Lombardi Award winners:

YEAR	PLAYER	POSITION
1971	Walt Patulski	Defensive End
1977	Ross Browner	Defensive End
1990	Chris Zorich	Defensive Tackle
1993	Aaron Taylor	Offensive Tackle

LONGO, TOM
Defensive Back (1963-65) ▪ 6-1, 195 ▪ Lyndhurst, NJ

A quarterback both in high school and on the freshman team at Notre Dame, Tom Longo was switched to defensive back in his sophomore season. In retrospect, it's obvious that coach Ara Parseghian made the right move: Quarterback John Huarte went on to win the Heisman Trophy in 1964, and Longo developed into one of the team's best defensive players.

As a sophomore, in 1963, Longo had 17 tackles and two interceptions. In 1964 he had four interceptions and led all defensive backs with 72 tackles. He also shared the team lead in passes broken up with 10. In his senior year, 1965, he had 73 tackles and four interceptions.

Longo played professionally with the New York Giants in 1969 and 1970 and with the St. Louis Cardinals in 1971.

LUJACK, JOHN
Quarterback (1943-47) ▪ 6-0, 180 ▪ Connellsville, PA

Shortly before the seventh game of the 1943 season, Notre Dame quarterback Angelo Bertelli left school to join the United States Marine Corps. After his departure, the undefeated Irish turned to sophomore running back John Lujack. In his first start, Lujack threw for two touchdowns, ran for another, and intercepted a pass in leading Notre Dame to a 26-0 victory over Army. But that was a mere prelude to what would turn out to be a spectacular career.

Lujack helped the Fighting Irish capture the national championship with a 9-1 record in 1943. He then left school and spent three years in the Navy during World War II. Upon his discharge he returned to South Bend. If there was any concern that Lujack's skills had deteriorated, they were quickly laid to rest. While running the offense out of the T formation, he passed for 778 yards and six touchdowns in 1946. He also played defensive back and served as the team's punter. In fact, his single biggest play that season occurred on defense, when he stopped Army fullback Doc Blanchard from scoring a touchdown to preserve a scoreless tie. Army was the top-ranked team in the Associated Press national poll at the time; Notre Dame was No. 2. By year's end, they had switched places.

John Lujack became a quarterback by necessity when Angelo Bertelli went off to war. Expectations were low as Lujack kicked off the 1943 season, which ended with the Fighting Irish winning the national championship.

Lujack was a consensus All-America selection in 1946 and finished second—behind

Army's Glenn Davis—in balloting for the Heisman Trophy. The following year, as a senior, he won the Heisman Trophy and was named Associated Press Male Athlete of the Year. It was an honor he deserved. Lujack completed 56 percent of his passes and threw for nine touchdowns in leading Notre Dame to another undefeated season and a second consecutive national championship.

After graduating from Notre Dame, Lujack entered the NFL. He played only four seasons—all with the Chicago Bears—but they were memorable. He led the team in scoring each year and twice was invited to play in the NFL Pro Bowl. In 1949 he set an NFL record by passing for 458 yards and six touchdowns in a game against the Chicago Cardinals. Lujack retired from the NFL in 1952 and returned to his alma mater as a backfield coach. He later entered private business, opening an automobile dealership in Davenport, Iowa.

John Lujack was inducted into the College Football Hall of Fame in 1960.

Career Statistics (Passing)

YEAR	ATT.	COMP.	YARDS	TD	PCT.
1943	71	34	525	4	.479
1946	100	49	778	6	.490
1947	109	61	777	9	.559
TOTAL	280	144	2,080	19	.514

Career Statistics (Rushing)

YEAR	CARRIES	YARDS	TD
1943	46	191	0
1946	23	108	1
1947	12	139	1
TOTAL	81	438	2

LYGHT, TODD

Cornerback (1987-90) ▪ 6-1, 184 ▪ Flint, MI

Two-time consensus All-American Todd Lyght was one of the most decorated athletes ever to play in the Notre Dame secondary. A wide receiver and defensive back at Luke M. Powers High in Flint, Michigan, he grew up in an athletic family: His father, William, played basketball at Morgan State; his brother, Trent, was a swimmer at Arizona State; and his sister, Cheryl, was a swimmer at the University of Rochester.

A prep All-American, Lyght made an immediate impact as a freshman at Notre Dame. He started in two games, played in 12, and finished the season with 29 tackles and one interception. The following year he became a full-time starter. He had 36 tackles and was named honorable mention All-America by the Associated Press.

In 1989, as a junior, Lyght became one of the best defensive backs in college football. He had 47 tackles and eight interceptions while running his streak of consecutive starts to 24; he played more minutes than any other Irish defensive player. A finalist for the Jim Thorpe Award (presented annually to the top defensive back in the country), Lyght was a unanimous first-team All-American.

That performance, naturally, led to great expectations for Lyght's senior year. *The Sporting News*, for example, named him "the best player in college football" in its pre-season report. As it turned out, Lyght's senior year was not quite as spectacular as his junior year. But it was impressive. Despite missing two games with a hamstring injury, he had 49 tackles and two interceptions and was a consensus All-American, earning first-team recognition from United Press International, the Walter Camp Foundation, and the American Football Coaches Association. He was a semifinalist for the Jim Thorpe Award.

Lyght was the fifth player chosen in the 1991 NFL draft. He played with the Los Angeles/St. Louis Rams from 1991 through 1996.

LYNCH, DICK
Halfback (1955-57) ▪ 6-0, 185 ▪ Bound Brook, NJ

Although better known as a professional football player with the New York Giants, Dick Lynch was one of Notre Dame's best all-purpose players in 1957.

He came to South Bend from Phillipsburg Catholic High School in Clinton, New Jersey. And although he was used sparingly as a sophomore and junior, he earned monograms each season. As a senior Lynch became the starting right halfback—and one of the team's most potent and reliable weapons. He rushed for 287 yards on 77 carries (second behind only Nick Pietrosante), caught a team-high 13 passes for 128 yards, and was second in scoring with 30 points. He also led the Irish in kickoff returns and punt returns and had 28 tackles from his position in the defensive secondary.

The Washington Redskins selected Lynch in the sixth round of the 1958 NFL Draft. After one season he joined the New York Giants. He retired in 1966.

LYNCH, JIM
Linebacker (1964-66) ▪ 6-1, 225 ▪ Lima, OH

A member of the College Football Hall of Fame, Jim Lynch grew up in Lima, Ohio, where he was captain of the high school football team and a member of the varsity baseball and basketball squads. He came from an athletic family that included an older brother, Tom, who went on to captain the football team at the U.S. Naval Academy.

In 1964, as a sophomore, Lynch weighed only 210 pounds; nevertheless, he caught the eye of first-year coach Ara Parseghian. Lynch started the first six games at outside linebacker before suffering a knee injury that forced him to the sideline for the remainder of the season. Still, he wound up with a respectable 41 tackles.

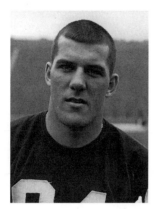

An outstanding athlete and scholar, Jim Lynch was named a first-team Academic All-American his senior year. His eleven-year career with the Kansas City Chiefs included the 1970 Super Bowl victory.

By the fall of 1965 Lynch was fully recovered. He returned to the starting lineup and had an outstanding season, recording a team-high 108 tackles in 252 minutes of playing time; he also broke up three passes and intercepted one. As the person who called signals, he was arguably the most important player on a defense that allowed just 73 points and less than two yards per rush. After the season he was named second-team All-America by the Newspaper Enterprise Association.

Lynch's best season was 1966. He served as captain of a team that won nine games, lost none, and tied one and brought Notre Dame its first consensus national championship in 17 years. Lynch led the team in tackles with 106; he also had three interceptions. Not surprisingly, he was a first-team selection on every prominent All-America team. Despite the extraordinary demands of football, he was also an exceptional student, as reflected by his status as a first-team Academic All-American.

Lynch, who won the Maxwell Award in 1966 as the top college football player in the nation (he was only the fourth Notre Dame player to win the award), finished his college career with 255 tackles and four interceptions. A second-round draft pick in 1967, he spent his entire 11-year NFL career with the Kansas City Chiefs and helped lead the team to a Super Bowl title in 1970. He was inducted into the College Football Hall of Fame in 1992.

M

MacAFEE, KEN
Tight End (1974-77) ▪ 6-4, 250 ▪ Brockton, MA

A three-time All-American and one of Notre Dame's all-time leading receivers, Ken MacAfee came to South Bend from Brockton, Massachusetts. He earned all-state and prep All-America honors in his junior and senior years and caught 10 touchdown passes each year to set a school record. He also competed for the varsity golf, track, and basketball teams and was a dean's list student.

Although he narrowed his athletic focus to football, not much changed for MacAfee in college. He continued to juggle the demands of the classroom and the practice field with admirable dexterity. In 1974, when he was a freshman, he caught 14 passes and scored one touchdown to earn his first monogram. As a sophomore he not only stepped into the starting lineup but also led the team in receiving with 26 catches for 333 yards and five touchdowns; United Press International named him first-team All-America.

After impressive prep and college careers, Ken MacAfee went on to play for the San Francisco 49ers. He left after just two years, however, to return to school and is now a successful oral surgeon.

In 1976 MacAfee led the Irish with 34 receptions for 482 yards and three touchdowns. He scored the team's only touchdown in a loss to eventual national champion Pittsburgh and had one of the best games of his career in a 21-18 victory over Alabama (coincidentally, MacAfee's father, Ken Sr., played wide receiver for the Crimson Tide). After the season he was honored as a first-team All-American by several organizations, including United Press International, the Football Writers Association of America, and the Walter Camp Foundation.

MacAfee's finest year, though, came in 1977 when he had 54 receptions for 797 yards and six touchdowns. He caught a team-high four passes for 45 yards in Notre Dame's

38-10 upset of Texas in the Cotton Bowl. A consensus first-team All-American, he finished third in voting for the Heisman Trophy (Texas running back Earl Campbell was the winner). He was also a first-team Academic All-American.

After graduating with honors, MacAfee was a first-round draft pick of the San Francisco 49ers. He spent just two years in the NFL before turning his attention to more scholarly pursuits. He eventually went to dental school and today is an oral surgeon.

With 128 receptions for 1,759 yards, MacAfee is fifth on Notre Dame's career pass receiving list.

Career Statistics (Receiving)

YEAR	NO.	YARDS	AVG.	TD
1974	14	146	10.4	1
1975	26	333	12.8	5
1976	34	483	14.2	3
1977	54	797	14.8	6
TOTAL	128	1,759	13.7	15

MacDONALD, TOM

Defensive Back (1961-63) ▪ 5-11, 180 ▪ Downey, CA

A defensive specialist in the final years of single-platoon football, Tom MacDonald became one of Notre Dame's career leaders in interceptions.

As a third-string halfback in 1961, his first year on the varsity, Macdonald had one interception and eight tackles. The following season he had 33 tackles and set a school record (later broken by Mike Townsend) with nine interceptions. As a senior, in 1963, he again led the team in interceptions with five. He was also sixth in tackles (47), first in punt returns (eight for 56 yards), and second in kickoff returns (eight for 146 yards). By the time he graduated, he was the school's all-time leader in interceptions with 15. That record was later surpassed by Luther Bradley, who finished his career in 1977 with 17 interceptions. It should be noted, however, that MacDonald remains the career leader among players who were allowed only three years of varsity eligibility.

Despite his collegiate accomplishments, MacDonald was not drafted until the thirteenth round in 1964. He did not play in the NFL.

Career Statistics (Interceptions)

YEAR	NO.	YARDS	AVG.	TD
1961	1	23	23.0	0
1962	9	81	9.0	0

1963	5	63	12.6	1
TOTAL	15	167	11.1	1

MACK, BILL

Halfback (1958-60) ▪ 6-0, 175 ▪ Allison Park, PA

Injuries prevented Bill "Red" Mack, a quick and talented running back, from reaching his potential. As a sophomore, in 1958, he was Notre Dame's starting left halfback and averaged nearly six yards per carry. The following season he missed the first two games with a knee injury and never fully recovered. Mack underwent surgery to repair the damaged knee in the spring of 1960 but played only two games in his senior year.

Physical problems notwithstanding, Mack had a six-year professional career after graduating from Notre Dame. He played with the Pittsburgh Steelers, Philadelphia Eagles, Atlanta Falcons, and Green Bay Packers.

MADDOCK, BOB

Guard (1939-41) ▪ 6-0, 189 ▪ Santa Ana, CA

At Santa Ana High School, Bob Maddock was an all-league guard. He played alongside Bill Musick, who went on to become a star fullback at the University of Southern California. Maddock, on the other hand, chose to leave the West Coast.

He enrolled at Notre Dame in the fall of 1938, made the varsity as a reserve lineman in 1939, and worked his way into the starting lineup in 1940. Along the way he lost nearly 15 pounds and became one of the team's quickest linemen. Maddock played professional football for the Chicago Cardinals in 1942 and 1946.

MAGGIOLI, ACHILLE

Halfback (1943-44) ▪ 5-11, 180 ▪ Mishawaka, IN

Achille "Chick" Maggioli began his college career at Indiana University when he made the football team as a walk-on. In 1943, after joining a Marine Corps Officers Training Program, he was transferred to the University of Notre Dame. He was a reserve during his first year in South Bend—the same year the Fighting Irish won their first national championship under Frank Leahy—but became a starter at left halfback for interim coach Ed McKeever in 1944.

Maggioli was called to active duty before the end of the 1944 season. When World War II ended he enrolled at the University of Illinois, where he completed his studies and helped the Illini win the 1946 Big 10 title. Maggioli was drafted by the Buffalo Bills of the All-America Football Conference in 1948. He also played with the Detroit Lions and Baltimore Colts before retiring in 1951. He returned to his hometown of Mishawaka, Indiana, in 1955 and became part owner of a restaurant. He was later inducted into the Indiana Football Hall of Fame.

MAHALIC, DREW
Linebacker (1972-74) ▪ 6-4, 222 ▪ Farmington, MI

Drew Mahalic played quarterback in high school; he played the position so well, in fact, that he was named Player of the Year in Michigan. At Notre Dame he was converted to outside linebacker, and the transition was remarkably smooth. Mahalic became a three-year starter and a vital member of the team's defense. He led the entire team in playing time as a sophomore with 287:31.

As a junior, in 1973, he spent less than half that much time on the field (primarily because Notre Dame's offense usually dictated the tempo of the game—the Irish, after all, went undefeated that year and outscored their opponents by a combined margin of 358-66) but still had 59 tackles. His fumble recovery and eight-yard return in the Sugar Bowl set up a 12-yard touchdown run by Eric Penick and helped the Irish defeat Alabama for the national title.

In 1974 Mahalic was second on the team with 117 tackles. A third-round draft pick of the Denver Broncos in 1975, he spent four years in the NFL, including three with the Philadelphia Eagles.

MARTIN, DAVE
Linebacker (1965-67) ▪ 6-0, 210 ▪ Roeland Park, KS

Dave Martin played fullback at Bishop Miege High School in Shawnee Mission, Kansas. At Notre Dame he switched to defense and became a three-year starter at outside linebacker. Although somewhat small, Martin was a smart player who could read an offense and react quickly to virtually any situation.

In his sophomore year he had 70 tackles. The next year he had 62 tackles, one interception, and two fumble recoveries in helping the Irish win their first consensus national championship in 17 years. He ran back his only interception 33 yards for a touchdown in a season-ending 51-0 victory over Southern California.

As a senior Martin was fourth on the team in tackles with 71. He played with the Kansas City Chiefs in 1968 and the Chicago Bears in 1969.

MARTIN, JIM

End/Tackle (1946-49) ▪ 6-2, 204 ▪ Cleveland, OH

Jim Martin had the good fortune to play at Notre Dame during a period of prolonged football prosperity. From 1946 through 1949 the Fighting Irish did not lose a game. They also won three national titles. But Martin wasn't merely along for the ride. Durable and talented, he played both ways throughout his career and was one of the primary reasons Notre Dame achieved such tremendous success on the football field.

No one ever doubted Martin's courage or determination. He came to South Bend after earning a Bronze Star in the U.S. Marine Corps during World War II. He started at end during his first three years, and in that time the Irish accumulated 26 victories, no losses, and two ties. They were national champions in 1946 and 1947. In 1949, with the temporary implementation of two-platoon football, many players began specializing in either offense or defense. Jim Martin continued to play both. He remained at end on defense, but switched to left tackle on offense. He was co-captain of a team that went 10-0 and captured another national title. Notre Dame was barely challenged that year; in fact, the Irish were seriously tested only once, in the final game of the season, when they held off Southern Methodist University, 27-20, to preserve a perfect season.

During Jim Martin's career with the Fighting Irish, they never lost a game and won three national titles. Martin made vital contributions on both offense and defense.

Martin was named first-team All-America by the Associated Press after the season. He also received the George Gipp Award, which is given annually to Notre Dame's outstanding athlete. After leaving South Bend, Martin joined the Cleveland Browns. He was traded after just one season and spent the next 12 years playing with the Detroit Lions. His finest year as a professional, 1962, he earned an invitation to the Pro Bowl.

Jim Martin was inducted into the College Football Hall of Fame in 1995.

MARX, GREG

Defensive Tackle (1970-72) ▪ 6-5, 265 ▪ Redford, MI

Defensive tackle Greg Marx was a consensus All-American in his senior year and a two-time Academic All-American. He went to Notre Dame in the fall of 1968 after an outstanding high school career. He missed the 1969 season with a fractured arm but by 1970 had demonstrated that he was one of the best linemen in the program.

In 1971, as a junior, Marx played more than 230 minutes and was second on the team with 85 tackles. He also earned first-team Academic All-America honors. In 1972, while serving as co-captain, he had 96 tackles and was a first-team selection on every major

All-America team. And he continued to perform equally well in the classroom, earning first-team Academic All-America honors for the second consecutive year.

Marx, who earned post-graduate scholarships from the NCAA and the National Football Foundation, was invited to play in the Hula Bowl and the College All-Star Game in 1973. He was a second-round draft pick of the Atlanta Falcons but spent only one season in the NFL. He later became an executive in the banking industry.

MASTRANGELO, JOHN
Guard (1944-46) • 6-1, 210 • Leechburg, PA

Poor eyesight prevented John Mastrangelo from being accepted by any of the armed services, so he remained at Notre Dame during World War II. With the help of contact lenses (he was one of the first football players to wear them on the field), he became a two-time All-American and one of the team's most outstanding linemen.

Mastrangelo earned four varsity letters in football at Vandergrift (Pennsylvania) High School. One of his boyhood idols was Knute Rockne, so it wasn't a shock that he decided to attend Notre Dame. He earned monograms as a reserve lineman in each of his first two years and became a starter in 1945. An exceptional open-field blocker and an intense competitor, Mastrangelo helped lead Notre Dame to a 7-2-1 record under interim coach Hugh Devore. After the season he was named first-team All-America by *The Sporting News* and second-team All-America by United Press and the International News Service, among others.

In 1946 when coach Frank Leahy and dozens of players returned from the armed forces, Mastrangelo held onto his job as the starting left guard. He even served as team captain for a game against Navy. As a senior he was one of the most valuable members of a Notre Dame team that went undefeated and finished first in the final Associated Press poll. He received first-team All-America honors from the International News Service, *Collier's* magazine, and *The Sporting News*, as well as second-team honors from the Associated Press and United Press.

A second-round draft choice of the Pittsburgh Steelers in 1947, Mastrangelo also played for the New York Yankees of the All-America Football Conference and the NFL's New York Giants in a four-year professional career.

MAVRAIDES, MENIL
Guard/End (1951-53) • 6-1, 205 • Lowell, MA

Menil "Minnie" Mavraides was a four-year star at Lowell High School, leading his team to the Massachusetts state title in his senior year. He earned his first monogram at

Notre Dame in 1951 as a second-string end. In 1952 he was a backup guard, and in 1953 he became a starter.

Mavraides also kicked field goals and extra points for the Irish; he was the team's fourth-leading scorer in 1953 with 27 points. He played professionally with the Philadelphia Eagles in 1954 and 1957.

MAXWELL AWARD

Since 1937 the Maxwell Award has been presented annually to the outstanding player in college football. Sponsored by the Maxwell Memorial Football Club of Philadelphia, the award honors the memory of Robert W. "Tiny" Maxwell, an All-American guard at Swarthmore College and the University of Chicago near the turn of the century.

Five players from Notre Dame have won the Maxwell Award.

YEAR	PLAYER	POSITION
1949	Leon Hart	End
1952	John Lattner	Halfback
1953	John Lattner	Halfback
1966	Jim Lynch	Linebacker
1977	Ross Browner	Defensive End

MAY 1

For each game played at Notre Dame Stadium, approximately 20,000 seats are reserved for contributing alumni. When demand for those tickets exceeds the available supply (as it often does), the school's ticket office conducts a computerized lottery using formal applications as entry blanks. The deadline for returning these applications is May 1. Frequently, of course, the deadline is missed, prompting otherwise sensible, mature, law-abiding adults to lose their minds (as well as their dignity) in an attempt to convince the ticket office staff that they *really* did have a legitimate excuse.

MAYES, DERRICK
Split End (1992-95) ▪ 6-1, 204 ▪ Indianapolis, IN

One of Notre Dame's all-time leading receivers, Derrick Mayes grew up in Indianapolis, where his mother was a junior high school principal. A *USA Today* prep All-American at North Central High School in 1991, he enrolled at Notre Dame in the fall of 1992 and made an immediate contribution. He caught only 10 passes as a freshman backup to Lake Dawson, but the first three of those receptions resulted in touchdowns.

In 1993 Dawson moved to flanker, leaving Mayes to share time at split end with Clint Johnson. Mayes had 24 receptions for 512 yards and two touchdowns, including seven catches (for 147 yards) in a 41-39 loss to Boston College. As a starter in 1994, Mayes blossomed. He caught a team-high 47 passes for 847 yards and 11 touchdowns and was named honorable mention All-America by United Press International.

As one of five senior captains in 1995, Mayes had his best season, catching 48 passes for 881 yards and six touchdowns. He had a career-high eight receptions against Northwestern and seven against Purdue. In a 31-26 loss to Florida State in the 1996 Orange Bowl, he caught six passes for 96 yards and two touchdowns and was named Notre Dame's MVP. After the season he was named second-team All-America by *Football News* and third-team All-America by the Associated Press. For the second consecutive year, he was named team MVP by the Monogram Club, and he was a semifinalist for the Fred Biletnikoff Award as the top receiver in the nation.

Derrick Mayes left Notre Dame as its all-time leader in reception yardage (2,512) and touchdown receptions (22), going on to join the world champion Green Bay Packers.

Mayes finished his college career as Notre Dame's all-time leader in reception yardage (2,512) and touchdown receptions (22). Through 1995 he was fourth in receptions with 129.

The Green Bay Packers selected Mayes in the second round of the 1996 NFL Draft.

Career Statistics (Receiving)

YEAR	NO.	YARDS	AVG.	TD
1992	10	272	27.2	3
1993	24	512	21.3	2
1994	47	847	18.0	11
1995	48	881	18.4	6
TOTAL	129	2,512	19.4	22

MAYL, GENE
End (1921-23) ▪ 6-1, 177 ▪ Dayton, OH

Eugene "Moose" Mayl was one of the Seven Mules of the early 1920s, the unheralded linemen whose work made it possible for Notre Dame's Four Horsemen backfield to achieve fame.

A starter at right end in his senior year (and a member of the Fighting Irish basketball team), Mayl went on to play for the NFL's Dayton Triangles in 1924 after earning a law degree from Notre Dame. He later went to work for the United States Department of Justice, serving as special counsel for the lands division from 1940 through 1953. He was also president of the Dayton Bar Association and attorney for the Archdiocese of Cincinnati.

McCOY, MIKE
Defensive Tackle (1967-69) ▪ 6-5, 274 ▪ Erie, PA

As a senior at Cathedral Prep in Erie, Pennsylvania, Mike McCoy was captain of the city championship wrestling team and an all-state football player. He entered Notre Dame in the fall of 1966; though he was ineligible for varsity competition as a freshman, there was little doubt that he would soon become a player of impact.

During spring practice in 1967 McCoy won the Hering Award as the team's top defensive lineman. That fall he split time at left tackle with Kevin Hardy and had 43 tackles. The next year, as a junior, he started every game and was third on the team (and first among linemen) with 72 tackles.

By the time he was a senior, McCoy was one of the best defensive linemen in the country. At 6-5, 274 pounds, he was the biggest player in Notre Dame's starting lineup, and yet he was also one of the quickest. That combination naturally made him a formidable opponent. McCoy had 88 tackles as a senior and was named Associated Press Lineman of the Year. He was a unanimous first-team All-American, a participant in the College All-Star Game, and sixth-place finisher in voting for the Heisman Trophy. He finished his college career with 203 tackles.

The Green Bay Packers chose McCoy in the first round of the 1970 NFL Draft. After six seasons in Green Bay, he went on to play for the Oakland Raiders, New York Giants, and Detroit Lions. He retired in 1980 and today works as a public speaker for Sports World Ministries.

McDONALD, DEVON
Defensive End (1989-92) ▪ 6-4, 241 ▪ Paterson, NJ

Born on November 8, 1969, in Kingston, Jamaica, Devon McDonald later came to the United States and settled in Paterson, New Jersey, where he and his twin brother, Ricardo, became star athletes at John F. Kennedy High School. While Ricardo accepted a scholarship from the University of Pittsburgh, Devon chose Notre Dame.

McDonald displayed flashes of brilliance in his college career, although knee injuries slowed his development. He did not play on the varsity as a freshman in 1988, and offseason arthroscopic knee surgery led to problems that kept him out of three games in 1989. By 1991, however, McDonald was a consistent starter at defensive end. He had 60 tackles and two sacks that season and was named honorable mention All-America by *Football News*.

Granted a fifth year of eligibility, McDonald returned in the fall of 1992 and had his best season. With a team-high 8.3 sacks and 47 tackles, he was again named honorable mention All-America by *Football News*. He was also named defensive MVP in Notre Dame's 28-3 victory over Texas A&M in the 1993 Cotton Bowl.

McDonald was drafted by the Indianapolis Colts in the fourth round of the 1993 NFL Draft.

McGILL, MIKE
Linebacker (1965-67) ▪ 6-2, 225 ▪ Hammond, IN

A four-sport star at Bishop Noll High School in Indiana, Mike McGill came to Notre Dame in the fall of 1964 and became a starter in 1965, his first year on the varsity. He played 217 minutes that season and had 88 tackles, third best on the team. A few months later, he won the Hering Award as outstanding linebacker, beating out returning All-American Jim Lynch among others.

In the fall of 1966, McGill seriously injured his knee in a 38-0 rout of Oklahoma and missed the rest of Notre Dame's championship season. But he returned to the starting lineup in 1967 and had his best season: With 93 tackles he was second only to Bob Olson. *The Sporting News* named him first-team All-America, and *Time* placed him on its second team.

McGill was a third-round draft pick of the Minnesota Vikings in 1968. He played with the Vikings for three seasons before joining the St. Louis Cardinals in 1971. He retired after the 1972 season.

McGOLDRICK, JIM
Left Guard (1936-38) ▪ 5-11, 175 ▪ Philadelphia, PA

The son of an Irish immigrant, Jim McGoldrick grew up in Philadelphia, where he played hockey and football and rowed on the crew team at West Catholic High School. He followed Notre Dame's football fortunes throughout his childhood, but his attraction to the school reached a peak in 1930 when he saw the Irish—led by Philadelphia native Tom Conley—trounce the University of Pennsylvania, 60-20.

Notre Dame did not really need another advantage in recruiting McGoldrick—he did not seriously consider any other schools—but it had one. The team's line coach was

Joe Boland, who played for the Irish in the 1920s and whose hometown was Philadelphia.

McGoldrick made the varsity in 1936, saw considerable playing time in 1937, and became a starter in 1938. He was also named team captain. Despite his modest stature (he wore a size six shoe), McGoldrick was a fierce competitor. He led the Irish to an 8-1 record and a No. 5 ranking in the Associated Press poll in his senior year. He was named to United Press International's All-America second team.

McGUIRE, GENE

Center/Tackle (1988-91) ▪ 6-4, 286 ▪ Panama City, FL

After seeing little playing time in his first two years on the varsity, Walter Eugene McGuire became a starting tackle in 1990. Unfortunately, he injured his knee in the third game of the season, a 37-11 victory over Purdue, and had to undergo arthroscopic surgery. His recovery, though, was swift: He was back in the starting lineup after missing just two games and was a vital performer for the remainder of the season on a line that helped the Fighting Irish rank among the national leaders in total offense.

McGuire moved to center in 1991 and started all 13 games. He was named honorable mention All-America by *Football News* and United Press International. Selected in the fourth round of the 1992 NFL Draft, he played with the New Orleans Saints (1992-93), Green Bay Packers (1995), and Miami Dolphins (1995-96).

McKEEVER, ED

Head Coach (1944) ▪ San Antonio, TX

In 1944, when head coach Frank Leahy was called to active duty by the U.S. Navy, it was no surprise that Notre Dame appointed Ed McKeever interim coach. McKeever, after all, had been Leahy's top assistant. Not only did he know the players and the program, but he also knew precisely what Leahy expected. He would make no major changes; rather, he would simply keep everything running smoothly during the coach's absence.

McKeever's relationship with the Fighting Irish actually began much earlier. He came to South Bend in the fall of 1930 after graduating from St. Edward's Prep School in Austin, Texas, where he was captain of the football team in his junior and senior years. McKeever played freshman football, basketball, and track at Notre Dame and appeared to have a promising career with the Fighting Irish. In the summer of 1931 he returned to his family home in Spofford, Texas, and took a job punching cattle. He returned to Notre Dame briefly in the fall, but when his father became ill, he withdrew from school and went back to Texas.

By the fall of 1932 McKeever had enrolled at Texas Tech. As a starting right halfback, he led the football team to a 30-5 record during his three years on the varsity. After graduation he stayed at Texas Tech as a backfield coach. He met Leahy at a coaching school in Lubbock, Texas, in the summer of 1938. Leahy, an assistant at Fordham, presented a clinic on line play; McKeever gave a clinic on backfield play. The two men formed an immediate friendship, and one year later, when Leahy was named the head coach at Boston College, he asked McKeever to be his backfield coach. After considering the offer for more than a week, McKeever finally accepted.

In 1941 Leahy became the head coach at Notre Dame. McKeever was offered a promotion at Boston College but turned the job down so that he could accompany Leahy to South Bend. Three years later that loyalty paid off when he was asked to guide the Fighting Irish during Leahy's tour of duty in World War II. McKeever did a fine job, leading the team to an 8-2 record and a top-10 finish in the final Associated Press rankings.

Ed McKeever stepped in as interim head coach for the Fighting Irish in 1944 when Frank Leahy was called to active duty. McKeever was an all-around athlete at Notre Dame as a student until his father fell ill in Texas and he returned home.

Shortly after the end of the season, the university announced that McKeever would remain as head coach and director of athletics for one more year. At a postseason football banquet, however, Notre Dame President Fr. J. Hugh O'Donnell talked at length about the school's tradition of excellence. Much credit was given to Leahy and the teams of the early 1940s; according to numerous reports, McKeever and the 1944 Fighting Irish were barely mentioned. This, of course, hurt McKeever deeply. Not long after the banquet he accepted an offer to become head coach at Cornell University.

Two years later he moved again, this time to the University of San Francisco, and in 1948 he became head coach of the Chicago Rockets in the All-America Football Conference. After just one season McKeever returned to the college ranks, as an assistant at Louisiana State University. In 1960 he became general manager of the Boston Patriots of the American Football League.

McKENNA, JIM
Quarterback (1935) ▪ Height and weight unavailable ▪ St. Paul, MN

Notre Dame's 18-13 victory over Ohio State on November 2, 1935, has been called the greatest football game of the first half of the twentieth century. And, indeed, that designation does not seem hyperbolic. Although both teams were unbeaten, Ohio State was a heavy favorite. The Buckeyes led 13-0 after three quarters and appeared to have the game in hand. Notre Dame, however, came charging back with three fourth-quarter touchdowns.

A frequently overlooked player in that dramatic contest was Jim McKenna, a reserve quarterback from St. Paul, Minnesota. McKenna was not on the Fighting Irish traveling squad but had sneaked aboard the train to Columbus anyway (his teammates had hidden him in a berth), simply because he wanted to see the game. When confronted by coach Elmer Layden in the locker room, McKenna explained that he didn't have a ticket. Leahy, impressed by the young man's determination, invited him to suit up. No one—least of all McKenna—expected him to play such a pivotal role in the game. Thanks to a quirk of the rule book, however, he did.

With 20 seconds remaining Ohio State led by a score of 13-12; Notre Dame had the ball on the Buckeye 19-yard line. Layden wanted to call a play known as "57-1", a pass in which two Irish receivers ran crossing patterns through the Ohio State defense. In 1935, however, quarterbacks called the plays. Signaling from the bench was not allowed; and if a play was to be sent in, it had to be delivered by an entering quarterback. Unfortunately, the Irish had only one healthy quarterback remaining on the sideline: Jim McKenna.

So Layden gave the play to McKenna, who ran onto the field, entered the huddle, and shared it with his teammates. With 13 seconds remaining Bill Shakespeare hit Wayne Millner with the winning touchdown pass.

McKenna's football career ended with that moment of glory. He dropped out of Notre Dame in 1936, re-entered in 1937, and dropped out again. He served as an aviation cadet during World War II. After the war McKenna worked for many years as a racetrack employee on the West Coast. He died in St. Paul in 1991.

McMULLAN, JOHN
Guard (1953-55) ▪ 5-10, 203 ▪ Hoboken, NJ

A four-year letterman and three-sport star at Demerest High School in Hoboken, New Jersey, John McMullan had to wait until his senior season before earning a monogram at Notre Dame. A reserve lineman in his first two seasons, he was named the starting right guard by coach Terry Brennan in 1955 and helped lead the team to an 8-2 record.

McMullan played with the New York Titans of the American Football League in 1960 and 1961.

MEGAPHONE

Since 1949 the winner of the Notre Dame-Michigan State football game has been presented with a megaphone. The megaphone, which bears the colors of both schools, is emblazoned with the scores of all previous contests. The award is sponsored by the alumni clubs of Notre Dame and Michigan State.

The Notre Dame-Michigan State rivalry dates back a century. The teams first met on the football field in 1897, with the Fighting Irish prevailing by a score of 34-6. The two teams have played 60 times; Notre Dame holds a 41-18-1 advantage. The schools faced each other every year from 1954 through 1994. Following a two-year break, the series resumed in 1997.

MEHRE, HARRY

Center (1919-21) ▪ 6-1, 190 ▪ Huntington, IL

Harry Mehre was a basketball star at Huntington High School. He went to Notre Dame on a basketball scholarship with no intention of playing football. But that all changed when Mehre was introduced to Knute Rockne. The coach did a quick appraisal of Mehre's physical attributes and began his sales pitch. Before long, Mehre was on the football field, working out as a freshman halfback.

By the time Mehre made the varsity in his sophomore year (1919), he had been switched to center. He earned his first monogram in 1920 and started the entire 1921 season. He was fortunate to play on some of the greatest Notre Dame teams: During his three years on the varsity, the Fighting Irish won 28 of 29 games.

Mehre played two seasons of professional football with the Minneapolis Marines before embarking on a long and productive coaching career. He started out as an assistant coach at the University of Georgia. In 1928 he was promoted to head coach and, over the next 10 years, led the Bulldogs to a 59-34-6 record. He resigned in 1938 to become head coach at the University of Mississippi, where he compiled a record of 31-8-1.

MELINKOVICH, GEORGE

Halfback/Fullback (1931-32, 1934) ▪ 6-0, 180 ▪ Tooele, UT

An All-American running back, George Melinkovich grew up on a ranch in Tooele, Utah. He started at fullback in 1931 and helped the Fighting Irish to a 6-2-1 record under first-year coach Hunk Anderson.

The following year Melinkovich was sensational. He led the team in rushing (503 yards on 88 carries), scoring (48 points), receiving (seven catches for 106 yards and one touchdown), and kickoff return average (41.0). After the season he was named first-team All-America by the North American Newspaper Alliance and second-team All-America by United Press, the International News Service, and the Newspaper Enterprise Association.

Melinkovich missed the 1933 season because of illness but returned to campus in 1934, which was something of a blessing to new coach Elmer Layden. With a shortage at halfback, Layden decided to make Melinkovich a starter at right half. It was a gamble that paid off. Melinkovich, nothing if not versatile, responded with another outstanding season, leading the Irish in both rushing (73 carries for 324 yards) and scoring (36 points).

MELLO, JIM
Fullback (1942-43, 1946) ▪ 5-11, 185 ▪ West Warwick, RI

Jim Mello was the starting fullback on Notre Dame's 1943 national championship team. His career was interrupted, though, when he was called to active duty with the Naval Air Corps in early 1944. For the next two seasons he played under Paul Brown at the Great Lakes Naval Training Station, where he was named to the All-Service team.

Mello returned to Notre Dame in 1946 and reclaimed his job at fullback. Although often overlooked in a backfield that included quarterback John Lujack and halfback Emil Sitko, he was instrumental in helping the Irish capture another consensus national title.

A nagging knee injury cut Mello's professional career short, although he did play parts of five seasons with the Los Angeles Rams, Chicago Cardinals, Chicago Rockets, and Detroit Lions. He retired from football in 1951 and began a long and successful career as a physical education teacher and administrator. He worked for many years as the head of physical education at the Mansfield Training School, a facility for the mentally retarded in Mansfield Depot, Connecticut. His innovative approach to working with the disabled formed the basis for the Special Olympics.

In 1985 Mello received the Notre Dame Alumni Association's Harvey G. Foster Award, which honors former athletes who have distinguished themselves through civic endeavors or university achievements.

MERCHANDISE

Notre Dame football fans are among the most zealous in all of sports. Remarkably, a great percentage of them have never even visited South Bend, Indiana. They have never seen the Golden Dome in person, never knelt before Touchdown Jesus. Although Notre Dame has its share of generous, supportive alumni and one of the most rabid student bodies in college sports, its popularity stems in large part from a unique ability to inspire allegiance among people who have no tangible attachment to the university. As Mike May of the Sporting Goods Manufacturers Association notes, "It seems like everyone is a subway alum of Notre Dame."

How else to explain the appeal of all things bearing the Fighting Irish logo? The sale of licensed college merchandise is a $2-billion-a-year business; according to *Team Licensing Business* magazine, industry analysts estimate Notre Dame's share of that pie to be as high as 35 percent. From California to Connecticut, fans of the Fighting Irish proclaim their loyalty through T-shirts, sweatshirts, bumper stickers, caps, and shorts. And there is no indication that interest will wane any time in the near future.

MERGENTHAL, ART

Left Tackle (1944) ▪ 6-2, 210 ▪ Bellevue, KY

After graduating from Bellevue High School, Art Mergenthal enrolled at Xavier University in Cincinnati where he played under coach Clem Crowe. His college career was interrupted when he enrolled in the U.S. Marine Corps and was sent to Parris Island. Mergenthal received a medical discharge, however, and when it came time to return to school he chose Notre Dame. The reason: Crowe had left Xavier in favor of an assistant coaching position with the Fighting Irish.

Interim Notre Dame coach Ed McKeever used Mergenthal as a backup guard early in the 1944 season but soon shifted him to tackle, where he became a starter. Mergenthal played with the Los Angeles Rams in 1945 and the Chicago Rockets of the All-America Football Conference in 1946.

METZGER, BERT

Guard (1928-30) ▪ 5-9, 149 ▪ Chicago, IL

In a 1929 game against Carnegie Tech, Notre Dame found itself being battered by a running back named Bull Karcis. As Karcis repeatedly burst through the line for 10-yard gains, a reserve guard for the Fighting Irish asked for an opportunity to stop the damage. Line coach Hunk Anderson and head coach Knute Rockne questioned the player's sanity but admired his heart. So they gave him a chance. And they never regretted it.

Bert Metzger helped Notre Dame defeat Carnegie Tech 7-0 that day. The fact that he was the smallest player on the field seemed not to matter in the least. He became one of Rockne's favorite players—and one of the most valuable members of a program that won national championships in 1929 and 1930.

Metzger's story is nothing short of amazing. He came to Notre Dame from Loyola Academy in Chicago, and he didn't have a scholarship. Undeterred, he made the football team as a walk-on. With a combination of quickness and intelligence, he began to impress the coaching staff and his teammates; in practice sessions Metzger often embarrassed bigger, stronger players. He climbed steadily through the ranks, moving from tenth team to second team early in his junior year. After the Carnegie Tech game, he was inserted into the starting lineup, and he stayed there until the final game of his senior year. In his two seasons as a starter, Notre Dame went 19-0 and outscored its opponents 410-112.

In addition to his defensive skills, Metzger was an exceptional blocker who made life much easier for running backs Marchy Schwartz, Marty Brill, and Joe Savoldi. In 1930 he was named first-team All-America by the Associated Press and United Press International. After college Metzger became an assistant coach at Catholic University in Washington, D.C. He left coaching after one year, however, and accepted a sales position with Bowman Dairy in his hometown of Chicago.

Bert Metzger was inducted into the College Football Hall of Fame in 1982.

MEYER, JOHN
Tackle (1963-64) ▪ 6-2, 212 ▪ Chicago, IL

John Meyer was a starting tackle during each of his two years on the Notre Dame varsity. In 1963 he had 32 tackles; he also played offensive tackle and accumulated a total of more than 285 minutes of field time.

A few months later, following spring practice, he was named the Hering Award winner as the "most consistent tackle." College football adopted the two-platoon system in 1964, and Meyer was used primarily on offense. He helped the Fighting Irish to a 9-1 record and a No. 3 ranking in the final Associated Press poll.

Meyer was drafted by the St. Louis Cardinals and Buffalo Bills in the eighth round of the 1965 NFL Draft. He played with the Houston Oilers in 1966.

MIESZKOWSKI, ED
Tackle (1943, 1945) ▪ 6-2, 205 ▪ Glen Ellyn, IL

A graduate of Chicago's Tilden Tech High School, Ed Mieszkowski made the varsity at Notre Dame in his freshman year but saw very little playing time. A knee injury incurred during spring practice sessions forced him to miss most of preseason training camp. He then aggravated the injury just a few days before the season opener and wound up sitting out the entire year.

Mieszkowski recovered from the injury and became a starter at left tackle in 1945. He played professionally for the Brooklyn Yankees in 1946 and 1947.

MILLER, CREIGHTON
Halfback (1941-43) ▪ 6-0, 187 ▪ Wilmington, DE

Creighton Miller was born in Cleveland, Ohio, and moved to Wilmington, Delaware, when he was a freshman in high school. An outstanding prep athlete who could have attended any number of colleges, Miller chose the University of Notre Dame because, well, because there really was no other choice. His father, Harry, had been a starting running back for the Fighting Irish from 1907 through 1909; his uncle Walter was a blocking back for George Gipp; another uncle, Don, was one of the legendary Four Horsemen; and his older brother Tom was already at Notre Dame, trying to carve out a career of his own.

Creighton Miller was the fifth member of the Miller family to play for the Fighting Irish. He continued the family tradition proudly despite a limiting medical condition.

As Miller later told a writer, "My father didn't ask me what college I wanted to attend. He told me what time the train left for South Bend."

Creighton proudly maintained the family tradition—he became one of the greatest running backs ever to wear a Notre Dame uniform—but not without a degree of hardship. In the spring of 1941 he informed incoming coach Frank Leahy that he would not be able to participate in spring football practice. Miller had a legitimate reason—a routine physical had revealed that his blood pressure was elevated, and doctors told him to avoid strenuous exercise indefinitely—but Leahy was not pleased. By nature skeptical of anyone who tried to avoid hard work, and notoriously intolerant of injuries and illnesses, he questioned whether Miller was true Notre Dame material.

As it turned out, he was. Miller survived a year as a backup fullback before stepping into the starting lineup as a halfback in 1942. Like many of his teammates, he enlisted in the U.S. Army in the spring of 1943. Another physical, however, confirmed the earlier diagnosis of hypertension. He spent six weeks in a military hospital before receiving his discharge.

When Miller returned to Notre Dame he encountered a more receptive Frank Leahy. The coach, upon hearing of Miller's discharge, realized that the kid had not been a slacker; he really did have a medical problem. So the two of them sat down and discussed a plan for the upcoming season. Generally speaking, Miller would be expected to practice as hard as everyone else; but if he felt fatigued or light-headed, he would be excused. For Leahy, a tough coach who believed all players should be treated the same, this was a difficult concession. But for the good of the team, and the well-being of Creighton Miller, it was necessary.

The arrangement worked well for all parties. Notre Dame went 9-1-0 and won its first consensus national championship under Leahy in 1943, and Miller was one of the primary reasons. He rushed for 911 yards on 151 carries (the second-highest single-season total in Notre Dame history at the time) and scored 13 touchdowns. He also had a team-high six interceptions. Miller finished fourth in voting for the Heisman Trophy (teammate Angelo Bertelli won the award) and was a consensus All-American.

Miller was also a fine sprinter who earned a varsity letter in track and field. He was a second-round draft pick of the Brooklyn Tigers in 1944 but chose instead to attend Yale Law School. He later became an attorney in Cleveland.

Creighton Miller was inducted into the College Football Hall of Fame in 1976.

MILLER, DON
Halfback (1922-24) ▪ 5-11, 160 ▪ Defiance, OH

One of Notre Dame's all-time leading rushers and a member of the famed Four Horsemen, Don Miller's career began humbly. A slight-built substitute on his high school team in Defiance, Ohio, he was a late bloomer whose pedigree was not apparent until his sophomore year at Notre Dame. Miller was one of five football-playing brothers, all of whom played for the Fighting Irish. The oldest, Harry "Red" Miller, was an All-American in 1909; Ray Miller, who went on to become mayor of the city of Cleveland, played left end behind Knute Rockne; Walter Miller was a starting fullback in 1917; and Gerry Miller was a reserve in the early 1920s.

It was Don Miller, though, who turned out to be the most successful athlete in the family. At once fearless and quick, he was the sort of player who demanded attention. Even Rockne, who rarely gushed about his players in public, was effusive in his praise of Miller. "Once in the open field, he was the most dangerous of the Four Horsemen," Rockne once said of Miller. "I would have to call him the greatest open-field runner I ever had."

Miller broke into the starting lineup in 1922 as a sophomore. He rushed for 472 yards on 87 carries, second only to Jim Crowley's 566 yards. In 1923 he led the team with 698 yards on 89 carries and was named first-team All-America by the International News Service. Interestingly, he was the only member of Notre Dame's backfield—which had not yet been dubbed the Four Horsemen—to receive first-team All-America honors. In 1924, as Notre Dame won its first consensus national championship, Miller rushed for 763 yards on 107 carries and scored five touchdowns. And yet, he was the only member of the Four Horsemen not to be named first-team All-America.

When Miller graduated from Notre Dame in 1925, he was second only to George Gipp on Notre Dame's career rushing list. With 1,933 yards on 283 carries, he was in thirteenth place heading into the 1996 season. He averaged 6.8 yards per carry, which remains a school record. Miller was not, however, merely a runner. He was also the team's leading receiver for three consecutive seasons, a varsity letterman in basketball, and president of his senior class.

Miller graduated with a degree in law in 1925. He played one year of professional football, with the Providence Steamroller, before turning to twin careers in coaching and law. He was an assistant coach first at Georgia Tech and later at Ohio State, but only during the fall months. The rest of the year he devoted his energy to working in the law firm of Miller, Hertz & Miller in Cleveland. In 1932, when the demands of his law practice increased, he left coaching.

President Franklin Roosevelt appointed Miller U.S. District Attorney for Northern Ohio in 1941. He later became national president of the U.S. Attorney's Association.

Miller was elected to the College Football Hall of Fame in 1970. He died in 1979.

Career Statistics (Rushing)

YEAR	ATT.	YARDS	AVG.	TD
1922	87	472	5.4	3
1923	89	698	7.5	9
1924	107	763	7.1	5
TOTAL	283	1,933	6.8	17

Career Statistics (Receiving)

YEAR	NO.	YARDS	AVG.	TD
1922	6	144	24	1
1923	9	149	16.5	1
1924	16	297	18.6	2
TOTAL	31	590	19.0	4

MILLER, HARRY

Halfback (1906-09) ▪ 6-0, 175 ▪ Defiance, OH

The first, although hardly the most well known, of several members of his family to play football at Notre Dame, Harry "Red" Miller was a four-year starter at left halfback. He led the Fighting Irish to a 7-0-1 record under coach Frank Longman in 1909 and was named third-team All-America by the Walter Camp Foundation.

Miller was the older brother of Don Miller, who was a member of the famous Four Horsemen backfield of 1924, and the uncle of halfback Creighton Miller, a consensus All-American in 1943.

MILLER, MICHAEL

Flanker (1991-94) ▪ 5-7, 160 ▪ Missouri City, TX

Michael Miller was one of the fastest players ever to wear a Notre Dame uniform. He was recruited out of Willowridge High School in Sugarland, Texas, where he was one of the top prep athletes in the nation. A high school All-American in football (he rushed for 635 yards and eight touchdowns and caught 35 passes for an additional 640 yards in his senior year), he was also one of the top sprinters in the country. Miller ran 10.32 seconds for 100 meters and 20.82 for 200 meters and won both events at the Texas state track meet.

Miller's size was something of a detriment in college; nevertheless, he eventually became a formidable threat as a flanker and kick return specialist. As a sophomore he scored on a 70-yard pass from Rick Mirer in a game against Northwestern. He averaged nearly 30 yards per return on kickoffs. As a junior Miller averaged 21.7 yards per reception, best on the team, and returned a punt 56 yards for a touchdown against Michigan. He started six games at flanker in 1994 before back and hamstring injuries forced him to the bench. His finest performance came on opening night against Northwestern when he caught seven passes for 142 yards and one touchdown.

Michael Miller was drafted by the Cleveland Browns in the fifth round of the 1995 NFL Draft.

MILLNER, WAYNE

End (1933-35) ▪ 6-0, 184 ▪ Salem, MA

Wayne Millner was born in Roxbury, Massachusetts, and grew up in nearby Salem. He enrolled at Notre Dame in 1932 and became a starter at left end after the first game of the 1933 season. In the final game of his first season on the varsity, Millner gained a degree of fame by leading the Irish to a 13-12 upset of previously unbeaten Army. He blocked an Army punt late in the fourth quarter and recovered the ball in the end zone for the game-winning touchdown.

Millner also caught the game-winning touchdown pass (from Bill Shakespeare) in an 18-13 victory over Ohio State in 1935; that game has long been considered one of the greatest in college football history. A three-year starter at left end, he was a true iron man who led the team in minutes played during each of his seasons on the varsity.

At the conclusion of the 1935 season Millner was named a consensus All-American. He played in the 1936 College All-Star Game and was selected in the eighth round of the NFL Draft by the Boston Redskins. In 1937 the Redskins moved to Washington and defeated the Chicago Bears, 28-21, in the NFL championship game. Millner figured prominently in that victory, catching touchdown passes of 55 yards and 78 yards from Sammy Baugh.

After a six-year professional career—interrupted by a stint in the U.S. Navy—Millner returned to South Bend to work as an assistant coach under Frank Leahy. He became head coach of the Philadelphia Eagles in 1952 but resigned shortly thereafter because of poor health. He was elected to the Pro Football Hall of Fame in 1968 and the College Football Hall of Fame in 1990.

MIRER, RICK

Quarterback (1989-92) ▪ 6-2, 217 ▪ Goshen, IN

Rick Mirer, Notre Dame's career leader in touchdown passes, began playing football at a very young age. His father, Ken, was a high school coach in Rick's hometown of Goshen, Indiana, and Rick began throwing a football around when he was barely old

enough to walk. At the age of eight he competed in the national Punt, Pass and Kick competition. By the time he reached high school, Mirer was considered a prodigy. He passed for 6,586 yards and 44 touchdowns in his prep career and was a consensus high school All-American; he was also named Indiana Player of the Year.

With Tony Rice playing quarterback ahead of him, Mirer was expected to do little more than watch and learn during his freshman year at Notre Dame. After Rice graduated in 1990, though, the job belonged to Mirer. He started all 12 games and played more minutes than any other offensive player as a sophomore, passing for 1,824 yards and eight touchdowns. *Football News* named him honorable mention All-America.

After setting numerous records in Notre Dame football—including touchdown passes and total offense—Rick Mirer was the second player selected in the 1993 NFL Draft, by the Seattle Seahawks.

Statistically, Mirer had his best season in 1991, completing 132 of 234 passes for 2,117 yards and 18 touchdowns. He also rushed for 306 yards and nine touchdowns on 75 carries while helping the Fighting Irish set single-season school records for points and total yards. His 2,423 yards of total offense was second on the school's all-time list, behind only Joe Theismann's 2,813 in 1970. He finished the season by completing 14 of 19 passes for 154 yards and two touchdowns in a 39-28 Sugar Bowl win over Florida. Afterward, he was named honorable mention All-America by *Football News*.

As a senior captain in 1992, Mirer set career records for total offense (6,691 yards) and touchdown passes (41). He completed 120 of 234 passes for 1,876 yards and rushed for an additional 158 yards. Named second-team All-America by *Football News* and United Press International, he was also a finalist for the Johnny Unitas Golden Arm Award and winner of the Most Exemplary Player Award from the Downtown Athletic Club and *Street & Smith's*. Although he put the ball in the air often, Mirer set a Notre Dame record for avoiding trouble: He was intercepted just 23 times in 698 passing attempts.

A first-round pick of the Seattle Seahawks, Mirer was the second player chosen in the 1993 NFL Draft. In his first three seasons with the Seahawks he completed 678 of 1,258 passes for 7,548 yards and 36 touchdowns. He also set an NFL rookie record for passing yards (2,833) in 1993.

Career Statistics (Passing)

YEAR	ATT.	COMP.	PCT.	YARDS	TD
1989	30	15	.500	180	0
1990	200	110	.550	1,824	8
1991	234	132	.564	2,117	18
1992	234	120	.513	1,876	15
TOTAL	**698**	**377**	**.540**	**5,997**	**41**

Career Statistics (Rushing)

YEAR	NO.	YARDS	AVG.	TD
1989	12	32	2.7	0
1990	98	198	2.0	6
1991	75	306	4.1	9
1992	68	158	2.3	2
TOTAL	**253**	**694**	**2.7**	**17**

MOHARDT, JOHN
Halfback (1918-21) ▪ 5-11, 170 ▪ Gary, IN

Known primarily as a blocker for the great George Gipp, Johnny Mohardt earned monograms in 1919, 1920, and 1921, a period during which the Notre Dame football team won 28 games and lost just one. Overshadowed by Gipp throughout much of his career, Mohardt became a star in his own right in 1921, his senior year. He rushed for a team-high 781 yards on 136 carries and also led the Irish in scoring with 72 points. He was named second-team All-America by *Collier's* magazine.

Mohardt graduated cum laude in the spring of 1922. He played professional football with the Chicago Cardinals and Chicago Bears; he also played one season of professional baseball with the Detroit Tigers. To Mohardt, though, sports was merely a means to an end. He used the money he made from baseball and football to help finance his education at Northwestern University Medical School. He later received a fellowship from the Mayo Clinic in Rochester and was a resident there in 1931, the year

Notre Dame coach Knute Rockne stopped in for treatment of phlebitis just a few weeks before he was killed in a plane crash. Rockne gave his former halfback a photograph and signed it with the words, "Very cordially to my friend, John Mohardt . . . Knute Rockne."

In 1933 Mohardt opened a private practice in Chicago. He was elected to the College of Surgeons and soon received appointments to the staffs of Northwestern Medical School and Cook County Hospital. He enlisted in the Army Medical Corps during World War II and served in North Africa and Italy. In 1955 he accepted an appointment as chief surgeon of the Veterans Administration hospital in Fort Bayard, New Mexico. Three years later he was named assistant director of the VA's surgical service in Washington, D.C.

MONOGRAM CLUB

Each Notre Dame athlete who earns a varsity letter becomes a member of the Notre Dame National Monogram Club. The club was formed in 1916. Its first president was J. Hugh O'Donnell, a center on the 1916 Fighting Irish football team and the thirteenth president of the university.

The Monogram Club supports a variety of endeavors, including the Rev. Thomas Brennan-Joe Boland Scholarship Fund, which provides financial assistance for the children of former monogram winners who enroll at Notre Dame, and the Sports Heritage Hall, which honors outstanding achievements of past Notre Dame athletes.

Each year the Monogram Club also recognizes a club member for his contributions to Notre Dame and to society at large. The 1995 winner was former Notre Dame athletic director Dick Rosenthal.

Additionally, the Notre Dame National Monogram Club MVP award is presented annually to the team's outstanding player, as determined by a vote of team members. Below is a list of the winners.

Year	Player(s)	
1967	Terry Hanratty (offense)	Tom Schoen (defense)
1968	Terry Hanratty (offense)	Bob Kuechenberg (defense)
1969	Bob Olson	
1970	Joe Theismann (offense)	Tim Kelly (defense)
1971	Dan Novakov (offense)	Walt Patulski (defense)
1972	Andy Huff (offense)	Jim O'Malley (defense)
1973	Dave Casper (offense)	Greg Collins (defense)
1974	Wayne Bullock (offense)	Greg Collins (defense)
1975	Al Wujiack (offense)	Steve Niehaus (defense)
1976	Al Hunter (offense)	Ross Browner (defense)
1977	Ken MacAfee	

1978	Joe Montana (offense)	Bob Golic (defense)
1979	Vagas Ferguson	
1980	Bob Crable	
1981	Bob Crable	
1982	Dave Duerson	
1983	Allen Pinkett	
1984	Allen Pinkett	
1985	Allen Pinkett	
1986	Tim Brown	
1987	Tim Brown	
1988	Tony Rice	
1989	Tony Rice	
1990	Raghib Ismail	
1991	Jerome Bettis	Rick Mirer
1992	Reggie Brooks	
1993	Jeff Burris	
1994	Derrick Mayes	
1995	Derrick Mayes	
1996	Renaldo Wynn	

MONTANA, JOE

Quarterback (1975, 1977-78) ▪ 6-2, 191 ▪ Monongahela, PA

Joe Montana arrived in South Bend as one of the most highly recruited prep athletes in the country. North Carolina State had offered him a basketball scholarship; he was a champion high jumper; *Parade* magazine had included him on its high school All-America football team. But the transition from high school to college was rocky. In fact, early in his career at Notre Dame, few people would have predicted that Montana would become arguably the greatest quarterback in NFL history.

As one of seven freshman quarterbacks in training camp, Montana was overwhelmed by the competition. He was quickly relegated to the junior varsity, where he spent the entire season. And even there he was merely a benchwarmer. In three games he attempted just six passes; he completed only one.

As a sophomore Montana unexpectedly began to develop a reputation for displaying uncommon grace under fire. First-year coach Dan Devine brought him in to replace injured starter Rick Slager in the third game of the season,

A two-time NFL MVP and three-time Super Bowl MVP, quarterback Joe Montana earned his reputation as the comeback kid at Notre Dame. He was just a sophomore when coach Dan Devine put him in for the injured Rick Slager—and the rest is history.

and Montana responded by leading the Fighting Irish to a 31-7 victory. On two other occasions that season he came off the bench to spark Notre Dame comebacks. In the eighth game of the year, however, he broke a finger and missed the rest of the season.

A separated shoulder forced Montana to miss the 1976 season. In 1977 he became a starter three games into the season, replacing Rusty Lisch. Once again, it was a dramatic performance in a reserve role that earned Montana the job. He came off the bench in the fourth quarter of a game against Purdue, with the Fighting Irish trailing 24-14. Montana then threw two touchdown passes as Notre Dame came away with a 31-24 victory. The next week, against Michigan State, he started the first of 21 consecutive games.

By the end of the 1977 season Montana's stock was rising. He completed 99 of 189 passes for 1,604 yards and 11 touchdowns. The Associated Press made him an honorable mention on its All-America team. More importantly, he led Notre Dame to a 38-10 victory over top-ranked Texas in the Cotton Bowl. Notre Dame won all nine of the games in which Montana started and captured the national championship.

In 1978 Montana had a tremendous senior season. He led Notre Dame to a 9-3 record (including a dramatic 35-34 victory over ninth-ranked Houston in the Cotton Bowl in which Montana threw the game-tying touchdown pass as time ran out) and once again received honorable mention status on the AP All-America team. He became only the third Fighting Irish quarterback to throw for more than 2,000 yards in a season; he also threw 10 touchdown passes.

Montana was chosen in the third round of the 1979 NFL draft. He was the eighty-second player selected overall and the third from Notre Dame. As it turned out, he was something of a bargain. Over the next 16 years, Montana would become one of the game's most successful and decorated quarterbacks. He led the San Francisco 49ers to four Super Bowl championships. He passed for more than 40,551 yards and threw 273 touchdown passes. He was twice named the NFL's Most Valuable Player; three times he was named MVP of the Super Bowl. He also led the NFL in completion percentage on five occasions and was named Associated Press Male Athlete of the Year in 1989 and 1990.

Joe Montana was traded to the Kansas City Chiefs in April 1993. He retired after the 1994 season.

Career Statistics (Passing)

YEAR	ATT.	COMP.	YARDS	TD	PCT.
1975	66	28	507	4	.424
1977	189	99	1,604	11	.524
1978	260	141	2,010	10	.542
TOTAL	515	268	4,121	25	.520

MORIARTY, LARRY

Fullback (1980-82) ▪ 6-2, 223 ▪ Santa Barbara, CA

Larry Moriarty was 22 years old by the time he showed up on the campus of Notre Dame in 1980. He had spent the previous year at Santa Barbara City College where he helped the football team to a top-10 national ranking; however, because injuries had shortened his high school career, that was the first time he had played football in nearly three years.

Moriarty gradually shed whatever rust had accrued and became a productive member of the Notre Dame offense. A backup fullback in 1980 and 1981, he became a starter in 1982 and rushed for 520 yards and five touchdowns on 88 carries. His rushing average of 5.9 yards per carry was best among Irish starters.

Moriarty continued to improve after he left Notre Dame and had a nine-year professional career. He played with the Houston Oilers from 1983 through 1986 and the Kansas City Chiefs from 1986 through 1991.

MOYNIHAN, TIM

Center (1926-29) ▪ 6-1, 195 ▪ Chicago, IL

Tim Moynihan was the captain of Notre Dame's 1929 national championship team. He made the varsity as a freshman and earned three monograms. In 1929 he was the starting center on a team that won all nine of its games under coach Knute Rockne.

Moynihan worked as an assistant coach for the Irish after he graduated. He also served on the coaching staffs at the University of Texas and Denver University and played professionally for two seasons with the Chicago Cardinals. He was a decorated veteran of the U.S. Marine Corps who served in the South Pacific during World War II.

MUNDEE, FRED

Center (1934-36) ▪ 6-1, 185 ▪ Youngstown, OH

Fred Mundee received all-state honors in basketball and football at South High School in Youngstown, Ohio. In college, however, he was somewhat slow to develop. He earned his first varsity letter in 1935 as a junior. The next year he surprised many observers in preseason camp, including coach Elmer Layden, by winning a heated battle for the starting center job.

Mundee graduated from Notre Dame in 1936 with a degree in journalism. From 1943 through 1945 he played center for the Chicago Bears.

MUTSCHELLER, JIM

End (1949-51) ▪ 6-1, 198 ▪ Beaver Falls, PA

In 1949 Notre Dame won a national championship under coach Frank Leahy. James Francis Mutscheller was a sophomore that year, playing his first full season of varsity football. As a backup to starter Bill Wightkin at left end, he not only contributed to the team's success, but he also laid the groundwork for an outstanding career.

Mutscheller became a starter in 1950. He led the team with a school-record 35 receptions for 426 yards and seven touchdowns; his 42 points also led the team. In 1951, as a senior, he was elected team captain. Again he was the top receiver for the Irish, with 20 catches for 305 yards and two touchdowns.

Mutscheller played tight end for the Baltimore Colts from 1954 through 1961.

N

NATIONAL CHAMPIONSHIPS

Several organizations release rankings of the best teams in college football. The national champion, however, is generally acknowledged to be the top-ranked team in either the Associated Press poll of sportswriters and broadcasters or the *USA Today*/CNN poll of coaches (known as the United Press International poll prior to 1991).

Since the first Associated Press poll was conducted in 1936, Notre Dame has won eight national championships (in 1943, 1946, 1947, 1949, 1966, 1973, 1977, and 1988), more than any other school; Oklahoma is second on the list with six. The coaches' poll has been in effect since 1950; in that time Notre Dame has won three national championships (in 1966, 1977, and 1988).

Prior to 1936 a variety of other rating systems were recognized by the NCAA. Notre Dame has won 11 consensus national titles dating back to 1924; however, the Fighting Irish have been named national champions by at least one legitimate poll on 19 separate occasions.

Notre Dame's Consensus National Championships

YEAR	RECORD	COACH
1924	10-0	Knute Rockne
1929	9-0	Knute Rockne
1930	10-0	Knute Rockne
1943	9-1	Frank Leahy
1946	8-0-1	Frank Leahy
1947	9-0	Frank Leahy
1949	10-0	Frank Leahy
1966	9-0-1	Ara Parseghian
1973	11-0	Ara Parseghian
1977	11-1	Dan Devine
1988	12-0	Lou Holtz

NEMETH, STEVE

Halfback (1943-44) ▪ 5-11, 166 ▪ South Bend, IN

Steve Nemeth grew up in the shadow of the Golden Dome. A three-year starter at Riley High School in South Bend, he made the varsity at Notre Dame in his junior year and was a second-string running back as a senior. He played on the national championship team of 1943.

After college Nemeth played with the Cleveland Rams of the NFL and the Chicago Rockets and Baltimore Colts of the All-America Football Conference.

NIEHAUS, STEVE

Defensive End/Defensive Tackle (1973-75) ▪ 6-5, 260 ▪ Cincinnati, OH

A consensus All-American in 1975, Steve Niehaus grew up in an athletic family in Cincinnati, Ohio. His father, Ralph, played for the Los Angeles Rams, and his older brother, John, was a defensive back at Alabama. But it was Steve who displayed the most early promise. At perennial power Moeller High School, he was an all-state and All-America lineman (playing offense and defense) and led the team to three consecutive city championships.

Niehaus's early years at Notre Dame were frustrating: He required knee surgery midway through each of his first two seasons. But as a junior, in 1974, coach Ara Parseghian moved him from defensive tackle to defensive end, and Niehaus responded with 95 tackles (third on the team), a performance that earned him first-team All-America recognition from *Football News*.

In 1975 he had a team-leading 113 tackles and was a first-team selection on every major All-America team. He finished twelfth in voting for the Heisman Trophy and was named defensive MVP by the Notre Dame National Monogram Club.

Niehaus finished his career with 290 tackles. He was a first-round draft choice of the Seattle Seahawks in 1976, but his NFL career lasted only four years. He later went into private business.

NIGHT GAMES

Few schools cling to tradition more than Notre Dame. And traditionally, the Fighting Irish do not play football games at night—at least, not at home.

In the last 15 years, however, as television contracts have played a greater role in determining the schedules of major college sports programs, Notre Dame has become more flexible. The Fighting Irish have played 27 games under the lights at Notre Dame Stadium, starting with the nationally televised season opener against Michigan in 1982.

This concession to progress has not, however, been embraced wholeheartedly. Prior to 1997 there were no permanent lights at Notre Dame Stadium. So when a television network wanted to broadcast a late afternoon, twilight, or night game from South Bend, it turned to Musco Mobile Lighting, Ltd. of Oskaloosa, Iowa. The company transported, via tractor trailer, anywhere from four to six lighting units to the campus. When the game ended, the lights went home. And Notre Dame Stadium fell dark again.

With the renovation and expansion of the stadium came the installation of permanent lighting. But, the Reverend E. William Beauchamp, the university's executive vice president, made it clear at the time that the lights did not signal any intention to add more night games to the schedule. In fact, their primary function remains unchanged: to aid television broadcasts of games that end in the late afternoon hours, as daylight is fading.

NOTRE DAME STADIUM

With the growing popularity of Notre Dame football in the 1920s came the need for a bigger and better stadium. Previously, the Fighting Irish had played their home games at 30,000-seat Cartier Field. But the team's phenomenal on-field success, combined with coach Knute Rockne's tireless marketing of the program, prompted university officials to embrace the notion of constructing a new facility.

It was Rockne who conceptualized the new stadium. Then, in 1929, architectural blueprints and bids were accepted from some of the most renowned contractors in the country. The contract was ultimately awarded to the Osborn Engineering Company, whose resumé included Yankee Stadium, Comiskey Park, and New York's Polo Grounds. Ground was broken in the summer of 1929; foundations were poured in April 1930. Four months later, 54,000-seat Notre Dame Stadium was open for business. It measured one-half mile in circumference and stretched 45 feet into the sky (a press box, with seating for 264 reporters,

In 1930 the 54,000-seat Notre Dame Stadium opened, and the Fighting Irish won their first game there on October 30, defeating SMU. The stadium was recently expanded to accommodate an additional 20,000 fans.

sat atop the stadium some 60 feet above the ground). Construction was completed at a cost of more than $750,000.

The Fighting Irish played their first game in Notre Dame Stadium on October 4, 1930, against Southern Methodist University. A modest crowd witnessed a 20-14 Notre Dame victory. One week later, before the start of a game against Navy, the stadium was officially dedicated. The crowd was larger this time, and the Fighting Irish managed to sustain the festive atmosphere with a 26-2 victory.

Notre Dame Stadium was truly a monument to Rockne. Not only did he play an active role in its design, but he also formulated a traffic and parking system that remained in effect for decades. Interestingly enough, although Rockne surely understood the symbiotic relationship between his program and its more influential fans, he wanted some distance between the two. For that reason he asked the stadium's designers to create minimal room on the sideline; in that way, Rockne hoped, well-meaning but intrusive sideline guests would be discouraged from visiting.

Sadly, Rockne never saw Notre Dame Stadium filled to capacity. He died in a plane crash in the spring of 1931. The following season the Fighting Irish defeated the University of Southern California in front of 50,731 fans (considered a sellout at the time). Today, of course, sellouts are the norm. Through 1995, the Fighting Irish had compiled a record of 248-71-5 at Notre Dame Stadium. Attendance since Opening Day in 1930 has averaged more than 52,200. The largest crowd was 61,296 on October 6, 1962, when Notre Dame lost to Purdue. Four years later, however, the school began recording attendance figures on the basis of paid attendance. Since that time Notre Dame has failed to sell out only one home game: a Thanksgiving contest against Air Force in 1973. So typically, attendance for games at Notre Dame Stadium is listed as 59,075.

That will change in the fall of 1997 when a $50 million expansion project is completed. Twenty thousand seats will be added to Notre Dame Stadium, boosting capacity to approximately 80,000. That would make Notre Dame Stadium the fourteenth-largest facility among the 107 schools playing Division I-A football. With its current capacity, Notre Dame ranks forty-fourth.

NOTRE DAME VICTORY MARCH

The nation's most famous college fight song was written, not surprisingly, by a pair of Notre Dame graduates, brothers Michael J. Shea (class of 1905) and John F. Shea (class of 1906). Michael wrote the words, and John wrote the music. The brothers' collaboration survived considerable geographic barriers: Michael was a parish priest in Ossining, New York, while John lived in Holyoke, Massachusetts. The distance would be no hindrance in today's high-tech world, but at the turn of the century, it was a serious problem. Nevertheless, the brothers Shea completed their work and copyrighted the song in 1908.

The "Notre Dame Victory March" was first performed in public that same year, at the Second Congregational Church in Holyoke. On Easter Sunday, 1909, it was given its debut on the campus of Notre Dame. The song was played by the University of Notre Dame band in the rotunda of the administration building as part of an Easter concert. It would be another decade before the song was played at a Fighting Irish athletic event.

Since then the "Notre Dame Victory March" has become synonymous with the spirit of college football. The song has been called one of the four most recognizable songs in U.S. history. (The others are "White Christmas," "God Bless America," and the "Star Spangled Banner.") If it seems a bit of hyperbole to place the "Notre Dame Victory March" in such fast company, it certainly is no stretch to suggest that the song is easily the most inspiring fight song in college athletics. And in fact, it was so honored in 1969, during the centennial celebration of college football.

Cheer, cheer for old Notre Dame,
Wake up the echoes cheering her name,
Send a volley cheer on high,
Shake down the thunder from the sky.
What though the odds be great or small
Old Notre Dame will win over all,
While her loyal sons are marching
Onward to victory.

As for the song's creators, Michael Shea, pastor of St. Augustine's Church, died in Ossining in 1938. John Shea, a Massachusetts state senator, died in Holyoke in 1955.

NOVAKOV, DAN
Center (1969-71) • 6-2, 225 • Cincinnati, OH

Dan Novakov first made a name for himself with an outstanding game at offensive tackle in the 1970 Cotton Bowl. By the following September, however, he had been moved to center, where he succeeded All-American Mike Oriard. Novakov was the team's starting center for two years. As a senior, in 1971, he was named offensive MVP by the National Monogram Club.

O'CONNOR, ZEKE
Left End (1944-47) ▪ 6-4, 215 ▪ Fort Montgomery, NY

William "Zeke" O'Connor was Notre Dame's starting left end in 1944 when the ranks of college teams were so depleted by the loss of athletes to the armed services that the NCAA declared freshmen eligible for varsity competition.

O'Connor attended high school at Mount St. Michael in New York. He was a three-sport star, earning all-state honors in basketball and leading his team to the All-Catholic title in football. Among his teammates at Mount St. Michael was Art Donovan, who also attended Notre Dame and who would one day become an All-Pro lineman with the Baltimore Colts.

West Point and the University of Southern California were the schools that most actively pursued O'Connor. But when Fighting Irish coach Hugh Devore jumped into the recruiting fray, O'Connor's father and high school coach were impressed; they both encouraged him to enroll at Notre Dame. O'Connor graduated from high school in January 1944 and immediately packed his bags and moved to South Bend. He registered for classes and joined the basketball team. The following fall, at the tender age of 17, he was thrown into the starting lineup on the football team.

O'Connor joined the U.S. Navy and played for the Great Lakes Naval Training Center team in 1945. He returned to Notre Dame in 1946 but, like so many other players, found the competition to be fierce. All around the country, thousands of college athletes who had been involved in the U.S. war effort were suddenly back on campus; and there wasn't room for all of them. Notre Dame won consecutive national championships in 1946 and 1947, but Zeke O'Connor failed to earn a varsity monogram in either season.

Despite his status as a bench-warmer, O'Connor was drafted in the fourth round by the Buffalo Bills of the All-America Football Conference. He also played for the New York Yankees and Cleveland Browns before moving to the Canadian Football League, where he became a star with the Toronto Argonauts.

ODYNIEC, NORMAN

Fullback (1956-58) ▪ 6-0, 180 ▪ Greensboro, NC

Norman Odyniec was a second-string fullback behind All-American Nick Pietrosante in 1957 and 1958. He played just 16 minutes and carried the ball only 11 times as a junior but managed to score two touchdowns. As a senior his playing time increased dramatically: He carried 58 times for 273 yards and had 31 tackles in the defensive backfield.

Odyniec was drafted by the Washington Redskins in 1959 but did not play in the NFL.

OLIVER, HARRY

Kicker (1980-81) ▪ 5-11, 185 ▪ Cincinnati, OH

Harry Oliver was the place-kicker on three consecutive state championship teams at Moeller High School in Cincinnati, where his coach was Gerry Faust. He spent two years on the junior varsity at Notre Dame before being promoted to the varsity in 1980. That season he made 18 of 23 field goals and 19 of 23 extra points for a total of 73 points—at the time just two short of the school's all-time record of 75, which was set by Dan Reeve in 1977. A left-footed, soccer-style kicker, Oliver twice kicked field goals of 50 yards or more and was the NCAA's third-ranked kicker with an average of 1.64 field goals per game. He was named third-team All-America by *Football News*.

As a senior Oliver made 28 of 30 extra points but hit only six of 13 field goal attempts. He did not play in the NFL.

OLSON, BOB

Linebacker (1967-69) ▪ 6-0, 226 ▪ Superior, WI

Bob Olson was one of the few Notre Dame players to be elected co-captain in both his junior and senior years. A two-time prep All-American at Superior High School, he made an easy transition to college football. Not only did he become a starter at Notre Dame in his sophomore year, but he also led the team in tackles with 98. The following year he had a team-high 129 tackles in just nine games.

Olson had his finest season in 1969 when he set a single-season school record for tackles with 142. In Notre Dame's 21-17 loss to Texas in the 1970 Cotton Bowl, he was named Outstanding Defensive Player. He received second-team All-America recognition from the Associated Press and was voted team MVP by the National Monogram Club. Olson was a fifth-round draft choice of the Boston Patriots in 1970.

O'MALLEY, JIM

Linebacker (1970-72) ▪ 6-2, 221 ▪ Youngstown, OH

Jim O'Malley overcame chronic knee problems to become a two-year starter at inside linebacker. An all-state selection in his senior year at Chaney High School in Youngstown, Ohio, he earned his first monogram at Notre Dame in 1970 as a second-string middle linebacker. He became a starter in 1971 and had 72 tackles, despite playing a modest 126 minutes.

As a senior, in 1972, O'Malley had his best season, leading the Fighting Irish in tackles with 122. He played with the Denver Broncos from 1973 through 1975.

ORIARD, MIKE

Center (1968-69) ▪ 6-3, 221 ▪ Spokane, WA

It isn't easy to make the Notre Dame football team as a walk-on; after all, the program annually attracts many of the finest high school players in the nation. Once in a while, though, an athlete slips through the cracks. He shows up in South Bend with neither a scholarship nor the proper pedigree but with enough heart and talent to merit a look from the coaching staff. Such was the case with Mike Oriard, who not only won a spot on the Fighting Irish roster, but also eventually became a second-team All-American.

Oriard earned his first monogram as a junior when he was a backup center behind Tim Monty. As a senior, in 1969, he moved into the starting lineup and was named co-captain, along with linebacker Bob Olson. The Irish went 8-2-1 that season under coach Ara Parseghian, and Oriard earned second-team All-America honors from *The Sporting News*. He won academic scholarships from the NCAA and the National Football Foundation but delayed his post-graduate studies until after he had completed his professional football career.

Oriard was a fifth-round draft choice of the Kansas City Chiefs, with whom he spent four seasons. He later wrote an autobiographical book about football entitled *The End of Autumn* and became a professor of literature at Oregon State University.

OSTROWSKI, CHET

End (1949-51) ▪ 6-1, 197 ▪ Chicago, IL

An English major with a fondness for the stories of Edgar Allan Poe, Chet Ostrowski was a two-year starter for the Fighting Irish at left end.

He came to South Bend in 1948 after starring for four years at Weber High School in Chicago. A backup on the 1949 championship team, he moved into the starting lineup in 1950 as a junior. In his senior year he was the team's second-leading receiver with 20 catches for 204 yards and one touchdown.

A tenth-round draft choice of the Washington Redskins in 1952, Ostrowski spent six years in the NFL.

OUTLAND TROPHY

First presented in 1946 by the Football Writers Association of America, the Outland Trophy is awarded to the outstanding interior lineman in college football. The award is named after Dr. John H. Outland, an 1898 graduate of the University of Kansas.

Three Notre Dame players have received the Outland Award.

YEAR	PLAYER	POSITION
1946	George Connor	Tackle
1948	Bill Fischer	Guard
1976	Ross Browner	Defensive End

P

PAGE, ALAN

Defensive End (1964-66) ▪ 6-5, 238 ▪ Canton, OH

A member of the College Football Hall of Fame and a participant in four Super Bowls, Alan Page is widely acknowledged as one of the finest athletes ever to attend the University of Notre Dame. He was also one of the most unique: A fiercely individualistic and intelligent young man, he carved out his own place in a sport that prizes conformity. In addition to being an exceptionally gifted football player, he was and is a true scholar; a man who has achieved greatness off the field as well as on it.

Alan Page could be called the Cal Ripken Jr. of football. After an outstanding career at Notre Dame, he went on to spend fifteen years in the NFL—without missing a single game.

Coincidentally, Page came to Notre Dame from Canton, Ohio, in 1963—the very same year Canton became the site of the Pro Football Hall of Fame. And it wasn't long before Page began to look like a player who would one day be feted in his hometown.

After an obligatory year on the freshman team, he became a starter at right defensive end in 1964 and made 41 tackles. The following season he had 30 tackles. As a senior Page had 63 tackles and was one of four consensus All-Americans on a team that won a national championship with a 9-0-1 record and whose only blemish was a 10-10 tie with second-ranked Michigan State. *The Sporting News, Time,* and several other groups named him first-team All-America; the Associated Press and United Press International each named him to its second team.

Page played in the College All-Star Game in 1967 and was drafted in the first round by the Minnesota Vikings a few months later. Although taller and leaner than the typical defensive lineman, Page was shifted to tackle shortly after he arrived in training camp in the summer of 1967. He adapted well, thanks in large part to his extraordinary agility; if he was smaller than most of the offensive linemen he faced, he was undeniably quicker. Throughout his career, in fact, Page stood as living testament to the argument that football is not merely a game of strength. He could, and often did, go around rather than through his opponent.

In 1971 Page had his best season. He registered 109 tackles and 10 assists and became the first defensive player to be named Player of the Year by the Associated Press; he was similarly honored by United Press International. Page helped lead the Vikings to four league or conference championships before being released during the 1978 season, ostensibly because the club was unhappy with his decision to embrace a distance running regimen that trimmed his weight to 225 pounds.

The Chicago Bears, however, were more than happy to offer Page a job, and he remained with the team until his retirement after the 1981 season. In 15 NFL seasons Page did not miss a single game. A nine-time All-Pro, he started 238 games and accumulated 1,431 tackles, 164 sacks, and 24 fumble recoveries.

Page's zest for life did not end with his retirement from the NFL—far from it. He became an avid marathon runner and a practicing attorney (he had earned his law degree while playing football). In 1992 he was appointed to a position as justice of the Minnesota Supreme Court. Page was elected to the Pro Football Hall of Fame in 1988 and the College Football Hall of Fame in 1993.

PALUMBO, SAM
Tackle (1951-54) ▪ 6-1, 208 ▪ Cleveland, OH

A graduate of Collinwood High School in Cleveland, Ohio, Sam Palumbo earned four monograms at Notre Dame. He joined the Fighting Irish in 1951 when freshmen were eligible for varsity competition and two-platoon football was enjoying a brief period of popularity.

Palumbo was a starting defensive tackle in 1951 and 1952. In 1953, when two-platoon football fell out of favor, he was the second-string left tackle behind Frank Varrichione. He returned to the starting lineup in 1954 when Varrichione was switched to right tackle.

Palumbo was a fourth-round draft choice of the Cleveland Browns in 1955. He left professional football in 1960 after stints with the Browns, Green Bay Packers, and Buffalo Bills.

PANELLI, JOHN
Fullback (1945-48) ▪ 5-11, 185 ▪ Morristown, NJ

John Rocco Panelli was an all-state fullback at Morristown High School in New Jersey in 1943. An admirer of Fighting Irish quarterback Angelo Bertelli, Panelli had his heart set on playing for Notre Dame.

In 1945, as a freshman, he earned a monogram as a second-string fullback behind Frank Ruggerio. His playing time was reduced in 1946 thanks to competition from a powerhouse backfield that included Jim Mello and Corwin Clatt at fullback, Emil Sitko and Terry Brennan at halfback, and John Lujack at quarterback—a group that helped the Irish capture a national championship.

The Irish won a second consecutive national title in 1947. Panelli, the starting fullback, rushed for 424 yards and four touchdowns on 72 carries. As a senior, in 1948, he rushed for 692 yards on 92 carries; he also scored eight touchdowns. Both were second best on the team, behind only Sitko, who was a consensus All-American.

Panelli played professionally with the Detroit Lions (1949-50) and Chicago Cardinals (1951-53).

PARSEGHIAN, ARA
Head Coach (1964-74) ▪ Akron, OH

Ara Parseghian was one of college football's most successful coaches. He came to Notre Dame in 1964 after eight years at Northwestern University and quickly restored

One of Notre Dame's most successful coaches, Ara Parseghian is also one college football's most successful coaches. His career winning percentage was an amazing .739.

the program-which had slipped under Joe Kuharich and Hugh Devore—to its previous luster.

The Fighting Irish won nine of 10 games in Parseghian's rookie season; the only blemish was a 20-17 loss to USC in the final game of the year. For directing such a remarkable turnaround (Notre Dame had won just two games the previous season), Parseghian was named College Coach of the Year. The Irish went 7-2-1 the next season, and then, in 1966, captured their first consensus national championship in 17 years.

That Notre Dame team was loaded with talent: quarterback Terry Hanratty, split end Jim Seymour, halfback Nick Eddy, linebacker Jim Lynch, and defensive end Alan Page, just to name a few. Over the course of 10 games the Irish overwhelmed their opponents by a combined margin of 362-38. The Fighting Irish did not lose a game that season, although they were held to a 10-10 tie by Michigan State in the penultimate game of the regular season. A 51-0 thrashing of USC in the season finale, however, clinched an undefeated season and secured the national title.

Parseghian did not come close to experiencing a losing season in South Bend; in fact, his teams never lost more than three games in a single year. In 1973 he had his most memorable season. The Fighting Irish went 11-0, outscoring their opponents 358-66

along the way. They met another unbeaten team, top-ranked Alabama, in the Sugar
Bowl. Their matchup was a rarity: a bowl that actually lived up to the pregame hype.
It ended with Bob Thomas kicking a 19-yard field goal with 4:26 remaining to give
Notre Dame a 24-23 victory.

Parseghian led the Irish to a 10-2 record in 1974. He then abruptly resigned. As much
as he loved it, the job of coaching the most popular college football team in the nation
had taken its toll. Parseghian was a passionate, driven man prone to personally demon-
strating plays and techniques during practice. He lived and died with each game; eventually, the stress began to affect his physical and emotional health. So he walked away
at the top of his profession. His career record at Notre Dame was 95-17-4; his 24-year
college coaching mark was 170-58-6, a winning percentage of .739.

After retiring from coaching, Parseghian went into broadcasting. He worked for
ABC Sports from 1975 through 1981 and for CBS Sports from 1982 through 1988. He was
inducted into the College Football Hall of Fame in 1980.

Parseghian's playing career was less spectacular. He enrolled in Akron University in
1941 but played just one season of football before enlisting in the U.S. Navy. After serving in World War II he entered Miami University in Ohio and became a starting halfback. He later played with the Cleveland Browns of the All-America Football
Conference, but injuries forced him to retire after just two seasons.

In 1950 Parseghian returned to his alma mater to work as an assistant coach under
Woody Hayes. When Hayes moved on to Ohio State in 1951, Parseghian became the
head coach. He compiled a record of 39-6-1 in five seasons, including a 9-0 mark in 1955.
That performance helped him land the head coaching job at Northwestern in 1956.
The Wildcats had less talent (and, not coincidentally, more stringent academic standards) than their Big 10 counterparts, but under Parseghian they managed to win more
games than they lost; they also went unbeaten (4-0) against Notre Dame, a feat that no
doubt impressed the brass in South Bend.

Career Coaching Record

YEAR	WON	LOST	TIED
1964	9	1	0
1965	7	2	1
1966	9	0	1
1967	8	2	0
1968	7	2	1
1969	8	2	1
1970	10	0	1
1971	8	2	0
1972	8	3	0
1973	11	0	0
1974	10	2	0
TOTAL	**95**	**17**	**4**

PASQUESI, TONY

Tackle (1952-54) ▪ 6-4, 212 ▪ Chicago, IL

A standout at St. Phillip's High School in Chicago, Tony Pasquesi made the Notre Dame varsity in his sophomore year but did not earn a monogram until he was a senior, in 1954. He played so well that season, however, that the Chicago Cardinals made him a third-round draft choice in 1955. He played for the Cardinals from 1955 through 1957.

PATULSKI, WALT

Defensive End (1969-71) ▪ 6-5, 235 ▪ Liverpool, NY

One of the greatest linemen in Notre Dame history, Walt Patulski grew up in Liverpool, New York, near Syracuse. He was a prep All-American at Christian Brothers Academy and among the most highly-recruited athletes of 1968.

Patulski lived up to expectations in South Bend. He started at left defensive end in the first game of his sophomore season—the first game in which he was eligible to start for the varsity—and he remained there for the next three years.

As a junior, in 1970, Patulski needed preseason surgery on his shoulder. He recovered fully and had 58 tackles, including 17 for minus 112 yards. He was named honorable mention All-America by United Press International.

Patulski was co-captain in 1971. He finished third on the team in tackles with 74 (including a team-high 17 for minus 129 yards) and was named UPI Lineman of the Year. He also won the Lombardi Trophy and received first-team honors from every prominent All-America team. His career statistics included 186 tackles and five fumble recoveries. He started every game from 1969 through 1971.

Patulski was the first player chosen in the 1972 NFL Draft. His professional career, however, was relatively short. He played with the Buffalo Bills from 1972 through 1975, missed the 1976 season because of a knee injury, joined the St. Louis Cardinals in 1977, and missed the 1978 season with a back injury. He retired in 1979 and later went into private business as a sales representative.

PENZA, DON

End (1951-53) ▪ 6-1, 200 ▪ Kenosha, WI

Don Penza was captain of the Fighting Irish in 1953. A solidly-built end, he was the team's fourth-leading receiver and a capable defensive player as well.

Penza came to Notre Dame from St. Catherine's High School in Kenosha, Wisconsin. He became a starter in his junior year and was named second-team All-America by United Press and *The Sporting News* in his senior year.

PERGINE, JOHN

Linebacker (1965-67) ▪ 6-0, 215 ▪ Norristown, PA

In high school John Pergine was an accomplished quarterback who threw for more than 1,000 yards in his junior year and was captain of the team in his senior year. While playing on the freshman team at Notre Dame, however, he was switched to linebacker. Although he weighed less than 190 pounds, he seemed naturally suited to the new position.

Pergine registered 15 tackles in less than 43 minutes of playing time as a sophomore. As a junior he moved into the starting lineup. He began the year at inside linebacker but moved to outside linebacker in the sixth game after an injury to Mike McGill. He finished the season with 98 tackles (second to consensus All-American Jim Lynch) and five interceptions and logged more playing time (261:55) than anyone on the team. The Fighting Irish won the national championship that year, and Pergine was named honorable mention All-America by the Associated Press.

In 1967 Pergine remained at outside linebacker and had another fine season. He was third on the team in tackles with 89 and first in interceptions with four. A United Press International second-team All-American, he was drafted by the Los Angeles Rams in 1968 and went on to play in the NFL for seven seasons.

PETITBON, JOHN

Halfback/Safety (1949-51) ▪ 6-0, 185 ▪ New Orleans, LA

At Jesuit High School in New Orleans, John Petitbon was a three-year member of the varsity football team. He earned his first monogram at Notre Dame as a sophomore as the starting safety on coach Frank Leahy's 1949 undefeated national championship team. In 1950 he became a two-way player, starting at left halfback as well as safety. He rushed for 388 yards on 65 carries and was second on the team in scoring with 30 points. He also caught 18 passes for 269 yards.

After the 1950 season Petitbon was named outstanding athlete in the New Orleans area by the New Orleans Athletic Club. In 1951, as a senior, he rushed for 221 yards and four touchdowns on 48 carries. He also led the team in punt returns and had two interceptions.

Petitbon played with the Dallas Texans, Cleveland Browns, and Green Bay Packers in his six-year NFL career.

PETERSON, ANTHONY

Linebacker (1990-93) ▪ 6-0, 223 ▪ Monongahela, PA

Great things were expected of Anthony Peterson in 1993—and not merely because he came from Monongahela, Pennsylvania, hometown of former Notre Dame star Joe Montana. A starter at inside linebacker, Peterson was Notre Dame's top returning tackler. In the season opener against Northwestern, however, he suffered a torn knee ligament that caused him to miss more than a month. He returned in the sixth game of the season, against Pittsburgh, but tore cartilage in the same knee on the third play of the game. He underwent arthroscopic surgery on October 19 and did not play again until January in the Cotton Bowl.

Despite his injuries, Peterson was selected by the San Francisco 49ers in the fifth round of the 1994 NFL Draft.

PIEPUL, MILT

Fullback (1938-40) ▪ 6-1, 206 ▪ Thompsonville, CT

In 1940 Milt Piepul became the first running back in 14 years to be named captain of a Notre Dame football team. He had earned the honor, in part, by rushing for a team-leading 427 yards and six touchdowns in his junior year.

Piepul was a prep star in Thompsonville, Connecticut, before going to Notre Dame. He received his first monogram in 1938 as a third-string fullback behind Mario Tonelli and Joe Thesing. He rushed for 137 yards on 40 carries that season. The following September he became a starter, and in 1940 he assumed the responsibilities of captain as well as place-kicker and linebacker. He was the team's second-leading rusher despite playing two games with an injured leg.

A second-team choice by *The Sporting News*, Piepul was Notre Dame's only All-American in 1940. He spent one season with the Detroit Lions before retiring from football.

PIETROSANTE, NICK

Fullback (1956-58) ▪ 6-2, 215 ▪ Ansonia, CT

Two-time All-American Nick Pietrosante became Notre Dame's starting fullback in his junior year after seeing little time as a sophomore. He made the most of the opportunity, rushing for a team-high 449 yards on 90 carries and registering 37 tackles on defense. After the season he was named third-team All-America by United Press and *The Sporting News*.

In his senior year Pietrosante was once again tireless. He was the team's leading rusher with 556 yards on 117 carries and also caught 10 passes for 78 yards. He was third in scoring with 26 points; with 44 tackles, he was also one of the team's defensive leaders. His post-season honors included an invitation to compete in the East-West Shrine Game and first-team All-America honors from the American Football Coaches Association.

Pietrosante, who graduated from Notre Dame High School (in New Haven, Connecticut) as well as the University of Notre Dame, was a first-round draft choice of the Detroit Lions in 1959. He played with the Lions and Cleveland Browns during an eight-year NFL career.

On February 6, 1988, Pietrosante died of cancer. His memory is honored each year with the presentation of the Nick Pietrosante Award, which is given to the Notre Dame football player who "best exemplifies the courage, loyalty, teamwork, dedication, and pride of the late Irish All-American fullback."

PILNEY, ANDY
Halfback (1933-35) ▪ 5-11, 175 ▪ Chicago, IL

Andy Pilney was a dependable and well-liked running back remembered primarily for his performance in Notre Dame's 18-13 victory over Ohio State in 1935—a game that is widely regarded as one of the best in college football history.

The Fighting Irish scored three touchdowns in the fourth quarter of that game, and Pilney played a major role in each of the drives: He returned a punt to the Ohio State 12-yard line and then completed a pass to the one to set up the first score; he threw three passes and caught another (for a total of 75 yards) on the second drive; on the final drive, he gained 32 yards on a single carry and set up the game-winning touchdown pass from quarterback Bill Shakespeare to end Wayne Millner in the final minute.

Pilney was a thoughtful, intelligent athlete who starred at Technical High School in Chicago, where he also served as president of the poetry club. He was a third-round draft choice of the Detroit Lions in 1936 but opted instead for a career in coaching.

PINKETT, ALLEN
Tailback (1982-85) ▪ 5-9, 181 ▪ Sterling, VA

Allen Pinkett, Notre Dame's career rushing leader, was born June 24, 1964, in Washington, D.C. At Park View High School in Sterling, Virginia, he twice earned all-state recognition as a defensive back and running back. He scored 57 career touchdowns and rushed for 4,700 yards. Small wonder that he was named high school All-American and had his choice of colleges to attend.

Pinkett selected Notre Dame and wasted little time getting acclimated. He started only one game as a freshman in 1982 but still rushed for 532 yards and five touchdowns. Although somewhat diminutive, he was a smart, explosive runner, characteristics that served him well throughout his career. Over the next three seasons he started in 36 consecutive games and rewrote the Notre Dame record books.

As a sophomore Pinkett rushed for 1,394 yards and 16 touchdowns and was named first-team All-America by *The Sporting News* and *Football News*. He set Notre Dame single-season records for touchdowns (18), points (110), and 100-yard rushing games (nine). He also missed Vagas Ferguson's yardage record by only 43 yards.

In 1984 Pinkett nearly matched those numbers. He rushed for 1,105 yards and 17 touchdowns on 275 carries and was named honorable mention All-America by the Associated Press and United Press International. As a senior captain in 1985, he gained 1,100 yards on 255 carries and scored 11 touchdowns. He was named first-team All-America by *Football News* and honorable mention All-America by AP and UPI. He also finished eighth in voting for the Heisman Trophy. For the third consecutive season he was voted MVP by his teammates.

Allen Pinkett *is* the Notre Dame record book. In the early eighties he set records for rushing touchdowns, rushing yards per game, touchdowns, carries, and points.

Pinkett finished his career with 4,131 yards rushing. He also set Notre Dame career records for touchdowns (53), rushing touchdowns (49), rushing yards per game (96.1), carries (889), and points (320). In addition to his ball-carrying ability, Pinkett was a superior receiver who caught 73 passes for 774 yards in his career.

A third-round draft pick in 1986, he spent his entire six-year NFL career with the Houston Oilers.

Career Statistics (Rushing)

YEAR	NO.	YARDS	AVG.	TD
1982	107	532	5.0	5
1983	252	1,394	5.5	16
1984	275	1,105	4.0	17
1985	255	1,100	4.3	11
TOTAL	889	4,131	4.6	49

Career Statistics (Receiving)

YEAR	NO.	YARDS	AVG.	TD
1982	9	94	10.4	0

1983	28	288	10.3	2
1984	19	257	13.5	1
1985	17	135	7.9	0
TOTAL	**73**	**774**	**10.6**	**3**

PIVEC, DAVE

End (1962-63) ▪ 6-3, 215 ▪ Baltimore, MD

Although never a starter, David John Pivec played two years of varsity football and saw significant playing time as a senior.

As a third-string end in 1962, he played 75 minutes and caught two passes for 32 yards. He also had 14 tackles and recovered two fumbles. In 1963, as a senior, Pivec backed up All-America split end Jim Kelly. He was the team's second-leading receiver (behind Kelly) with six catches for 76 yards and one touchdown. As a defensive back he had 22 tackles.

A fourteenth-round draft choice of the Chicago Bears in 1965, Pivec played tight end for the Los Angeles Rams from 1966 through 1968 and for the Denver Broncos in 1969. As a professional he caught 14 passes for 146 yards. He scored one touchdown.

PLISKA, JOE

Halfback (1911-14) ▪ 5-10, 172 ▪ Chicago, IL

Joe Pliska was a starting halfback at Notre Dame from 1912 through 1914, but he was overshadowed by some of his more famous teammates, including quarterback Gus Dorais and end Knute Rockne.

Pliska played with the Hammond Pros for one season. A lieutenant in the Army Air Corps, he was seriously injured in an accident in 1918. Disabled for much of his adult life, he died of pneumonia at the age of 49.

POLISKY, JOHN

Tackle (1925-27) ▪ 5-7, 192 ▪ Bellaire, OH

A stocky player with a buoyant personality, John Polisky was affectionately—and deservedly—known as "Bull." He was born in Pittsburgh and attended high school in Ohio and Texas. Throughout his travels, football remained a constant in his life.

After graduating from St. Edward's High School in Austin, Texas, Polisky enrolled at Notre Dame in the fall of 1924. Although he was not quite capable of cracking the lineup of a team so deep and talented that it would win the national championship, he made an impression on coach Knute Rockne that carried over into the following season. In fact, Polisky was a starter at right tackle for three years. As a senior, in 1927, he was a second-team All-American.

Polisky worked as an assistant coach at Notre Dame while completing requirements for a law degree in 1928. He played briefly with the Chicago Bears before opening his own law practice in Whiting, Indiana. Less than two years later, though, he was drawn back to the football field, this time as an assistant at Rice University in Houston. He later became an assistant at Creighton University under another Notre Dame alumnus, Marchmont Schwartz.

POTTIOS, MYRON
Guard (1958-60) ▪ 6-2, 220 ▪ Van Voorhis, PA

A second-team high school All-American, Myron Pottios came to Notre Dame in the fall of 1957. He became the team's starting center in his sophomore year and was shifted to right guard and linebacker as a junior. In the first three games of the 1959 season he had a team-leading 24 tackles. Unfortunately, he suffered a severe knee injury in the fourth game and missed the remainder of the season.

After undergoing off-season surgery to repair torn ligaments, Pottios was named captain of the 1960 Fighting Irish. His recovery was impressive: He led the team in tackles with 74 and was named first-team All-America by *Time*. Pottios was a bright spot in a generally dismal season for Notre Dame, which won only two of ten games; no other player received All-America honors.

Pottios was a second-round draft pick of the Pittsburgh Steelers in 1961. In his 13-year NFL career he also played for the Washington Redskins and Los Angeles Rams.

POWLUS, RON
Quarterback (1994-96) ▪ 6-2, 222 ▪ Berwick, PA

Ron Powlus became a celebrity at a relatively early age. He played for one of the premier prep football programs in the country, leading Berwick High School to a 37-5 record in his three years as a starting quarterback. His senior year the Bulldogs went undefeated and captured the Pennsylvania state championship and the number one ranking in the nation. Powlus threw for more than 2,900 yards and 31 touchdowns; he also rushed for 677 yards and 20 touchdowns. After the season he was named national player of the year by *USA Today* and *Parade* magazine. In three seasons he completed a remarkable 445 of 791 passes for 7,339 yards and 62 touchdowns; he rushed for 1,679 yards and 45 touchdowns.

In addition to his football achievements, he was a two-year starter on the Berwick basketball team and captain of the baseball team.

Powlus took that impressive resumé to South Bend in the fall of 1993. He was competing for a starting job in preseason camp when he suffered a broken right clavicle. The injury was aggravated during a practice session in October, and he wound up on the bench for the entire season. He also skipped contact drills in spring practice the following year.

By the fall, however, Powlus was healthy and eager to play. Coach Lou Holtz named him the starting quarterback during summer camp, and he went on to have a sensational sophomore year. Powlus showed no signs of rust in his first game in nearly two years, completing 18 of 24 passes for 291 yards and four touchdowns in a 42-15 victory over Northwestern. He set a Notre Dame single-season record with 19 touchdown passes and led the Irish in minutes played. He was named Player of the Game at the 1995 Fiesta Bowl.

As a junior Powlus started the first 10 games of the season before braking his wrist in a 58-21 victory over Navy. He missed the last regular season game and the Orange Bowl. Nevertheless, he had another impressive year, passing for 1,853 yards and 12 touchdowns. In just two seasons Powlus established himself as potentially one of the best quarterbacks in Notre Dame history. Already he was second on the school's career list for touchdown passes with 31 (Rick Mirer was first with 41); he was eighth in completions with 243.

Powlus underwent surgery just one day after breaking his wrist. A metal rod was inserted into the bone to stabilize the joint, but doctors expected him to be fully recovered by the start of the 1996 season; in fact, he was named tri-captain. Powlus went on to have his finest season in '96, completing 125 of 213 passes for 1,834 yards and eleven touchdowns. He was intercepted four times.

Career Statistics

YEAR	ATT.	COMP.	YARDS	TD	INT.	PCT.
1994	222	119	1,729	19	9	.536
1995	217	124	1,853	12	7	.571
1996	232	133	1,942	12	4	.573
TOTAL	671	376	5,524	43	20	.560

POZDERAC, PHIL
Offensive Tackle (1978-81) ▪ 6-9, 270 ▪ Garfield Heights, OH

After playing behind All-American Tim Foley in his first two seasons, Phil Pozderac became a starter at offensive tackle in 1980. A big, durable player, he started all 12 games that year and accumulated a team-high 315 minutes of playing time. Pozderac started again in 1981. He was a fifth-round draft choice of the Dallas Cowboys in 1982 and spent six seasons with the team before retiring in 1987.

PRITCHETT, WES
Linebacker (1985-88) ▪ 6-6, 251 ▪ Atlanta, GA

A fiery competitor whose enthusiasm was contagious, Wesley Andrew Pritchett was a two-year starter at linebacker. He had 70 tackles as a junior in 1987 and a team-high 112 in 1988 while helping the Fighting Irish win a national championship. *The Sporting News* named Pritchett second-team All-America after the '88 season, and he was invited to play in the Hula Bowl and the East-West Shrine Game.

A sixth-round draft pick of the Miami Dolphins in 1989, Pritchett played with the Buffalo Bills (1989-90) and Atlanta Falcons (1991).

PRO FOOTBALL HALL OF FAME
Six former Notre Dame players have been inducted into the National Football League Hall of Fame in Canton, Ohio. The first was Curly Lambeau, who played for the Irish in 1918 and later went on to found the Green Bay Packers.

PLAYER	NFL TEAMS	POSITION	YEAR INDUCTED
Curly Lambeau	Green Bay	Fullback/Coach	1963
George Trafton	Chicago	Center	1964
Wayne Millner	Boston, Washington	End	1968
George Connor	Chicago	Center	1975
Paul Hornung	Green Bay	Halfback	1986
Alan Page	Minnesota, Chicago	Defensive End	1988

PUPLIS, ANDY
Quarterback (1935-37) ▪ 5-8, 168 ▪ Chicago, IL

Although he rarely passed the ball, Andy Puplis was a two-year starter at quarterback who led the Fighting Irish to 6-2-1 records in 1936 and 1937. He was chosen by coach Elmer Layden primarily because of his ability to call the right play in most situations—and because he was an outstanding all-around athlete (he was captain of the football team and an all-city shortstop on the baseball team at Harrison High School in Chicago).

Puplis played for the Chicago Cardinals in 1943.

Q

QUINN, STEVE

Center (1965-67) ▪ 6-1, 225 ▪ Northfield, IL

A reserve center on the 1966 national championship team, Steve Quinn won the Hering Award in spring practice just a few months later as "most improved lineman." He was a starter in 1967 when the Fighting Irish went 8-2. Quinn was not selected in the 1968 NFL Draft but did play one season with the Houston Oilers.

R

RADIO

For the past 29 years Notre Dame football games have been broadcast on radio by the Mutual Broadcasting System. The Fighting Irish are the only football team—professional or collegiate—whose entire schedule is broadcast nationally on radio. More than 300 stations across the United States carry the games; a portion of the schedule is also broadcast globally via the Armed Forces Radio Network.

Since 1980, play-by-play duties have been handled by Tony Roberts, a multiple winner of the Washington, D.C. Sportscaster of the Year Award. Tom Pagna, who played college football for Ara Parseghian at Miami of Ohio, has provided color commentary since 1985. He is a former executive director of the University of Notre Dame Alumni Association.

As part of its Notre Dame pregame radio coverage, the Mutual Broadcasting Network also carried "The Lou Holtz Show," a weekly 30-minute television show featuring the Fighting Irish coach, until his retirement following the 1996 season.

RASSAS, NICK

Defensive Back (1963-65) ▪ 6-0, 185 ▪ Winnetka, IL

Nicholas Charles Rassas began his college career as a walk-on and ended it as a consensus first-team All-American. Despite the fact that he wasn't offered a scholarship, he insisted on going to Notre Dame, where his father had been a receiver in the late 1930s.

Once given an opportunity, Rassas displayed both the talent and drive needed for success at the highest level of college football. He earned his first monogram in 1964 as a starting safety; occasionally, he also played offensive halfback. He had 51 tackles and one interception and led the team in punt returns with 15 for 153 yards.

In 1965 Rassas was one of the best all-purpose players in college football. He had 53 tackles and a team-high six interceptions; more impressive, though, was his performance as a return specialist. Rassas led the nation in punt returns with 24 for 459 yards and three touchdowns. His 19.1-yard average per return still stands as a Notre Dame single-season record; his career average of 15.7 is also a school record.

Rassas finished his improbable career with 106 tackles, seven interceptions, and four touchdowns. A consensus first-team All-American in 1965, he was the only Notre Dame player to participate in the 1966 College All-Star Game. A second-round draft pick of the Atlanta Falcons and San Diego Chargers in 1966, he played three seasons of professional football before entering the private sector. He is currently manager of First National Bank of Chicago Foundation/First Chicago Investment Advisors.

RATIGAN, BRIAN

Linebacker (1989-92) ▪ 6-4, 226 ▪ Council Bluffs, IA

Brian Ratigan started only two games in his college career; nevertheless, he was a sturdy, reliable athlete who earned four monograms as a linebacker and special teams player. Ratigan's best season was 1991 when he played in all 13 games and started against Penn State and Hawaii. He finished the season with 25 tackles in 66:08 of playing time.

An accomplished basketball player, Ratigan led Saint Albert High School to the Iowa Class 2-A state championship in 1989.

Although he was not drafted, Ratigan played with the Indianapolis Colts in 1994.

RATKOWSKI, RAY

Halfback (1958-60) ▪ 6-1, 185 ▪ Glendale, NY

A reserve running back during his three-year college career, Ray Ratkowski had his best season in 1959. He carried the ball 26 times and played 133 minutes. His lone touchdown came on a 43-yard interception in a season-opening 28-8 victory over North Carolina. Ratkowski played less in his senior year but still caught the eye of NFL scouts. He was drafted in 1961 by the Boston Patriots of the American Football League. His professional career lasted just one season.

RATTERMAN, GEORGE

Quarterback (1945-46) ▪ 6-0, 165 ▪ Fort Thomas, KY

George Ratterman was one of the first Notre Dame athletes to win four monograms in a single year. As a junior (in 1945-46) he was enrolled in the Navy's V-12 program and earned varsity letters in football, basketball, baseball, and tennis. He was named to several all-star teams in basketball.

Most of Ratterman's notoriety, however, stems from his success in the fall of 1946 as a T formation quarterback—he split time with future Heisman Trophy winner Johnny Lujack. Ratterman completed 8 of 18 passes for 114 yards to help the Irish win the national championship with an 8-0-1 record.

Although he was overshadowed by Lujack in college, Ratterman had the more successful professional career. He played with the Buffalo Bills (1947-49) and New York Yankees (1950-51) of the All-America Football Conference and the Cleveland Browns (1952-56).

REAGAN, RONALD

Former United States President Ronald Reagan did not attend the University of Notre Dame; and he was only five years old when George Gipp began his playing career in South Bend. Nevertheless, Reagan, Gipp, and the Fighting Irish have become forever linked in American pop and political culture.

Reagan, then a budding Hollywood movie star, campaigned feverishly for the role of George Gipp in the 1940 film *Knute Rockne, All-American*. His sentimental portrayal of the Fighting Irish halfback, which included a melodramatic deathbed scene, helped solidify the legend of "The Gipper." That Gipp was actually a pool-hustling rogue who was, at least temporarily, thrown out of school for failing to attend classes did not matter to the film's producers. And it did not matter to Reagan. The film depicted Gipp as a clean-living hero. And Reagan benefited enormously from the resulting publicity.

Reagan turned all of his attention to politics and many years later was shrewd enough to realize that his most famous movie line could be used as an effective campaign tool. Thus, "Win One for the Gipper" became Ronald Reagan's campaign slogan.

REGNER, TOM

Offensive Guard/Defensive Tackle (1964-66) ▪ 6-1, 245 ▪ Kenosha, WI

Tom Regner was a consensus All-American offensive guard who helped lead the Fighting Irish to a 9-0-1 record and a national championship in 1966. But he began his college career as a defensive tackle.

In 1964, as a sophomore, Regner had 68 tackles (fifth best on the team and first among linemen) in 262 minutes of playing time. The following year, coach Ara Parseghian moved him to offense. It should have been a difficult transition, but Regner was a gifted athlete (he was captain of the baseball team and won the Wisconsin state championship in the shot put at St. Joseph's High School) who adjusted quickly. He played 303 minutes and earned second-team All-America honors from the Newspaper Enterprise Association.

By 1966 Regner was one of the top guards in college football. He was also the most experienced offensive lineman on the Notre Dame roster. The Irish were loaded with talent that year, but no player was more vital to the team's success than Regner. That fact was acknowledged after the season when he was named to the first team of nearly every All-America squad (*Life* magazine was a notable exception). An outstanding student, he was also named first-team Academic All-America.

Regner played with the Houston Oilers for six seasons. He retired from professional football in 1972 and today works as marketing manager for Allied-Sysco Food Services, Inc.

REHDER, TOM

Offensive Tackle/Defensive Tackle/Tight End (1984-87) ▪ 6-7, 263 ▪ Santa Maria, CA

As versatile as he was physically impressive, Thomas Bernard Rehder played three positions in four seasons at Notre Dame.

A reserve defensive tackle as a freshman in 1984, he started nine games at tight end in 1985, catching 13 passes for 182 yards and one touchdown. First-year coach Lou Holtz moved Rehder to offensive tackle in 1986, and he started in eight of 11 games. A case of pneumonia kept him out of spring drills in 1987, but he was at full strength by the fall and wound up starting in all but one game.

Rehder was a third-round draft pick of the New England Patriots in 1988. He spent five seasons in the NFL.

REILLY, JIM

Offensive Tackle (1967-69) ▪ 6-2, 247 ▪ Yonkers, NY

A three-year starter at left offensive tackle, Jim Reilly was a graduate of Hackley Prep in Tarrytown, New York. He won state high school championships in the shot put and discus prior to enrolling at Notre Dame, but football was clearly the family sport—one brother, Mike, played at Brown University and another brother, Tom, played at George Washington.

Reilly was an important player on two of the best offensive teams in Notre Dame history. He averaged more than 250 minutes a season and was a starting offensive lineman in 1969, when the Irish rolled up 4,489 yards of total offense, and in 1970, when they compiled a record 5,105 yards and scored 330 points. He was also an exceptional student who earned first-team Academic All-America honors in 1969.

The Buffalo Bills drafted Reilly in 1971. He played with the team for two seasons.

RESTIC, JOE
Safety/Punter (1975-78) ▪ 6-2, 190 ▪ Milford, MA

Two-time Academic All-American Joe Restic was one of the top defensive players on the 1977 national championship squad. He had 51 tackles and a team-high six interceptions from his free safety position. In Notre Dame's 38-10 victory over Texas in the Cotton Bowl, he had four tackles before being forced out of the game with a knee injury late in the first half.

By the fall of 1978, Restic was fully recovered and back in the starting lineup. He had 51 tackles and three interceptions in his final season and finished his career with 161 tackles and 13 interceptions (tied for third on Notre Dame's all-time list).

Defense, however, was only one of Restic's talents. The son of former Harvard football coach Joe Restic Sr., he was a star quarterback, defensive back, and punter at Milford High School, as well as a member of the National Honor Society. At Notre Dame, he continued to excel as an athlete and a student. In addition to being an outstanding free safety, Restic was the team's punter for four years. With a career average of 40.2 yards per kick, he is fifth on the school's all-time list; his 51.6-yard average against Air Force in 1975 (when he was a freshman) still stands as a single-game record.

Despite the demands of football, Restic was also an exceptional student who was named first-team Academic All-America in 1977 and 1978.

Career Statistics (Punting)

YEAR	NO.	YARDS	AVG.
1975	40	1,739	43.5
1976	63	2,627	41.7
1977	45	1,713	38.1
1978	61	2,330	38.2
TOTAL	**209**	**8,409**	**40.2**

Career Statistics (Interceptions)

YEAR	NO.	YARDS	AVG.
1975	0	0	0.0
1976	4	92	23.0
1977	6	25	4.2
1978	3	59	19.7
TOTAL	**13**	**176**	**13.5**

RICE, TONY
Quarterback (1987-89) ▪ 6-1, 200 ▪ Woodruff, SC

All-American quarterback Tony Rice was one of the best athletes ever to play for the University of Notre Dame. He came to South Bend from Woodruff High School where he was a *Parade* All-American and South Carolina player of the year. As dangerous a runner as he was a passer, Rice scored 460 points in high school and accumulated more than 7,000 yards of total offense. His career at Notre Dame was only slightly less impressive.

Rice sat out his freshman year for academic reasons. He did, however, win the MVP award in the school's annual Bookstore Basketball Tournament in the spring. In the fall of 1987 he became the starting quarterback when senior Terry Andrysiak went down with a broken collarbone in the fourth game of the season. Rice finished the season with 663 yards passing and 337 yards rushing; he scored seven touchdowns and passed for one.

Over the course of the next two seasons Rice was arguably the best quarterback in college football. An accurate passer and elusive runner, he led the Fighting Irish to a 24-1 record, including a national championship in 1988. He ran for 700 yards and threw for 1,176 that season; he also scored nine touchdowns and passed for eight as the Irish went 12-0. Rice was the first quarterback since Paul Hornung in 1956 to lead the team in rushing. He capped a great season by rushing for 75 yards and passing for 213 in a 34-21 Fiesta Bowl victory over West Virginia. After the season he was named honorable mention All-America by *Football News*, *The Sporting News*, and the Associated Press.

Rice was named first-team All-America by *Football News* in 1989 after rushing for 884 yards (a school record for a quarterback), passing for 1,122, and leading the Fighting Irish to a 12-1 record. He finished fourth in voting for the Heisman Trophy and received the Johnny Unitas Golden Arm Award as the top quarterback in college football.

Rice finished his career with 1,921 yards rushing, the most by a Notre Dame quarterback. Through 1995, his 4,882 yards of total offense was fourth on the all-time list.

Despite his accomplishments at Notre Dame, Rice was not selected in the 1990 NFL Draft. Rather than sign a free-agent contract, he accepted an offer to play for the Saskatchewan Roughriders of the Canadian Football League.

Career Statistics (Passing)

YEAR	ATT.	COMP.	YARDS	PCT.	TD
1987	82	35	663	.427	1
1988	138	70	1,176	.507	8
1989	137	68	1,122	.496	2
TOTAL	357	173	2,961	.485	11

Career Statistics (Rushing)

YEAR	ATT.	YARDS	AVG.	TD
1987	89	337	3.8	7
1988	121	700	5.8	9
1989	174	884	5.1	7
TOTAL	**384**	**1,921**	**5.0**	**23**

RIFFLE, CHUCK

Guard/Fullback (1937-39) ▪ 6-0, 200 ▪ Warren, OH

Charles Francis Riffle was born in Dillonvale, Ohio, and moved to Warren, Ohio, at the age of eight. A small, frail boy, he was cut from the Warren Harding High School football team as a sophomore. Over the course of the next two years, though, he gained more than 50 pounds and became one of the team's best linemen; he also played basketball and baseball.

Riffle played fullback in his first year on the Fighting Irish varsity, but as a junior, in 1938, he was switched to guard. He broke into the starting lineup as a senior. Riffle later played with the NFL's Cleveland Browns (1944) and the New York Yankees of the All-America Football Conference.

RINGS

More than three dozen Notre Dame graduates have played in the Super Bowl, and nearly two dozen have won Super Bowl rings. A more exclusive club, though, is one whose members have won Super Bowl rings and NCAA championship rings. Only eight members of the Fighting Irish have accomplished this feat.

PLAYER	NCAA TITLE	NFL TEAM	SUPER BOWL TITLE
Rocky Bleier	1966	Pittsburgh	1975, 1976, 1979, 1980
Jim Lynch	1966	Kansas City	1970
Bob Kuechenberg	1966	Miami	1973, 1974
Terry Hanratty	1966	Pittsburgh	1976
Dave Casper	1973	Oakland	1977
Steve Sylvester	1973	Oakland	1977, 1981, 1984
Joe Montana	1977	San Francisco	1982, 1985, 1989, 1990
Bobby Leopold	1977	San Francisco	1982
Ricky Watters	1988	San Francisco	1995

ROBINSON, JACK

Center (1932-34) ▪ 6-3, 200 ▪ Huntington, NY

That Jack Robinson became an All-American in 1934 was a minor miracle. He had a privileged childhood in affluent Huntington, Long Island, and was a starting center in his sophomore season at Notre Dame. But then his luck turned.

In June of 1933, while he was home for summer vacation, Robinson discovered a cyst on his right eye. Surgery to remove the cyst proved only marginally successful, and he was unable to return to school. In fact, he spent much of the next year in the hospital: He had a second operation in February of 1934 and a third in the summer. Around that same time, his father died of a heart attack.

Robinson eventually made it back to South Bend, but only one week before the start of the 1934 season. Incredibly enough, his skills hadn't eroded. He reclaimed his job at center within a matter of weeks and went on to play the best football of his career. He was a consensus All-American, earning second-team honors from the Associated Press and United Press International and first-team honors from the All-America Board and the North American Newspaper Alliance.

Robinson was Notre Dame's only All-American in 1934.

ROCKNE, KNUTE

Left End (1910-13) ▪ Head Coach (1918-30) ▪ 5-8, 165 ▪ Voss, Norway

The most successful college football coach in history was born Knute Rokne on March 4, 1888. The family name was changed to "Rockne" when Knute's father, a carriage maker, moved to Chicago in 1893 to establish a business. The rest of the family soon followed.

Young Knute was introduced to the game of football on the sandlots of Chicago's Logan Square District. He was a small, thin boy who often came home from those early pickup games with bumps and bruises all over his body. So concerned were his parents that they once forbid him to play the game any longer. By the time he was in high school however, Knute had his family's blessing. He loved football, and he seemed to have a natural gift for it.

The coach with the highest winning percentage in the history of football, Knute Rockne put Notre Dame on the map. In addition to transforming its football program into the one we know today, Rockne was also responsible for developing a national reputation for the university.

Still, it took Rockne some time to reach Notre Dame. He worked as a mail dispatcher with the Chicago Post Office for four years after high school while continuing to play football (and other sports) at the various athletic clubs in Chicago. Eventually Rockne saved enough money for college. In 1910 he bought a train ticket for South Bend where he hoped to make a name for himself.

Success came slowly for Rockne, who found that his size was a disadvantage in the world of college football. He sat the bench as a freshman, and the experience was so discouraging that he nearly quit the sport. In track and field, though, Rockne fared much better. His size was not a detriment, and his strength and courage proved valuable assets in his chosen event, the pole vault. (He set a school record of 12 feet, 4 inches.) Rockne's success in track and field gave him the confidence to continue playing football. He became a starter in his sophomore year and was captain of the team as a senior. That season, 1913, the Fighting Irish went undefeated (7-0); along the way they upset a powerful Army team, 35-13.

But there was much more to Knute Rockne than football. He also picked up some spare change by boxing during his time in South Bend. He wrote for the school newspaper and was an active member of the campus theater. He was a flutist in the school orchestra. Above all else, though, he was a student: Rockne worked his way through school as a chemistry research assistant and graduated magna cum laude. He then entered Notre Dame's graduate program in chemistry. At the same time, he assisted coach Jesse Harper with the football team. When Harper retired after the 1917 season, Rockne stepped into his job. And a legend was born.

It was under Rockne that Notre Dame rose to national prominence. The team's popularity began to transcend the world of college football; indeed, it is fair to say that Notre Dame's first generation of "subway alumni" came of age during Rockne's tenure.

In his 13-year career as head coach Rockne compiled a 105-12-5. His winning percentage of .881 is the best in the history of college (or professional) football. He coached five undefeated teams, including the 1924 national champions, who were led by the famous Four Horsemen. Rockne also led the Fighting Irish to consensus national titles in 1929 and 1930.

On and off the field, Rockne was a progressive thinker. He understood the value of promotion, and so he became the first coach to take his team around the country. Notre Dame would play anyone—anywhere. With rivalries on both coasts, as well as in the Midwest, Notre Dame became the first truly "national" program in college football. Rockne also was responsible for redesigning the equipment used by his teams. He created lighter pads and more aerodynamic uniforms and, of course, was a brilliant strategist. He introduced the shift to the Notre Dame play book. As the ball was snapped, all four backs were in motion, prompting mass confusion on the part of the defense. So effective and confounding was the shift that it was eventually outlawed. Rockne was also the first major college football coach to wholeheartedly embrace the forward pass.

If he was not quite the saintly genius depicted in the 1940 film *Knute Rockne, All-American*, he was, at the very least, an innovator. Rockne was a truly gifted coach and motivator who laid the foundation for all that Notre Dame football has become. Throughout his adult life, he displayed the versatility and boundless energy that marked his college days. At various times he served as Notre Dame's business manager, athletic director, ticket distributor, equipment manager, and track coach. He even helped design Notre Dame Stadium. He was a popular and successful public speaker. He authored three books.

Rockne's career would surely have been even more impressive if it were not cut short by tragedy. After the 1930 season he accepted an offer to do some promotional work in Los Angeles. Rockne boarded Transcontinental-Western Flight 599 in Kansas City on March 31, 1931. The plane encountered bad weather and crashed in a field near Bazaar, Kansas. All passengers and crew members were killed.

In 1951 the National Football Foundation opened the College Football Hall of Fame. Knute Rockne was among the first inductees.

Career Coaching Record

YEAR	WON	LOST	TIED
1918	3	1	2
1919	9	0	0
1920	9	0	0
1921	10	1	0
1922	8	1	1
1923	9	1	0
1924	10	0	0
1925	7	2	1
1926	9	1	0
1927	7	1	1
1928	5	4	0
1929	9	0	0
1930	10	0	0
TOTAL	105	12	5

ROSENTHAL, DICK
Athletic Director (1987-95)

Former Notre Dame athletic director Richard A. Rosenthal grew up in St. Louis, Missouri. An All-American basketball player at McBride High School, he first came to South Bend in 1950. For three years he was a starter on the basketball team, helping the Fighting Irish to records of 16-10, 19-5, and 22-3.

In his senior year Rosenthal, a 6-5, 210-pound forward, averaged 20.7 points as captain of a team that reached the Mideast Regional Final of the NCAA basketball tournament and was ranked sixth in the final Associated Press poll. By the time he graduated, he was Notre Dame's all-time leading scorer with 1,227 points (through 1995 he was twenty-second on the career list). He received All-America honors in his junior and senior seasons.

After his senior year Rosenthal was named MVP of a college all-star team that toured with the Harlem Globetrotters. He later played two seasons with the Fort Wayne Zollner Pistons of the NBA, averaging 7.8 points and 4.5 rebounds in 1954-55 and 2.8 points and 2.9 rebounds in 1956-57. In between, he served briefly in the military.

Rosenthal was more than just an athlete, though. At Notre Dame's 1954 graduation ceremony, he was presented with the Byron Kanaley Award as the top senior student-athlete. He went on to attend the Senior Bank Management School at Columbia University and the Graduate School of Banking at the University of Wisconsin. In 1957 he took a position as vice president of the Indiana Bank and Trust Company in Fort Wayne, Indiana. He later became chief executive officer of the St. Joseph Bank and Trust Company in South Bend, a position he held for 25 years.

On August 4, 1987, he returned to his alma mater, succeeding Gene Corrigan as director of athletics at the University of Notre Dame. Under his guidance the school made a number of changes in its athletic programs, including the addition of 50 women's scholarships and five women's varsity sports. He also played a vital role in the school's decision to join the Big East Conference in all sports except football and in helping the Fighting Irish football team land a unique—and lucrative—network television contract with NBC.

Dick Rosenthal returned to his alma mater after more than two decades in the business world to serve as its athletic director. In 1991, he was named the 37th most powerful person in sports by *The Sporting News*—and was the only college athletic director to make the list.

While he was athletic director, Rosenthal also served on the NCAA Council and was a member of the NCAA Gender Equity Task Force and the Postseason Football Subcommittee of the NCAA Special Events Committee. In 1991, *The Sporting News* listed Rosenthal thirty-seventh on its list of the 100 most powerful people in sports; he was the only college athletic director to make the list.

RUDDY, TIM

Center (1990-93) ▪ 6-3, 286 ▪ Dunmore, PA

Although he received all-state honors at Dunmore High School and led his team to the Pennsylvania state Class A title, Tim Ruddy was never just a football player. He was also one of the best shot putters in the state. And he was no slouch in the classroom. In fact, Ruddy maintained a 4.0 grade point average in high school.

That combination of intelligence and athletic ability made Ruddy one of the most prized recruits in the nation. He chose Notre Dame and enrolled in the College of

Engineering in the fall of 1990. Although he started only two games in his first two years, he continued to excel in the classroom, earning a 3.9 GPA.

As a junior Ruddy stepped into a starting role and was among the team's top three offensive players in minutes played. He helped the Fighting Irish finish among the nation's leaders in total offense, rushing, and scoring. Most impressive of all, he improved his GPA to a perfect 4.0 in the fall semester. He received the 1992 Student-Athlete Award from the Notre Dame Club of St. Joseph Valley and was a GTE/CoSIDA National Academic All-America selection.

In 1993 Ruddy continued to juggle athletic and academic responsibilities with uncommon skill. A senior tri-captain, he led the team in minutes played, despite missing a starting assignment with a pulled abdominal muscle. After the season he was named first-team All-America by *College & Pro Football Newsweekly* and second-team All-America by the Associated Press and United Press International. The academic honors continued to roll in as well: first-team Academic All-America, 1994 Cotton Bowl Scholar-Athlete, and post-graduate scholarships (totaling $28,000) from the National Football Foundation and the NCAA.

All were well deserved. Ruddy, a mechanical engineering major, carried a 4.0 GPA in his senior year and graduated with a cumulative GPA of 3.859. He was chosen by the Miami Dolphins in the second round of the 1994 NFL Draft.

RUDNICK, TIM
Defensive Back (1971-73) ▪ 5-10, 187 ▪ Chicago, IL

Tim Rudnick found his way into the starting lineup late in his junior year when Notre Dame coach Ara Parseghian decided to switch to a four-man defensive backfield. He had 21 tackles and three interceptions and also returned nine kickoffs for 122 yards.

As a senior, in 1973, Rudnick started at right cornerback on a defense that allowed just 66 points all season. He was seventh on the team in tackles with 43 and second in interceptions with three. Drafted by the Baltimore Colts in 1974, Rudnick played just one season in the NFL.

RUETTIGER, DANIEL
Defensive End (1975) ▪ 5-7, 184 ▪ Joliet, IL

Daniel Ruettiger earned exactly one varsity letter at Notre Dame, but thanks to the magic of Hollywood, he remains one of the school's most famous alumni.

"Rudy" was neither big enough nor quick enough to play major college football. Nevertheless, he pursued his dream of attending Notre Dame—and wearing the blue and gold of the Fighting Irish—with unabashed vigor. A working-class kid from Joliet, Illinois, he first attended Rockport College on a baseball and wrestling scholarship. He later worked as a turbine operator for Commonwealth Edison, served two years in the U.S. Navy, and graduated from Holy Cross Junior College.

He enrolled at Notre Dame in the fall of 1974 at the age of 26 and, against astronomical odds, made the football team as a walk-on.

In truth, Reuttiger was little more than a tackling dummy. But his spirit and determination earned him respect from coaches and players alike. In 1975, in the final game of his senior year, Ruettiger fulfilled his lifelong ambition by playing 27 seconds against Georgia Tech. When the final gun sounded, he was carried off the field on the shoulders of his teammates.

Nearly two decades later the story of Daniel Ruettiger found a larger audience. Screenwriter Angelo Pizzo and director David Anspaugh, who had previously demonstrated a flair for capturing the drama of athletics in the film *Hoosiers*, teamed up on *Rudy*. Ruettiger's brief moment of glory was recreated in the fall of 1992 during a game against Boston College. It was the first time since *Knute Rockne, All-American* in 1940 that a major motion picture had been filmed on the campus of Notre Dame. As 60,000 fans stood and cheered wildly, actor Sean Astin, in the title role, was carried off the field.

Daniel Ruettiger is arguably the biggest Notre Dame fan ever. His lifelong love of the university led to his never-ending persistence to play for the Fighting Irish. His dream came true in 1975, and he took the field in the last game of his senior year. At the conclusion of that game, he became the only player to be carried off the field at Notre Dame Stadium.

The movie was released in the fall of 1993 (its world premier, appropriately enough, was in South Bend) and became both a commercial and critical success. Daniel Ruettiger parlayed his fame into a career as a motivational speaker.

RUETZ, JOE
Guard/Quarterback (1935-37) ▪ 6-0, 184 ▪ South Bend, IN

Joe Ruetz was born in Racine, Wisconsin. His family moved to South Bend when he was in junior high school. He was a football and track star at South Bend Central High where he developed a heated cross-town rivalry with a future teammate (and Notre Dame coach) named Joe Kuharich, who starred for Riley High School.

Ruetz earned a monogram as a second-string left guard in his sophomore year with the Fighting Irish. The next season, however, a shortage of quarterbacks prompted coach Elmer Layden to move Ruetz to the backfield. In 1937, as a senior, he returned to his natural position—left guard—and helped the Irish post a 6-2-1 record. He later played for two seasons with the Chicago Rockets of the All-America Football Conference.

RUTKOWSKI, ED
Halfback/Quarterback (1960-62) ▪ 6-2, 195 ▪ Kingston, PA

A prep All-American, Edward John Rutkowski became something of a utility man at Notre Dame. He began his varsity career in 1960 as a second-string halfback, rushing for 76 yards on 25 carries. The next year he returned to the position he had played in high school, quarterback, but saw only 47 minutes of playing time. He completed one of five passes for 25 yards, rushed for 41 yards on eight carries, and had seven tackles as a defensive back.

In 1962 Rutkowski was moved to halfback again, and his field time increased significantly. He rushed for 52 yards on 16 carries and had 17 tackles; he was also one of the team leaders in kickoff and punt return yardage.

Rutkowski's versatility helped him in the professional ranks: In his four seasons with the Buffalo Bills he played flanker, halfback, and quarterback.

RYAN, TIM
Offensive Guard/Center/Linebacker (1987-90) ▪ 6-4, 266 ▪ Kansas City, MO

Versatility and adaptability were Tim Ryan's trademarks. He started out as a linebacker in his freshman year, was switched to center in preseason workouts the following summer, and finally settled in as a guard early in the 1988 season. He was named honorable mention All-America by the Associated Press as a sophomore and by *The Sporting News* as a junior.

In 1990, as a senior, Ryan started all 12 games and logged more playing time than any offensive lineman except center Mike Heldt. He played with the Tampa Bay Buccaneers from 1991 through 1993.

Ryan, by the way, was not the most successful athlete in the family: His first cousin is Danny Ferry, a former College Basketball Player of the Year at Duke who went on to play with the NBA's Washington Bullets and Cleveland Cavaliers.

RYDZEWSKI, FRANK
Center (1915-17) ▪ 6-1, 214 ▪ Chicago, IL

A two-year starter at center, Frank Rydzewski helped lead Notre Dame to a 6-1 record in Jesse Harper's last season as head coach. He was a consensus All-American, receiving first-team honors from the Newspaper Enterprise Association and the International News Service and second-team recognition from *Collier's*.

After graduation Rydzewski embarked on a professional career. In six seasons he played with six different teams, including the Chicago Cardinals and Chicago Bears. He later served as an Illinois state commander of the American Legion.

RYMKUS, LOU

Tackle (1940-42) ▪ 6-4, 218 ▪ Chicago, IL

Lou Rymkus, one of the best players on coach Frank Leahy's 1942 squad, was born in Carbondale, a coal mining town in southern Illinois. His father died when he was only six years old. When the mines began to shut down during the Great Depression, his mother moved the family to Chicago in the hope of finding work. For a time it appeared that Lou might have to drop out of school entirely, but when his older brother found employment in a stockyard and an aunt offered free housing, the family's financial situation began to improve.

Lou enrolled at Tilden Tech in his freshman year and, because of his size (he was already six feet tall and weight 220 pounds), was quickly recruited by the football coach. The game came naturally to him, and by the end of his sophomore year he was named all-state. He repeated that accomplishment as a junior and senior. But football wasn't Rymkus's only talent; he also won city and state championships as a heavyweight wrestler. Several large universities in the Midwest—including Purdue, Wisconsin, and Northwestern—actively pursued Rymkus. Notre Dame did not become involved in the recruiting process until late in his senior year, when an assistant coach saw him play a game in Indiana. The coach was so impressed that he invited Rymkus to visit the campus; and Rymkus was so impressed during his visit to the campus that he decided to attend Notre Dame. Despite all his options, the choice wasn't particularly difficult. Like most kids in the Midwest, Rymkus knew all about the Fighting Irish; he had grown up with an ear next to the radio on Saturday afternoons. If Notre Dame wanted him, then that's where he would play.

It turned out to be a good decision for both parties. Rymkus was a back-up at left tackle during his sophomore year under coach Elmer Layden and as a junior under Leahy. As a senior he moved to right tackle and became a starter. The Irish went 7-2-2. After the season Rymkus was named MVP by his teammates. He was selected by the Washington Redskins in the fifth round of the 1943 National Football League Draft. He spent the 1943 season with the Redskins; after World War II he played for six more seasons with the Cleveland Browns.

S

SALMON, LOUIS

Fullback (1900-03) ▪ Head Coach (1904) 5-10, 175 ▪ Syracuse, NY

Louis "Red" Salmon was Notre Dame's first great running back. He scored 36 career touchdowns, which stood as a school record until 1985 when it was broken by Allen

Pinkett. He still holds the record for points per game in a single season: 11.7 in 1903. Salmon scored 105 points in nine games, a statistic that takes on greater weight when you consider that each touchdown was, at that time, worth only five points.

Salmon started at halfback in his freshman year and then started at fullback for three years. He was team captain in 1902 and 1903. The Fighting Irish compiled a record of 28-6-4 during his time in South Bend, including an 8-0-1 mark in 1903; they did not allow a single point that entire season, and Salmon was named third-team All-America by the Walter Camp Foundation.

In an era when touchdowns were worth only five points, Louis "Red" Salmon scored 105 points in just nine games. After graduating from Notre Dame, he served one year as the team's head coach.

Salmon graduated with a degree in civil engineering in 1904. That same year he was named head coach of the Notre Dame football team. He held the position for just one season, leading the Irish to a 5-3 record.

SAVOLDI, JOE

Fullback (1928-30) ▪ 5-11, 200 ▪ Three Oaks, MI

Joe Savoldi's career—both during and after his time at Notre Dame—was unique. An elusive running back, he made the varsity in 1928, his sophomore year, and led the team in rushing as a junior with 597 yards on 112 carries. What should have been a marvelous senior year, however, ended in ignominy. With three games remaining, Savoldi was asked to withdraw from school. The reason: He had secretly married his girlfriend.

There was, of course, no specific rule prohibiting married players from attending Notre Dame or representing the football team; however, it was understood at the time that the Catholic church did not approve of secret marriages or marriages outside the church. Savoldi was a Catholic, and Notre Dame was a Catholic university. By violating a law of the church, he had heaped embarrassment upon the university. So in October of 1930, he was asked to leave.

Savoldi immediately signed with the Chicago Bears, but his professional career lasted only one season. In later years, secrecy proved to be his specialty. He served in the Office of Strategic Services during World War II and then became a professional wrestler, billing himself as "The Mystery Man of World War II."

SCANNELL, TIM

Offensive Guard (1982-85) ▪ 6-4, 278 ▪ State College, PA

Although Tim Scannell's father, Bob, was a vice president at Penn State University, the family's ties to Notre Dame ran much deeper. Bob Scannell, after all, had earned three monograms as an end for the Fighting Irish in the 1950s; and Tim's grandfather, John, was chairman of the physical education department for four decades. So when it came time to choose a college, Tim Scannell opted for South Bend, Indiana, over State College, Pennsylvania.

Scannell was a three-year starter at offensive guard, earning second-team All-America honors from *Football News* in his senior year. He also served as a team captain.

SCARPITTO, BOB

Halfback (1958-60) ▪ 5-11, 180 ▪ Rahway, NJ

One of Notre Dame's best all-around players in the late 1950s, Bob Scarpitto came to South Bend from Rahway, New Jersey. He earned his first varsity letter in 1958 as a second-string running back. The next year, as a junior, he moved into the starting lineup and became the team's leading scorer (48 points) and receiver (15 receptions for 297 yards and four touchdowns) and logged more playing time (288 minutes) than any other halfback.

In 1960 Scarpitto again led the Fighting Irish in scoring (with 30 points). He was second in receiving (eight receptions for 164 yards) and third in rushing (51 for 228). He also led the team in kickoff returns (10 for 230).

Scarpitto also played baseball at Notre Dame, but football was his first love. He played professionally with the San Diego Chargers, Denver Broncos, and Boston Patriots.

SCHAEFER, DON

Quarterback/Fullback (1953-55) ▪ 5-11, 190 ▪ Pittsburgh, PA

A third-string quarterback in his sophomore year, Don Schaefer enjoyed far greater success when he moved to fullback for his last two seasons at Notre Dame.

Schaefer led the Fighting Irish with 766 yards on 141 carries in 1954—an average of 5.4 yards per attempt. In 1955 he rushed for 638 yards on 145 carries—again best on the team. He was also third in scoring with 34 points and fourth in receiving with 6 catches for 36 yards. After the season he received first-team All-America honors from the International News Service, *Collier's*, and *Look*, as well as second-team honors from the Associated Press and *The Sporting News*. He was also a first-team Academic All-American.

Schaefer was a third-round draft pick of the Philadelphia Eagles in 1956. His NFL career, however, lasted just one season.

SCHOEN, TOM

Safety (1965-67) ▪ 5-11, 178 ▪ Euclid, OH

When Tom Schoen arrived at Notre Dame in the fall of 1964, he dreamed of becoming a star quarterback. Before he left South Bend he did become a star; and he did play quarterback. But the two accomplishments did not occur simultaneously.

As a sophomore, in 1965, Schoen served as a backup to starting quarterback Bill Zloch. The following year, with the arrival of Terry Hanratty, it became apparent that there would be no room at quarterback for Schoen. So coach Ara Parseghian decided to take advantage of Schoen's natural athletic ability and move him to the defensive backfield. It was a move that proved beneficial to everyone involved. Schoen became a two-year starter for the Fighting Irish. In 1966 he had seven interceptions, two touchdowns, and led the team in punt return yardage. In sum, he was a pivotal player on a Notre Dame team that captured the national championship.

Although the Fighting Irish lost two games the following year and failed to defend their title, Schoen had another outstanding season: 52 tackles and four interceptions, and 42 punt-returns for 447 yards and one touchdown. In a game against Pittsburgh, he set an NCAA record for punt yardage with 167 yards on nine returns. Not surprisingly, when the season ended Schoen was a consensus All-American and was invited to play in the East-West Shrine Game. He was drafted in the eighth round of the 1968 NFL Draft by the Cleveland Browns. After retiring from professional football, Schoen took a job as a manufacturing representative for Easco Sports Sales.

SCHOLTZ, BOB

Center (1957-59) ▪ 6-2, 240 ▪ Tulsa, OK

A three-year starter at center, Bob Scholtz was one of the most reliable players on the admittedly mediocre Notre Dame teams of the late 1950s. He was third on the team in tackles as a junior, with 51 in 285 minutes of playing time. As a senior he led the Fighting Irish with 85 tackles.

Scholtz, an amateur pilot who graduated from Notre Dame in 1960 with a degree in electrical engineering, was a third-round draft pick of the Detroit Lions; he played for them from 1960 through 1964. He also spent two seasons with the New York Giants.

SCHRADER, JIM

Center (1951-53) ▪ 6-2, 210 ▪ Carnegie, PA

A graduate of Scott Township High School in Carnegie, Pennsylvania, Jim Schrader went on to become a two-year starter at center for Notre Dame. He played behind future All-American Art Hunter in his sophomore year but became a starter as a junior when Hunter moved to end. He also started as a senior in 1953.

Schrader was a second-round draft pick of the Washington Redskins in 1955. He also played for the Philadelphia Eagles in a professional career that lasted nearly a decade.

SCHWARTZ, MARCHMONT

Halfback (1929-31) ▪ 5-11, 167 ▪ Bay St. Louis, MS

Marchmont "Marchy" Schwartz was born in New Orleans and raised in Bay St. Louis, Mississippi, where he attended St. Stanislaus High School. He first enrolled at Loyola University in New Orleans but decided to transfer to Notre Dame after hearing Knute Rockne speak at a basketball tournament.

Schwartz was a backup to Jack Elder at left halfback on the 1929 national championship team and moved into the starting lineup in 1930. He had an impressive season, rushing for 927 yards on just 124 carries—an average of 7.5 per carry. And although he wasn't the team's quarterback, he led the Irish in passing, completing 17 of 56 passes for 319 yards and three touchdowns. His 54 points also led the team. Notre Dame won a second consecutive national championship that year, thanks in no small part to Schwartz. It was his 54-yard touchdown run in the fourth quarter that lifted the Irish to a 7-6 victory over Army in the penultimate game of the year. After the season he was a consensus All-American.

In 1931 Schwartz was a unanimous first-team All-American. He rushed for 692 yards on 146 carries and passed for 174 yards. Once again he led the Irish in scoring. He was also the team's punter (in fact, his 15 punts against Army in 1931 still stands as a Notre Dame single-game record). His finest performance came against Carnegie Tech when he rushed for 188 yards and two touchdowns on 23 carries. At the time of his graduation he was second on the school's career rushing list (behind George Gipp) with 1,945 yards.

When his playing career ended, Marchy Schwartz went into coaching, first as an assistant at Notre Dame and the University of Chicago, and later as head coach at Creighton and Stanford. He was inducted into the College Football Hall of Fame in 1974.

Career Statistics (Rushing)

YEAR	ATT.	YARDS	AVG.	TD
1929	65	326	5.0	3
1939	124	927	7.5	9
1931	146	692	4.7	5
TOTAL	335	1,945	5.8	17

SCIBELLI, JOE
Tackle (1958) • 6-0, 225 • Springfield, MA

Joe Scibelli played just one year of football at Notre Dame. While sharing the left tackle spot with Frank Geremia in 1958, he had 23 tackles.

A tenth-round draft pick of the Los Angeles Rams in 1961, he spent 14 years in the NFL.

SCOTT, VINCE
Guard (1944-46) • 5-8, 195 • Hamilton, Ontario

Although his college career was unspectacular, Vince Scott became a successful professional football player after graduating from Notre Dame. He earned only one monogram, as a second-string guard in his junior year. As a senior, in 1946, when dozens of players returned from the armed services, he was relegated to reserve status.

In 1947, though, Scott signed a professional contract with the Buffalo Bills of the All-America Football Conference. When the AAFC folded in 1949, Scott signed with the Hamilton Tiger-Cats of the Canadian Football League. He played with Hamilton for 14 years before retiring in 1963. In 1982 he was inducted into the Canadian Football Hall of Fame.

SCULLY, JOHN

Center/Offensive Tackle (1977-80) ▪ 6-5, 255 ▪ Huntington, NY

After two years as a backup tackle, John Scully was given the difficult task of succeeding All-American Dave Huffman at center in 1979. He handled the assignment impressively, starting 11 games and earning a reputation as one of the more promising offensive linemen in the country.

The following year, as a senior tri-captain, Scully was not merely one of the best centers in the country—he was *the* best. A consensus first-team All-American, he played in the East-West Shrine Game and was a fourth-round draft choice of the Atlanta Falcons. He played with Atlanta until his retirement in 1990.

SEILER, PAUL

Offensive Tackle (1964-66) ▪ 6-4, 235 ▪ Algona, IA

A starting offensive tackle in 1966 when the Fighting Irish were consensus national champions, Paul Seiler came to South Bend from Algona, Iowa, where he was a star lineman for Bishop Garrigan High School. Although he was a second-string tackle in his sophomore and junior years, he did not earn a monogram until he was a senior when he succeeded Bob Meeker as the starting left tackle.

In light of his relative lack of experience, Seiler's performance as a senior was extraordinary. The Irish led the nation in scoring in 1966, and Seiler's line play was an important part of their success. Three of Notre Dame's starting offensive linemen earned All-America honors after the season, including Seiler, who was named to *The Sporting News*'s second team and United Press International's third team.

Seiler played in the 1967 College All-Star Game and was drafted in the first round by the New York Jets. He played with the Jets in 1967 but missed the 1968 season while serving in the military. He returned to the Jets in 1969, missed the 1970 season because of an injury, and then played with the Oakland Raiders from 1971 through 1973. He played in the World Football League for two years after leaving the NFL.

SEVEN MULES

The Notre Dame football team of 1924 was one of the greatest in the school's history. The Fighting Irish went 10-0 that year and, under seventh-year coach Knute Rockne, captured their first national championship.

The 1924 squad, of course, featured the legendary Four Horsemen—the backfield made famous by sportswriter Grantland Rice in the wake of the team's dramatic victory over Army at the Polo Grounds in New York.

But, as with any championship team, the Fighting Irish of 1924 were more than a handful of star players. The Four Horsemen may have "formed the crest of the South Bend cyclone," as Rice wrote, but they had considerable assistance. The Seven Mules were the men who opened the holes for the Four Horsemen. They toiled in the trenches, receiving far less glory (as is always the case with linemen) but no less satisfaction.

Their names were Joe Bach, tackle; Chuck Collins, end; Ed Hunsinger, end; Noble Kizer, guard; Rip Miller, tackle; Adam Walsh, center; and John Weibel, guard.

Without the Seven Mules, Notre Dame would not have won a national title, and the Four Horsemen might well have ridden into obscurity.

Miller was the last surviving member of the Seven Mules; he died in 1992.

SEYMOUR, JIM

Split End (1966-68) ▪ 6-4, 205 ▪ Berkley, MI

One of Notre Dame's all-time leading receivers, Jim Seymour grew up in Berkley, Michigan. He led his high school football team to the Detroit Catholic championship; he also starred in basketball and track. In South Bend Seymour was a three-year starter at split end. His career is forever linked with that of Terry Hanratty, who was the team's starting quarterback during those same years. In leading Notre Dame to a national championship in 1966 and a 24-4-2 overall record from 1966 through 1968, the duo became recognized as perhaps the greatest passing combination in the school's history.

Seymour's talent was apparent from the beginning. He caught 13 passes for 276 yards and three touchdowns in his first varsity game, a 26-14 victory over Purdue. It was a sensational debut; in fact, Seymour still holds the school's single-game record for pass reception yardage and shares the record for touchdowns. Both marks were set that very first day.

He went on to catch 48 passes for 862 yards and eight touchdowns in his rookie season, a performance that merited inclusion on several All-America teams. In 1967 he had 37 receptions for 515 yards and four touchdowns and was named first-team All-America by United Press International and Central Press. In 1968, as a senior, he had 53 receptions for 736 yards and four touchdowns. UPI, *The Sporting News*, the American Football Coaches Association, and the Walter Camp Foundation each named him first-team All-America.

Seymour played in the 1969 College All-Star Game and was a first-round draft pick of the Los Angeles Rams. He spent just three seasons in the NFL, all with the Chicago Bears, during which he caught 21 passes for 385 yards. He is second on Notre Dame's career receiving list with 138 catches.

Career Statistics (Receiving)

YEAR	NO.	YARDS	AVG.	TD
1966	48	862	17.9	8
1967	37	515	13.9	4
1968	53	736	13.9	4
TOTAL	138	2,113	15.3	16

SHAKESPEARE, BILL

Halfback/Punter (1933-35) ▪ 5-11, 179 ▪ Staten Island, NY

William V. Shakespeare ("The Bard," as he was affectionately known in South Bend) was one of Notre Dame's best players in the 1930s. A native of Staten Island, New York, he arrived on campus in 1932 but did not earn his first monogram until 1934, when he was a junior. Shakespeare was the team's starting left halfback; he also handled punting duties.

In 1935 Shakespeare led the Fighting Irish in rushing with 374 yards on 104 carries. He also completed 19 passes, scored four touchdowns, and averaged more than 40 yards per punt. (His 86-yard kick against Pittsburgh still stands as a school record.) His greatest achievement, though, came against Ohio State in one of the most memorable games in college football history. The Fighting Irish rallied from a 13-0 deficit in the fourth quarter to post an 18-13 victory. The winning touchdown was scored on a 19-yard pass from Shakespeare to Wayne Millner with only seconds remaining.

After the season Shakespeare received second-team All-America honors from United Press International and *The Sporting News* and first-team honors from the All-America Board. He set a Notre Dame career punting record with 3,705 yards on 91 attempts.

Shakespeare was a first-round draft choice of the NFL's Pittsburgh Pirates in 1936. He chose instead to accept a position as a sales trainee with the Thor Power Tool Company. He worked as a service engineer in New York and Los Angeles before being assigned to the company's export division in 1940. He was eventually transferred to one of Thor's subsidiaries, the Cincinnati Rubber Manufacturing Company, where he rose to become president.

Shakespeare served in the U.S. Army during World War II. He enlisted as a private, quickly achieved the rank of sergeant, and then entered the Infantry Officers Candidate School in Fort Benning, Georgia. He was awarded the Bronze Star for his conduct at the Battle of the Bulge.

Bill Shakespeare died in 1974. He was inducted into the College Football Hall of Fame in 1983.

Career Statistics (Punting)

YEAR	ATT.	YARDS	AVG.
1933	5	266	53.2
1934	41	1,638	40.0
1935	45	1,801	40.0
TOTALS	**91**	**3,705**	**40.7**

SHANNON, DAN
Linebacker/End (1951-54) ▪ 6-0, 190 ▪ Chicago, IL

At Mount Carmel High School in Chicago, Dan Shannon was one of coach Terry Brennan's best players. The two were reunited in 1954 when Brennan became the head coach at Notre Dame. Shannon was a senior co-captain then, and he helped make Brennan's transition to the college game a smooth one.

In fact, the Fighting Irish went 9-1 and were ranked fourth in the Associated Press final poll-the best performance by any of Brennan's teams. Shannon, a starting end, was one of the premier players on that squad. He caught 11 passes for 215 yards and three touchdowns and was named second-team All-America by *The Sporting News*.

The highlight of Shannon's career, though, came in November of 1952 when he forced a fumble in the closing minutes of a game against fourth-ranked Oklahoma. The Irish recovered the fumble and went on to upset the Sooners, 28-21.

Shannon was drafted by the Chicago Bears but did not play in the NFL.

SHAW, LAWRENCE
Tackle (1919-21) ▪ 6-0, 185 ▪ Lawrence, IA

Lawrence "Buck" Shaw had virtually no high school football experience yet went on to become an All-American at Notre Dame and, later, an immensely successful coach.

When he was 10 years old, Shaw's family moved to Stuart, Iowa, where football had been abolished because of a fatality on the playing field. The sport was not reinstated until 1917, Shaw's senior year. He played just three high school games, but that was enough to pique his interest. The following year, when he arrived at Creighton University, he decided to try out for the football team. Shaw played only one game that season, thanks to a flu epidemic that wiped out most of Creighton's schedule.

In 1919 Shaw transferred to Notre Dame and, as a walk-on, became a second-string tackle behind Frank Coughlin. He was elevated to starter in 1920 and in 1921 earned second-team All-America honors from *Football World*.

Despite his success as a player, Shaw did not really consider coaching as a career until late in his senior year when Knute Rockne told him of a few openings and offered to give him a recommendation. Shaw's first job was line coach at the University of Nevada. In 1924 he became head coach at North Carolina State, and from 1925 through 1928 he was head coach at Nevada. In 1929 he became an assistant at Santa Clara, and in 1936 he was promoted to head coach. In seven seasons Shaw led Santa Clara to two Sugar Bowl victories. During one memorable stretch, the team won 16 consecutive games, including 11 without allowing a touchdown.

Santa Clara dropped football in 1942, and Shaw eventually moved on to the professional ranks. In 1946 he became the first coach of the San Francisco 49ers. Shaw remained with the 49ers until 1955. In 1956 he returned to the college game as the first head of the U.S. Air Force Academy. Two years later, though, he was back in the NFL, coaching the Philadelphia Eagles. The Eagles won just two games in Shaw's first season, but in 1960 they captured a divisional title with a 10-2 record. In the NFL championship game they upset Vince Lombardi's Green Bay Packers, 17-13. A few months later, Shaw announced his retirement.

In 1972 Buck Shaw was inducted into the College Football Hall of Fame. He died in 1977, at the age of 77.

SHELLOGG, ALEC
Right Tackle (1936-37) ▪ 6-1, 209 ▪ New Castle, PA

Alec Shellogg was a starter at right tackle in his junior year (1937). He was elected team captain for the 1938 season but withdrew from school unexpectedly in late January. Shellogg gave no explanation for his withdrawal, and university officials said only that he (and his twin brother, Fred, who also withdrew) had committed a "rules infraction." In keeping with the policy of the time, they declined further comment.

Shellogg later played professionally with the NFL's Brooklyn Dodgers and Chicago Bears.

SHILLELAGH
Shillelagh is a town in Ireland famous for its tall and sturdy oak trees. Hence, the dictionary definition: shillelagh—a heavy club or cudgel. This is another bit of Irish folklore that has been embraced by the Notre Dame community. Each year the Fighting

Irish play games against USC and Purdue. The winner of each game takes possession of a shillelagh symbolic of victory.

Joe McLaughlin, a merchant seaman and longtime Notre Dame football fan, brought one of the shillelaghs from Ireland and donated it as a trophy. Since 1957, it has been presented annually to the winner of the Notre-Purdue game.

The story behind the jewel-encrusted shillelagh presented to the winner of the Notre Dame-USC game is a bit more interesting—and harder to swallow, since it has never been verified. Supposedly, it was brought to South Bend from Ireland by Howard Hughes's personal pilot. Regardless of its origin, the trophy is a beauty. It is adorned with emerald-studded shamrocks reflecting the date and score of each Notre Dame victory; each USC victory is symbolized by a ruby-studded Trojan helmet.

The words "From the Emerald Isle" are engraved on the shillelagh.

SIMMONS, FLOYD

Halfback/Fullback (1945-47) ▪ 6-0, 195 ▪ Portland, OR

At Jefferson High School in Portland, Oregon, Floyd Weston Simmons played baseball, hockey, and track in addition to football. He entered Notre Dame in 1945 after serving 21 months in the U.S. Navy and began his college football career as a reserve halfback. In 1946 he contributed to Notre Dame's national championship by rushing for 229 yards on 36 carries (an average of 6.4 yards); he scored two touchdowns.

In 1947 Simmons was moved to fullback where he backed up John Panelli. He gained 73 yards on 26 carries and caught four passes for 32 yards. In addition to playing football, Simmons competed in the javelin and shot put for the Fighting Irish track and field team. He played professional football with the Chicago Rockets of the All-America Football Conference in 1948.

SITKO, EMIL

Running Back (1946-49) ▪ 5-8, 175 ▪ Fort Wayne, IN

Emil "Red" Sitko never experienced defeat at Notre Dame. He had the good fortune to play on some of the greatest Fighting Irish teams in history. And it's fair to say that he contributed significantly to the program's accomplishments during that time.

Although small in stature, Sitko was a huge presence in the Notre Dame backfield. As a junior and senior he was a consensus All-American, and in 1949 he finished eighth in voting for the Heisman Trophy. One of his teammates, Leon Hart, won the award that year.

Sitko entered Notre Dame after serving in World War II and immediately landed a spot in the starting lineup. But it wasn't until his sophomore year, in 1947, that he displayed signs of greatness. As the starting right halfback, he carried the ball only 60 times but accumulated 426 yards, an average of more than seven yards per carry. Still, Sitko was overshadowed by such stars as George Connor, Bill Fischer, and Heisman Trophy winner John Lujack, who led the Fighting Irish to a second consecutive national championship under coach Frank Leahy.

Sitko led the team in rushing in 1948 with 742 yards and nine touchdowns on 129 carries. He also caught seven passes for 70 yards. In 1949 he picked up 712 yards on 120 carries and won the Walter Camp Trophy as the outstanding college player in the nation. He also played a pivotal role in Notre Dame's drive toward another national championship. Sitko finished his career with 2,226 yards rushing—second only to George Gipp on the school's all-time list (he is currently seventh). He had a brief professional career, playing for three years with the San Francisco 49ers and Chicago Cardinals.

Emil Sitko died on December 15, 1973. He was elected to the College Football Hall of Fame in 1984.

Another famous Notre Dame "Red," Emil Sitko was a two-time consensus All-American. He was instrumental in the Fighting Irish's national champion wins in 1946, '47, and '49.

Career Statistics

YEAR	ATT.	YARDS	AVG.	TD
1946	54	346	6.4	3
1947	60	426	7.1	4
1948	129	742	5.8	9
1949	120	712	5.9	9
TOTAL	362	2,226	6.1	25

SKOGLUND, BOB

End (1944-46) ▪ 6-1, 198 ▪ Chicago, IL

When Bob Skoglund was just an 11-year-old boy, he spent a memorable Saturday afternoon sitting on the Notre Dame bench. The visit had been arranged by his older brother, Len, who was the team's starting wide receiver at the time. The younger Skoglund was duly impressed. After a standout career at Loyola Academy in Chicago—where he earned varsity letters in football, track and boxing—he chose the obvious path and enrolled at Notre Dame.

A serious student, Skoglund skipped freshman football in the fall of 1943 so that he could concentrate on his classwork, a decision that at once impressed and aggravated head coach Frank Leahy. But by the middle of the second semester Skoglund was an A-student, so he decided to join the Fighting Irish for spring football practice. Before long he had established himself there as well. He earned his first monogram in 1944, backing up Zeke O'Connor at left end. The next year he became a starter and led the team in receiving with nine catches for 100 yards. With the arrival of Jim Martin (a future All-American) and Leon Hart (a future Heisman Trophy winner) in 1946, however, Skoglund had to settle for a bit less playing time.

Due to relaxed wartime eligibility rules, Skoglund could have played one more season. He chose instead to complete his degree and accept an offer to play for the Green Bay Packers. Sadly, a kidney infection took his life in 1949. He was 24 years old.

SMAGALA, STAN
Defensive Back (1986-89) ▪ 5-11, 186 ▪ Burbank, CA

An all-city tailback at St. Laurence High School in Burbank, California, Stan Smagala went on to become a three-year starter at cornerback for the Fighting Irish. Although not particularly big, Smagala had excellent speed and quickness and deceptive hitting ability. One of the highlights of his career was a 64-yard interception return for a touchdown against USC. The play helped spark eventual national champion Notre Dame to a 27-10 victory in the final game of the 1988 regular season.

Smagala played with the Dallas Cowboys in 1990 and the Pittsburgh Steelers in 1992 and 1993.

SMITH, CHRIS
Fullback/Tailback/Linebacker (1981-84) ▪ 6-2, 231 ▪ Cincinnati, OH

In Notre Dame's 1983 Liberty Bowl victory over Boston College, junior fullback Chris Smith ran for 104 yards on 18 carries. It was a performance that clearly illustrated his versatility, for Smith had previously been known primarily as a blocking back.

There might have been many more 100-yard games if not for the fact that he shared the backfield with Allen Pinkett, Notre Dame's all-time leading rusher. As it was, though, Smith was largely overshadowed throughout his career. After rushing for 421 yards on 77 carries as a junior, he gained 260 yards on 61 carries as a senior in 1984. Both times he was second on the team behind Pinkett.

A gifted all-around athlete, Smith played tailback as a freshman and linebacker as a sophomore before settling in at fullback in 1983.

SMITH, IRV

Tight End (1989-92) ▪ 6-4, 246 ▪ Browns Mills, NJ

A superior blocker and receiver, Irvin Martin Smith was born in Trenton, New Jersey, and grew up in Browns Mills. He played linebacker, free safety, and tight end at Pemberton Township High School and was a *Parade* All-American in his senior year.

As a second-string tight end at Notre Dame, Smith caught a total of only eight passes in his first three seasons; however, he was technically sound—especially when blocking—and it was only a matter of time before his numbers began to improve.

With the graduation of All-American Derek Brown in 1992, Smith got his chance. He started every game as a senior, caught 20 passes for 262 yards and two touchdowns, and led all receivers in minutes played (257:34). The team's leading receiver (three catches for 38 yards) in a 28-3 Cotton Bowl victory over Texas A&M, he was named second-team All-America by the Newspaper Enterprise Association and honorable mention All-America by *Football News*. A few months later Smith was drafted in the first round by the New Orleans Saints.

SMITH, JOHN

Guard (1925-27) ▪ 5-9, 165 ▪ Hartford, CT

A member of the College Football Hall of Fame, John "Clipper" Smith was born on December 12, 1905, in Hartford, Connecticut. He was captain of his high school team in 1923 and enrolled at Notre Dame in the fall of 1924. According to popular legend, when Fighting Irish coach Knute Rockne was first introduced to Smith, he was unimpressed. "You're too small to play football," the coach reportedly said.

But Smith was not easily discouraged. He earned a monogram as a backup guard in 1925 and became a starter in 1926. As a senior, in 1927, he served as captain of a team that went 7-1-1. A smart, aggressive player who used quickness to compensate for a lack of size, Smith was a consensus All-American in 1927, earning first-team honors from the Associated Press, United Press, the International News Service, and *Collier's*. It was in *Collier's* that noted sportswriter Grantland Rice wrote of Smith, "There were fewer outstanding guards . . . Captain Smith of Notre Dame, one of the fast, alert, aggressive types, had no superior. He had to face a killing schedule, and yet his play remained high class."

Smith was also an outstanding student, graduating in the top 10 percent of his class. He worked as an assistant coach at Notre Dame while completing requirements for his law degree and later worked as an assistant at Trinity College and Georgetown University before accepting a position as head football coach and athletic director at North Carolina State. He moved on to Duquesne in 1935 and pulled off one of the biggest upsets of the 1936 season when his team defeated perennial national power

Pittsburgh, 7-0. Duquesne won seven of nine games that season, including a 13-12 victory over Mississippi State in the Orange Bowl.

Smith also coached at Villanova before leaving football to take a position with the Pratt and Whitney Aircraft Corporation in his hometown of Hartford. He was inducted into the College Football Hall of Fame in 1975.

SMITH, RICHARD

Guard/Fullback (1925-26) ▪ 5-11, 195 ▪ Combined Lock, WI

Richard "Red" Smith was a second-string guard in 1925. The following season he played both guard and fullback, though he did not start at either position. He earned two monograms at Notre Dame.

As a professional, Smith played quarterback for the Green Bay Packers (1927, 1929), New York Yankees (1928), Newark Tornadoes (1930), and New York Giants (1931). He eventually went into coaching. In 1936 he was named head coach of the Boston Shamrocks of the first American Football League, and he later joined the Packers as a line coach.

SMITH, ROD

Defensive Back/Flanker (1988-91) ▪ 6-0, 186 ▪ St. Paul, MN

One of the fastest players ever to wear a Notre Dame uniform, Rod Smith began his career as a flanker before switching to the defensive secondary in his sophomore year. He made the move seem almost effortless, playing more than 96 minutes and starting three games at cornerback in 1989. The following year, as a junior, he started four games and had 29 tackles.

As a senior, in 1991, Smith played both cornerback and strong safety, accumulating more than 284 minutes of playing time. He was second on the team (behind Demetrius DuBose) with 69 tackles; he also had three interceptions. Perhaps the best performance of his career came in a 39-28 victory over Florida in the 1992 Sugar Bowl; he had a career-high 18 tackles.

Smith was a second-round draft pick of the New England Patriots in 1992. After three seasons with the Patriots, he played with the Carolina Panthers in 1995 and the Minnesota Vikings in 1996.

An outstanding all-around athlete, Smith was the 1987 Minnesota state high school champion in the 100 meters, 200 meters, and long jump. He also competed on the track team at Notre Dame for two years.

SMITH, TONY
Split End (1989-91) ▪ 6-2, 191 ▪ Gary, IN

An all-state receiver and punter at Roosevelt High School in Gary, Indiana, Anthony Duane Smith did not play on the Notre Dame varsity as a freshman; however, by the time he was a senior, he was the team's leading receiver.

Smith improved in each of his three seasons with the Fighting Irish. He had two receptions in 1989 and 15 in 1990. As a senior, in 1991, he caught 42 passes for 789 yards and four touchdowns and was named honorable mention All-America by *Football News*. In Notre Dame's 39-28 victory over Florida in the 1992 Sugar Bowl, he caught seven passes for 79 yards.

Smith played with the Kansas City Chiefs in 1992.

SMITHBERGER, JIM
Defensive Back (1965-67) ▪ 6-1, 1990 ▪ Grundy, VA

As captain of the Welch High School football team in 1963, Jim Smithberger was named West Virginia's player of the year. He earned his first monogram in 1965 as a second-string safety playing behind All-American Nick Rassas. In 1966, as a junior, he was moved to defensive back and became a starter on one of Notre Dame's best teams. Smithberger had 54 tackles and four interceptions in 261 minutes of playing time as the Fighting Irish went unbeaten and captured the national championship. He was also named honorable mention Academic All-America.

In his senior year Smithberger had 41 tackles and two interceptions; he also broke up seven passes. *The Sporting News* named him second-team All-America, and he was a first-team Academic All-American. Although a fifth-round draft pick of the Philadelphia Eagles in 1968, Smithberger did not play in the NFL.

SNOW, JACK
End/Flanker (1962-64) ▪ 6-2, 215 ▪ Long Beach, CA

An all-city baseball and football player at St. Anthony's High School in Long Beach, California, Jack Snow came to Notre Dame in the fall of 1961. The following year, as a sophomore split end, he made the varsity but played sparingly and failed to earn a monogram.

In 1963, however, Snow's playing time increased dramatically. While dividing time between split end and flanker, he caught six passes for 82 yards (second on the team). He also had 21 tackles and one interception as a defensive back and averaged better than 38 yards per attempt as a punter.

Two major changes in 1964 had a significant impact on Snow's career: the advent of two-platoon football, which allowed him to concentrate on offense, and the emer-

Jack Snow was a versatile player, excelling on both offense and defense. After graduating from Notre Dame, he spent eleven years with the Los Angeles Rams.

gence of John Huarte as the best quarterback in college football. Huarte won the Heisman Trophy on the strength of a performance that included 16 touchdown passes and 114 completions for 2,062 yards. More than half the time, his target was Jack Snow. With 60 catches for 1,114 yards and nine touchdowns, Snow was the NCAA's second-leading receiver. He also set single-season school records for yardage, receptions, and touchdowns. One of his best efforts came in a season-opening 31-7 victory over Wisconsin; he caught nine passes for a school-record 217 yards and two touchdowns.

Snow, a consensus first-team All-American, was fifth in voting for the Heisman Trophy in 1964. A few months later he was drafted in the first round by the Los Angeles Rams, with whom he would spend his entire 11-year career. One of the Rams' all-time leading receivers, he caught 340 passes for 6,012 yards and 45 touchdowns. He became a broadcaster when his playing career ended.

SNOWDEN, JIM
Fullback/Tackle (1961, 1963-64) ▪ 6-4, 235 ▪ Youngstown, OH

A four-sport star at East Youngstown High School, Jim Snowden at first seemed to make the transition to college football with relative ease. He was Notre Dame's fourth-leading rusher in 1961 with 169 yards on 32 carries. He sat out the 1962 season, and when he returned in 1963 he was used primarily as a backup defensive tackle. He played 115 minutes and had 15 tackles.

In 1964, as a senior, Snowden was a second-string offensive tackle. His talent was spotted by numerous NFL scouts, however, and he was drafted in the fifth round by the Washington Redskins and Kansas City Chiefs. He played tackle and defensive end for the Redskins from 1965 through 1971.

SPANIEL, FRANK
Halfback (1947-49) ▪ 5-10, 184 ▪ Vandergrift, PA

Together with Emil Sitko and Larry Coutre, Frank Spaniel gave the Fighting Irish the most potent rushing attack in college football in 1949.

A reserve in his first two years on the varsity, Spaniel assumed a more important role as a senior with the graduation of three-year starter Terry Brennan. He met the challenge impressively, rushing for 496 yards on 80 carries (a 6.2-yard average) and scoring 42 points. He was third on the team in both categories. He was also fourth in receiving (16 receptions for 212 yards and three touchdowns) and second in kickoff and punt return yardage.

Spaniel played for the Baltimore Colts and Washington Redskins in 1950, his only year in the NFL.

SPORTS HERITAGE HALL

Located in the Joyce Center, the Sports Heritage Hall represents a history of Notre Dame athletics. Organized by decade, the display includes the name of every athlete who has ever won a monogram at Notre Dame—in any sport. It also features rare photographs, trophies, and other memorabilia.

The Sports Heritage Hall was donated to the school by the Notre Dame National Monogram Club in 1988.

STAMS, FRANK

Defensive End/Linebacker/Fullback ▪ (1984-88) 6-4, 237 ▪ Akron, OH

After rushing for more than 2,300 yards at St. Vincent-St. Mary High School in Akron, Ohio, Frank Stams accepted a scholarship to Notre Dame, where he hoped to become a great college running back. Instead, he became a great defensive end on one of Notre Dame's greatest teams: the 1988 national championship squad.

Of course, the trip took some time. Stams did indeed begin his college career in the backfield: He was the team's starting fullback as a sophomore in 1985. The following year, though, Lou Holtz took over as head coach and Stams began making the transition to defense. A broken leg suffered during spring practice forced him to miss virtually the entire 1986 season, but he played in 11 games in 1987, backing up Darrell "Flash" Gordon at outside linebacker.

As a senior in 1988 Stams started all 12 games at defensive end. The speed and agility that had made him an outstanding fullback served him well in his new position: He had 51 tackles and seven sacks and was named Lineman of the Year by the Moose Krause Chapter of the National Football Foundation. A consensus All-American, he earned first-team recognition from the Associated Press, United Press International, and *Football News*.

A second-round NFL draft choice, Stams played with the Los Angeles Rams (1989-91), Cleveland Browns (1992-94), and Carolina Panthers (1995-96).

STEINKEMPER, BILL
Tackle (1934-36) ▪ 6-2, 210 ▪ Chicago, IL

Bill Steinkemper was a three-year starter on the varsity at DePaul Academy in Chicago, where he received all-state honors as a fullback. He was switched to tackle at Notre Dame and earned his first monogram in his sophomore year. In 1936, as a senior, he was the team's starting left tackle.

Steinkemper played with the Chicago Bears in 1943.

STICKLES, MONTY
End (1957-59) ▪ 6-4, 225 ▪ Poughkeepsie, NY

A two-time All-American, Monty Stickles was one of the most accomplished ends in Notre Dame history. He broke into the starting lineup in 1957, his first year on the varsity, and was the team's second-leading receiver with 11 receptions for 183 yards and three touchdowns; his 32 points (he also kicked 11 PATs and one field goal) was best on the team. With 27 tackles, he also proved himself to be a capable defensive player.

In 1958 Stickles led the Fighting Irish in scoring (60 points), receiving (20 receptions for 328 yards and 7 touchdowns), and minutes played (358). After the season he was named first-team All-America by *The Sporting News*.

Stickles was Notre Dame's third-leading receiver in 1959 with 11 receptions for 285 yards and two touchdowns. He also kicked 16 extra points and three field goals for a total of 37 points. On defense he had another superior season, recording 52 tackles (fourth on the team). He was named first-team All-America by *The Sporting News* and United Press International and second-team All-America by the Associated Press.

Stickles finished his career with 42 receptions for 746 yards and 12 touchdowns. He kicked 42 field goals and made 110 tackles. In 1960 he was invited to play in the College All-Star Game and the East-West Shrine Game. He was a first-round draft choice of the San Francisco 49ers in 1960. He played with the 49ers for eight years before joining the New Orleans Saints for one season. He later returned to San Francisco and took a job as a marketing executive with the 49ers.

Career Statistics (Receiving)

YEAR	REC.	YARDS	AVG.	TD
1957	11	183	16.6	3
1958	20	328	16.4	7
1959	11	235	21.3	2
TOTAL	42	746	17.8	12

STONEBREAKER, MICHAEL
Linebacker (1986, 1988, 1990) ▪ 6-1, 228 ▪ River Ridge, LA

Although his college career was twice interrupted, Michael Stonebreaker is generally considered one of Notre Dame's best linebackers.

After a stellar career at John Curtis High School in River Ridge, Louisiana (he was named the state's defensive MVP in his senior year), Stonebreaker came to South Bend in the fall of 1986. He appeared in 10 games as a freshman, with his playing time increasing each week (he had 19 of his 21 tackles in the last five games). Expected to challenge for a starting job as a sophomore, Stonebreaker instead sat out the season because of academic difficulties. By the time he returned in 1988, he had developed into one of the best linebackers in the country. He was second on the team with 104 tackles and earned first-team All-America honors from the Associated Press, the Walter Camp Foundation, the Newspaper Enterprise Association, *College and Pro Football Newsweekly*, and *Football News*. He also finished third in voting for the Butkus Award, presented annually to college football's top linebacker.

Stonebreaker missed the 1989 season after suffering a broken kneecap and a dislocated hip in an auto accident. By 1990, however, he had recovered fully. He had a team-high 95 tackles and was a consensus first-team All-American. As in 1988, he finished third in voting for the Butkus Award.

The Chicago Bears drafted Stonebreaker in the ninth round in 1991. He played with the Bears in 1991 and the Atlanta Falcons in 1993 and 1994.

STREETER, GEORGE
Safety (1985-88) ▪ 6-2, 212 ▪ Chicago, IL

George Streeter was a starter in the Notre Dame secondary for the better part of three seasons. He broke into the lineup midway through his sophomore year after strong safety Brandy Wells suffered a knee injury. Streeter finished the 1986 season with 44 tackles. The next year he had 56 tackles and was second in minutes played among members of the defense. As a senior, in 1988, he started in all 12 games and had 49 tackles and three interceptions. He logged more minutes (276:21) than any other defensive player and was named honorable mention All-America by *Football News* and *The Sporting News*.

Streeter played with the Chicago Bears in 1989 and the Los Angeles Raiders in 1990.

STROHMEYER, GEORGE
Center (1946-47) ▪ 5-9, 195 ▪ McAllen, TX

George Strohmeyer grew up in McAllen, Texas, near the Mexican border. At home Strohmeyer had been a sensational athlete, earning 24 varsity letters in four years of high school competition. He was an all-state selection in football, basketball, baseball, and track, as well as city champion in wrestling and boxing. There was, it seemed, no sport he could not master.

George Strohmeyer was an amazing athlete who competed in football, basketball, baseball, track, wrestling, and boxing—in high school. He continued to prove his athletic prowess as a freshman at Notre Dame when he earned the position of starting center.

So when he arrived at Notre Dame in the summer of 1946, Strohmeyer carried an immense chip on his shoulder. He stunned coaches and teammates alike by boldly declaring that he would soon be the starting center. This, of course, was an outrageous prediction for a freshman. Notre Dame was the most competitive college football program in the country. And in 1946 the competition was particularly fierce. Several players had returned to campus after serving in the military. They all had talent; they had all earned monograms in the past. It was pure foolishness for a freshman to expect to be able to break into such a lineup.

Nevertheless, that is precisely what Strohmeyer did. In practice he outplayed both Bill Walsh, the starting center in 1945, and Art Statuto, a senior who had played on the varsity from 1943 through 1945. Throughout the preseason Strohmeyer impressed the coaching staff and alienated his teammates by dominating practices sessions with his hitting ability and his incessant chattering. He was cocky, but he was also capable of backing up his words. Strohmeyer did indeed become the starting center that season. He was a vital member of one of the greatest teams Notre Dame has ever produced—a team that went 8-0-1 and captured the national championship. After the season Strohmeyer was selected to virtually every All-America team.

Oddly enough, though, that season was the highlight of his career. He showed up for summer practice in 1947 unfit and overweight and lost the starting job to Walsh. The next year Strohmeyer left school and signed a professional contract with the Brooklyn Dodgers of the All-American Football Conference. He also played with the Chicago Hornets.

STUHLDREHER, HARRY
Quarterback (1922-24) ▪ 5-7, 151 ▪ Massillon, OH

The quarterback in Notre Dame's famous Four Horsemen backfield of 1924, Harry Stuhldreher grew up in Massillon, Ohio. As a boy he watched Knute Rockne play professional football with the Massillon Tigers, and the experience stayed with him through his high school years. After graduating from Kiski Prep, he enrolled at Notre

Dame and, under Rockne's guidance, began forging his own identity in the world of college football.

Small but self-assured, and blessed with a strong passing arm, Stuhldreher was a natural leader who became the team's starting quarterback midway through his sophomore season in the fall of 1922. He scored five touchdowns that year and passed for three more. In 1923 he passed for 205 yards and three touchdowns and rushed for 50 yards and two touchdowns. But it wasn't until his senior year that he received widespread recognition.

Exhibiting a confidence that was sometimes mistaken for arrogance, Stuhldreher helped direct the Fighting Irish to a 10-0 record and a national championship in 1924. He completed 25 of 33 passes for 471 yards and four touchdowns; he also rushed for two touchdowns and was the team's leading punt returner. When the season ended, Stuhldreher was a consensus All-American.

Of course, he was not the only Irish player to be so honored that year. Halfback Jim Crowley and fullback Elmer Layden also were first-team All-Americans. Together with halfback Don Miller they comprised the most famous backfield in college football history. Christened "The Four Horsemen" by sportswriter Grantland Rice in a story that appeared in the *New York Herald Tribune* on October 19, 1924, all four players eventually found their way into the

Harry Stuhldreher was the quarterback of the famous Four Horsemen of the early 1920s. A strong leader who made a memorable impact at Notre Dame, Stuhldreher continued his career in football both as a coach and an athletic director.

College Football Hall of Fame. For Stuhldreher, enshrinement came in 1958, long after he had left the game of football.

After a brief professional playing career, Stuhldreher became head coach at Villanova in 1925. In 1936 he was named director of athletics and head football coach at the University of Wisconsin. He left coaching in 1947 with a career record of 110-87-15.

Stuhldreher later went into private business with the United States Steel Corporation in Pittsburgh. A man of many talents (he authored two books and wrote short stories and nonfiction pieces that appeared in *The Saturday Evening Post*), he died in 1965 at the age of 63.

Career Statistics (Passing)

YEAR	ATT.	COMP.	YARDS	TD	PCT.
1922	15	8	68	3	.533
1923	19	10	205	3	.526
1924	33	25	471	4	.757
TOTAL	**118**	**69**	**744**	**10**	**.584**

Career Statistics (Rushing)

YEAR	ATT.	YARDS	AVG.	TD
1922	26	49	1.9	5
1923	26	50	1.9	2
1924	17	19	1.1	3
TOTAL	69	118	1.7	10

SULLIVAN, GEORGE

Tackle (1943-44, 1946-47) ▪ 6-3, 206 ▪ Walpole, MA

At Walpole High School, George Sullivan was a four-sport athlete whose greatest success came in track and field. He won the shot put at the Massachusetts state championship in 1942 and 1943, a fact that naturally increased interest on the part of college recruiters.

Sullivan eventually settled on Notre Dame, where he enrolled in the fall of 1943. He played behind starting left tackle Jim White that season and earned the first of four football monograms. In 1944 he became a starter, but he missed the 1945 season while serving in the U.S. Navy.

When Sullivan returned to South Bend in 1946, he faced tremendous competition for a starting job. Head coach Frank Leahy moved him to the other side of the line (right tackle), where he played behind Ziggy Czarobski, a future All-American. Another All-American, George Connor, started at left tackle. As a senior, Sullivan again played behind Czarobski. Before graduating, he helped the Irish win consecutive national championships. He also won three monograms in track and field and was president of both his junior class and the Monogram Club.

A sixth-round draft pick of the Boston Yanks in 1948, Sullivan played one season in the NFL.

SWATLAND, DICK

Offensive Guard (1965-67) ▪ 6-2, 235 ▪ Stamford, CT

Dick Swatland was captain of the football team at Stamford High School in 1962, but it wasn't until three years later that he played in a varsity game at Notre Dame. Like all freshmen in 1963, he was ineligible for varsity competition; in 1964 he missed the entire season with an injury. Finally, in 1965, he earned his first monogram as a reserve guard.

A few months later, at spring practice, Swatland won the Hering Award as most improved lineman. Then, in 1966, he stepped into a starting role, played 227 minutes, and helped the Fighting Irish win a national title.

Swatland was granted an additional year of eligibility because of his injury, so he returned in 1967. The team's best offensive lineman that season, he earned second-team All-America honors from *Time*. Swatland played with the Houston Oilers in 1968.

SWEENEY, CHUCK

End (1935-37) ▪ 6-0, 179 ▪ Bloomington, IL

Chuck Sweeney was a basketball and football star at Trinity High School in Bloomington, Illinois. He came to Notre Dame in the fall of 1934 after working as a seaman on a freighter during the summer months. Not content to be merely a football player, Sweeney also tried out for the basketball team. He played with the Fighting Irish as a freshman and sophomore but eventually turned all of his attention to football.

Sweeney earned his first football monogram in 1936 and became a starter in 1937. He had several outstanding games, both offensively and defensively, as he helped the Irish to a 6-2-1 record. In a 9-7 victory over Navy, for example, Sweeney tackled halfback Allan McFarland in the end zone for the winning safety. He was a consensus All-American in 1937, receiving first-team honors from both the Associated Press and United Press International.

SWISTOWICZ, MIKE

Halfback (1946-49) ▪ 5-11, 195 ▪ Chicago, IL

A graduate of Tilden Tech in Chicago, Michael Paul Swistowicz suffered a series of injuries that restricted his playing time during his first three years in a Fighting Irish uniform.

Although he earned four monograms, he did not crack the starting lineup until his senior year. Swistowicz was one of the best defensive players on a team that went 10-0 and captured a national championship in 1949. In addition to his work in the secondary, he was a capable running back who rushed for 53 yards on 11 carries.

Swistowicz was a fifth-round draft pick of the New York Bulldogs in 1950. He played for the New York Yankees and the Chicago Cardinals that year—his only season of professional football.

SYLVESTER, STEVE

Offensive Tackle (1972-74) ▪ 6-4, 241 ▪ Milford, OH

An all-state tackle at Cincinnati's Moeller High School, Steve Sylvester needed two years to adapt to the rigors of big-time college football. A little-used reserve as a sophomore in 1972, he climbed steadily up the depth chart over the course of the next few months. By the fall of 1973, as the Fighting Irish prepared for what would turn out to be a successful run toward a national title, Sylvester had become the team's starting right tackle. He led all linemen in playing time with more than 288 minutes, and his skill at opening holes was one reason Notre Dame rushed for a school-record 3,502 yards in 1973—a mark that still stands.

Sylvester returned at right tackle in 1974. And although the Irish did not successfully defend their national title, Sylvester's efforts did not go unrecognized: The Associated Press and *Football News* each named him third-team All-America. A tenth-round draft choice of the Oakland Raiders in 1975, Sylvester spent nine years in the NFL—all with the Raiders. By the time he retired, he had acquired three Super Bowl rings.

SZYMANSKI, DICK

Center/Linebacker (1951-54) ▪ 6-2, 215 ▪ Toledo, OH

When Dick Szymanski came to Notre Dame in the fall of 1951, two-platoon football was the rule rather than the exception. This meant more opportunities for more players, including freshmen.

Szymanski immediately earned a place in coach Frank Leahy's starting lineup as a middle linebacker. He moved to right linebacker in 1952 but, with the return of single-platoon football in 1953, settled for splitting time at center with Jim Schrader. He had the job to himself as a senior in 1954.

The Baltimore Colts drafted Szymanski in the second round in 1955. He spent his entire 13-year NFL career in Baltimore.

SZYMANSKI, FRANK

Center (1943-44) ▪ 6-0, 190 ▪ Detroit, MI

An all-state tackle at Detroit Northwestern High School, Frank Szymanski showed up at Notre Dame with superior credentials and hopes for a long and brilliant career. He ended up with neither, though he was hardly anonymous during his time in South Bend.

Szymanski was a second-string center who saw considerable playing time in 1943 when the Fighting Irish won the national championship with a 9-1 record under coach Frank Leahy. He entered the Navy's V-12 program after the '43 season and was not expected to play for the Irish in 1944; however, while assigned to the Naval Pre-Flight School in St. Mary's, California, he contracted rheumatic fever and was given a medical discharge. Szymanski returned to South Bend in the fall and rejoined the football team midway through the season. He played his first game, against Army, after just one week of practice. And although his presence was not enough to boost the Irish to victory (they lost to the Cadets—who went on to win the national championship behind running backs Glen Davis and Doc Blanchard—by a score of 59-10), he was given a hero's welcome.

Notre Dame did not lose another game that season and finished with an 8-2 record. In the spring of 1945 Szymanski was named captain-elect for the upcoming season. But he did not have an opportunity to fulfill that obligation because it was discovered that he had already signed a professional contract with the Chicago Bears. Szymanski was under the impression that the contract would not become effective until after he completed his college football career. And indeed, the National Football League later determined that, since Szymanski wasn't a free agent (he had one more year of eligibility after the 1945 season), the contract was null and void. That summer, though, the Big 10 issued a ruling that declared ineligible any player who "enters into an agreement or signs a contract" with any professional team. Szymanski could have fought the ruling, but to avoid "embarrassing the university" (his words at the time), he resigned as captain and left the football team.

The Detroit Lions, still convinced of Szymanski's talent, made him the number one pick in the 1945 NFL Draft. He left the Lions after the 1947 season and later played briefly with the Green Bay Packers and Philadelphia Eagles. In 1956 he was appointed auditor general of the state of Michigan by Governor G. Mennen Williams, and in 1959 he became a probate judge of Wayne County. He held that position until his death in 1987.

T

TAYLOR, AARON
Guard/Tackle (1990-93) ▪ 6-4, 299 ▪ Concord, CA

A two-time consensus All-American, Aaron Taylor was one of the most decorated line-men in Notre Dame history. He played high school football at DeLaSalle High in Concord, California, where he not only received all-state honors in two consecutive seasons but was also a first-team pick on *USA Today's* prep All-America team in 1989.

By the time he was a sophomore, Taylor had worked his way into the Fighting Irish starting lineup as an offensive guard. He started all 12 games as a junior, in 1992, and was a consensus All-American. He was also a semifinalist for the Lombardi Award, given annually to the outstanding line-man in college football.

Taylor's senior year was even more memorable. He moved to left tackle and helped lead the Irish to an 11-1 record and a number two ranking in the national polls. When the season ended he received just about every award possible for an offensive lineman: unanimous first-team All-American; Lombardi Award winner; finalist for the Outland Trophy (given annually to the outstanding interior lineman in college football); Nick Pietrosante Award (presented to the Irish player who best exemplifies the courage, pride, and dedication of the late Irish fullback).

Offensive lineman Aaron Taylor earned every possible honor his senior year, including first-team All-America, the Lombardi Award, and the Nick Pietrosante Award. After graduating a semester early, Taylor was drafted by the Green Bay Packers.

On top of his athletic achievements, Taylor was a solid student who carried a 3.229 grade point average in the spring semester of his junior year; he graduated one semester early. A first-round pick of the Green Bay Packers, he was the sixteenth player chosen in the 1994 NFL draft.

TAYLOR, BOBBY
Cornerback (1992-94) ▪ 6-3, 201 ▪ Longview, TX

Bobby Taylor was the only returning starter in the Fighting Irish secondary in 1994. As if that weren't enough pressure, several publications—including *The Sporting News* and *Street & Smith's*—listed him as the top defensive back in the country in their preseason forecasts.

Not that he didn't deserve the attention. Throughout his career Taylor had known nothing but success. A *USA Today* and *Parade* High School All-American in 1991, he came to Notre Dame as one of the most highly recruited prep athletes in the country. In addition to his football prowess, Taylor had been an outstanding basketball player: He scored 1,225 points in high school and was named Texas 5-A Player of the Year. He also ran track—no great surprise considering his lineage: Taylor's father, Robert, was a silver medalist in the 100 meters and a member of the winning 400-meter relay team at the 1972 Olympic Games in Munich, Germany.

In his first year at Notre Dame, Taylor adapted quickly to the college game. He became a starter five games into the 1992 season and received more playing time than any other freshman. As a sophomore, in 1993, he had 51 tackles and four interceptions. He was a finalist for the Jim Thorpe Award, given annually to the NCAA's best defensive back. He was also a first-team All-America selection by the Football Writers Association of America.

As a junior Taylor was equally impressive. He had 46 tackles and one interception and proved to be a true leader. In the fifth game of the year, a 34-15 victory over Stanford, Taylor blocked one field goal, broke up a touchdown pass, and recorded six tackles. He also fractured his hand. But the injury did not cause him to miss a single game; instead, he played with a cast on his arm for three weeks. When the season was over Taylor was named Defensive Back of the Year by the Columbus Touchdown Club. He was Notre Dame's only All-American.

Taylor left school after his junior year to play professional football. He was taken by the Philadelphia Eagles in the second round of the NFL Draft.

Career Statistics

YEAR	INT.	YARDS	AVG.	TD	TACKLES
1992	0	0	0	0	37
1993	4	100	25	1	51
1994	1	38	38	0	46
TOTAL	**5**	**138**	**27.6**	**1**	**134**

TELEVISION

Notre Dame has the largest following of any team in college football, so it's not surprising that the Fighting Irish have a unique relationship with cable and network television. A total of 174 Notre Dame games have been televised nationally, dating back to a 27-21 victory over Oklahoma in 1952. The Irish have traditionally fared quite well in these games: their record, through 1995, was 116-55-3.

Of course, the networks that have chosen to broadcast Notre Dame football games have also done quite well. In fact, the three highest-rated televised college football games in history have all involved Notre Dame: Notre Dame 21, USC 21 (November 30, 1968); Notre Dame 10, Michigan State 10 (November 9, 1966); USC 38, Notre Dame 10 (November 20, 1970).

So vast and loyal is the team's following that in 1991 Notre Dame became the first school with a private network television contract. NBC paid $30 million for the privilege of broadcasting Fighting Irish home games—and not just in the United States. Included in this deal was an agreement to provide live coverage of Notre Dame home games to 60 million households in 32 countries around the world.

The five-year contract has since been extended through the year 2000.

TERLEP, GEORGE

Left Halfback (1943-44) ▪ 5-8, 166 ▪ Elkhart, IN

George Terlep was a member of Notre Dame's 1943 national championship team but did not earn a monogram. The following year, however, he split time at left halfback with Chick Maggioli. His roommate was starting halfback Bob Kelly, who led the team in rushing.

After World War II, Terlep, a member of the Navy's V-12 program, played with the Buffalo Bills and the Cleveland Browns of the All-America Football Conference.

TERRELL, PAT

Defensive Back/Split End (1986-89) ▪ 6-0, 195 ▪ St. Petersburg, FL

Patrick Christopher Terrell was an All-American wide receiver at Lakewood High School in St. Petersburg, Florida. In his junior year at Notre Dame he was switched from split end to free safety and quickly became one of the most valuable members of a defense that helped win a national championship in 1988. Terrell started six games and had 38 tackles and two interceptions.

The following year, as a senior, he started in all 13 games. He had 44 tackles and was second on the team in interceptions with five. In a 21-6 victory over Colorado in the

1990 Orange Bowl, he had nine tackles and one fumble recovery. After the season, Gannett News Service named him first-team All-America.

Terrell was a second-round draft pick of the Los Angeles Rams in 1990. After leaving the Rams in 1993, he played with the New York Jets (1994-95) and Carolina Panthers (1996).

THAYER, TOM

Offensive Lineman (1979-82) ▪ 6-5, 268 ▪ Joliet, IL

Tom Thayer was a versatile athlete who played three different positions in his three years as a starter on the offensive line. He led the offense in minutes played as a junior tackle in 1981. The following year, as a senior, he started seven games at guard and four at center. Thayer was a fourth-round draft pick in 1983. He spent eight seasons with the Chicago Bears and one with the Miami Dolphins.

THEISMANN, JOE

Quarterback (1968-70) ▪ 6-0, 170 ▪ South River, NJ

When Joe Theismann was a boy growing up in New Jersey, his family's name was pronounced "Thees-man." It wasn't until he arrived in South Bend and became one of the best quarterbacks in college football that he changed the pronunciation to "Thise-man." Actually, the metamorphosis wasn't really Theismann's idea at all; rather, it was the brainchild of the Notre Dame Sports Information Department, which was promoting Theismann as a player worthy of consideration for college football's greatest honor. Thus the publicity campaign revolved around the slogan "Theismann . . . as in Heisman."

Joe "Thees-man" became known as Joe "Thise-man" when the Notre Dame Sports Information Department developed a promotion, "Theismann . . . as in Heisman." Although he never won the coveted award, his outstanding ability did not go unnoticed: He was drafted by the Miami Dolphins in 1971 and had an outstanding professional career in the CFL

Theismann came to Notre Dame in 1967. The following year, as a sophomore, he served as a backup to Terry Hanratty. In 1969 he became a starter and quickly eased concerns that he was too small to play major college football. Although he stood only six feet tall, Theismann was strong and smart and had a quick release. He also knew how to run with the ball, which made him one of the best all-around players ever to wear a Notre Dame uniform. As a junior he passed for 1,531 yards and 13 touchdowns in leading the Fighting Irish to an 8-2-1 record. Notre Dame lost to No. 1-ranked Texas, 21-17, in the Cotton Bowl, but Theismann set records for passing yardage (231) and total yardage (279).

Theismann's senior year was exceptional. He completed 58 percent of his passes for 2,529 yards (a school record) and led Notre Dame to a 10-0-1 record. In perhaps his most memorable performance, he completed 33 of 58 passes for 526 yards against USC. He capped his college career by completing nine of 16 passes for 179 yards in a 24-11 upset of top-ranked Texas in the 1971 Cotton Bowl. Theismann finished his career with 4,411 yards passing and more than 1,000 yards rushing. He was an Academic All-American in his senior season and finished second, behind Stanford's Jim Plunkett, in voting for the Heisman Trophy.

Theismann was selected by the Miami Dolphins in the fourth round of the 1971 NFL Draft (if not for his size, he surely would have gone sooner). When he learned that the Dolphins planned to use him as a defensive back, Theismann declined their offer and signed instead with the Toronto Argonauts of the Canadian Football League. In three seasons in the CFL, he passed for more than 6,000 yards and 40 touchdowns. Along the way he managed to convince NFL teams that his size wasn't really a detriment. Theismann joined the Washington Redskins in 1974. In 1978 he became the team's starting quarterback, and for the next eight years he was one of the league's best offensive players. He led the Redskins to NFC championships in 1982 and 1983; he was also named NFL Player of the Year in '83.

Theismann's football career ended on November 18, 1985, when he suffered a compound fracture of his right leg while being tackled by New York Giants linebacker Lawrence Taylor. In 12 NFL seasons he threw for more than 25,000 yards and 160 touchdowns. After retiring from professional football, Theismann moved on to a second career as a television color commentator.

Career Statistics (Passing)

Year	Att.	Comp.	Yards	TD	Pct.
1968	49	27	451	2	.551
1969	192	108	1,531	13	.562
1970	268	155	2,529	16	.578
TOTAL	509	290	4,411	31	.569

THOMAS, BOB
Kicker (1971-73) ▪ 5-10, 178 ▪ Rochester, NY

Bob Thomas, who kicked the game-winning field goal in Notre Dame's 1973 Sugar Bowl victory, graduated from McQuaid High School in Rochester, New York, where he was an all-city selection in both football and soccer.

Thomas began kicking for the Fighting Irish in 1971. He was nearly flawless on extra points during his three-year career, hitting 98 of 101 attempts (good for third on the school's all-time percentage list). He also made 21 of 38 field goal attempts. In 1971 Thomas led the team in scoring with 36 points. He was second (behind Andy Huff) in 1972 with 55 points and first in 1973 with 70 points. He was also named first-team Academic All-America in his senior year.

But the highlight of Thomas's collegiate playing career was undoubtedly the 1973 Sugar Bowl when he kicked a 19-yard field goal with 4:26 left in the game to give the Fighting Irish a 24-23 victory over Alabama. Both teams were unbeaten coming into the game, and the victory assured Notre Dame of a national championship.

Drafted by the Los Angeles Rams in 1974, Thomas played in the NFL for 11 seasons, with stops in Chicago, New York, Detroit, and San Diego. He made 303 of 330 extra point attempts and 151 of 239 field goal attempts.

Career Statistics

YEAR	PAT	FG	POINTS
1971	21-22	5-9	36
1972	34-34	7-11	55
1973	43-45	9-18	70
TOTAL	**98-101**	**21-38**	**161**

TICKETS

Official capacity at Notre Dame Stadium (prior to the expansion that is expected to be completed in 1997) is 59,075. Since the Fighting Irish have failed to sell out only one home game since 1966, it's something of an understatement to say that seats are hard to obtain. It's not impossible, but the odds are greatly improved if one is a Notre Dame student or an influential alumnus.

Tickets to home games are distributed as follows: 20,000 to contributing alumni; 16,000 to season-ticket holders; 10,500 to Notre Dame and St. Mary's students; 5,000 to the visiting team; 2,479 to university administrators; 2,096 to box-seat holders; and 3,000 to university faculty and staff.

These are merely guidelines—on special occasions the distribution is modified. For example, one game each season is considered a "Parents' Game." On that day, the parents of any current undergraduate student are guaranteed two tickets.

In 1995 a ticket to a Notre Dame home game cost $30.

TOBIN, GEORGE

Guard (1942, 1946) ▪ 5-10, 195 ▪ Arlington, MA

George Tobin was a second-string guard in 1942. The next year he entered the Navy and became a starting guard for Iowa Pre-Flight, whose only loss in 1943 was to Notre Dame. Competition was intense when he returned to South Bend in 1946. The Irish had numerous experienced players returning after serving in the armed forces, and there simply wasn't enough playing time for everyone. So Tobin settled for being a reserve guard.

Before the start of the 1947 season, however, he was offered a contract with the NFL's New York Giants. Tobin consulted with Notre Dame coach Frank Leahy before signing. The truth, Leahy said, was this: Tobin would probably receive more playing time in New York than he would at Notre Dame. Tobin thanked the coach and accepted the offer. He played with the Giants for one season and later returned to South Bend to complete his degree.

TONEFF, BOB

Tackle (1949-51) ▪ 6-2, 230 ▪ Barberton, OH

Bob Toneff was a three-year starter and an All-American in his senior year. He entered Notre Dame in 1948 and earned his first monogram as the starting right defensive tackle on Frank Leahy's 1949 championship team. In 1950 Toneff started on both offense and defense; in 1951 he was primarily an offensive player. Clearly, though, he was one of the best offensive linemen in the country. The Associated Press named him first-team All-America, and *The Sporting News* and United Press each placed him on its second team.

Toneff was a second-round draft pick of the San Francisco 49ers in 1952. He played with the 49ers until 1958 and with the Washington Redskins from 1959 through 1964.

TONELLI, MARIO

Fullback (1936-38) ▪ 5-11, 188 ▪ Chicago, IL

After prepping at Chicago's DePaul Academy where he was an all-state running back, Mario Tonelli enrolled at Notre Dame in the fall of 1935. He was a reserve fullback in 1936, his first year on the varsity, and a starter in the 1937 season opener against Drake. A series of injuries limited his playing time for much of the year; however, in the final game of the season he scored the winning touchdown in a 20-13 victory over the University of Southern California.

As a senior Tonelli was the team's second-leading rusher with 259 yards on 42 carries—an average of 6.2 yards per carry. After graduation he signed with the Chicago

Cardinals. Tonelli entered the armed services in 1941. One year later he was among the American soldiers who fought at Bataan in the Philippines. He was part of the infamous Bataan Death March, in which U.S. and Filipino soldiers marched 200 miles in seven days without food or water.

Reported missing in action on New Year's Eve, 1942, Tonelli was released from a Japanese prisoner of war camp in 1945. Although he lost 60 pounds during his imprisonment, he eventually regained his strength and played one more season with the Cardinals. Coincidentally, his number at Notre Dame, in Chicago, and even in the last of several POW camps was 58.

TORAN, STACEY
Defensive Back (1980-83) ▪ 6-4, 206 ▪ Indianapolis, IN

At 6-4, 206 pounds, Stacey Toran had a body better suited for basketball than football. In fact, he earned all-state honors in both sports at Broad Ripple High School; and he once made a game-winning 50-foot shot at the buzzer in the semifinals of the Indiana state high school basketball tournament.

But it was football that defined Toran at Notre Dame. A four-year starter at cornerback, he was named honorable mention All-America by *The Sporting News* in 1982 after playing more than 316 minutes and finishing third on the team with 77 tackles. As a senior, in 1983, he was elected captain of the defense. Unfortunately, injuries kept him out of two games and limited his effectiveness for much of the season. He had only 23 tackles (the lowest total of his four-year career) and did not intercept a pass.

A sixth-round NFL draft choice, Toran played with the Los Angeles Raiders from 1984 through 1988.

TOUCHDOWN JESUS
On the south side of the Hesburgh Library is a 132-foot-high stone mosaic modeled after Millard Sheet's painting, *The World of Life*, depicting Christ as a teacher surrounded by his apostles and a group of saints and scholars. The mural, which can be seen from Notre Dame Stadium, portrays Christ with his hands raised above his head. And that is why it is often referred to as "Touchdown Jesus."

Touchdown Jesus is a Notre Dame hallmark. The mural is actually part of the Hesburgh Library and can be seen from the stadium.

TOWNSEND, MIKE

Defensive Back (1971-73) ▪ 6-3, 183 ▪ Hamilton, OH

Mike Townsend was one of Notre Dame's finest all-around athletes in the early 1970s. He was a two-year starter in the defensive backfield and made the Irish basketball team as a walk-on. His older brother, Willie, was a split end at Notre Dame.

In 1972, as a junior, Townsend started at left cornerback and led the nation with a school-record 10 interceptions. As a senior safety he helped lead Notre Dame to an 11-0 record and a national championship. He had 26 tackles, three interceptions, three fumble recoveries, and was a consensus All-American.

Townsend was drafted by the Minnesota Vikings in 1974 but chose instead to play for the Florida Sharks of the World Football League. He never played in the NFL.

Career Statistics

YEAR	INT.	YARDS	AVG.	TD
1971	0	0	0	0
1972	10	39	3.9	0
1973	3	47	15.7	0
TOTAL	**13**	**86**	**6.6**	**0**

TRAFTON, GEORGE

Center (1919) ▪ 6-2, 190 ▪ Chicago, IL

George Trafton was the starting center on the undefeated (9-0) 1919 Notre Dame team coached by Knute Rockne. His college career was brief, however; he was dismissed from the Fighting Irish after just one season when it was learned that he was playing semipro football on the side.

As it turned out, the loss was Notre Dame's. Trafton went on to become one of the top linemen in the early years of professional football. He started out in 1920 as a member of Decatur Staley, which became the Chicago Staleys in 1921 and the Chicago Bears in 1922.

An unapologetically tough man, Trafton earned a reputation for dirty play during his 13 seasons. It was a reputation he probably deserved. In 1920, for example, Rock Island center Harry Gunderson was so beat up that he left a game early after an encounter with Trafton. A gash over Gunderson's left eye required 11 stitches, another in his lip required two stitches, and he had a broken hand. Another Rock Island player once suffered a broken leg after running out of bounds and being tackled into a fence by Trafton. After the game, Trafton left hurriedly in a taxi cab—while still wearing his uniform—to avoid being assaulted by a mob of spectators.

"You had to be tough to stay alive in those days," Trafton would say many years later. "And believe me, bub, I lived."

A star on the George Halas-coached teams known as the Monsters of the Midway, Trafton received All-Pro honors in 1923, 1924, and 1926. He retired in 1932 after 201 games and 158 hours of playing time. In 1964 he was inducted into the Pro Football Hall of Fame.

TRIPUCKA, FRANK

Quarterback (1945-48) ▪ 6-2, 172 ▪ Bloomfield, NJ

After waiting three years for a chance to quarterback the Fighting Irish, Frank Tripucka made the most of the opportunity.

A reserve in 1945, he became John Lujack's backup in 1946 and 1947. Lujack won the Heisman Trophy in '47 but graduated in the spring of '48, leaving the job to Tripucka. He responded by completing 53 of 91 passes for 660 yards. After the season he was invited to play on the College All-Star Team.

The Philadelphia Eagles chose Tripucka in the first round of the 1949 NFL Draft. In his 15-year NFL career, he also played for the Detroit Lions, Chicago Cardinals, Dallas Texans, and Denver Broncos.

TWOMEY, TED

Tackle (1928-29) ▪ 6-1, 205 ▪ Duluth, MN

Harry Stuhldreher, quarterback for the famed Four Horsemen, once said of Ted Twomey, "He was so tough and so mean, Knute Rockne wouldn't let him scrimmage against his own teammates." Maybe so, but the Fighting Irish coach was more than happy to have Twomey in the lineup on game day. He was a two-year starter at tackle and a second-team All-American in his senior year (1929) when Notre Dame won the national championship.

When his playing days were over, Twomey began a 20-year career as an assistant coach. Among his employers were Georgia, Kentucky, Texas, and Florida. He never became a head coach, though, and in the late 1940s he left the field and went into private business.

U

UNIFORM

Although the crowd at Notre Dame Stadium seems to be awash in a sea of traditional Irish green on game days, Notre Dame's official home colors are actually gold and blue. Since Lou Holtz became head coach in 1986, the Fighting Irish have worn green jerseys just once: during a 41-24 loss to Colorado in the 1995 Fiesta Bowl.

Throughout history, though, Notre Dame has been remarkably inconsistent on this issue. In the 1920s, for example, coach Knute Rockne's varsity team wore blue, while the freshman team usually wore green. But on those rare occasions when the opponent's uniform color was also blue, Rockne would have the varsity squad switch to green simply to avoid confusion. Of course, sometimes Rockne's intentions were less benign; he was, after all, nothing if not cunning. So it was that when Notre Dame met Navy (which also wore blue) in 1927, Rockne dressed his reserves in green and sent them out as starters. The starting unit, meanwhile, sat on the bench, dressed in blue. Rockne waited until Navy scored its first touchdown, just five minutes into the game, and then summoned his starters from the sideline. Together they stripped off their blue jerseys, revealing green jerseys underneath. Then they marched onto the field to face the bewildered Midshipmen. From that moment on, the day went exactly as Rockne had hoped: Notre Dame rallied to win the game, 19-6.

The Fighting Irish frequently wore green during the 1930s, '40s, and '50s, although it was never officially adopted as the team's color; instead, teams periodically switched from green to blue—and back to green again—with little or no reason. Hugh Devore's 1963 team, for example, wore blue for its first eight games, then switched to green for the season finale against Syracuse at Yankee Stadium. The strategy backfired, and the Orangemen came away with a 14-7 victory. But Devore could hardly be faulted for trying something different—after all, Notre Dame had won only two games all season.

Ara Parseghian's teams in the 1960s and '70s always wore navy blue. Dan Devine's teams switched to green, however, in 1977, starting with a 49-19 victory over USC. Then, in 1981, first-year head coach Gerry Faust opted for royal blue jerseys with gold and white stripes on the sleeves. Three years later, in 1984, the stripes were eliminated and the color was changed to navy blue. Holtz arrived two years later and made one subtle change to the jersey: the addition of the Notre Dame logo on the shoulder. Since then the jersey has remained virtually unchanged.

The rest of the Notre Dame home uniform has undergone fewer transformations over the years, with players typically wearing gold helmets and gold pants.

URBAN, GASPER
Guard/Tackle (1943, 1946-47) ▪ 6-2, 200 ▪ Lynn, MA

An all-state lineman from Lynn Classical High School in Massachusetts, Gasper George Urban earned his first monogram at Notre Dame in 1943 as a second-string guard on a team that went 9-1 and captured the national championship. He missed the 1944 and 1945 seasons while serving in the U.S. Marine Corps during World War II but returned to campus in 1946, just in time to help the Irish win another national title.

In 1947, as a backup behind All-American tackle George Connor, Urban was part of a third national championship team. He played with the Chicago Rockets of the All-America Football Conference in 1948.

V

VAIRO, DOM
Right End (1932-34) ▪ 6-2, 196 ▪ Calumet, MI

Early in his first year at Notre Dame, Dominic Vairo reported to freshman football practice and discovered that, through some error in the equipment office, his uniform was missing. Although he denied responsibility in the incident, Vairo was charged with the cost of replacing the uniform. Unfortunately, he didn't have the money, so he left the football team.

Although his career got off to a rough start, Vairo soon proved that he belonged in South Bend. He earned his first varsity monogram as a sophomore, in 1932, and split time at left end with Wayne Millner in 1933. As a senior he switched to right end and was elected team captain.

Vairo played with the Green Bay Packers in 1935 before retiring from football.

VARRICHIONE, FRANK
Guard/Tackle (1951-54) ▪ 6-0, 210 ▪ Natick, MA

A three-year starter at tackle, Frank Varrichione came to Notre Dame from Aquinas Institute in Rochester, New York, where he spent his final year of high school. He was one of 10 children.

Varrichione played on the varsity as a freshman and became a starter at offensive guard as a sophomore in 1952. In 1953 and 1954 he was a two-way starter at tackle. In his senior year he helped lead Notre Dame to a 9-1 record under first-year coach Terry Brennan. After the season he was named first-team All-America by *The Sporting News* and second-team All-America by United Press and the International News Service.

In 1955 Varrichione was a first-round draft pick of the Pittsburgh Steelers, with whom he spent six seasons. He also played with the Los Angeles Rams for five seasons.

VASYS, ARUNAS

Linebacker (1963-65) ▪ 6-2, 220 ▪ Cicero, IL

In 1963, during his first season on the varsity, Arunas Vasys was a seldom-used end. The next year he was switched to linebacker by coach Ara Parseghian, and his playing time immediately began to increase. Vasys had 35 tackles in 1964 and 22 in 1965. He was never a first-team player—primarily because he played behind the likes of All-American Jim Lynch—but he did become a consistently productive linebacker.

Vasys, who also ran track for the Fighting Irish, played for the Philadelphia Eagles from 1966 through 1968.

VERGARA, GEORGE

Guard/End (1922-23) ▪ 6-1, 187 ▪ Bronx, NY

George Vergara began his college career at Fordham. He transferred to Notre Dame and became the starting right end in 1922, helping the Irish to an 8-1-1 record. He played guard the following season and would have been a starter on the 1924 national championship squad if not for the fact that he had already used up all of his eligibility (he had played a small amount of varsity football during his freshman year at Fordham).

Vergara completed his degree requirements while serving as freshman football coach at Notre Dame. He played for the Green Bay Packers in 1925. He later entered the field of politics and in 1956 was elected mayor of New Rochelle.

W

WADSWORTH, MIKE

Center (1963-65) ▪ Athletic Director (1995-present) ▪ Height and weight unavailable ▪ Toronto, Canada

Mike Wadsworth's appointment as athletic director of the University of Notre Dame was announced on August 1, 1994. He arrived on campus the following April and succeeded Dick Rosenthal in August of 1995. Wadsworth brought a wealth of administrative, athletic, and financial experience to the position. In fact, his background is as diverse as that of any man who has ever held the job.

A solid but not exceptional player for the Fighting Irish, Mike Wadsworth flourished in the Canadian Football League. He returned to South Bend in 1995 to succeed Dick Rosenthal as the university's athletic director.

He first became associated with Notre Dame when he arrived on campus as a freshman in the fall of 1962. The son of Canadian Football League All-Star John "Bunny" Wadsworth, Mike came to South Bend from De La Salle High School in Toronto. (His high school team lost only three games during his three years on the varsity.) Wadsworth attended Notre Dame on a football scholarship. He was not an exceptional player, but he was good enough to earn a varsity letter as a defensive lineman in 1964. Although knee injuries limited his playing time throughout his college career, Wadsworth had the good fortune to play on Ara Parseghian's first two teams at Notre Dame, which posted a combined record of 16-3-1 and laid the foundation for the national championship squad of 1966.

Wadsworth graduated from Notre Dame in the spring of 1966 with a degree in political science. He spent the next five years playing professionally in the CFL; he was even named Rookie of the Year. Simultaneously, he worked on a law degree at Osgoode Hall Law School in Toronto. Wadsworth earned a reputation for toughness and intelligence, qualities that were on display daily in the summer of 1969 when he led a boycott of training camp. His efforts helped CFL players secure a new agreement with the league that included, among other things, an improved preseason pay scale. Wadsworth later accepted an invitation to become the first president of the CFL Players' Association.

After retiring from professional football Wadsworth embarked on a career in law. He worked as an attorney—primarily in litigation—for 10 years and had the opportunity to argue several cases before the Canadian Supreme Court. Never one to be content with a single job, however, Wadsworth also pursued his love of journalism and broadcasting. He wrote columns for the *Toronto Daily Star* and provided radio and television commentary on CFL games.

In 1981 Wadsworth left the practice of law and entered the business world. He became vice president for administration of Tyco Laboratories in Exeter, New Hampshire. But even that was not enough of a challenge. While working for Tyco, Wadsworth enrolled in the Harvard Graduate School of Business. In 1984 he joined Crownx, Inc., a Canadian corporation. By 1987 he had risen to the position of senior vice president of U.S. operations for Crown Life Insurance Company. In that capacity Wadsworth managed a staff of 2,100. And he did so with dexterity, helping the company stage a remarkable turnaround (from $24 million in losses to $10 million in earnings) in just two years time.

In 1989 Wadsworth left Crownx to become Canada's ambassador to Ireland. He resided in Dublin until late 1994.

WALLACE, JOHN
End/Tackle (1923-26) ▪ 6-0, 180 ▪ Calumet City, IL

John Wallace received his first monogram in 1924 as a second-string tackle on Notre Dame's unbeaten national championship team. The next year he moved to a new position—end—and into the starting lineup. He split time with Joe Maxwell in 1926.

Wallace was an assistant coach under Knute Rockne in 1927. He played professionally with the Chicago Bears in 1928 and the Dayton Triangles in 1929. He later became a city judge in his hometown of Calumet City, Illinois.

WALLNER, FRED
Fullback/Guard (1948-50) ▪ 6-2, 212 ▪ Greenfield, MA

A winner of three monograms and a starter on the 1949 national championship team, Fred Wallner was fortunate to make it to Notre Dame. In 1946, during his senior year in high school, he was critically injured in an automobile accident. Thanks to a complete recovery, he was a reserve fullback for the Fighting Irish by 1948.

In 1949 coach Frank Leahy took advantage of Wallner's size by moving him to guard, where he played alongside All-Americans Leon Hart and Jim Martin. He also started at linebacker, along with another future All-American named Jerry Groom. Wallner started both ways again in 1950. After graduating from Notre Dame, he played professionally with the Chicago Cardinals and Houston Oilers.

WALSH, ADAM

Center (1922-24) ▪ 6-0, 187 ▪ Hollywood, CA

When Notre Dame won its first consensus national championship in 1924, much of the credit went to the backfield known collectively as the Four Horsemen. Less publicized, but no less important, were the efforts of the Seven Mules, a group of linemen who made it possible for the Four Horsemen to run free. Center Adam Walsh was the heart and soul of that group.

Walsh was born in Churchville, Iowa, and grew up in California. He lettered in football, baseball, basketball, and track at Hollywood High School; he was captain of the undefeated 1919 football team. In 1922 he earned his first monogram at Notre Dame as the starting center on a team that went 8-1-1 under coach Knute Rockne. He started again in 1923 and was named captain in 1924, helping the Irish to a 10-0 record in his senior year.

Among Walsh's more notable accomplishments that season was a heroic effort against Army, in which he played nearly the entire game with two broken hands. Despite this handicap, he did not make a single bad snap from center, and he even intercepted a pass late in the fourth quarter to secure a six-point Notre Dame victory. After the game, Rockne declared Walsh's performance the greatest he had ever seen by a center. Walsh was also a pivotal figure in a memorable goal-line stand that helped the Irish defeat Stanford, 27-10, in the Rose Bowl. After the season he received All-America honors from several organizations, including the International News Service, Newspaper Enterprise Association, and *Collier's* magazine.

Fiercely competitive and ambitious, Walsh also competed in basketball and track and field. To help pay for his college education, he worked 30 hours a week at the Northern Indiana Gas & Electric Company. A mechanical engineering major, he never completed the requirements for his degree (he fell behind after missing a semester because of a severe throat infection). Instead, he married during his senior year and took a job as a coach to support his family.

Walsh's first stop after South Bend was the University of Santa Clara, where he was named head football coach and athletic director at the age of 23. In four seasons he compiled a record of 19-18-2. Despite Santa Clara's comparatively small size (300 students in 1925), Walsh insisted on a big-time schedule that included California, Stanford, and the University of Southern California.

In 1929 he accepted a job as line coach at Yale, and in 1934 he moved again, this time to Harvard. (He was the first person to serve on the varsity football staffs of the archrivals.) Walsh's stay at Harvard was brief, though. In 1935 he was named head coach at Bowdoin College in Brunswick, Maine. While there he transformed Bowdoin into one of the premier small-college programs in the East. His 1937 team, for instance, allowed just 27 points the entire season. And his 1938 team won the New England small-college championship. His eight-year record was 34-16-2.

When Bowdoin made a decision to drop football during World War II, Walsh took a leave of absence and became an assistant coach at his alma mater. One year later, in 1945, he was named head coach of the National Football League's Cleveland Rams. In his first season he guided the team to a 13-2 record and the league championship and was named NFL Coach of the Year. Despite his success in the professional ranks, Walsh returned to Bowdoin in 1947. He remained there until 1958, when he went into private business. In 1961 he was appointed U.S. Marshal for the District of Maine.

Walsh was inducted into the College Football Hall of Fame in 1968. He died in 1986.

WALSH, BILL
Center (1945-48) ▪ 6-3, 205 ▪ Shawnee Mission, KS

Bill Walsh was Notre Dame's starting center in 1945 when he was just a freshman. He backed up George Strohmeyer in 1946 and then reclaimed the job in 1947. That season, on a team that captured the national championship, Walsh shared iron man honors with captain Bill Fischer: Each played 300 minutes.

Walsh earned his fourth monogram in 1948, again as the starting center. He was a third-round draft pick of the Pittsburgh Steelers, with whom he played five seasons. He later went into coaching and for four years worked as an assistant at Notre Dame.

WATTERS, RICKY
Running Back/Flanker (1987-90) ▪ 6-2, 205 ▪ Harrisburg, PA

Born on April 7, 1969, in Harrisburg, Pennsylvania, Richard James Watters was a three-sport star at McDevitt High School and a prep All-American in football. A second-string tailback behind Mark Green, he played in all 12 games as a freshman at Notre Dame, rushing for 373 yards and three touchdowns on 69 carries. He started at flanker in his sophomore year and led the Irish in receiving with 15 catches for 286 yards. With 19 punt returns for 253 yards and two touchdowns, he also succeeded 1987 Heisman Trophy winner Tim Brown as the team's primary weapon on special teams.

After Green's graduation in 1988, Watters returned to tailback. He rushed for 791 yards on 118 carries (second on the team behind quarterback Tony Rice) and caught 13 passes for 196 yards. He also returned 15 punts for 201 yards, including one for a 97-yard

touchdown. He started in Notre Dame's 21-6 victory over Colorado in the Orange Bowl, but a bruised knee limited him to just two carries. After the season he was named honorable mention All-America by *The Sporting News* and *Football News*.

Watters was a senior captain in 1990. He rushed for 579 yards and eight touchdowns on 108 carries and was named honorable mention All-America by *Football News*. Although he began the year slowly, Watters finished impressively, with a 174-yard rushing effort against Tennessee and a 114-yard game against Penn State in November.

With 1,814 rushing yards, Watters finished his career in fourteenth place on Notre Dame's all-time rushing list. He was drafted in the second round by the San Francisco 49ers in 1991 and helped lead the team to NFC and Super Bowl titles in 1994. In his first five seasons in the NFL he rushed for 4,113 yards and 36 touchdowns on 990 carries. He also caught 202 passes for 1,884 yards and nine touchdowns and played in four Pro Bowls. Watters was traded to the Philadelphia Eagles in 1995.

Ricky Watters started his collegiate career by playing in all twelve games his freshman year. He finished it with 1,814 yards rushing, fourteenth on Notre Dame's all-time list.

Career Statistics (Rushing)

YEAR	NO.	YARDS	AVG.	TD
1987	69	373	5.4	3
1988	30	71	2.4	0
1989	118	791	6.7	10
1990	108	579	5.4	8
TOTAL	**325**	**1,814**	**5.6**	**21**

Career Statistics (Receiving)

YEAR	NO.	YARDS	AVG.	TD
1987	6	70	11.7	0
1988	15	286	19.1	2
1989	13	196	15.1	0
1990	7	58	8.3	0
TOTAL	**41**	**610**	**14.9**	**2**

WAYMER, DAVE
Defensive Back/Flanker (1976-79) ▪ 6-3, 188 ▪ Charlotte, NC

Dave Waymer was a versatile athlete who played defensive back and split end at West Charlotte High School in North Carolina. And it took some time for the coaching staff at Notre Dame to determine how best to utilize his talents.

Waymer alternated between flanker and cornerback as a freshman. The next year, 1977, he started at flanker and caught 10 passes for 164 yards, including a 68-yard touchdown reception from Joe Montana in a 69-14 victory over Georgia Tech. In a 38-10 victory over Texas in the Cotton Bowl—a victory that clinched a national championship—Waymer had three catches for 38 yards.

Despite his obvious ability as a receiver, Waymer was moved to cornerback in his last two seasons. He had 51 tackles and three interceptions as a junior; as a senior tri-captain he had 41 tackles and four interceptions. A second-round draft choice of the New Orleans Saints in 1980, Waymer played in the NFL for 13 years. In addition to the Saints (1980-89), he also played for the San Francisco 49ers (1990-91), and Los Angeles Raiders (1992).

WENDELL, MARTY
Fullback/Center/Guard (1944, 1946-48) ▪ 5-11, 198 ▪ Chicago, IL

In the fall of 1948 Marty Wendell became only the second player in Notre Dame history to letter at three different positions.

A graduate of St. George High School in Evanston, Illinois, where he received all-state honors, Wendell earned his first monogram as a freshman fullback in 1944. After a year of military service, he returned to South Bend in 1946 and was promptly reassigned to the center position by coach Frank Leahy. In 1947 he became the starting right guard, a position he held for two seasons.

Wendell, who was vice-president of the class of 1948, was named first-team All-America by *Collier's* magazine in his senior year. He played with the Chicago Hornets of the All-America Football Conference in 1949.

WESTON, JEFF
Defensive Tackle (1974-78) ▪ 6-4, 258 ▪ Rochester, NY

At Cardinal Mooney High School in Rochester, New York, Jeff Weston was a two-way tackle who earned all-state and All-America honors. As a freshman at Notre Dame in 1974, he backed up Mike Fanning at defensive tackle. But with 31 tackles in 91 minutes of playing time, it was apparent that he would quickly find a place in the starting lineup.

Weston was second on the team (behind Steve Niehaus) in tackles with 101 in 1975. His finest performance—actually, one of the best performances by any Notre Dame defensive lineman—came in a 31-10 victory over Navy. He made five solo tackles and assisted on 17 others, caused one fumble and recovered another, and returned an interception 53 yards for a touchdown.

Unfortunately, Weston's sophomore year represented a career zenith. He suffered a serious knee injury in 1976 and played in only one game. In 1977 he returned to the starting lineup and had 57 tackles, but he required a second surgical procedure in the spring of 1978. He recovered in time for the 1978 season (he was granted an additional year of eligibility because of the injury in 1976) and had 51 tackles. But he was unable to fulfill the promise of his sophomore year.

Weston played with the New York Giants from 1979 through 1982.

WETOSKA, BOB

End (1956-58) ▪ 6-3, 225 ▪ Minneapolis, MN

After playing a reserve role during his first two years on the varsity, Bob Wetoska earned a spot in the starting lineup in 1958. He responded with 12 catches for 210 yards (third best on the team). He also had 38 tackles. Most impressive of all, he was named first-team Academic All-America.

Wetoska was a fifth-round draft choice of the Washington Redskins in 1959; however, he never played for Washington. Instead, he changed positions (from end to tackle) and enjoyed a 10-year career with the Chicago Bears.

WHITTINGTON, MIKE

Linebacker (1977-79) ▪ 6-2, 219 ▪ Miami, FL

When starting outside linebacker Bobby Leopold went down with an injury with four games left in the 1978 season, Mike Whittington was asked to fill in. He handled the assignment so well that coach Dan Devine made room in the starting lineup for both players the following season. Whittington had 197 tackles in his career, including 108 as a senior. He was second on the team that year behind Bob Crable, who set a record with 187 tackles.

Whittington played with the New York Giants from 1980 through 1983.

WIGHTKIN, BILL

End (1946-49) ▪ 6-2, 198 ▪ Santa Monica, CA

Overshadowed by Notre Dame's other end—Heisman Trophy winner and All-American Leon Hart—Bill Wightkin was nonetheless an important member of the undefeated 1949 national championship squad.

He graduated from Catholic Central High School in Detroit and made the varsity at Notre Dame in his freshman year, although he saw little action. Wightkin earned his first monogram as a sophomore, playing behind Hart at right end. In 1949, however, with the temporary implementation of two-platoon football, Wightkin became the starting left end on offense; he also saw considerable time on defense.

The Chicago Bears selected Wightkin in the eighth round of the 1950 NFL Draft. He spent his entire professional career with the Bears, retiring in 1957.

WILLIAMS, BOB

Quarterback (1948-50) ▪ 6-1, 180 ▪ Towson, MD

Bob Williams, a consensus All-American in 1949, was one of Notre Dame's greatest quarterbacks. Born in Cumberland, Maryland, Williams attended Loyola High School in Towson near Baltimore. He was a versatile athlete who received all-state honors in basketball, football, and baseball; in his senior year he was named high school All-America in football.

Despite those accolades, Williams was not vigorously pursued by major college football programs. Notre Dame, in fact, expressed only minor interest and did not offer him a scholarship until June of his senior year. The recruiting process caused Williams considerable distress, because he wanted nothing more than to attend Notre Dame. He had first visited the campus when he was only eight years old. Williams's brother, Harold, was a student then, and he introduced Bob to football coach Elmer Layden. Bob was, of course, star-struck. For the next 10 years he prepared for the day when he would enroll at Notre Dame and wear the uniform of the Fighting Irish.

But he very nearly didn't make it. Williams was offered a scholarship only after another recruit decided to go elsewhere, opening up a spot on the roster. He gladly accepted, and before long it was clear that Notre Dame had stumbled upon an exceptional talent.

Williams was a backup to starting quarterback Frank Tripucka in 1948. The following year, as a junior, he stepped into the starting lineup and led the Fighting Irish to a 10-0 record and a national championship. Williams was nothing short of sensational that season. He completed 83 of 147 passes for 1,374 yards and 16 touchdowns, breaking Angelo Bertelli's records for yardage and touchdowns; he also rushed for 63 yards and one touchdown and averaged 39.2 yards as the team's punter. In a 34-21 victory over

Michigan State, he set a single-game school record by completing 13 of 16 passes. Of course, that was reflective of his performance throughout the year: His passing efficiency rating of 161.4 still stands as a Notre Dame single-season record. When the season ended Williams not only received All-America honors, but he was also fifth in voting for the Heisman Trophy (his teammate, end Leon Hart, was first).

The Fighting Irish went into "rebuilding" mode in 1950 and lost as many games as they won (their record was 4-4-1). But Williams enjoyed another good season, completing 99 of 210 passes for 1,035 yards and 10 touchdowns. He was named first-team All-America by the Associated Press and finished sixth in the Heisman Trophy voting.

Williams was a first-round draft choice of the Chicago Bears in 1951. After three seasons in the NFL he retired from professional football. He later became president of a savings and loan in Baltimore.

Bob Williams was inducted into the College Football Hall of Fame in 1988.

Career Statistics

YEAR	ATT.	COMP.	YARDS	TD	PCT.
1948	14	8	110	0	.571
1949	147	83	1,374	16	.565
1950	210	99	1,035	10	.471
TOTAL	371	190	2,519	26	.512

WILLIAMS, LARRY
Offensive Guard/Tackle (1981-84) ▪ 6-6, 276 ▪ Santa Ana, CA

Two-time All-American Larry Williams weighed less than 225 pounds when he arrived at Notre Dame in the fall of 1981. By the time he was a senior, he had added more than 50 pounds to his frame and become one of the top offensive linemen in college football.

Williams, who was captain of the football and basketball teams at Mater Dei High School, earned his first Notre Dame monogram as a freshman and became a starting tackle as a sophomore. In 1983, as a junior, he was named second-team All-America by *Football News*, despite an ankle injury that kept him out of the last two regular-season games. He switched to guard as a senior and had little trouble making the adjustment. United Press International named him second-team All-America, while the Associated Press and *Football News* placed him on their third teams.

Although not drafted until the tenth round in 1985, Williams enjoyed a seven-year NFL career with stops in Cleveland, San Diego, New Orleans, and New England.

WOLSKI, BILL

Halfback (1963-65) ▪ 5-11, 195 ▪ Muskegon, MI

William F. Wolski went to Notre Dame from Muskegon, Michigan. He earned his first monogram in 1963 when, as a sophomore halfback, he was the team's second-leading rusher with 320 yards on 70 carries. The next year he led the team with 657 yards on 136 carries and was fourth in receiving with eight catches for 130 yards. He also led the team in scoring with 66 points. Wolski's finest performance that season came in a 28-6 victory over Stanford; he scored three touchdowns, including one on a 54-yard pass from quarterback John Huarte, who went on to win the Heisman Trophy.

In 1965 Wolski was the senior member of a talented backfield that also included halfback Nick Eddy and fullback Larry Conjar. Wolski rushed for 452 yards on 103 carries and again led the team in scoring with 52 points. A fifth-round draft choice of the Atlanta Falcons in 1966, Wolski spent just one season in the NFL.

Career Statistics (Rushing)

YEAR	NO.	YARDS	AVG.	TD
1963	70	320	4.6	2
1964	136	657	4.8	9
1965	103	452	4.4	8
TOTAL	**309**	**1,429**	**4.6**	**19**

WORDEN, NEIL

Fullback (1951-53) ▪ 5-11, 185 ▪ Milwaukee, WI

One of Notre Dame's all-time leading rushers, Neil Worden was a tough, hard-working fullback who came by his nickname, "Bull," honestly.

Prior to going to Notre Dame, he played football and basketball and ran track for Pulaski High School in Milwaukee, Wisconsin. He was named all-city and all-state in his senior year. In his first year on the Fighting Irish varsity, Worden was named the starting fullback by coach Frank Leahy. He led the team in rushing with 676 yards on 181 carries. He was also the leading scorer with 48 points. As a junior Worden was second on the team in rushing (150 carries for 504 yards) and first in scoring (60 points). He was one of the most reliable players on a team that finished third in the final Associated Press rankings.

As a senior Worden led the Irish to a 9-0-1 record and a No. 2 ranking. He was the team's leading rusher (859 yards on 145 carries) and scorer (66 points). By the time he graduated, Worden had rushed for 2,039 yards, third on the school's all-time rushing list. Heading into the 1996 season, he stood in eighth place.

Worden was a first-round draft choice of the Philadelphia Eagles in 1954. His NFL career, however, lasted only two seasons.

Career Statistics (Rushing)

YEAR	ATT.	YARDS	AVG.	TD
1951	181	676	3.7	8
1952	150	504	3.4	10
1953	145	859	5.9	11
TOTAL	**476**	**2,039**	**4.3**	**29**

WRIGHT, HARRY
Guard/Quarterback (1940-42) • 6-0, 190 • Hempstead, NY

Harry Wright had an unusual career. He started out as a reserve fullback in 1940, became the starting quarterback in 1941, and then—with the emergence of Angelo Bertelli as one of the best passers in college football—moved to right guard in 1942. Not exactly a glamorous exchange for Wright; as it turned out, though, he had his greatest success as a lineman, earning second-team All-America honors from *The Sporting News* in his senior year.

WUJCIAK, AL
Offensive Guard (1973-75) • 6-2, 228 • Newark, NJ

A 60-foot shot-putter in high school, Al Wujciak led Essex Catholic to the Garden State track and field championship in his senior year. At Notre Dame he did not earn a football monogram until 1974 when, as a junior, he not only became a starter at left guard but also wound up playing 335 minutes, third highest on the team. As a pulling guard he proved to be a proficient blocker, helping the Irish accumulate 3,119 yards rushing during the regular season.

Wujciak started again as a senior and was named offensive MVP by the Monogram Club.

WYNN, RENALDO
Defensive End (1993-96) • 6-3, 275 • Chicago, IL

Renaldo Levalle Wynn, Notre Dame's top defensive player in 1996, was born September 3, 1974, in Chicago. A prep All-American who played fullback and linebacker for DeLaSalle High School, he began his college career as an outside linebacker. Just three games into his freshman season, though, Wynn was moved to defensive end. He became a fixture at that position for the better part of four years.

With each successive season, Wynn demonstrated improvement. He had 19 tackles as a freshman, 47 as a sophomore, and 57 as a junior. In 1996, as a senior, he had 61 tackles and was voted Most Valuable Player by the Monogram Club.

WYNNE, CHET

Fullback (1918-21) ▪ 6-0, 168 ▪ Norton, KS

A self-proclaimed "scrub" during his first two and a half seasons on the Notre Dame varsity, Chet Wynne got his break during the Army game in 1920. Teammate and star halfback George Gipp encouraged coach Knute Rockne to stick with Wynne even though Wynne had fumbled the football shortly after entering the game. Rockne gave Wynne a second chance, and he went on to become the team's starting fullback for much of that season and the entire 1921 season. He led the team with four interceptions in his senior year. He was also captain of the track team.

Wynne played for the Rochester Jeffersons in 1922. He later held head coaching positions at Creighton, Auburn, and the University of Kentucky.

WYNNE, ELMER

Fullback (1925-27) ▪ 6-1, 188 ▪ Topeka, KS

Elmer Wynne went to Notre Dame from Topeka, Kansas. He arrived in South Bend in the fall of 1924, the year in which the famed Four Horsemen led the Fighting Irish to a 10-0 record. Wynne earned varsity monograms as a second-string fullback in his sophomore and junior years and then became a starter in his senior year.

After graduating with a law degree, Wynne played professional football for the Chicago Bears and Dayton Triangles. He later settled in Denver, Colorado, where he worked as an industrial relations manager for Safeway grocery stores.

Y

YARR, TOMMY

Center (1929-31) ▪ 5-11, 195 ▪ Dabob, WA

Tommy Yarr was a two-year starter at center. He went to Notre Dame in 1928 after an outstanding career at Chimacum Prep in Dabob, Washington. In 1929 he was a third-string center whose play was largely unimpressive; certainly he did not appear to be a future star.

College Football Hall-of-Famer Tommy Yarr was a superior player on offense and defense under Knute Rockne. He stayed on with the Fighting Irish after graduation as an assistant coach before joining the Chicago Cardinals in 1933.

In 1930, however, Knute Rockne made Yarr a starting center, and Yarr seized the opportunity with great zeal. He became one of Notre Dame's most dependable all-around players, excelling on both offense and defense. In the closing minutes of the season opener against Southern Methodist, for example, he intercepted two passes to secure a 20-14 victory. The Irish went on to win all 10 of their games and capture the national championship.

Yarr was elected team captain in 1931 and proved himself worthy of that honor by, among other things, playing the last three games of the season with a cast on his hand. He was a first-team All-America selection by the Associated Press; United Press International named him to its second team.

Yarr worked as an assistant coach at Notre Dame in 1932 before signing a contract with the Chicago Cardinals in 1933. His professional career lasted just one season, though, and he soon returned to coaching—this time as the head coach at Carroll College. In 1987 he was inducted into the College Football Hall of Fame.

YONAKER, JOHN

End (1942-43) ▪ 6-4, 222 ▪ Dorchester, MA

The leading receiver on Notre Dame's 1943 national championship team, John Yonaker was also the biggest player in the starting lineup. He prepped at Mechanic Arts High School in Boston, where he received All-New England honors his junior and senior years.

Yonaker earned his first monogram in 1942 as a third-string end. The next year coach Frank Leahy gave him an opportunity to start, and he did not disappoint. Yonaker led the team in receiving with 15 catches for 323 yards. He scored four touchdowns, including one on a 30-yard pass in Notre Dame's most important game of the year, a 26-0 victory over third-ranked Army. That same year he also won the national Amateur Athletic Union indoor shot put title with a toss of 50 feet, 2 1/2 inches. He was invited to play in the 1944 College All-Star Game and was a consensus All-American.

The Philadelphia Eagles selected Yonaker in the first round of the 1945 NFL Draft. He played with the Cleveland Browns of the All-America Football Conference, as well as the NFL's New York Yankees and Washington Redskins and the Montreal Alouettes of the Canadian Football League. He retired from professional football in 1952.

YOUNG, BRYANT

Defensive Tackle (1990-93) ▪ 6-3, 277 ▪ Chicago Heights, IL

An All-American in 1993, Bryant Young grew up in Chicago Heights, Illinois. He earned four varsity letters as a defensive end at Bloom Township High School and was a *Parade* prep All-American in 1989. He also earned four letters in wrestling (and finished third in the state tournament as a senior) and three letters in track and field.

In his freshman year at Notre Dame, Young was primarily a special-teams player. He became a starter at defensive tackle in his sophomore year and finished fourth on the team in tackles. As a junior he led the Irish in both sacks and tackles for lost yardage. He logged more minutes than any other defensive lineman and was named honorable mention All-America by *Football News*.

Bryant Young started his Notre Dame career on special teams but, by his senior, had become one of the team's top defensive linemen. He was selected in the first round of the NFL Draft by the San Francisco 49ers.

Young was one of four captains in 1993. He finished third on the team in tackles (67) and first in sacks (6). In the 1994 Cotton Bowl he had nine tackles and one sack as Notre Dame defeated Texas A&M, 24-21. Young started the last 26 games of his college career. He was named a first-team All-American by the American Football Coaches Association and a second-team

All-American by the Associated Press and United Press International, among others.

The San Francisco 49ers selected Young in the first round of the 1994 NFL Draft. The seventh player chosen overall, he adapted quickly to life in the NFL, recording six sacks and 49 tackles in his rookie year.

Career Statistics

YEAR	TACKLES	SACKS	YDS.
1990	8	0	0
1991	50	4	28
1992	51	7.5	64
1993	67	6.5	49
TOTAL	**176**	**18**	**141**

Z

ZALEJSKI, ERNIE

Halfback (1946, 1948-49) ▪ 5-11, ▪ 185 South Bend, IN

South Bend native Ernie Zalejski enrolled at Notre Dame after serving in World War II. He earned a monogram as a freshman running back on the 1946 national championship team, but a knee injury forced him to miss the 1947 season and limited his playing time in 1948. In 1949 Zalejski was a second-string halfback and the team's fifth-leading rusher with 171 yards on 29 carries. He also caught five passes—four of which resulted in touchdowns—and scored 30 points.

Zalejski played one year of professional football with the Baltimore Colts.

ZAVAGNIN, MARK

Linebacker (1979-82) ▪ 6-2, 228 ▪ Evergreen Park, IL

Linebacker Mark Zavagnin came to Notre Dame from Chicago's St. Rita High School, where he earned all-city, all-state, and Catholic All-America honors. He became a starter at weakside linebacker for the Fighting Irish in his sophomore year and was second on the team in tackles (behind Bob Crable) in 1980 and 1981.

As a senior, in 1982, Zavagnin took over for the graduated Crable at middle linebacker and led the team in tackles with 113. He was named second-team All-America by *Football News* and third-team All-America by the Associated Press.

ZELLARS, RAY

Fullback (1991-94) ▪ 5-11, 221 ▪ Pittsburgh, PA

Ray Zellars rushed for nearly 500 yards in his senior year, despite missing three full games with an ankle injury. He went to Notre Dame from Oliver High School in

Pittsburgh, where he rushed for 1,237 yards and 11 touchdowns as a senior and led his team to the City League championship. He was a two-time all-state selection at tailback. Football was just one of Zellars's talents, though; he was also captain of the track, wrestling, and baseball teams—and he was student council president.

After carrying the ball just 32 times during his first two years at Notre Dame, Zellars became the starting fullback as a junior. He rushed for 494 yards on 99 carries and scored five touchdowns—which was five more than he had scored in his first two seasons combined. His best game, appropriately enough, came against Pittsburgh when he rushed for 67 yards and two touchdowns on just 12 carries. After the season Zellars was named honorable mention All-America by *Football News*.

Most publications predicted big things for Zellars prior to the 1994 season; *The Sporting News*, for example, rated him third among all fullbacks in college football. In the fourth game of the season, a 39-21 victory over Purdue, he seemed to be on his way to meeting those grand expectations, rushing for a career-best 156 yards and one touchdown on only 14 carries (an average of 11.1 yards per attempt). The next week, however, Zellars sprained his ankle against Stanford. The injury kept him on the sideline for the better part of a month. He missed games against Boston College, Brigham Young, and Navy and carried just five times in a backup role against Florida State.

A sprained ankle interrupted Ray Zellars's senior year, a year in which he was predicted to dominate offense in college football. But he finished the year healthy and well enough to impress the New Orleans Saints, who drafted him in the second round.

Zellars finished the season with 466 yards on 79 carries. His size and strength—and his performance when he was healthy—sufficiently impressed NFL scouts. He was drafted by the New Orleans Saints in the second round of the 1995 NFL Draft.

Career Statistic (Rushing)

YEAR	ATT.	YARDS	AVG.	TD
1991	6	51	8.5	0
1992	26	124	4.8	0
1993	99	494	5.0	5
1994	79	466	5.9	3
TOTAL	210	1,135	5.4	8

ZETTEK, SCOTT

Defensive Tackle (1976-80) ▪ 6-5, 245 ▪ Elk Grove Village, IL

Although bothered by injuries throughout his career, Scott Zettek was a talented, determined lineman who eventually earned All-America honors.

Zettek had 21 tackles as a freshman in 1976. A few months later, in spring drills, he suffered the first of several knee injuries. He returned to the lineup in the fall of 1977 and had 51 tackles, but knee problems kept him on the sideline for most of the 1978 season. He underwent surgery in the spring of 1979. That fall, in what was originally supposed to be his senior season, Zettek played in eight games and had 61 tackles. He missed three games because of a sprained knee.

Granted an additional year of eligibility because of his physical problems, Zettek returned in 1980 and had his finest, healthiest season. He was the team's third-leading tackler with 70 and was named first-team All-America by the Associated Press and *Football News*. Zettek was an eighth-round draft choice of the Chicago Bears in 1982, but he did not play in the NFL.

ZILLY, JACK

Right End (1943, 1946) ▪ 6-2, 200 ▪ Southington, CT

Born November 11, 1921, in Southington, Connecticut, Jack Zilly was a three-sport star (basketball, football, and track) at Lewis High School. He played right end behind John Yonaker on Notre Dame's 1943 national championship squad. After the season he was assigned to active duty in the U.S. Navy.

Zilly served in the Pacific until his discharge in the spring of 1946. He returned to Notre Dame in the fall and helped the Fighting Irish win another national championship. After graduation he played six years of professional football with the Los Angeles Rams and Philadelphia Eagles. He retired in 1952 and accepted a position with the Industrial Distributing Corporation of Los Angeles. In 1955 Zilly returned to football as an assistant coach with the Rams, and the following year he became an assistant at Notre Dame.

ZONTINI, LOU

Halfback (1937-39) ▪ 5-9, 181 ▪ Whitesville, WV

One of Lou Zontini's greatest athletic accomplishments was an 84-yard touchdown run against the University of Minnesota in 1938. Little did he know that a few years later the play would be edited into the final cut of the film *Knute Rockne, All-American*, and that his effort would become part of Notre Dame folklore.

If that was the most memorable moment of his career, however, it was not the only one worth preserving. Zontini started at right halfback for two years and was second on the team in rushing in 1938 with 319 yards; primarily, though, he was appreciated for his blocking skills. Zontini played for the Chicago Cardinals and Cleveland Rams before joining the Navy in 1943. He later spent two seasons with the Buffalo Bills. He retired from professional football in 1948 and entered private business.

ZORICH, CHRIS
Defensive Tackle (1988-90) ▪ 6-1, 266 ▪ Chicago, IL

One of the most decorated players in Notre Dame history, Christopher Robert Zorich was born on March 13, 1969, in Chicago, Illinois. A four-year starter at linebacker at Vocational High School, he was named all-state and honorable mention All-America in his senior year.

Zorich was switched to nose tackle early in his freshman year at Notre Dame. He had some difficulty making the adjustment and did not see any time with the varsity that season. Never one to shy away from hard work, Zorich applied himself to the task of learning his new position. By the time he was a sophomore, he was a fixture in the starting lineup of a team that went on to win a national championship. He finished the season with 70 tackles, third best on the team, and was named first-team All-America by the Newspaper Enterprise Association.

As a junior, in 1989, Zorich had 92 tackles in 12 games. A consensus first-team All-American, he was named Lineman of the Year by United Press International and was a finalist for the Lombardi Award, which is presented annually to college football's out-standing lineman.

In 1990, as a senior, Zorich missed two games because of a partially dislocated kneecap; nevertheless, he was the most honored lineman in college football. A unanimous first-team All-American, he also won the Lombardi Award and was a semifinalist for the Outland Award. In the final game of his career, the 1991 Orange Bowl, he had 10 tackles and was named Notre Dame MVP.

Zorich returned to his hometown in 1991 as a second-round draft pick of the Chicago Bears. He had 15.5 sacks in his first five seasons as a professional. One of the strongest players ever to wear a Notre Dame uniform (he could bench press more than 475 pounds), Zorich also had an immense capacity for compassion. He founded the Chris Zorich Foundation, which funds several noteworthy community outreach programs in the Chicago area and, in 1995, was named one of *USA Weekend*'s Most Caring Athletes for his charitable work. He returns to his old neighborhood on Chicago's south side each Thanksgiving to distribute food to needy families.

APPENDICES

All-Time Roster

A

Abraham, Byron, 1983
Achterhoff, Jay, 1973-75
Adamonis, Stan, 1937
Adams, John (Tree), 1942-44
Adamson, Ken, 1957-59
Adell, Bernie, 1979-81
Adent, Joe, 1994
Agnew, Ed, 1930
Agnone, John, 1945-46
Ahern, Bill, 1960-62
Akers, Jeremy, 1993-95
Alaniz, Steve, 1986-88
Albert, Frank, 1937-39
Ale, Arnold, 1988
Alessandrini, Jack, 1950-52
Alexander, Ben, 1931-32
Alexander, Harry, 1965-66
Alge, Brad, 1986-88
Allan, Denny, 1968-70
Allen, Joe, 1988-90
Allen, Wayne, 1962
Allison, Bill (Tex), 1916-17
Allocco, Frank, 1972-75
Allocco, Rich, 1974
Alm, Jeff, 1986-89
Alvarado, Joe, 1971-73
Ambrose, John, 1919
Ames, Dick, 1938
Anderson, Eddie, 1918-21
Anderson, Heartley (Hunk), 1918-21
Anderson, Shawn, 1987-89
Andler, Ken, 1974-75
Andretti, Pete, 1963-65

Andres, Bill, 1917
Andrews, Frank (Bodie), 1916-17
Andrysiak, Terry, 1984-87
Andrzejewski, Mark, 1992
Angsman, Elmer, 1943-45
Anson, George, 1894
Antonietti, Mark, 1985
Arboit, Ennio, 1936-37
Arboit, Pete, 1937-39
Archer, Art, 1944
Archer, Clyde, 1938
Armbruster, Steve, 1994
Arment, Bill, 1974
Armstrong, Lennox, 1911
Arndt, Russ, 1922-24
Arrington, Dick, 1963-65
Arrix, Bob, 1952
Ashbaugh, Russell (Pete), 1941-42, 46-47
Askin, John, 1983-86
Atamian, John, 1962-64
Augustine, Charlie, 1959-60
Autry, Jon, 1980-83
Azzaro, Joe, 1964-67

B

Babey, Joe, 1993-95
Bach, Joe, 1923-24
Bachman, Charlie, 1914-16
Bagarus, Steve, 1939-40
Bahan, Leonard (Pete), 1917-19
Bailie, Roy, 1929-30
Bake, Tom, 1974
Baker, Brian, 1992-94
Baker, Jeff, 1988-91

Bakich, Huntley, 1991-93

Balentine, Norm, 1988-89

Ballage, Pat, 1982-85

Balliet, Calvin, 1973-74

Banas, Steve, 1931-33

Banicki, Fred, 1949

Banks, Braxston, 1986-88

Banks, Mike, 1973-76

Banks, Robert, 1983-86

Barber, Bob, 1938

Barber, Ty, 1978-80

Bardash, Virgil, 1950-52

Barnard, Jack, 1962

Barnett, Reggie,1972-74

Barrett, John, 1893-94

Barrett, Billy, 1949-51

Barry, George, 1923

Barry, Ken, 1995

Barry, Norm, 1917-20

Barry, Norm, 1940-41

Bars, Joe, 1981-84

Barstow, Fred, 1931-34

Bartlett, Jim, 1949-50

Barz, Bill, 1968-70

Batuello, Joe, 1981

Bauer, Ed, 1972-75

Baugus, James, 1986

Baujan, Harry, 1913-16

Bavaro, Mark, 1981-84

Beach, Joe, 1933-34

Beacom, Pat, 1903-06

Beams, Byron, 1954-55

Bechtold, Joe, 1938

Becker, Doug, 1974-77

Becker, Harry, 1933-35

Beckwith, Jason, 1990-93

Becton, Lee, 1991-94

Bednar, George, 1961-63

Begley, Gerry, 1947-49

Beh, Carleton, 1914

Behmer, Brian, 1981-84

Beinor, Ed, 1936-38

Belden, Bill, 1935

Belden, Bob, 1966-68

Belden, Tony, 1978-81

Belisle, Kurt, 1994-95

Bell, Greg, 1980-83

Belles, Steve, 1986-89

Benda, Joe, 1925-27

Benigni, George, 1944

Bennett, Anson, 1898

Bennett, Corey, 1994-95

Bercich, Pete, 1990-93

Bereolos, Hercules, 1939-41

Berezney, Pete, 1943-45

Berger, Alvin (Heine), 1911-14

Bergman, Alfred (Dutch), 1910-11, 13-14

Bergman, Arthur (Dutch), 1915-16, 19

Bergman, Joe (Dutch), 1921-23

Bergmann, Jon, 1991-94

Berkey, Ken, 1916

Berry, Bert, 1993-95

Berta, Bill, 1938

Berteling, John (Doc), 1906-07

Bertelli, Angelo, 1941-43

Berve, Ben, 1906

Beschen, Dick, 1958

Best, Art, 1972-74

Bettis, Jerome, 1990-92

Beuerlein, Steve, 1983-86

Biagi, Frank, 1938-39

Bianco, Don, 1951

Bice, Len, 1931

Bigelow, Jim, 1952-54

Bill, Bob, 1959-61

Binkowski, Ben, 1936-38

Binz, Frank, 1908

Bisceglia, Pat, 1953-55

Bitsko, Mickey, 1961

Bleier, Bob (Rocky), 1965-67

Bleyer, Bob, 1980

Bleyer, Frank, 1977

Bliey, Ron, 1962-63

Blunt, Leon, 1994

Bobb, James, 1984-86

Bock, Tom, 1978-79, 81

Bodine, Jerry, 1989

Boeringer, Art (Bud), 1925-26

Boerner, Chris, 1980-81

Boggs, Pat, 1977

Boji, Byron, 1949-51

Boland, Joe, 1924-26

Boland, Ray, 1932

Bolcar, Ned, 1986-89

Bolger, Matt, 1941

Bolger, Tom, 1971-73

Bonar, Bud, 1933-34

Bonder, Frank, 1974

Bondi, Gus, 1927-29

Bone, Rod, 1979-82

Bonvechio, Sandy, 1963-64

Borer, Harold, 1938

Borowski, Chuck, 1936

Bosse, Joe, 1954-55

Bossu, Augie, 1936-38

Bossu, Frank, 1968-70

Bossu, Steve, 1974

Boulac, Brian, 1960-62

Boushka, Dick, 1977-80

Boushka, Mike, 1978-81

Bouwens, Seraphine, 1897

Boyd, Walter, 1989-90

Boyle, Rich, 1958

Boznanski, Brent, 1992

Bracken, Bob, 1904-06

Bradley, Luther, 1973, 75-77

Brady, Jim, 1927-28

Brancheau, Ray, 1931-33

Brandy, Joe, 1917, 19-20

Brantley, Tony, 1973-75

Bray, Jim, 1926-28

Brennan, Tom, 1938

Brennan, Jim, 1944, 46-47

Brennan, Joe, 1909

Brennan, Mike, 1986-89

Brennan, Terry, 1945-48

Brennan, Terry, 1967-69

Brenneman, Mark, 1971, 73-74

Brent, Francis, 1901

Brew, Frank, 1937-38

Briick, Herb, 1970-72

Brill, Marty, 1929-30

Brocke, Jim, 1963

Brock, Tom, 1940-42

Brogan, John, 1905

Brooks, Mark, 1981-84

Brooks, Reggie, 1989-92

Brooks, Tony, 1987-88, 90-91

Broscoe, Eddie, 1936-38

Brosey, Cliff, 1939-40

Brown, Bob, 1895-96

Brown, Chris, 1980-81, 82-83

Brown, Cliff, 1971-73

Brown, Dean, 1986-89

Brown, Derek, 1988-91

Brown, Earl, 1936-38

Brown, Earl, 1892

Brown, Frank, 1926

Brown, Harvey, 1921-23

Brown, Ivan, 1973

Brown, Roger, 1946-47

Brown, Tim, 1984-87

Browner, Jim, 1975-78

Browner, Ross, 1973-77

Browner, Willard, 1976

Bruni, Todd, 1979-81

Bruno, Bill, 1934-36

Brutz, Jim, 1939-41

Bryant, Junior, 1989-92

Bucci, Don, 1951-53

Bucci, Elvo, 1976

Buchanan, Pete, 1978, 80-81

Buches, Steve, 1968-70

Buczkiewicz, Ed, 1952

Budka, Frank, 1961-63

Budynkiewicz, Ted, 1947-48

Buehner, Rick, 1977-78

Bufton, Scott, 1986-87

Bulger, Jim, 1970-71

Bullock, Wayne, 1972-74

Buoniconti, Nick, 1959-61

Burdick, Henry, 1906-08

Burgener, Mike, 1965-67

Burger, Bob, 1978-80

Burger, Tom, 1981

Burgmeier, Ted, 1974-77

Burke, Ed, 1960-62

Burke, Frank, 1944

Burke, John, 1907

Burke, Kevin, 1956-58

Burnell, Max, 1936-38

Burnell, Max, 1959-60

Burnett, Al, 1945

Burns, Bill, 1962-63

Burns, Paul, 1949-51

Burris, Jeff, 1990-93

Bush, Hardy, 1913-14

Bush, Jack, 1949-51

Bush, Joe, 1951-52, 55

Bush, Bob, 1977

Bush, Roy, 1945

Buth, Doug, 1974-75

Butler, Dave, 1983-86

Butler, Frank, 1930

Byrne, Bill, 1926

Byrne, John, 1921

Byrne, Tom, 1925-27

Byrne, Tom, 1985-87

C

Cabral, Walter, 1951-54

Caito, Leo, 1960

Caldwell, George, 1932-34

Calhoun, Mike, 1976-78

Callaghan, Leo, 1954

Callan, Mike, 1988-90

Callicrate, Dom, 1905-07

Cameron, Alexander, 1921

Campbell, Stafford, 1889
Canale, Frank, 1931-32, 34
Cannon, Jack, 1927-29
Capers, Tony, 1968
Caprara, Joe, 1949-50
Carberry, Glen (Judge), 1920-22
Carey, Tom, 1951-54
Carey, Tony, 1964-65
Carideo, Frank, 1928-30
Carideo, Fred, 1933-35
Carmody, James, 1930
Carney, John, 1983-86
Carney, Mike, 1974-76
Carollo, Joe, 1959-61
Carrabine, Gene, 1951-52
Carrabine, Luke, 1954
Carretta, Kevin, 1993-95
Carroll, Jim, 1962-64
Carroll, Joe, 1993-94
Carter, Don, 1947
Carter, Mansel, 1980-82
Carter, Phil, 1979-82
Carter, Ray, 1983-85
Carter, Tom, 1949-50
Carter, Tom, 1990-92
Cartier, Dezera, 1889
Cartier, George, 1887
Case, Jay, 1975, 77-79
Casey, Dan, 1894-95
Cash, Tony, 1944
Casper, Dave, 1971-73
Cassidy, Bill, 1929
Cassidy, Thaddeus, 1938-40
Castin, Jack, 1960
Castner, Paul, 1920-22
Cavalier, John, 1936
Cavanaugh, Tom, 1895-96
Cavanaugh, Vince, 1930-31
Cengia, Scott, 1994-95
Cerney, Bill, 1922-24
Champion, Cikai, 1994-95
Chand, Parvez, 1981
Chandler, Bill, 1944
Chanowicz, Stan, 1935
Chapleau, Tom, 1987
Chauncey, Jim, 1974
Chevigny, Jack, 1926-28
Chidester, Abraham (Abe), 1893-94
Chlebeck, Andy, 1940
Christensen, Ross, 1974-77
Christman, Norb, 1928-31
Chryplewicz, Pete, 1992-95

Chura, Pat, 1984
Church, Augie (Sonny), 1934-35
Church, Durant, 1904
Cibula, George, 1943
Cichy, Steve, 1978-81
Ciechanowicz, Emil, 1947-48
Ciesielski, Dick, 1956, 58-59
Cieszkowski, John, 1969-72
Cifelli, Gus, 1946-49
Clark, Bill, 1959-60
Clark, Oswald, 1945
Clark, Willie, 1990-93
Clasby, Bob, 1979-82
Clasby, Ed, 1944
Clatt, Corwin (Cornie), 1942, 46-47
Clear, Eugene, 1904
Clement, B., 1908
Clements, Bill, 1960
Clements, Jack, 1971
Clements, Tom, 1972-74
Clevenger, Chris, 1994-95
Clifford, Jerry, 1935-37
Clinnen, Walter, 1908, 10
Clippinger, Art, 1910
Cloherty, John, 1969-71
Coad, Dick, 1904
Coady, Ed, 1888-89
Coady, Pat, 1892
Coady, Tom, 1888-89
Cobbins, Lyron, 1993-95
Cody, Francis (Lew), 1925
Cohen, Maurice (Pat), 1926
Cofall, Stan, 1914-16
Colella, Phil, 1945
Coleman, Charles, 1901
Coleman, Herb, 1942-43
Coleman, Linc, 1987
Collins, Chuck, 1922-24
Collins, Eddie, 1926-29
Collins, Fred, 1925-28
Collins, Greg, 1972-74
Collins, Joe, 1908-10
Collins, Leo, 1966
Colosimo, Jim, 1957-59
Colrick, John, 1927-29
Compton, Doug, 1981
Condeni, Dave, 1978-81
Conjar, Larry, 1965-66
Conley, Tom, 1928-30
Connell, Ward (Doc), 1922-24
Connor, George, 1946-47
Connor, Joe, 1935

Connor, John, 1948-49
Connor, Sean, 1988
Connors, Ben, 1918-19
Conway, Denny, 1964-65
Cook, Bill, 1912-13
Cook, Ed, 1953-54
Cook, Harold, 1922
Cooke, Larry, 1954-56
Cooney, John, 1985-86
Corbisiero, John, 1944
Corby, Sidney, 1894-96
Corgan, Mike, 1937-38
Corry, Clarence, 1894
Corsaro, Dan, 1983
Corson, Bob, 1957
Costa, Don, 1958
Costa, Paul, 1961, 63-64
Costello, Al, 1932-34
Cotter, Bob, 1969
Cotter, Dick, 1948-50
Cotton, Forrest (Fod), 1920-22
Coughlin, Bernie, 1922, 24-25
Coughlin, Danny, 1920-21
Coughlin, Frank, 1916, 19-20
Courey, Mike, 1977-80
Coutre, Larry, 1946-49
Covington, Ivory, 1994-95
Covington, John, 1990-93
Cowhig, Gerry, 1942-46
Cowin, Jeff, 1969
Coyne, Bob, 1954
Crable, Bob, 1978-81
Crawley, Pat, 1892
Creaney, Mike, 1970-72
Creevey, John, 1942-46
Creevey, Tom, 1973
Creevy, Dick, 1940-42
Creevy, Tom, 1942
Crews, Ron, 1975
Crimmins, Bernie, 1939-41
Criniti, Frank, 1966-68
Cripe, Clarence, 1907
Crippin, Jeff, 1978-79
Cronin, Art, 1934-36
Cronin, Carl, 1929-31
Cronin, Dick, 1945
Crotty, Jim, 1957-59
Crotty, Mike, 1969-71
Crounse, Mike, 1986, 88-89
Crowe, Clem, 1923-25
Crowe, Ed, 1925
Crowe, Emmett, 1936-38

Crowley, Charlie, 1910-12
Crowley, Jim, 1922-24
Cullen, Jack, 1960-61
Cullen, John, 1892-93
Cullinan, Joe (Jepers), 1900-03
Cullins, Ron, 1974-75
Culver, Al, 1929-31
Culver, Rodney, 1988-91
Curley, Bob, 1943
Cusack, Joe, 1887-88
Cusack, Pat, 1983-85
Cushing, Tom, 1983
Cusick, Frank, 1942
Cyterski, Len, 1951
Czaja, Mark, 1976-77, 79
Czarobski, Zygmont (Ziggy), 1942-43, 46-47

D

Dabiero, Angelo, 1959-61
Dahl, Bob, 1988-90
Dahman, Ray (Bucky), 1925-27
Dailer, Jim, 1944, 47-48
Dainton, Bill, 1965
D'Alonzo, Al, 1944-45
Daly, Charles, 1899
Daly, Mike, 1896-97
Dampeer, John, 1970-72
Danbom, Larry, 1934-36
Dancewicz, Frank, 1943-45
Daniels, Bert, 1908
Dansby, Melvin, 1993-94
Darcy, John, 1936
Daut, John, 1949
Davila, Jenaro, 1895
Davin, David, 1954
Davis, Greg, 1988-91
Davis, Irwin, 1933-34
Davis, Ray, 1943
Davis, Shawn, 1989-90
Davis, Travis, 1991-94
Davitt, Harold, 1901
Davlin, Mike, 1944
Dawson, Lake, 1990-93
deArrietta, Jim, 1968-69
DeBuono, Dick, 1945
DeCicco, Nick, 1977
Dee, John, 1944
DeFranco, Joe, 1937-39
DeGree, Ed, 1920-22
DeGree, Walter (Cy), 1916-17, 19
deHueck, Ian, 1984
deManigold, Marc, 1989-90

Demmerle, Pete, 1972-74
Dempsey, John, 1894
DeNardo, Ron, 1957
Denchfield, Art, 1927
Denisoff, Mike, 1988
Dennery, Vince, 1962-64
Denson, Autry, 1995
Denvir, Mike, 1995
DePola, Nick, 1960
DePrimio, Dennis, 1969-71
Desch, Gus, 1921-22
DeSiato, Tom, 1979-80
Desmond, Bill, 1902
Detmer, Marty, 1978-80
Devine, Ed, 1968
Devine, Tom, 1971-72
Devore, Hugh, 1931-33
Dew, Billy, 1927-28
Dewan, Darryll, 1970-72
DiBernardo, Rick, 1982-85
DiCarlo, Mike, 1961-63
Dickerson, Sydney, 1889
Dickerson, Ty, 1976-77, 79
Dickman, Dan, 1967
Dickson, George, 1949
Diebold, Clarence, 1900
Diedrick, Larry, 1985
Diener, John, 1906-08
Dienhart, Joe, 1924
Dike, Ken, 1976-77
Dillard, James, 1988
Dillon, Dan, 1903
Diminick, Gary, 1971-73
Dimmick, Ralph, 1908-10
DiNardo, Gerry, 1972-74
DiNardo, Larry, 1968-70
Dingens, Greg, 1982-85
Dingens, Matt, 1985-86
Dinkle, Nicholas, 1892-94
Dionne, Louis, 1908
DiOrio, Doug, 1987-89
Ditton, James, 1907
Dixon, Sherwood, 1916-17
Djubasak, Paul, 1957
Doar, Jim
Doarn, John, 1926-28
Dobbins, Marc, 1987-89
Doerger, Tom, 1982-85
Doherty, Brian, 1971-73
Doherty, Kevin, 1973-75
Doherty, Pat, 1912
Dolan, Bill, 1911-12

Dolan, Pat, 1955-57
Dolan, Sam (Rosey), 1906-09
Domin, Tom, 1976-77
Donahue, James, 1991
Donahue, John, 1898
Donoghue, Dick, 1927-30
Donohue, Pete, 1967
Donovan, Bob (Smousherette), 1906
Donovan, Dick, (Smoush), 1903-05
Donovan, Red, 1918
Doody, Frank, 1938, 40
Dooley, Jim, 1919-21
Dorais, Charles (Gus), 1910-13
Dorais, Joe, 1915-16
Dorsey, Eric, 1982-85
Doughty, Mike, 1994-95
Dove, Bob, 1940-42
Dover, Steve, 1977-78
Downs, Bill, 1905
Downs, Morris, 1905
Doyle, Pat, 1957-59
Doyle, Nick, 1906
Draper, Bill, 1903-05
Drennan, William, 1922
Drew, Dave, 1970-72
Driscoll, Leo, 1977
Dubenetzky, John, 1974-76
DuBose, Demetrius, 1989-92
DuBrul, Ernest, 1892-93
Duerson, Dave, 1979-82
Duffy, John, 1907-10
Dugan, Bill, 1907
Dugan, Mike, 1957-58
Duggan, Eddie, 1911-14
Dumas, Ray, 1986-88
Duncan, Bob, 1977
Duncan, Ernest, 1899
Dunlay, Jim, 1950-51
Dunn, Ed, 1934-3
Dunphy, Ray, 1912
Duranko, Pete, 1963-66
Dushney, Ron, 1966-68
Dwan, Alan, 1906
Dwyer, Gene, 1942
Dwyer, Pete, 1908-10

E
Earley, Bill, 1940-42
Earley, Fred, 1943, 45-47
Earley, Mike, 1966
Earley, Rich, 1988-89
Eason, Tony, 1985-86

Eastman, Tom, 1974-76
Eaton, Tom, 1968-70
Ebert, Rick, 1988
Ebli, Ray, 1940-41
Eckman, Mike, 1969
Ecuyer, Al, 1956-58
Eddy, Nick, 1964-66
Edison, Jarvis, 1994-95
Edmonds, Wayne, 1953-55
Edwards, Gene (Red), 1924-26
Edwards, Howard (Cap), 1908-09
Edwards, Marc, 1993-95
Eggeman, Fred, 1906
Eggeman, Joe, 1923
Eggeman, John, 1897-99
Eggert, Herb, 1924
Eichenlaub, Ray, 1911-14
Eilers, Pat, 1987-89
Elder, Jack, 1927-29
Ellis, Clarence, 1969-71
Ellis, Howard, 1915
Ellis, Randy, 1979-82
Elser, Don, 1933-35
Elward, Allen (Mal), 1912-15
Ely, Gene, 1936-37
Emanuel, Denny, 1936-37
Emerick, Lou, 1950
Endress, Frank, 1944
Enright, Rex, 1923, 25
Epstein, Frank, 1950
Espenan, Ray, 1946-49
Etten, Nick, 1962-63
Etter, Bill, 1969, 71-72
Eurick, Terry, 1974-77
Evans, Fred (Dippy), 1940-42

F
Fagan, Bill, 1897
Failla, Paul, 1991-93
Fallon, Jack, 1944-45, 46, 48
Fallon, Patrick, 1988
Fanning, Mike, 1972-74
Fansler, Mike, 1902-04
Faragher, Jim, 1900-01
Farley, John, 1897-1900
Farmer, Jim, 1983
Farmer, Robert, 1993-95
Farrell, Dan, 1992-94
Farrell, Joe, 1962-64
Farrell, Joe, 1987-89
Farrell, Tom, 1923
Farren, John, 1989-91

Fasano, Angelo, 1978-80
Favorite, Mike, 1981-83
Fay, Ed, 1944-45
Fazio, Joe, 1981, 83-84
Fedorenko, Nick, 1974
Feeney, Al, 1910-13
Fehr, Frank, 1887-89
Feigel, Chuck, 1948-50
Feltes, Norm, 1922
Fennessey, John, 1897
Ferguson, Vagas, 1976-79
Figaro, Cedric, 1984-87
Filley, Pat, 1941-44
Fine, Tom, 1973-74
Finegan, Charles (Sam), 1911-14
Finnegan, Robbie, 1981-84
Finneran, Jack, 1937-39
Fischer, Bill, 1945-48
Fischer, Mark, 1980-82
Fischer, Ray, 1968
Fitzgerald, Art, 1944
Fitzgerald, Dick, 1953-55
Fitzgerald, Freeman (Fitz), 1912-15
Fitzgerald, Ted, 1985, 87-88
Fitzgibbons, James, 1889
Fitzpatrick, Bill, 1926
Fitzpatrick, George, 1916, 19
Flanagan, Christie, 1925-27
Flanagan, Jim, 1943
Flanigan, Jim, 1990-93
Flanigan, John (Thunder), 1917
Flanigan, John, 1892-93
Flannery, Bryan, 1986-89
Fleming, Charles, 1898-99
Fleming, Steve, 1889
Fleurima, Reggie, 1993-94
Flemons, Lester, 1982-84
Flinn, Neil, 1922
Flood, Dave, 1950-52
Flood, John, 1981
Flor, Ollie, 1958-59
Flynn, Bill, 1945, 48-50
Flynn, Charles, 1889
Flynn, Dave, 1950
Flynn, Jack, 1921-22
Flynn, John, 1931-32
Flynn, Tom, 1976-78
Fogel, John, 1935-37
Foley, Joe, 1931
Foley, John, 1987
Foley, Tim, 1976-79
Foley, Tom, 1910

Foos, Ben, 1994-95
Ford, Bill, 1960
Ford, Brian, 1993-94
Ford, Gerald, 1943
Ford, Jim, 1940
Fortin, Al, 1898-1901
Fortunato, Steve, 1988
Forystek, Gary, 1975-77
Foster, Harvey, 1936-37
Fox, Harry, 1936
Fox, Roger, 1966
Frampton, John, 1947-48
Francis, Al, 1955
Francisco, D'Juan, 1986-89
Francisco, Hiawatha, 1983-86
Frantz, George, 1915-16
Frascogna, Mike, 1993-95
Frasor, Dick, 1951-54
Frawley, George, 1942
Frederick, John, 1925-27
Freebery, Joe, 1967-68
Freeman, Tom, 1984-87
Freeze, Chet, 1907-08
Freistroffer, Tom, 1970-72
Frericks, Tom, 1974
Friday, Jimmy, 1995
Friske, Joe, 1923
Fromhart, Wally, 1933-35
Frost, Bob, 1938
Fry, Willie, 1973, 75-77
Fuentes, David, 1991-92
Funk, Art, 1902-05
Fuqua, Joe, 1987
Furjanic, Tony, 1982-85
Furlong, Nick, 1902-03
Furlong, Nick, 1967-69

G
Gaffney, John, 1953-54
Gagnon, Robb, 1980
Galanis, John, 1974-75
Galardo, Armando, 1952-53
Galen, Albert, 1895
Gallagher, Bill, 1969-71
Gallagher, Frank, 1936
Gallagher, John, 1895
Gallagher, Tom, 1938-40
Galloway, Tom, 1985-86
Gambone, John, 1973
Gander, Del, 1949-51
Ganey, Mike, 1943-45
Gann, Mike, 1981-84

Gardner, John, 1968
Gargan, Joe, 1912-13
Gargiulo, Frank, 1959-60
Garner, Terry, 1970-72
Garunde, 1908
Garvey, Art (Hector), 1920-21
Gasparella, Joe, 1944-45
Gasseling, Tom, 1968-70
Gasser, John, 1968-69
Gatewood, Tom, 1969-71
Gatti, Mike, 1986-88
Gaudreau, Bill, 1951
Gaul, Frank, 1945, 47-48
Gaul, Frank, 1933-35
Gay, Bill, 1947-50
Gaydos, Bob, 1955-57
Gebert, Al (Bud), 1928-29
Geers, Mike, 1977
Geniesse, Oswald, 1924
George, Don, 1953-54
Geremia, Frank, 1956-58
Gibbons, Tom, 1977-80
Gibbs, Bill, 1993-95
Gibson, Herbert, 1992-94
Gibson, Oliver, 1990-94
Gildea, Hubert, 1931-32
Gillen, Charles, 1900-02
Gipp, George, 1917-20
Girolami, Tony, 1940
Glaab, John, 1944-45
Gladieux, Bob, 1966-68
Gleason, Joe (Red), 1935-37
Gleason, Marc, 1987
Gleckler, Ed, 1974
Glueckert, Charles, 1922-24
Glynn, Ed (Cupid), 1909
Glynn, Ralph, 1899-1900
Gmitter, Don, 1964-66
Goberville, Tom, 1961-63
Goeddeke, George, 1964-66
Goeke, John, 1895
Goheen, Justin, 1991-94
Golic, Bob, 1975-78
Golic, Greg, 1981-83
Golic, Mike, 1981-84
Gompers, Bill, 1945-47
Goode, Ty, 1995
Goodman, Ron, 1972-74
Gordon, Darrell (Flash), 1985-88
Gores, Tom, 1969
Gorman, Tim, 1965-66
Gorman, Tom, 1986-89

Gorman, Tom (Kitty), 1931-33
Gottsacker, Harold, 1936-38
Grable, Charles, 1965
Grabner, Hank, 1918
Gradel, Ted, 1986-87
Grady, Bill, 1914
Graham, Kent, 1987-88
Graham, Pete, 1986-89
Graham, Tracy, 1992-94
Gramke, Joe, 1978-81
Graney, Mike, 1958
Grant, Chet, 1916, 20-21
Grasmanis, Paul, 1992-95
Grau, Frank, 1960-61
Gray, Gerry, 1959, 61-62
Gray, Ian, 1979-80
Gray, Ricky, 1982-84
Graziani, Larry, 1976
Green, Mark, 1985-88
Greeney, Norm, 1930-32
Greisbach, Matt, 1995
Grenda, Ed, 1969
Grieb, John, 1985-86
Griffin, Mike, 1983-84, 86-87
Griffith, Dan, 1958, 60
Griffith, Kevin, 1979, 81-82
Griggs, Ray, 1989-92
Grimm, Donn, 1987-90
Grindinger, Dennis, 1976-78
Groble, George, 1954-56
Grogan, Pete, 1980
Groom, Jerry, 1948-50
Grooms, Scott, 1980-81, 83-84
Grothaus, Walt, 1945, 47-49
Grunhard, Tim, 1986-89
Gubanich, John, 1938-40
Guerrera, Jim, 1992
Guglielmi, Ralph, 1951-54
Guilbeaux, Benny, 1995
Guillory, Lamar, 1989-90, 92
Gullickson, Tom, 1974
Gulyas, Ed, 1969-71
Gunderman, Reuben, 1931
Gushurst, Fred (Gus), 1912-13
Gustafson, Phil, 1969
Guthrie, Dave, 1904
Guthrie, Tom, 1944
Gutowski, Denny, 1970-72

H
Hack, Jim, 1934, 36
Hackett, Billy, 1987-89

Hadden, H.G., 1895
Haffner, George, 1959-60
Hagan, Lowell, 1932-33
Hagerty, Bob, 1966
Haggar, Joe, 1970, 72
Hagopian, Gary, 1969
Hague, Harry, 1907
Haines, Kris, 1975-78
Haley, Dave, 1966-67
Hall, Justin, 1988-92
Halter, Jordan, 1989-93
Hamby, Jim, 1949, 51
Hamilton, Brian, 1991-94
Hamilton, Don, 1908-09
Hankerd, John, 1977-80
Hankins, Bret, 1989
Hanley, Dan, 1930, 33-34
Hanlon, Bob, 1943
Hanousek, Dick, 1924-25
Hanratty, Terry, 1966-68
Harchar, John, 1973
Hardy, Kevin, 1964-67
Hardy, Russell, 1915
Hargrave, Bob, 1939-41
Harmon, Joe, 1922-24
Harrington, Vince, 1922-24
Harris, Gregory, 1985-87
Harris, Jim, 1930-32
Harrison, Randy, 1974-78
Harshman, Dan, 1965-67
Hart, Kevin, 1977-79
Hart, Leon, 1946-49
Hart, Speedy, 1976-77
Hartman, Pete, 1972-73
Hartweger, Pete, 1988
Hartwig, Steve, 1978-79
Harvat, Paul, 1911-12
Harvey, Tad, 1937-39
Hautman, Jim, 1976-78
Hawkins, B.J., 1990
Hayduk, George, 1971-73
Hayes, Art, 1898-1900
Hayes, Dave, 1917, 19-20
Hayes, Jackie, 1939-40
Haywood, Mike, 1982-86
Healy, Pat, 1959
Healy, Ted, 1987-89
Healy, Tom, 1903-05
Healy, Waldo, 1897
Heap, Joe, 1951-54
Hearden, Tom, 1924-26
Heath, Cliff, 1938

Heaton, Mike, 1965-67
Heavens, Jerome, 1975-78
Hebert, Carl, 1955-57
Heck, Andy, 1985-88
Hecomovich, Tom, 1959-61
Hedrick, Gene, 1955-56
Heenan, Pat, 1959
Heffern, Shawn, 1983-86
Heimkreiter, Steve, 1975-78
Hein, Jeff, 1971-73
Heldt, Mike, 1987-90
Helwig, John, 1948-50
Heman, Dick, 1945
Hempel, Scott, 1968-70
Hendricks, Dick, 1953-54
Heneghan, Curt, 1966-68
Henley, James, 1892
Henneghan, Bill, 1960
Henning, Art, 1906-08
Hentrich, Craig, 1989-92
Hepburn, Joseph, 1887-89
Hering, Frank, 1896
Herwit, Norm, 1928
Hesse, Frank, 1893, 95-96
Heywood, Bill, 1946
Hickey, Karl, 1988-89
Hickey, Louis, 1934-36
Hickman, Bill, 1957
Hicks, Bill, 1912
Higgins, Bill, 1948-50
Higgins, Luke, 1942
Higi, Joe, 1921
Hilbert, Steve, 1981
Hill, Greg, 1971-73
Hillerman, Karl, 1985
Hines, Mike, 1941
Ho, Reggie, 1987-88
Hoebing, Bob, 1945
Hoerster, Ed, 1960-62
Hofer, Bill, 1936-38
Hoffman, Frank (Nordy), 1930-31
Hogan, Don, 1939-41
Hogan, Don, 1962
Hogan, John, 1926
Hogan, Paul, 1918
Holden, Germaine, 1991-94
Hollendoner, Frank, 1937-38
Holdener, Mark, 1992
Hollister, Chet, 1989, 91
Holmes, George (Ducky), 1914, 16
Holohan, Pete, 1978-80
Holton, Barry, 1917, 20

Holtz, Skip, 1986
Holzapfel, Mike, 1966-68
Hooten, Herman, 1970-71
Hoppel, Leo, 1936
Horan, Bill, 1936
Horansky, Ted, 1976-79
Hornback, Eddie, 1979
Horney, John, 1964-66
Hornung, Paul, 1954-56
Host, Paul, 1930-32
Houck, George, 1887
Houser, Max, 1923-24
Howard, Al, 1929-30
Howard, Bobby, 1995
Howard, Joe, 1981-84
Howard, Walter, 1985-87
Huarte, John, 1962-64
Huber, Bill, 1942
Hudak, Ed, 1947-49
Hudson, Greg, 1986-87
Huff, Andy, 1969, 71-72
Huffman, Dave, 1975-78
Huffman, Tim, 1977-80
Huffman, Steve, 1986
Hufford, Larry, 1978-79
Hughes, Ernie, 1974-77
Hughes, Robert, 1991-93
Hughes, Tom, 1954-56
Humbert, Jim, 1969-71
Humenik, Dave, 1961-62
Hunsinger, Ed, 1922-24
Hunter, Al, 1973, 75-76
Hunter, Art, 1951-53
Hunter, Tony, 1979-82
Hurd, Bill, 1967
Hurlbert, Jim, 1926-27
Hurley, Bill, 1926-27
Hutzell, Oscar, 1906

I
Ismail, Raghib, 1988-90
Ivan, Ken, 1963-65
Izo, George, 1957-59

J
Jackson, Ernie, 1968
Jackson, Milt, 1982-84, 86
Jacobs, Frank, 1987-89
James, Johnny, 1922
James, Mike, 1984-85
Jandric, David, 1988-89
Jarosz, Joe, 1986-88

Jarrell, Adrian, 1989-93
Jaskwhich, Chuck, 1930-32
Jeffers, Jack, 1947-48
Jefferson, Alonzo, 1983-87
Jewett, Harry, 1887-88
Jeziorski, Ron, 1964-66
Jockisch, Bob, 1967-68
Johnson, Anthony, 1986-89
Johnson, Chris, 1986
Johnson, Clint, 1991-93
Johnson, Frank (Rodney), 1945, 47-49
Johnson, Joe, 1981-84
Johnson, Lance, 1990-93
Johnson, Malcolm, 1995
Johnson, Matt, 1989-92
Johnson, Murray, 1950
Johnson, Pete, 1974-78
Johnson, Phil, 1977-78
Johnson, Ron, 1968-70
Johnston, Frank, 1949-50
Johnston, Mike, 1980-83
Jonardi, Ray, 1949-50
Jones, Andre, 1987-90
Jones, Anthony, 1992
Jones, Bill, 1926-27
Jones, Eric, 1989-91
Jones, Jerry, 1915-16
Jones, Keith (Deak), 1911-14
Jones, Ray, 1911
Joseph, Bob, 1951-52
Joyce, Tom, 1905
Jurkovic, Mirko, 1988-91
Just, Jim, 1956-58
Juzwik, Steve, 1939-41

K
Kaczenski, Rick, 1994-95
Kadish, Mike, 1969-71
Kafka, Mike, 1974
Kairis, Matt, 1986
Kane, Mickey, 1920-22
Kantor, Joe, 1961-64
Kapish, Bob, 1949-51
Kapish, Gene, 1953-55
Kaplan, Clarence, 1929-30
Karcher, Ken, 1981-82
Karr, Jim, 1938
Kasper, Cy, 1919-20
Kassis, Tom, 1928-30
Katchik, Joe, 1951
Keach, Leroy, 1906
Keane, Steve, 1983

Kearns, John, 1892
Keefe, Emmett, 1912-15
Keefe, Frank, 1926
Keefe, Larry, 1924
Keefe, Walter, 1904-06
Kegaly, John, 1954
Kegler, Bill, 1896-97
Kell, Paul, 1936-38
Kelleher, Bill, 1911-14
Kelleher, Dan, 1974-76
Kelleher, John, 1938-39
Keller, Dick, 1953-54
Kelley, Ed, 1895
Kelley, Mike, 1981-84
Kelly, Al (Red), 1909
Kelly, Bob, 1943-44
Kelly, Bob, 1950-51
Kelly, Chuck, 1974
Kelly, Gerald, 1965-66
Kelly, Jim, 1940
Kelly, Jim, 1961-63
Kelly, Jim, 1964, 66
Kelly, Joe, 1944
Kelly, Johnny, 1936
Kelly, Johnny, 1937-39
Kelly, Kevin, 1981-84
Kelly, Luke, 1908-11
Kelly, Pete, 1938-40
Kelly, Tim, 1968-70
Kelly, Will, 1916
Kenneally, Tommy, 1927-29
Kennedy, Charles, 1967-69
Kennedy, John, 1908
Keough, Frank, 1892-94
Kersjes, Frank, 1930
Kerr, Bud, 1937-39
Kidd, Don, 1979-80
Kiel, Blair, 1980-83
Kienast, Phil, 1961
Kiernan, Mike, 1981, 84-85
Kilburg, Jeff, 1994-95
Kiley, Roger (Rodge), 1919-21
Kiliany, Dennis, 1967-68
Killian, Chuck, 1986-88
Kinder, Randy, 1993-95
Kineally, Kevin, 1973
King, Hollis (Hoot), 1913-15
King, Tom, 1916-17
Kinsherf, Jim, 1987-89
Kiousis, Marty, 1949
Kirby, Harley, 1901-02
Kirby, Maurice, 1893

Kirk, Bernie, 1918-19

Kissner, Larry, 1980-81

Kizer, Noble, 1922-24

Klees, Vince, 1973-75

Kleine, Wally, 1983-86

Klusas, Tim, 1992-94

Knafelc, Greg, 1977-79

Knapp, Lindsay, 1989-92

Knight, Thomas, 1993

Knott, Dan, 1973, 75-77

Koch, Bob, 1938-40

Koch, Dave, 1949

Koegel, Tim, 1977-81

Kohanowich, Al, 1951-52

Koken, Mike, 1930-32

Kolasinski, Dan, 1960

Kolski, Steve, 1960-62

Kondrk, John, 1970-72

Kondrla, Mike, 1968

Konieczny, Rudy, 1965-66

Kopczak, Frank, 1934-36

Kopka, Kevin, 1995

Kordas, Jim, 1992-94

Koreck, Bob, 1959-60

Kornman, Russ, 1972-75

Korth, Howard, 1938-40

Kos, Gary, 1968-70

Kosikowski, Frank, 1946-47

Kosky, Ed, 1930-32

Kostelnik, Tom, 1962-64

Kouris, John, 1992-93

Kovalcik, George (Jake), 1936, 38

Kovaleski, Mike, 1983-86

Kovatch, John, 1939-41

Kowalkowski, Scott, 1987-90

Kowalski, George, 1914

Kozak, George, 1931

Krall, Rudy, 1944

Kramer, Jeff, 1994-95

Kramer, Pat, 1978-82

Krause, Ed (Moose), 1931-33

Krembs, Dave, 1927

Krimm, John, 1978-81

Krivik, Stan, 1945

Krug, Tom, 1994-95

Krupa, Ed, 1942-43

Kuchta, Frank, 1956-57

Kucmicz, Mike, 1965-66

Kudlacz, Stan, 1941-42

Kuechenberg, Bob, 1966-68

Kuffel, Ray, 1943

Kuh, Dick, 1948

Kuharich, Joe, 1935-37

Kulbitski, Vic, 1943

Kunz, George, 1966-68

Kunz, Jeff, 1984-87

Kunz, Matt, 1995

Kuppler, George, 1898-1900

Kurth, Joe, 1930-32

Kurzynske, Jim, 1945

Kutzavitch, Bill, 1961

Kvochak, Chris, 1985-87

L

LaBorne, Frank, 1931-33

Lacheta, Chet, 1990-91

LaFollette, Clarence, 1923

Lahey, Jim, 1937

Lahey, Matt, 1992

Laiber, Joe, 1939-41

Lalli, Mike, 1989, 91-92

Lally, Bob, 1947-49

Lamantia, Pete, 1966

Lambeau, Earl (Curly), 1918

Lambert, Steve, 1968

Lamonica, Daryle, 1960-62

Lanahan, John, 1940-42

Landolfi, Chuck, 1967-68

Landry, Jack, 1948-50

Lane, Greg, 1990-93

Laney, Tom, 1973-74

Lanigan, Craig, 1989-91

Lantry, Joe, 1906

Lanza, Chuck, 1984-87

Lark, Antwon, 1988-89

Larkin, Art (Bunny), 1912-14

Larkin, Ed, 1938

Larkin, Mike, 1981-82, 84-85

Larsen, John, 1911

Larson, Fred (Ojay), 1918, 20-21

Lasch, Bob, 1953-54

Lathrop, Ralph (Zipper), 1911-14

Lattner, Johnny, 1951-53

Lauck, Chick, 1966-68

Lautar, John, 1934-36

Lavin, John, 1966-68

Law, John, 1926-29

Lawrence, Don, 1956-58

Lawrence, Steve, 1983-86

Lawson, Tom, 1967-69

Layden, Elmer, 1922-24

Layden, Mike, 1933-35

Leahy, Bernie, 1929-31

Leahy, Frank, 1928-29

Leahy, James, 1968
Leahy, Ryan, 1992-95
LeBlanc, Joe, 1911
LeBlanc, Mark, 1980-82
Lebrau, John, 1944
LeCluyse, Len, 1946-47
Leding, Mike, 1931-32
Lee, Al, 1938-40
Lee, Jack, 1951-54
Lee, Jay, 1911
Lehmann, Bob, 1961-63
Lemek, Ray, 1953-55
Lennon, Peter, 1898
Leon, John 1977-79
Leonard, Bill, 1945-47
Leonard, Bob, 1938-40
Leonard, Jim, 1931-33
Leonard, Rob, 1991-93
Leonard, Tony, 1984
Leopold, Bobby, 1976-79
Leppig, George, 1926-28
Lesko, Al, 1945, 48
Levens, Dorsey, 1989-90
Levicki, John, 1934-36
Lewallen, Brian, 1968-69
Lewis, Aubrey, 1955-57
Lezon, Todd, 1985
Lieb, Tom, 1921-22
Liebenstein, Mike, 1980-81
Liggio, Tom, 1960-61
Likovich, John, 1974-76
Lillis, Paul, 1939-41
Lima, Chuck, 1955-57
Limont, Mark, 1944
Limont, Paul, 1942-43, 46
Lind, Mike, 1960-62
Linehan, Ed, 1892
Linehan, John, 1960
Lins, George, 1896-1901
Lippincott, Marty, 1986-88
Lisch, Rusty, 1976-77, 79
Listzwan, Tom, 1928
Littig, Edward, 1897
Lium, John, 1966
Livergood, Bernie, 1922-24
Livingstone, Bob, 1942, 46-47
Loboy, Alan, 1963-64
Lockard, Frank (Abbie), 1917-18
Locke, Joe, 1927, 29
Lodish, Mike, 1957-59
Logan, Les, 1920-22
Lohman, Mike, 1986

Lombardo, Carmelo, 1918
Loncaric, Lou, 1954-56
Lonergan, Frank (Happy), 1901-03
Long, Harry, 1963-65
Longhi, Ed, 1936-38
Longo, Tom, 1963-65
Loop, Paul, 1958
Lopienski, Tom, 1972-75
Loula, Jim, 1960
Lower, Harold, 1912
Lozano, Rick, 1990-92
Lozi, Dennis, 1972-73
Luecke, Dan, 1960
Lueken, Jeff, 1979-81
Luhn, Henry, 1887
Lujack, Johnny, 1943, 46-47
Lukats, Nick, 1930, 32-33
Lyden, Mike, 1943
Lyell, Will, 1993
Lyght, Todd, 1987-90
Lynch, Dick, 1955-57
Lynch, Ed, 1907-09
Lynch, Jim,1964-66
Lynch, John, 1992-93
Lynn, Brad, 1937
Lyon, Francis, 1896
Lytle, Dean, 1991-93

M
Maarleveld, John, 1981
MacAfee, Ken, 1974-77
MacDonald, Tom, 1961-63
MacDonald,Tom, 1992, 94
Machtolf, Dave, 1983-84
Maciag, Dick, 1970, 72
Mack, Bill (Red), 1958-60
Maddock, Bob, 1939-41
Madigan, Edward (Slip), 1916-17, 19
Magee, Brian, 1992-95
Maggioli, Achille, (Chick), 1943-44
Magevney, Hugh (Red), 1921
Maglicic, Ken, 1962-64
Magnotta, Mike, 1959-60
Mahaffey, Tom, 1931-32
Mahalic, Drew, 1972-74
Maher, Willie (Red), 1921-23
Mahoney, Dick, 1930-31
Mahoney, Gene, 1927
Mahoney, Jim, 1948-49
Maiden, Alton, 1993-94
Male, Chuck, 1978-79
Malone, Grover, 1915-16, 19

Malone, Mike, 1968

Maloney, James, 1887

Maloney, Jerry, 1994

Maloney, Jim, 1908-09

Maloney, John, 1938

Mangialardi, Fred, 1951-53

Mannelly, Bernard, 1989, 91-92

Manzo, Lou, 1956-58

Marchand, Gerry, 1950

Marelli, Ray, 1925-26

Mariani, John, 1970-72

Marino, Nunzio, 1944

Markowski, Joe, 1953

Marquardt, Clarence, 1938

Mart, John, 1934-36

Marrero, Keith, 1981

Marsh, Drew, 1991, 93

Marshall, George, 1988-90

Marshall, Tim, 1980-81, 83

Marshall, Walt, 1935-37

Marsico, Joe, 1966

Martell, Gene, 1953-55

Martin, Bill, 1910

Martin, Bob, 1952-53

Martin, Dave, 1965-67

Martin, Jim, 1946-49

Martin, Jim (Pepper), 1934-36

Martin, Mike, 1968, 70

Martin, Pierre, 1989

Martinovich, Rob, 1976-79

Martz, Bob, 1985

Martz, George, 1944

Marx, Greg, 1970-72

Maschmeier, Tom, 1974-75

Masini, Mike, 1980-81

Massey, Bob, 1930

Massey, Jim, 1969

Masterson, Bernie, 1938

Mastrangelo, John, 1944-46

Masztak, Dean, 1978-81

Mathews, Lee, 1908-10

Mathews, James (Marty), 1914

Mattera, Vince, 1963-64

Mattes, Francis, 1888

Matthews, Ed, 1938

Matz, Paul, 1951-54

Maune, Neil, 1979, 81-83

Mavraides, Menil (Minnie), 1951-53

Maxwell, Joe, 1960-62

Maxwell, Joe, 1924-26

May, Paul, 1965-66

Mayer, Frank, 1925-26

Mayes, Derrick, 1992-95

Mayl, Gene, 1921-23

Mazziotti, Tony, 1933-35

Mazur, John, 1949-51

McAdams, Vince (Bennie), 1926

McAvoy, Tom, 1905

McBride, Bob, 1941-42, 46

McBride, Mike, 1972-73

McBride, Oscar, 1991-94

McCabe, Harold (Dinger), 1925-26

McCabe, John, 1983-85

McCarthy, Chris, 1994

McCarthy, Bill, 1951

McCarthy, Bill, 1934-36

McCarthy, Frank, 1927

McCarthy, Jack, 1935-37

McCarthy, William, 1895

McCarty, Pat, 1936-37

McConnell, Dan, 1993-95

McCormick, Keith, 1978-79

McCormick, Nevin (Bunny), 1936-37

McCoy, Mike, 1967-69

McCullough, Mike, 1993-95

McDaniels, Steve, 1975-77

McDermott, Ed, 1902-03

McDermott, Frank, 1921

McDermott, James, 1892

McDevitt, Dan, 1988

McDonald, Angus, 1896, 98-99

McDonald, Devon, 1989-92

McDonald, Paul, 1907-08

McDonnell, John, 1954-56

McDonough, Joe, 1938

McDougal, Kevin, 1990-93

McGannon, Bill, 1938-40

McGarry, Rob, 1979-80

McGee, Coy, 1945-48

McGehee, Ralph, 1946-49

McGill, Karmeeleyah, 1989-92

McGill, Mike, 1965-67

McGinley, John, 1956-57

McGinn, Dan, 1963-65

McGinnis, Dan, 1910-12

McGinnis, John, 1942

McGlew, Henry (Fuzzy), 1900-03

McGlinn, Mike, 1991-94

McGoldrick, Jim, 1936-38

McGovern, George, 1936

McGrath, Bob, 1936

McGrath, Chester (Mugsy), 1910-11

McGrath, Frank, 1923

McGrath, Jack, 1926-28

McGraw, Pat, 1970-72
McGuff, Al, 1932
McGuffey, David, 1984-85
McGuire, Bob, 1917
McGuire, Gene, 1988-91
McGuire, Mike, 1974
McGurk, Jim, 1945-46
McHale, John, 1940
McHale, John, 1968-70
McHugh, Tom, 1951-53
McHugh, Tom, 1984-86
McInerny, Arnold, 1915-16
McIntyre, John, 1938-39
McKenna, Jim, 1935
McKeon, Tom, 1889
McKillip, Leo, 1948-50
McKinney, Charles, 1926-27
McKinley, Tom, 1966-68
McLane, Mark, 1974-76
McLaughlin, Dave, 1941
McLaughlin, John, 1994-95
McLaughlin, Tom, 1911-13
McLaughlin, Pat, 1974-75
McLoone, Mike, 1988
McMahon, Joe, 1934-36
McMahon, Johnny, 1936-38
McManmon, Art, 1929-30
McMullan, John, 1923-25
McMullan, John, 1953-55
McMurry, Andrew, 1975
McNally, Vince, 1925-26
McNamara, Regis, 1929-31
McNamara, Ted, 1988-89
McNeil, Tim, 1987
McNeill, Chuck, 1941
McNerny, Larry, 1903-05
McNichols, Austin, 1946
McNulty, Mike, 1898-99
McNulty, Paul, 1922
McSorley, John, 1926-27
McShane, Kevin, 1986, 88-89
Meadows, Dave, 1983
Meagher, Jack, 1916
Meagher, John, 1888
Meeker, Bob, 1963-65
Megin, Bernard, 1936
Mehre, Harry, 1919-21
Melady, Eugene, 1887-88
Melinkovich, George, 1931-32, 34
Mello, Jim, 1942-43, 46
Menie, Tom, 1970-71
Meno, Chuck, 1956

Mense, Jim, 1953-55
Mergenthal, Art, 1944
Merkle, Bob, 1964
Merkle, Rob, 1989
Merlitti, Jim, 1967-69
Mertes, Al, 1906-08
Meschievitz, Vince, 1950
Meter, Bernie (Bud), 1942-43, 46
Meter, Brian, 1992-93
Metzger, Bert, 1928-30
Meyer, Howard, 1975-78
Michalik, Rick, 1985-86
Michaels, Andrew, 1940
Michaels, Bill, 1947
Michuta, John, 1933-35
Mieszkowski, Ed, 1943, 45
Mihalko, Ryan, 1988-91
Mikacich, Jim, 1959-61
Milbauer,Frank, 1922-23
Miles, Frank, (Rangy), 1918
Miller, Alvin, 1983-86
Miller, Creighton, 1941-43
Miller, Don, 1922-24
Miller, Earl, 1918
Miller, Edgar (Rip), 1922-24
Miller, Fred, 1926-28
Miller, Gerry, 1922-24
Miller, Harry (Red), 1906-09
Miller, Howard, 1921
Miller, John, 1914-16
Miller, Michael, 1991-94
Miller, Ray, 1911-12
Miller, Steve, 1934-36
Miller, Tom, 1940-42
Miller, Walter, 1915-19
Miller, Ward, 1916
Millheam, Curtis (Duke), 1931
Millner, Wayne, 1933-35
Mills, Rupert (Rupe), 1913-14
Milota, Jim, 1954, 56
Minik, Frank, 1960-62
Minor, Kory, 1995
Minnix, Bob, 1969-71
Mirer, Rick, 1989-92
Misetic, Steve, 1993-94
Mishler, Ron, 1978-81
Miskowitz, Lew, 1973
Mitchell, Dave, 1977-78
Mitoulas, Bill, 1994-95
Mittelhauser, Tom, 1963
Mixon, Leo, 1922
Modak, Dan, 1949-50

Mohardt, Johnny, 1918-21
Mohn, Bill, 1918
Monahan, Bill, 1897-99
Monahan, Mark, 1992-95
Monahan, Tom, 1960
Monahan, Tom, 1984-86
Mondron, Bob, 1955
Montana, Joe, 1975, 77-78
Montroy, Jack, 1928
Monty, Tim, 1966-68
Mooney, Al, 1937-39
Moore, Dan, 1925-26
Moore, Elton, 1973-76
Moore, LaRon, 1991-92, 94-95
Morales, Alfred, 1916
Morgan, Larry (Red), 1917
Morgan, Steve, 1910-12
Moriarity, Mike, 1906, 08-09
Moriarty, George, 1933-35
Moriarty, Kerry, 1974
Moriarty, Larry, 1980-82
Moriarty, Trevor, 1988-91
Moritz, Charles H., 1896
Morrin, Dan, 1971-73
Morris, Rodney, 1980-82
Morrison, James, 1894
Morrison, Paul, 1938
Morrison, Rich, 1986-87
Morrissey, Joe, 1926-28
Morrissey, Rockne, 1952-53
Morse, Jim, 1954-56
Morse, Jim, 1976-77
Morse, 1894
Mortell, John, 1938
Mosca, Angelo, 1956
Moscardelli, Chris, 1990-91
Mosley, Emmett, 1993-95
Mosley, John, 1980-83
Moynihan, Brendan, 1978-79
Moynihan, Tim, 1926-29
Mudron, Pat, 1968, 70
Muehlbauer, Mike, 1957-59
Mueller, Art, 1934
Muessel, 1893
Mulcahey, Jim, 1937
Mullen, Jack, 1894-99
Muller, Nick, 1962
Mullins, Larry (Moon), 1927-30
Mundee, Fred, 1934-36
Munger, Harold, 1911-12
Muno, Kevin, 1977
Munro, Jim, 1954-56

Munson, Frank, 1905-07
Murphy, Dan, 1904
Murphy, Denny, 1960-62
Murphy, Emmett, 1930-32
Murphy, Fred, 1892
Murphy, Gene, 1921-22
Murphy, George, 1940-42
Murphy, Jerry, 1916
Murphy, Johnny, 1936-37
Murphy, John, 1908
Murphy, John, 1894-96
Murphy, John, 1981
Murphy, Terry, 1976-77
Murphy, Tim, 1921-23
Murphy, Tom, 1950-52
Murphy, Tom, 1927-29
Murphy, Tom, 1981-83
Murray, Joe, 1897-98
Murray, John, 1961-62
Murrin, George, 1925-27
Musuraca, Jim, 1970-72
Mutscheller, Jim, 1949-51
Myers, Gary, 1956-58

N
Naab, Dick, 1959-61
Nadolney, Romanus (Peaches), 1918
Nagurski, Bronko, 1956-58
Nash, Joe, 1926-29
Nash, Tom, 1968-69
Nau, Jeremy, 1991-94
Naughton, David, 1897
Naughton, Mike, 1971-73
Naylor, Rick, 1980-83
Nebel, Ed, 1958-59
Neece, Steve, 1973-74
Neff, Bob, 1940-42
Neidell, David, 1987
Neidert, Bob, 1968-70
Nelson, Patrick, 1887
Nemeth, Steve, 1943-44
Nichols, John, 1930
Nickel, Russ, 1936
Nicola, Norm, 1962-64
Nicula, George, 1953-55
Niehaus, Steve, 1972-75
Niemiec, John, 1926-28
Niezer, Charles, 1897
Nightingale, Chuck, 1970
Nigro, Mark, 1986
Nissi, Paul, 1960
Noon, Tom, 1926

Noppenberger, John, 1923
Norman, Mark, 1979
Norri, Eric, 1966-68
Nosbusch, Kevin, 1972-74
Novakov, Dan, 1969-71
Novakov, Tony, 1973-75
Nowack, Art, 1953
Nowers, Paul (Curly), 1912-13
Noznesky, Pete, 1954-55
Nusskern, John, 1949
Nyere, George, 1901-03

O

Oaas, Torgus (Turk), 1910-11
Oberst, Gene, 1920, 22-23
O'Boyle, Harry, 1924-26
O'Brien, Coley, 1966-68
O'Brien, Dick, 1940-41
O'Brien, Johnny (One Play), 1928-30
O'Brien, Johnny, 1938-40
O'Brien, Tom, 1956
O'Connor, Bill (Bucky), 1942, 46-47
O'Connor, Bill (Zeke), 1944, 46
O'Connor, Dan, 1968
O'Connor, Dan, 1902
O'Connor, Paul (Bucky), 1928-30
O'Connor, Phil, 1945
Odem, James, 1913-15
O'Donnell, Hugh, 1914-15
O'Donnell, John, 1972, 74
O'Donnell, Leo, 1914
Odyniec, Norm, 1956-58
O'Flynn, Ed, 1906
O'Hara, Charlie, 1960-63
O'Hara, Francis, 1896
O'Hara, Jim, 1981-82
O'Hara, Joe, 1916, 19
O'Haren, Dave, 1984
O'Leary, James, 1907
O'Leary, Tom, 1965-67
Oleksak, Mark, 1986
Oliver, Harry, 1980-81
Olosky, Marty, 1961-63
O'Loughlin, Bill, 1936-38
Olson, Bob, 1967-69
O'Malley, Dom, 1899-1900, 02
O'Malley, Hugh, 1966
O'Malley, Jim, 1970-72
O'Meara, Walt, 1938-40
O'Neil, Bill, 1911
O'Neil, Bob, 1951-52
O'Neil, John, 1904

O'Neill, Bob, 1938-39
O'Neill, Hugh, 1916
O'Neill, Jeff, 1984
O'Neill, Joe, 1934-36
O'Neill, Mike, 1991
Opela, Bruno, 1945
O'Phelan, John, 1903
Oracko, Steve, 1945, 47, 49
O'Regan, Tom, 1887
O'Reilly, Chuck, 1936-37
O'Reilly, Martin, 1940
Oriard, Mike, 1968-69
Ornstein, Gus, 1994
Orsini, Steve, 1975-77
Osterman, Bob, 1939-40
Ostrowski, Chet, 1949-51
O'Toole, Dan, 1970-72
Owen, Tom, 1918
Owens, Bill, 1957

P

Page, Alan, 1964-66
Pagley, Lou, 1978
Paine, Bob, 1907-08
Palladino, Bob, 1943
Pallas, Pete, 1977-78
Palmer, Ralph, 1895-96
Palumbo, Sam, 1951-54
Palumbo, Scott, 1995
Panelli, John, 1945-48
Paolone, Ralph, 1950
Papa, Bob, 1964
Papa, Joe, 1938-40
Parenti, Chris, 1991-93
Parise, Tom, 1973-75
Parisien, Art, 1925-26
Parker, Mike, 1971-73
Parry, Tom, 1944
Parseghian, Mike, 1974
Pasquesi, Tony, 1952-54
Paterra, Frank, 1951-52
Patten, Paul, 1940-41
Patton, Eric, 1969-71
Patulski, Walt, 1969-71
Payne, Randy, 1974-75
Pawelski, Don, 1981
Pearcy, Van, 1982-83
Pearson, Dudley, 1917, 19
Pearson, Jeff, 1986-87
Peasenelli, John, 1940, 42
Pendergast, Kevin, 1991-93
Penick, Eric, 1972-74

Penman, Gene,1962

Penza, Don, 1951-53

Pergrine, John, 1965-67

Perko, John, 1943

Perkowski, Joe, 1959-61

Perona, Mike, 1995

Perrino, Mike, 1982-85

Perry, Brian, 1994

Perry, Art, 1949-50

Pesavento, Pat, 1985

Peters, Marty, 1933-35

Peterson, Anthony, 1990-93

Peterson, Elmer, 1940

Petitbon, John, 1949-51

Petitgout, Luke, 1995

Pfefferle, Dick, 1932, 34-35

Pfeiffer, Bill, 1961-63

Phelan, Bob, 1919-21

Phelan, Jim, 1915-17

Phelan, Vince, 1986-87

Phelps, Robert, 1995

Philbin, Dave, 1916-17

Philbrook, George, 1908-11

Phillips, Denny, 1961-63

Phillips, John, 1918

Piccin, Tony, 1983-84

Piccone, Cammille (Pic), 1942

Pick, John, 1900-01

Piel, Ed, 1901

Piepul, Milt, 1938-40

Pierce, Bill, 1930-32

Pietrosante, Nick, 1956-58

Pietrzak, Nick, 1956-58

Pilney, Andy, 1933-35

Pinkett, Allen, 1982-85

Pinn, Frank, 1954

Pinn, Frank, 1986

Pivarnik, Joe, 1931-33

Pivec, Dave, 1962-63

Plain, George

Plantz, Ron, 1982-85

Pliska, Joe, 1911-14

Ploszek, Mike, 1974

Poehler, Fred, 1951-52

Pohlen, Pat, 1973-75

Pojman, Henry, 1933-35

Polisky, John (Bull), 1925-27

Pollard, William, 1989-92

Pomarico, Frank, 1971-73

Poorman, George, 1989-91

Pope, Al, 1969

Pope, Stephen, 1992

Porter, Paul, 1945

Poskon, Dewey, 1967-69

Postupack, Joe, 1939

Potempa, Gary, 1971-73

Potter, Tom, 1945-46

Pottios, Myron, 1958-60

Powers, John, 1897

Powers, John, 1917

Powers, John, 1959-61

Powlus, Ron, 1994-95

Pozderac, Phil, 1978-81

Prelli, Joe, 1924-25, 27

Prendergast, Dick, 1955-57

Prinzivalli, David, 1987-89

Prinzivalli, Domenic, 1985-87

Pritchett, Wes, 1985-88

Prokop, George, 1918-20

Prokop, Joe, 1940-41

Provissiero, John, 1928

Prudhomme, Edward, 1887-89

Pszeracki, Joe, 1973-74

Puntillo, Chuck, 1957-58

Puntillo, Tony, 1985-86

Puplis, Andy, 1935-37

Purcell, Rick, 1989

Purk, Gary, 1981

Putzstuck, John, 1980-81

Q

Quehl, Steve, 1972-73, 75

Quinlan, Mike, 1892

Quinn, Dan, 1986-87

Quinn, Jim, 1926

Quinn, Mark, 1977

Quinn, Steve, 1965-67

Quinn, Tom, 1966-68

Quist, David, 1993-95

R

Raba, Elmer, 1945

Racanelli, Vito, 1967

Race, Joe, 1935-37

Raich, Nick, 1953-54

Rakers, Jim, 1962-63

Rankin, George, 1969-70

Ransavage, Jerry, 1926-28

Rascher, Norb, 1932

Rassas, George, 1938, 40

Rassas, Kevin, 1966-67

Rassas, Nick, 1963-65

Raterman, John, 1969-71

Ratigan, Brian, 1989-92

Ratkowski, Ray, 1958-60
Ratterman, George, 1945-46
Rausch, Lorenzo, 1914
Rausch, Peter, 1987, 90-91
Ray, John, 1944
Rayam, Hardy, 1976-79
Ready, Bob, 1951-54
Reagan, Bob, 1921-23
Redder, Corey, 1994
Reedy, Joe, 1925
Reese, Frank, 1921, 23-24
Reeve, Dave, 1974-77
Regner, Tom, 1964-66
Rehder, 1984-87
Reid, Don, 1967-69
Reilly, Clarence, 1924
Reilly, Jack, 1928
Reilly, Jim, 1967-69
Rellas, Chris, 1943
Renaud, Charles, 1943
Restic, Joe, 1975-78
Reynolds, Frank, 1956-58
Reynolds, Lawrence, 1908
Reynolds, Paul, 1951-52, 54-55
Reynolds, Tom, 1967
Rhoads, Tom, 1965-66
Rice, John, 1979-81
Rice, Tony, 1987-89
Richerson, Mike, 1981, 84
Ridder, Tim, 1995
Ridgley, Troy, 1988-91
Riffle, Chuck, 1937-39
Rigali, Bob, 1952-53
Rigali, Joe, 1924-25
Riley, Charlie, 1925-27
Riley, Tom, 1984-86
Riney, Jeff, 1992-93
Rini, Tom, 1958-59
Riordan, Will, 1941
Rively, Clair, 1939
Roach, John, 1923-26
Roach, Tom, 1932-33
Robb, Aaron, 1985-88
Robertson, Bob, 1935
Robinson, Jack, 1932-34
Robinson, Marvin, 1991
Robinson, Tyrone, 1972
Robst, Paul, 1951, 53
Roby, Charles, 1892-93
Rockne, Knute, 1910-13
Roddy, Marty, 1981, 83-84
Roddy, Steve, 1987-88

Rodenkirk, Don, 1976
Rogenski, Steve, 1936, 38
Rogers, John, 1930-31
Rogers, Scott, 1983-84
Rogers, Sean, 1995
Roggeman, Tom, 1983-84
Rohan, Andy, 1973-74
Rohrs, George, 1931
Rokich, Pete, 1984-86
Rolle, Richard, 1993-94
Ronchetti, Pete, 1916-17
Ronzone, Matt, 1934
Roolf, Jim, 1971-72
Rosenthal, Jacob (Rosy), 1894-96
Rossum, Allen, 1994-95
Roth, Jesse, 1908
Rovai, Fred, 1944-46
Roy, Norb, 1959-61
Royer, Dick, 1956-58
Ruckelshaus, John, 1925
Ruddy, Tim, 1990-93
Rudnick, Tim, 1971-73
Rudzinski, Joe, 1979-82
Ruell, Ulric, 1908
Ruettiger, Dan, 1975
Ruetz, Joe, 1935-37
Rufo, John, 1974
Ruggerio, Frank, 1943-45
Russell, Bill, 1945-46
Russell, Marv, 1973-75
Rutkowski, Ed, 1960-62
Rutkowski, Frank, 1974
Ruzicka, Jim, 1967, 69
Ryan, Billy, 1907-10
Ryan, Jim, 1917
Ryan, Jim, 1965-66
Ryan, Tim, 1987-90
Rydzewski, Frank, 1915-17
Rykovich, Julie, 1943
Rymkus, Lou, 1940-42

S
Sabal, Al, 1957-59
Sack, Allen, 1964-66
Saddler, LeShane, 1991-94
Sadowski, Ed, 1936
Saggau, Bob, 1938-40
Saggau, Tom, 1948
Salmon, Louis (Red), 1900-03
Salvino, Bob, 1954
Sample, Jeremy, 1991-94
Samuel, Al, 1972-74

Sanders, Cy, 1918-19

Sandri, Winston, 1988-90

Sanford, Charles, 1889

Sarb, Pat, 1973

Sass, James, 1986-87

Satterfield, Bob, 1987-88

Sauget, Dick, 1964

Sauget, Rich, 1991-92

Savoldi, Joe, 1928-30

Sawicz, Paul, 1973

Sawkins, Edward, 1887-88

Scales, Ed, 1973

Scanlan, Ray, 1906

Scannell, Bob, 1954-56

Scannell, Tim, 1982-85

Scarpitto, Bob, 1958-60

Schaack, Ed, 1892

Schaaf, Jim, 1956-58

Schaefer, Don, 1953-55

Scharer, Eddie, 1924-25

Schilling, Joe, 1936

Schillo, Fred, 1892-94, 96-97

Schiralli, Angelo, 1966

Schiralli, Rocco, 1932-34

Schiro, Bumper, 1981-82

Schivarelli, Pete, 1969-70

Schlezes, Ken, 1970-72

Schmid, Charles, 1940

Schmidt, Oscar, 1894

Schmitt, Bill, 1906-09

Schmitz, Steve, 1975-77

Schneider, J.S., 1899

Schnurr, Fred, 1966

Schoen, Tom, 1965-67

Scholtz, Bob, 1957-59

Schrader, Jim, 1951-53

Schramm, Paul, 1954-56

Schreiber, Tom, 1944-45

Schrenker, Henry, 1938, 40

Schrenker, Paul, 1933-34

Schroffner, Stefan, 1993-94

Schultz, Herb, 1927

Schulz, Clay, 1959-61

Schumacher, Larry, 1967-69

Schuster, Ken, 1944

Schwartz, Charles, 1929

Schwartz, Marchy, 1929-31

Scibelli, Joe, 1958

Scott, Vince, 1944-46

Scruggs, Martin, 1989-91

Scully, John, 1977-80

Seaman, Neil, 1957-58

Seaman, Tom, 1950-52

Seasly, Mike, 1985-86

Secret, Bob, 1961

Sefcik, George, 1959-61

Seiler, Leo, 1960

Seiler, Paul, 1964-66

Selcer, Dick, 1956-58

Setzer, Rusty, 1988-90

Sexton, Jim, 1988-91

Seyfrit, Frank (Si), 1920-21

Seymour, Jim, 1966-68

Shakespeare, Bill, 1933-35

Shamla, Dick, 1934

Shanahan, George, 1918

Shannon, Brian, 1988-90

Shannon, Dan, 1951-54

Sharkey, Ed, 1974

Sharp, Art, 1913-14

Shaughnessy, Frank (Shag), 1901-04

Shaughnessy, Rodney, 1921

Shaughnessy, Tom, 1914

Shaw, Lawrence (Buck), 1919-21

Shay, George (Dinny), 1927-29

Shea, Bill (Red), 1920-21

Sheahan, Jim, 1968

Sheehan, Clarence, 1903-06

Sheeketski, Joe, 1930-32

Shellogg, Alec, 1936-37

Shellogg, Fred, 1936-37

Sheridan, Benny, 1937-39

Sheridan, Phil, 1938-40

Sheridan, Phil, 1963-65

Sherlock, Jim, 1960-62

Sherman, Kevin, 1981

Shey, Chris, 1989

Shields, Bob, 1926

Shields, Jack, 1980-82

Shiner, Mike, 1980-83

Shulsen, Dick, 1955-56, 58

Siewe, Bill, 1979-80

Signaigo, Joe, 1943, 46-47

Silver, Nate, 1902-05

Simien, Erik, 1989-90

Simmons, Floyd, 1945-47

Simon, Jack, 1961-63

Simon, Tim, 1973-75

Simonich, Ed, 1936-38

Sinnott, Roger, 1893

Sipes, Sherrill, 1954-56

Sitko, Emil, 1946-49

Sitko, Steve, 1937-39

Skall, Russell, 1947

Skat, Al, 1943

Skoglund, Bill, 1966

Skoglund, Len, 1935-37

Slackford, Fred (Fritz), 1915-16, 19

Slafkosky, John, 1961-62

Slager, Rick, 1974-76

Slovak, Emil, 1945-46

Smagala, Stan, 1986-89

Smalls, Michael, 1988-89

Smith, Art, 1911

Smith, Bill, 1933-34

Smith, Chris, 1981-84

Smith, Darnell, 1994-95

Smith, Dick (Red), 1925-26

Smith, Gene, 1973, 75-76

Smith, Gene, 1910-11

Smith, Glen, 1910-11

Smith, Howard, 1927

Smith, Hunter, 1995

Smith, Irv, 1983

Smith, John (Clipper), 1925-27

Smith, Kevin, 1983

Smith, Lancaster (Lank), 1946-48

Smith, Maurice (Clipper), 1917-20

Smith, Nick, 1989-92

Smith, Pete (Red), 1921

Smith, Rod, 1988-91

Smith, Scott, 1970-71

Smith, Shawn, 1989-90

Smith, Sherman, 1972-74

Smith, Tony, 1989-91

Smith, Tony, 1987

Smith, Wade, 1993

Smithberger, Jim, 1965-67

Snell, Ed, 1936

Snowden, Jim, 1961, 63-64

Snow, Jack, 1962-64

Snow, Paul, 1966-68

Snyder, Jim, 1943

Solari, Fred, 1933-35

Sollmann, Scott, 1994-95

Sorensen, Dan, 1985-86

Southall, Corny, 1985-88

Spalding, Tom, 1917

Spaniel, Frank, 1947-49

Spears, Kenny, 1990

Spence, Marv, 1984-87

Spencer, Jamie, 1995

Spickelmier, Jon, 1994-95

Spielmaker, Daane, 1980-83

Springer, Frank, 1887-88

Spruell, Byron, 1984-87

Staab, Fred, 1930

Stafford, Charles, 1992-95

Stams, Frank, 1984-88

Stanczyak, Al, 1945

Standring, Jay, 1968-69

Stange, Gus, 1922-23

Stanitzek, Frank, 1954

Stanley, Basil, 1917

Stansfield, John, 1910

Statuto, Art, 1943-47

Staudt, Clement, 1900

Stec, Greg, 1992-94

Steenberge, Pat, 1970-71

Steiner, Art, 1902-03

Steinkemper, Bill, 1934-36

Stelmazek, Ed, 1945

Stenger, Brian, 1966-68

Stepaniak, Ralph, 1969-71

Stephan, Jack, 1974

Stephan, Leo. 1914-15

Stephens, Clay, 1961-63

Stephens, Jack, 1952

Stevenson, Harry, 1937-39

Stevenson, Martin, 1912

Stewart, Ralph, 1944

Stickles, Monty, 1957-59

Stilley, Ken, 1933-35

Stine, Raleigh (Rollo), 1917-18

Stock, Jim, 1972-75

Stoker, Todd, 1990

Stokes, Clement, 1995

Stone, Chris, 1979-82

Stone, Dan, 1979-80

Stone, Jim, 1977-80

Stonebreaker, Michael, 1986, 88, 90

Streeter, George, 1985-88

Strohmeyer, George, 1946-47

Stroud, Clarke, 1950

Stroud, Cliff, 1993-94

Studebaker, John, 1893-94

Studer, Dean, 1954-56

Stuhldreher, Harry, 1922-24

Sullivan, Bob, 1938

Sullivan, Danny, 1936-37

Sullivan, George, 1943-44, 46-47

Sullivan, Joe, 1933-34

Sullivan, John, 1937-38

Sullivan, Larry, 1940-42

Sullivan, Tim, 1971-73

Sullivan, Tom, 1908

Sullivan, Tom, 1963-65

Susko, Larry, 1972-73

Swatland, Dick, 1965-67
Swearingen, Tim,1967-68
Sweeney, Bob, 1973-74
Sweeney, Chuck, 1935-37
Swendsen, Fred, 1969-71
Swenson, Mark, 1991-92
Swistowicz, Mike, 1946-49
Swoboda, Dave, 1981
Swonk, Frank, 1897
Sylvester, Steve, 1972-74
Szatko, Greg, 1972-73
Szor, Denis, 1962-63
Szymanski, Dick, 1951-54
Szymanski, Frank, 1943-44

T

Tafelski, Mike, 1986-87
Talaga, Tom 1963-65
Taliaferro, John, 1991-93
Tanczos, Dan, 1983-84, 86
Tatum, Kinnon, 1993-95
Taylor, Aaron, 1990-93
Taylor, Bob, 1951-53
Taylor, Bobby, 1992-94
Taylor, James, 1896
Taylor, Pernell, 1985-87
Tereschuk, John, 1970-71
Terlaak, Bob, 1930
Terlep, George, 1943-44
Terrell, Pat, 1986-89
Tharp, Jim, 1943
Thayer, Tom, 1979-82
Theisen, Charles, 1936, 38
Theismann, Joe, 1968-70
Thernes, Matt, 1934-35
Thesing, Joe, 1937-39
Thomann, Rick, 1969-71
Thomas, Bob, 1971-73
Thomas, Deane, 1948
Thomas, Frank, 1920-22
Thomas, John, 1976-79
Thorne, Marcus, 1993-95
Thornton, Pete, 1964-65
Tobin, George, 1942, 46
Tobin, John (Red), 1932-33
Toczylowski, Steve, 1944
Todorovich, Mike, 1943
Toneff, Bob, 1949-51
Tonelli, Mario, 1936-38
Toran, Stacey, 1980-83
Torrado, Rene, 1967
Toth, Ron, 1956-58

Townsend, Mike, 1971-73
Trafton, George, 1919
Traney, Leon, 1945
Trapp, Bil, 1969-71
Traver, Les, 1959-61
Tripp, Tim, 1978-81
Tripucka, Frank, 1945-48
Trombley, Cliff, 1925
Trumper, Ed, 1943
Tuck, Ed, 1966-68
Tuck, Sweeney, 1938
Tull, Bob, 1976-77
Twomey, Ted, 1928-29
Tyner, Stuart, 1991-92

U

Underwood, Jay, 1981, 83, 85
Unis, Joe, 1977-79
Unis, Tom, 1976
Urban, Gasper, 1943, 46-47

V

Vainisi, Jack, 1945
Vairo, Dom, 1932-34
VanDenburgh, Tom, 1977
Vangen, Willard, 1946
Van Huffel, Al, 1965-66
Van Rooy, Bill, 1930
Van Summern, Bob, 1945
Varrichione, Frank, 1951-54
Vasys, Arunas, 1963-65
Vaughan, Charles, 1911
Vaughan, Pete, 1908-09
Vehr, Nick, 1978-80
Vejar, Laurie, 1931-32
Vergara, George, 1922-23
Vezie, Manny, 1926-29
Vinson, Dave, 1976-77
Viola, Gene, 1959-61
Viracola, Mike, 1981-84
Virok, Ernie, 1945
Visovatti, Mike, 1987
Vlk, George, 1928-30
Voedisch, John (Ike), 1925-27
Voelkers, John, 1913-15
Von Wyl, Hal, 1982, 84-85
Vuillemin, Ed, 1966-67

W

Wachtel, Chris, 1994
Wack, Steve, 1968
Wackowski, John, 1984

Wadsworth, Mike, 1963-65

Wagasy, Bill, 1993-95

Wagner, Earl, 1899

Waldorf, Rufus, 1904-06

Waldron, Ronayne, 1943

Wallace, John, 1923-26

Wallace, Leon, 1992-95

Wallner, Fred, 1948-50

Walls, Bob, 1974

Walsh, Adam, 1922-24

Walsh, Bill, 1895

Walsh, Bill, 1945-48

Walsh, Bob, 1941

Walsh, Bob, 1946

Walsh, Charles (Chile), 1925-27

Walsh, Earl, 1919-21

Walsh, Mike, 1981

Ward, Gilbert (Gillie), 1914, 16

Ward, Bob, 1955-57

Ward, Reggie, 1984-87

Warner, Jack, 1940-41

Washington, Bob, 1971-73

Washington, Dick, 1953

Wasilevich, Max, 1973

Waters, Fred, 1897

Watters, Ricky, 1987-90

Waybright, Doug, 1944, 47-49

Waymer, Dave, 1976-79

Webb, Bob, 1940

Webb, Mike, 1970-71, 73

Weber, Robin, 1973-74, 76

Webster, Mike, 1963-64

Weibel, john, 1922-24

Weidner, Fred, 1934

Weiler, Jim, 1973, 76

Weinle, Jerry, 1982-84

Weissenhofer, Ron, 1982, 84-86

Weithman, Jim, 1950-52

Welch, Bob, 1944

Welch, Bob, 1986

Wells, Brandy, 1984-87

Wendell, Marty, 1944, 46-48

Wengierski, Tim, 1966

West, Rod, 1987-89

Wetoska, Bob, 1956-58

Wheeler, Lucian, 1895

Whelan, Brian, 1981

Whelan, Ed, 1950

Whelan, Jack, 1951-52

Whelan, Jim, 1925

Whipple, Ray, 1915-16

White, Bob, 1945

White, Carl, 1911

White, Don, 1957-59

White, Eddie, 1925-27

White, Jim, 1942-43

White, Richard, 1918

White, Steve, 1983-84

Whiteside, Bill, 1949-50

Whittington, Mike, 1977-79

Wightkin, Bill, 1946-49

Wilcox, Percy, 1920

Wilke, Bob, 1934-36

Wilke, Henry, 1957-59

Wilke, Roger, 1959-61

Wilkens, Dick, 1955

Willertz, Steve, 1984

Williams, Bo, 1928

Williams, Bob, 1956-58

Williams, Bob, 1948-50

Williams, Fred (Cy), 1910

Williams, George, 1959-61

Williams, George, 1987-90

Williams, Joel, 1983-86

Williams, Larry, 1981-84

Williams, Scott, 1969

Williams, Ted, 1938

Williamson, Greg, 1980-81

Wilson, George, 1953-55

Wilson, Troy, 1983-86

Winegardner, Jim, 1966-68

Winsouer, Paul, 1935-36

Winter, Frank, 1898-1901

Wisne, Gerald, 1966-68

Witchger, Jim, 1968-70

Wittereid, George, 1916

Wittliff, Phil, 1968

Witucki, Jack, 1954

Wodecki, Darryl, 1988, 90

Woebkenberg, Harry, 1974-76

Wojcihovski, Vic, 1934-36

Wolf, George (Louie), 1915

Wolski, Bill, 1963-65

Wood, Fay, 1907-08

Wood, Greg, 1962

Wooden, Shawn, 1991, 93-95

Worden, Neil, 1951-53

Wozneak, Joe, 1979

Wright, Harry, 1940-42

Wright, Jim, 1968-70

Wright, Tom, 1970

Wroblewski, Tom, 1977-79

Wujciak, Al, 1973-75

Wunsch, Harry, 1931-33

Wynn, Renaldo, 1993-95
Wynne, Chet, 1918-21
Wynne, Elmer, 1925-27

Y
Yarr, Tommy, 1929-31
Yeager, Leslie (Dutch), 1915-16
Yoder, Jim, 1969-70
Yonakor, John, 1942-43
Yonto, Joe, 1945
Young, Barry, 1981-82
Young, Bryant, 1990-93
Young, Jacob, 1907
Young, John (Tex), 1933
Young, Tyler, 1992
Yund, Walter, 1911-12

Z
Zackrison, Kurt, 1987-88
Zajeski, Ben, 1953-54
Zalejski, Ernie, 1946, 48-49
Zaleski, John, 1986
Zambroski, Tony, 1949-51
Zancha, John, 1949-50

Zanot, Bob, 1972-73, 75
Zappala, Tony, 1973-76
Zataveski, Mark, 1991-94
Zavagnin, Mark, 1979-82
Zehler, Bill, 1945
Zeigler, Dusty, 1993-94
Zielony, Dick, 1969-70
Ziemby, Wally, 1940-42
Zikas, Mike, 1969-71
Zilly, Jack, 1943, 46
Zimmerman, Jeff, 1967-68
Ziznewski, Jay, 1968
Zloch, Bill, 1963-65
Zloch, Chuck, 1968-70
Zloch, Jim, 1972-73
Zmijewski, Al, 1946-49
Zoia, Clyde, 1917
Zontini, Lou, 1937-39
Zorich, Chris, 1988-90
Zubek, Bob, 1966
Zuber, Tim, 1970
Zuendel, Joe, 1938
Zurowski, Dave, 1964-66
Zwers, Joe, 1935-37

All-Time Scores

1887
Nov. 23, Michigan, 0-8
Record: 0-1-0

1888
April 20, Michigan, 6-26
April 21, Michigan, 4-10
Dec. 6, Harvard Prep, 20-0
Record: 1-2-0

1889
Nov. 14, at Northwestern, 9-0
Record: 1-0-0

1892
Oct. 19, South Bend High School, 56-0
Nov. 24, Hillsdale, 10-10
Record: 1-0-1

1893
Oct. 25, Kalamazoo, 34-0
Nov. 11, Albion, 8-6
Nov. 23, De LaSalle, 28-0
Nov. 30, Hillsdale, 22-10
Jan. 1, at Chicago, 0-8
Record: 4-1-0
1894
Oct. 13, Hillsdale, 14-0
Oct. 20, Albion, 6-6
Nov. 15, Wabash, 30-0
Nov. 22, Rush Medical, 18-6
Nov. 29, Albion, 12-19
Record: 3-1-1

1895
Oct. 19, Northwestern Law, 20-0
Nov. 7, Illinois Cycling Club, 18-2
Nov. 22, Indianapolis Artillery, 0-18

Nov. 28, Chicago Physicians & Surgeons, 32-0
Record: 3-1-0

1896
Oct. 8, Chicago Physicians & Surgeons, 0-4
Oct. 14, Chicago, 0-18
Oct. 27, South Bend Commercial Athletic Club, 46-0
Oct. 31, Albion, 24-0
Nov. 14, Purdue, 22-28
Nov. 20, Highland Views, 82-0
Nov. 26, Beloit, 8-0
Record: 4-3-0

1897
Oct. 13, Rush Medical, 0-0
Oct. 23, DePauw, 4-0
Oct. 28, Chicago Dental Surgeons, 62-0
Nov. 6, at Chicago, 5-34
Nov. 13, St. Viator, 60-0
Nov. 25, Michigan State, 34-6
Record: 4-1-1

1898
Oct. 8, at Illinois, 5-0
Oct. 15, Michigan State, 53-0
Oct. 23, at Michigan, 0-23
Oct. 29, DePauw, 32-0
Nov. 5, Indiana, 5-11
Nov. 19, at Albion, 60-0
Record: 4-2-0

1899
Sept. 27, Englewood High School, 29-5
Sept. 30, Michigan State, 40-0
Oct. 4, Chicago, 6-23
Oct. 14, Lake Forest, 38-0
Oct. 18, Michigan, 0-12
Oct. 23, Indiana, 17-0
Oct. 27, Northwestern, 12-0
Nov. 4, Rush Medical, 17-0
Nov. 18, Purdue, 10-10
Nov. 30, Chicago Physicians & Surgeons, 0-5
Record: 6-3-1

1900
Sept. 29, Goshen, 55-0
Oct. 6, Englewood High School, 68-0
Oct. 13, South Bend Howard Park, 64-0
Oct. 20, Cincinnati, 58-0
Oct. 25, Indiana, 0-6
Nov. 3, Beloit, 6-6
Nov. 10, Wisconsin, 0-54

Nov. 17, Michigan, 0-7
Nov. 24, Rush Medical, 5-0
Nov. 29, Chicago Physicians & Surgeons, 5-0
Record: 6-3-1

1901
Sept. 28, South Bend Athletic Club, 0-0
Oct. 5, Ohio Medical University, 6-0
Oct. 12, Northwestern, 0-2
Oct. 19, Chicago Medical College, 32-0
Oct. 26, Beloit, 5-0
Nov. 2, Lake Forest, 16-0
Nov. 9, Purdue, 12-6
Nov. 16, Indiana, 18-5
Nov. 23, Chicago Physicians & Surgeons, 34-0
Nov. 28, South Bend Athletic Club, 22-6
Record: 8-1-1

1902
Sept. 27, Michigan State, 33-0
Oct. 11, Lake Forest, 28-0
Oct. 18, Michigan (at Toledo), 0-23
Oct. 25, Indiana, 11-5
Nov. 1, Ohio Medical University, 6-5
Nov. 8, Knox, 5-12
Nov. 15, American Medical, 92-0
Nov. 22, DePauw, 22-0
Nov. 27, Purdue, 6-6
Record: 6-2-1

1903
Oct. 3, Michigan State, 12-0
Oct. 10, Lake Forest, 28-10
Oct. 17, DePauw, 56-0
Oct. 24, American Medical, 52-0
Oct. 29, Chicago Physicians & Surgeons, 46-0
Nov. 7, Missouri Osteopaths, 28-0
Nov. 14, Northwestern, 0-0
Nov. 21, Ohio Medical University, 35-0
Nov. 26, Wabash, 35-0
Record: 8-0-1

1904
Oct. 1, Wabash, 12-4
Oct. 8, American Medical, 44-0
Oct. 15, Wisconsin (at Milwaukee), 0-58
Oct. 22, Ohio Medical University, 17-5
Oct. 27, Toledo Athletic Association, 6-0
Nov. 5, Kansas, 5-24
Nov. 19, DePauw, 10-0
Nov. 24, Purdue, 0-36
Record: 5-3-0

1905
Sept. 30, North Division High School (Chicago), 44-0
Oct. 7, Michigan State, 28-0
Oct. 14, Wisconsin (at Milwaukee), 0-21
Oct. 21, Wabash, 0-5
Oct. 28, American Medical, 142-0
Nov. 4, DePauw, 71-0
Nov. 11, Indiana, 5-22
Nov. 18, Bennett Medical College (Chicago), 22-0
Nov. 24, Purdue, 0-32
Record: 5-4-0

1906
Oct. 6, Franklin, 26-0
Oct. 13, Hillsdale, 17-0
Oct. 20, Chicago Physicians & Surgeons, 28-0
Oct. 27, Michigan State, 5-0
Nov. 3, Purdue, 2-0
Nov. 10, Indiana (at Indianapolis), 0-12
Nov. 24, Beloit, 29-0
Record: 6-1-0

1907
Oct. 12, Chicago Physicians & Surgeons, 32-0
Oct. 19, Franklin, 23-0
Oct. 26, Olivet, 22-4
Nov. 2, Indiana, 0-0
Nov. 9, Knox, 22-4
Nov. 23, Purdue, 17-0
Nov. 28, St. Vincent's (Chicago), 21-12
Record: 6-0-1

1908
Oct. 3, Hillsdale, 39-0
Oct. 10, Franklin, 64-0
Oct. 17, Michigan, 6-12
Oct. 24, Chicago Physicians & Surgeons, 88-0
Oct. 29, Ohio Northern, 58-4
Nov. 7, Indiana (at Indianapolis), 11-0
Nov. 13, Wabash, 8-4
Nov. 18, St. Viator, 46-0
Nov. 26, Marquette, 6-0
Record: 8-1-0

1909
Oct. 9, Olivet, 58-0
Oct. 16, Rose Poly, 60-11
Oct. 23, Michigan State, 17-0
Oct. 30, Pittsburgh, 6-0
Nov. 6, Michigan, 11-3
Nov. 13, Miami (Ohio), 46-0
Nov. 20, Wabash, 38-0
Nov. 25, Marquette, 0-0

Record: 7-0-1

1910
Oct. 8, Olivet, 48-0
Oct. 22, Butchel (Akron), 51-0
Nov. 5, Michigan State, 0-17
Nov. 12, Rose Poly, 41-3
Nov. 19, Ohio Northern, 47-0
Nov. 24, Marquette, 5-5
Record: 4-1-1

1911
Oct. 7, Ohio Northern, 32-6
Oct. 14, St. Viator, 43-0
Oct. 21, Butler, 27-0
Oct. 28, Loyola (Chicago), 80-0
Nov. 4, Pittsburgh, 0-0
Nov. 11, St. Bonaventure, 34-0
Nov. 20, Wabash, 6-3
Nov. 30, Marquette, 0-0
Record: 6-0-2

1912
Oct. 5, St. Viator, 116-7
Oct. 12, Adrian, 74-7
Oct. 19, Morris Harvey, 39-0
Oct. 26, Wabash, 41-6
Nov. 2, Pittsburgh, 3-0
Nov. 9, St. Louis, 47-7
Nov. 28, Marquette (at Chicago), 69-0
Record: 7-0-0

1913
Oct. 4, Ohio Northern, 87-0
Oct. 18, South Dakota, 20-7
Oct. 25, Alma, 62-0
Nov. 1, Army, 35-13
Nov. 7, Penn State, 14-7
Nov. 22, Christian Brothers (St. Louis), 20-7
Nov. 27, Texas, 30-7
Record: 7-0-0

1914
Oct. 3, Alma, 56-0
Oct. 10, Rose Poly, 103-0
Oct. 17, Yale, 0-28
Oct. 24, South Dakota (at Sioux Falls), 33-0
Oct. 31, Haskell, 20-7
Nov. 7, Army, 7-20
Nov. 14, Carlisle (at Chicago), 48-6
Nov. 26, Syracuse, 20-0
Record: 6-2-0

1915
Oct. 2, Alma, 32-0
Oct. 9, Haskell, 34-0
Oct. 23, Nebraska, 19-20
Oct. 30, South Dakota, 6-0
Nov. 6, Army, 7-0
Nov. 13, Creighton, 41-0
Nov. 25, Texas, 36-7
Nov. 27, Rice, 55-2
Record: 7-1-0

1916
Sept. 30, Case Tech, 48-0
Oct. 7, Western Reserve, 48-0
Oct. 14, Haskell, 26-0
Oct. 28, Wabash, 60-0
Nov. 4, Army, 10-30
Nov. 11, South Dakota (at Sioux Falls), 21-0
Nov. 18, Michigan State, 14-0
Nov. 25, Alma, 46-0
Nov. 30, Nebraska, 20-0
Record: 8-1-0

1917
Oct. 6, Kalamazoo, 55-0
Oct. 13, Wisconsin, 0-0
Oct. 20, Nebraska, 0-7
Oct. 27, South Dakota, 40-0
Nov. 3, Army, 7-2
Nov. 10, Morningside, 13-0
Nov. 17, Michigan State, 23-0
Nov. 24, Washington & Jefferson, 3-0
Record: 6-1-1

1918
Sept. 28, Case Tech, 26-6
Nov. 2, Wabash, 67-7
Nov. 9, Great Lakes, 7-7
Nov. 16, Michigan State, 7-13
Nov. 23, Purdue, 26-6
Nov. 28, Nebraska, 0-0
Record: 3-1-2

1919
Oct. 4, Kalamazoo, 14-0
Oct. 11, Mount Union, 60-7
Oct. 18, Nebraska, 14-9
Oct. 25, Western Michigan, 53-0
Nov. 1, Indiana (at Indianapolis), 16-3
Nov. 8, Army, 12-9
Nov. 15, Michigan State, 13-0
Nov. 22, Purdue, 33-13
Nov. 27, Morningside, 14-6
Record: 9-0-0

1920
Oct. 2, Kalamazoo, 39-0
Oct. 9, Western Michigan, 42-0
Oct. 16, Nebraska, 16-7
Oct. 23, Valparaiso, 28-3
Oct. 30, Army, 27-17
Nov. 6, Purdue, 28-0
Nov. 13, Indiana (at Indianapolis), 13-10
Nov. 20, Northwestern, 33-7
Nov. 25, Michigan State, 25-0
Record: 9-0-0

1921
Sept. 24, Kalamazoo, 56-0
Oct. 1, DePauw, 57-10
Oct. 8, Iowa, 7-10
Oct. 15, Purdue, 33-0
Oct. 22, Nebraska, 7-0
Oct. 29, Indiana (at Indianapolis), 28-7
Nov. 5, Army, 28-0
Nov. 8, Rutgers (at Polo Grounds, NYC), 48-0
Nov. 12, Haskell, 42-7
Nov. 19, Marquette, 21-7
Nov. 24, Michigan State, 48-0
Record: 10-1-0

1922
Sept. 30, Kalamazoo, 46-0
Oct. 7, St. Louis, 26-0
Oct. 14, Purdue, 20-0
Oct. 21, DePauw, 34-7
Oct. 28, Georgia Tech, 13-3
Nov. 4, Indiana, 27-0
Nov. 11, Army, 0-0
Nov. 18, Butler, 31-3
Nov. 25, Carnegie Tech, 19-0
Nov. 30, Nebraska, 6-14
Record: 8-1-1

1923
Sept. 29, Kalamazoo, 74-0
Oct. 6, Lombard, 14-0
Oct. 13, Army (at Ebbets Field, Brooklyn), 13-0
Oct. 20, Princeton, 25-2
Oct. 27, Georgia Tech, 35-7
Nov. 3, Purdue, 34-7
Nov. 10, Nebraska, 7-14
Nov. 17, Butler, 34-7
Nov. 24, Carnegie Tech, 26-0
Nov. 29, St. Louis, 13-0
Record: 9-1-0

1924
Oct. 4, Lombard, 40-0
Oct. 11, Wabash, 34-0
Oct. 18, Army (at Polo Grounds), 13-7
Oct. 25, Princeton, 12-0
Nov. 1, Georgia Tech, 34-3
Nov. 8, Wisconsin, 38-3
Nov. 15, Nebraska, 34-6
Nov. 22, Northwestern (at Soldier Field), 13-6
Nov. 29, Carnegie Tech, 40-19
Record: 10-0-0

1925
Sept. 26, Baylor, 41-0
Oct. 3, Lombard, 69-0
Oct. 10, Beloit, 19-3
Oct. 17, Army (at Yankee Stadium, NYC), 0-27
Oct. 24, Minnesota, 19-7
Oct. 31, Georgia Tech, 13-0
Nov. 7, Penn State, 0-0
Nov. 14, Carnegie Tech, 26-0
Nov. 21, Northwestern, 13-10
Nov. 26, Nebraska, 0-17
Record: 7-2-1

1926
Oct. 2, Beloit, 77-0
Oct. 9, Minnesota, 20-7
Oct. 16, Penn State, 28-0
Oct. 23, Northwestern, 6-0
Oct. 30, Georgia Tech, 12-0
Nov. 6, Indiana, 26-0
Nov. 13, Army, 7-0
Nov. 20, Drake, 21-0
Nov. 27, Carnegie Tech, 0-19
Dec. 4, USC, 13-12
Record: 9-1-0

1927
Oct. 1, Coe, 28-7
Oct. 8, Detroit, 20-0
Oct. 15, Navy (at Baltimore), 19-6
Oct. 22, Indiana, 19-6
Oct. 29, Georgia Tech, 26-7
Nov. 5, Minnesota, 7-7
Nov. 12, Army, 0-18
Nov. 19, Drake, 32-0
Nov. 26, USC (at Soldier Field), 7-6
Record: 7-1-1

1928
Sept. 29, Loyola (New Orleans), 12-6

Oct. 6, Wisconsin, 6-22
Oct. 13, Navy (at Soldier Field), 7-0
Oct. 20, Georgia Tech, 0-13
Oct. 27, Drake, 32-6
Nov. 3, Penn State (at Philadelphia), 9-0
Nov. 10, Army (at Yankee Stadium), 12-6
Nov. 17, Carnegie Tech, 7-27
Dec. 1, USC, 14-27
Record: 5-4-0

1929
Oct. 5, Indiana, 14-0
Oct. 12, Navy (at Baltimore), 14-7
Oct. 19, Wisconsin (at Soldier Field), 19-0
Oct. 26, Carnegie Tech, 7-0
Nov. 2, Georgia Tech, 26-6
Nov. 9, Drake (at Soldier Field), 19-7
Nov. 16, USC (at Soldier Field), 13-12
Nov. 23, Northwestern, 26-6,
Nov. 30, Army (at Yankee Stadium), 7-0
Record: 9-0-0

1930
Oct. 4, SMU, 20-14
Oct. 11, Navy, 26-2
Oct. 18, Carnegie Tech, 21-6
Oct. 25, Pittsburgh, 35-19
Nov. 1, Indiana, 27-0
Nov. 8, Pennsylvania, 60-20
Nov. 15, Drake, 28-7
Nov. 22, Northwestern, 14-0
Nov. 29, Army (at Soldier Field), 7-6
Dec. 6, USC, 27-0
Record: 10-0-0

1931
Oct. 3, Indiana, 25-0
Oct. 10, Northwestern (at Soldier Field), 0-0
Oct. 17, Drake, 63-0
Oct. 24, Pittsburgh, 25-12
Oct. 31, Carnegie Tech, 19-0
Nov. 7, Pennsylvania, 49-0
Nov. 14, Navy (at Baltimore), 20-0
Nov. 21, USC, 14-16
Nov. 28, Army (at Yankee Stadium), 0-12
Record: 6-2-1

1932
Oct. 8, Haskell, 73-0
Oct. 15, Drake, 62-0
Oct. 22, Carnegie Tech, 42-0
Oct. 29, Pittsburgh, 0-12

Nov. 5, Kansas, 24-6
Nov. 12, Northwestern, 21-0
Nov. 19, Navy (at Cleveland), 12-0
Nov. 26, Army, 21-0
Dec. 10, USC, 0-13
Record: 7-2-0

1933
Oct. 7, Kansas, 0-0
Oct. 14, Indiana, 12-2
Oct. 21, Carnegie Tech, 0-7
Oct. 28, Pittsburgh, 0-14
Nov. 4, Navy (at Baltimore), 0-7
Nov. 11, Purdue, 0-19
Nov. 18, Northwestern, 7-0
Nov. 25, USC, 0-19
Dec. 2, Army (at Yankee Stadium), 13-12
Record: 3-5-1

1934
Oct. 6, Texas, 6-7
Oct. 13, Purdue, 18-7
Oct. 20, Carnegie Tech, 13-0
Oct. 27, Wisconsin, 19-0
Nov. 3, Pittsburgh, 0-19
Nov. 10, Navy (at Cleveland), 6-10
Nov. 17, Northwestern, 20-7
Nov. 24, Army (at Yankee Stadium), 12-6
Dec. 8, USC, 14-0
Record: 6-3-0

1935
Sept. 28, Kansas, 28-7
Oct. 5, Carnegie Tech, 14-3
Oct. 12, Wisconsin, 27-0
Oct. 19, Pittsburgh, 9-6
Oct. 26, Navy (at Baltimore), 14-0
Nov. 2, Ohio State, 18-13
Nov. 9, Northwestern, 7-14
Nov. 16, Army (at Yankee Stadium), 6-6
Nov. 23, USC, 20-13
Record: 7-1-1

1936
Oct. 3, Carnegie Tech, 21-7
Oct. 10, Washington (St. Louis), 14-6
Oct. 17, Wisconsin, 27-0
Oct. 24, Pittsburgh, 0-26
Oct. 31, Ohio State, 7-2
Nov. 7, Navy (at Baltimore), 0-3
Nov. 14, Army (at Yankee Stadium), 20-6
Nov. 21, Northwestern, 26-6

Dec. 5, USC, 13-13
Record: 6-2-1

1937
Oct. 2, Drake, 21-0
Oct. 9, Illinois, 0-0
Oct. 16, Carnegie Tech, 7-9
Oct. 23, Navy, 9-7
Oct. 30, Minnesota, 7-6
Nov. 6, Pittsburgh, 6-21
Nov. 13, Army (at Yankee Stadium), 7-0
Nov. 20, Northwestern, 7-0
Nov. 27, USC, 13-6
Record: 6-2-1

1938
Oct. 1, Kansas, 52-0
Oct. 8, Georgia Tech, 14-6
Oct. 15, Illinois, 14-6
Oct. 22, Carnegie Tech, 7-0
Oct. 29, Army (at Yankee Stadium), 19-7
Nov. 5, Navy (at Baltimore), 15-0
Nov. 12, Minnesota, 19-0
Nov. 19, Northwestern, 9-7
Dec. 3, USC, 0-13
Record: 8-1-0

1939
Sept. 30, Purdue, 3-0
Oct. 7, Georgia Tech, 14-6
Oct. 14, SMU, 20-19
Oct. 21, Navy (at Cleveland), 14-7
Oct. 28, Carnegie Tech, 7-6
Nov. 4, Army (at Yankee Stadium), 14-0
Nov. 11, Iowa, 6-7
Nov. 18, Northwestern, 7-0
Nov. 25, USC, 12-20
Record: 7-2-0

1940
Oct. 5, College of Pacific, 25-7
Oct. 12, Georgia Tech, 17-14
Oct. 19, Carnegie Tech, 61-0
Oct. 26, Illinois, 26-0
Nov. 2, Army (at Yankee Stadium), 7-0
Nov. 9, Navy (at Baltimore), 13-7
Nov. 16, Iowa, 0-7
Nov. 23, Northwestern, 0-20
Dec. 7, USC, 10-6
Record: 7-2-0

1941
Sept. 27, Arizona, 38-7
Oct. 4, Indiana, 19-6
Oct. 11, Georgia Tech, 20-0
Oct. 18, Carnegie Tech, 16-0
Oct. 25, Illinois, 49-14
Nov. 1, Army (at Yankee Stadium), 0-0
Nov. 8, Navy (at Baltimore), 20-13
Nov. 15, Northwestern, 7-6
Nov. 22, USC, 20-18
Record: 8-0-1

1942
Sept. 26, Wisconsin, 7-7
Oct. 3, Georgia Tech, 6-13
Oct. 10, Stanford, 27-0
Oct. 17, Iowa Pre-Flight, 28-0
Oct. 24, Illinois, 21-14
Oct. 31, Navy (at Cleveland), 9-0
Nov. 7, Army (at Yankee Stadium), 13-0
Nov. 14, Michigan, 20-32
Nov. 21, Northwestern, 27-20
Nov. 28, USC, 13-0
Dec. 5, Great Lakes (at Soldier Field), 13-13
Record: 7-2-2

1943
Sept. 25, Pittsburgh, 41-0
Oct. 2, Georgia Tech, 55-13
Oct. 9, Michigan, 35-12
Oct. 16, Wisconsin, 50-0
Oct. 23, Illinois, 47-0
Oct. 30, Navy (at Cleveland), 33-6
Nov. 6, Army (at Yankee Stadium), 26-0
Nov. 13, Northwestern, 25-6
Nov. 20, Iowa Pre-Flight, 14-13
Nov. 27, Great Lakes, 14-19
Record: 9-1-0

1944
Sept. 30, Pittsburgh, 58-0
Oct. 7, Tulane, 26-0
Oct. 14, Dartmouth (at Fenway Park, Boston), 64-0
Oct. 21, Wisconsin, 28-13
Oct. 28, Illinois, 13-7
Nov. 4, Navy (at Baltimore), 13-32
Nov. 11, Army (at Yankee Stadium), 0-59
Nov. 18, Northwestern, 21-0
Nov. 25, Georgia Tech, 21-0
Dec. 2, Great Lakes, 28-7
Record: 8-2-0

1945
Sept. 29, Illinois, 7-0
Oct. 6, Georgia Tech, 40-7
Oct. 13, Dartmouth, 34-0
Oct. 20, Pittsburgh, 39-9
Oct. 27, Iowa, 56-0
Nov. 3, Navy (at Cleveland), 6-6
Nov. 10, Army (at Yankee Stadium), 0-48
Nov. 17, Northwestern, 34-7
Nov. 24, Tulane, 32-6
Dec. 1, Great Lakes, 7-39
Record: 7-2-1

1946
Sept. 28, Illinois, 26-6
Oct. 5, Pittsburgh, 33-0
Oct. 12, Purdue, 49-6
Oct. 26, Iowa, 41-6
Nov. 2, Navy (at Baltimore), 28-0
Nov. 9, Army (at Yankee Stadium), 0-0
Nov. 16, Northwestern, 27-0
Nov. 23, Tulane, 41-0
Nov. 30, USC, 26-6
Record: 8-0-1

1947
Oct. 4, Pittsburgh, 40-6
Oct. 11, Purdue, 22-7
Oct. 18, Nebraska, 31-0
Oct. 25, Iowa, 21-0
Nov. 1, Navy (at Cleveland), 27-0
Nov. 8, Army, 27-7
Nov. 15, Northwestern, 26-19
Nov. 22, Tulane, 59-6
Dec. 6, USC, 38-7
Record: 9-0-0

1948
Sept. 25, Purdue, 28-27
Oct. 2, Pittsburgh, 40-0
Oct. 9, Michigan State, 26-7
Oct. 16, Nebraska, 44-13
Oct. 23, Iowa, 27-12
Oct. 30, Navy (at Baltimore), 41-7
Nov. 6, Indiana, 42-6
Nov. 13, Northwestern, 12-7
Nov. 27, Washington, 46-0
Dec. 4, USC, 14-14
Record: 9-0-1

1949
Sept. 24, Indiana, 49-6

Oct. 1, Washington, 27-7
Oct. 8, Purdue, 35-12
Oct. 15, Tulane, 46-7
Oct. 29, Navy (at Baltimore), 40-0
Nov. 5, Michigan State, 34-21
Nov. 12, North Carolina (at Yankee Stadium), 42-6
Nov. 19, Iowa, 28-7
Nov. 26, USC, 32-0
Dec. 3, SMU, 27-20
Record: 10-0-0

1950
Sept. 30, North Carolina, 14-7
Oct. 7, Purdue, 14-28
Oct. 14, Tulane, 13-9
Oct. 21, Indiana, 7-20
Oct. 28, Michigan State, 33-36
Nov. 4, Navy (at Cleveland), 19-10
Nov. 11, Pittsburgh, 18-7
Nov. 18, Iowa, 14-14
Dec. 2, USC, 7-9
Record: 4-4-1

1951
Sept. 29, Indiana, 48-6
Oct. 5, Detroit (at Briggs Stadium, Detroit), 40-6
Oct. 13, SMU, 20-27
Oct. 20, Pittsburgh, 33-0
Oct. 27, Purdue, 30-9
Nov. 3, Navy (at Baltimore), 19-0
Nov. 10, Michigan State, 0-35
Nov. 17, North Carolina, 12-7
Nov. 24, Iowa, 20-20
Dec. 1, USC, 19-12
Record: 7-2-1

1952
Sept. 27, Pennsylvania, 7-7
Oct. 4, Texas, 14-3
Oct. 11, Pittsburgh, 19-22
Oct. 18, Purdue, 26-14
Oct. 25, North Carolina, 34-14
Nov. 1, Navy (at Cleveland), 17-6
Nov. 8, Oklahoma, 27-21
Nov. 15, Michigan State, 3-21
Nov. 22, Iowa, 27-0
Nov. 29, USC, 9-0
Record: 7-2-1

1953
Sept. 26, Oklahoma, 28-21
Oct. 3, Purdue, 37-7

Oct. 17, Pittsburgh, 23-14
Oct. 24, Georgia Tech, 27-14
Oct. 31, Navy, 38-7
Nov. 7, Pennsylvania, 28-20
Nov. 14, North Carolina, 34-14
Nov. 21, Iowa, 14-14
Nov. 28, USC, 48-14
Dec. 5, SMU, 40-14
Record: 9-0-1

1954
Sept. 25, Texas, 21-0
Oct. 2, Purdue, 14-27
Oct. 9, Pittsburgh, 33-0
Oct. 16, Michigan State, 20-19
Oct. 30, Navy (at Baltimore), 6-0
Nov. 6, Pennsylvania, 42-7
Nov. 13, North Carolina, 42-13
Nov. 20, Iowa, 34-18
Nov. 27, USC, 23, 17
Dec. 4, SMU, 26-14
Record: 9-1-0

1955
Sept. 24, SMU, 17-0
Oct. 1, Indiana, 19-0
Oct. 7, Miami (Fla.), 14-0
Oct. 15, Michigan State, 7-21
Oct. 22, Purdue, 22-7
Oct. 29, Navy, 21-7
Nov. 5, Pennsylvania, 46-14
Nov. 12, North Carolina, 27-7
Nov. 19, Iowa, 17-14
Nov. 26, USC, 20-42
Record: 8-2-0

1956
Sept. 22, SMU, 13-19
Oct. 6, Indiana, 20-6
Oct. 13, Purdue, 14-28
Oct. 20, Michigan State, 14-47
Oct. 27, Oklahoma, 0-40
Nov. 3, Navy (at Baltimore), 7-33
Nov. 10, Pittsburgh, 13-26
Nov. 17, North Carolina, 21-14
Nov. 24, Iowa, 8-48
Dec. 1, USC, 20-28
Record: 2-8-0

1957
Sept. 28, Purdue, 12-0
Oct. 5, Indiana, 26-0

Oct. 12, Army (at Philadelphia), 23-21
Oct. 26, Pittsburgh, 13-7
Nov. 2, Navy, 6-20
Nov. 9, Michigan State, 6-34
Nov. 16, Oklahoma, 7-0
Nov. 23, Iowa, 13-21
Nov. 30, USC, 40-12
Dec. 7, SMU, 54-21
Record: 7-3-0

1958
Sept. 27, Indiana, 18-0
Oct. 4, SMU, 14-6
Oct. 11, Army, 2-14
Oct. 18, Duke, 9-7
Oct. 25, Purdue, 22-29
Nov. 1, Navy (at Baltimore), 40-20
Nov. 8, Pittsburgh, 26-29
Nov. 15, North Carolina, 34-24
Nov. 22, Iowa, 21-31
Nov. 29, USC, 20-13
Record:6-4-0

1959
Sept. 26, North Carolina, 28-8
Oct. 3, Purdue, 7-28
Oct. 10, California, 28-6
Oct. 17, Michigan State, 0-19
Oct. 24, Northwestern, 24-30
Oct. 31, Navy, 25-22
Nov. 7, Georgia Tech, 10-14
Nov. 14, Pittsburgh, 13-28
Nov. 21, Iowa, 20-19
Nov. 28, USC, 16-6
Record: 5-5-0

1960
Sept. 24, California, 21-7
Oct. 1, Purdue, 19-51
Oct. 8, North Carolina, 7-12
Oct. 15, Michigan State, 0-21
Oct. 22, Northwestern, 6-7
Oct. 29, Navy (at Philadelphia), 7-14
Nov. 5, Pittsburgh, 13-20
Nov. 12, Miami (Fla.), 21-28
Nov. 19, Iowa, 20-28
Nov. 26, USC, 17-0
Record: 2-8-0

1961
Sept. 30, Oklahoma, 19-6
Oct. 7, Purdue, 22-20

Oct. 14, USC, 30-0
Oct. 21, Michigan State, 7-17
Oct. 28, Northwestern, 10-12
Nov. 4, Navy, 10-13
Nov. 11, Pittsburgh, 26-20
Nov. 18, Syracuse, 17-15
Nov. 25, Iowa, 21-42
Dec. 2, Duke, 13-37
Record: 5-5-0

1962
Sept. 29, Oklahoma, 13-7
Oct. 6, Purdue, 6-24
Oct. 13, Wisconsin, 8-17
Oct. 20, Michigan State, 7-31
Oct. 27, Northwestern, 6-35
Nov. 3, Navy (at Philadelphia), 20-12
Nov. 10, Pittsburgh, 43-22
Nov. 17, North Carolina, 21-7
Nov. 24, Iowa, 35-12
Dec. 1, USC, 0-25
Record: 5-5-0

1963
Sept. 28, Wisconsin, 9-14
Oct. 5, Purdue, 6-7
Oct. 12, USC, 17-14
Oct. 19, UCLA, 27-12
Oct. 26, Stanford, 14-24
Nov. 2, Navy, 14-35
Nov. 9, Pittsburgh, 7-27
Nov. 16, Michigan State, 7-12
Nov. 28, Syracuse (at Yankee Stadium), 7-14
Record: 2-7-0

1964
Sept. 26, Wisconsin, 31-7
Oct. 3, Purdue, 34-15
Oct. 10, Air Force, 34-7
Oct. 17, UCLA, 24-0
Oct. 24, Stanford, 28-6
Oct. 31, Navy (at Philadelphia), 40-0
Nov. 7, Pittsburgh, 17-15
Nov. 14, Michigan State, 34-7
Nov. 21, Iowa, 28-0
Nov. 28, USC, 17-20
Record: 9-1-0

1965
Sept. 18, California, 48-6
Sept. 25, Purdue, 21-25
Oct. 2, Northwestern, 38-7

Oct. 9, Army (at Shea Stadium, NYC), 17-0
Oct. 23, USC, 28-7
Oct. 30, Navy, 29-3
Nov. 6, Pittsburgh, 69-13
Nov. 13, North Carolina, 17-0
Nov. 20, Michigan State, 3-12
Nov. 27, Miami (Fla.), 0-0
Record: 7-2-1

1966
Sept. 24, Purdue, 26-14
Oct. 1, Northwestern, 35-7
Oct. 8, Army, 35-0
Oct. 15, North Carolina, 32-0
Oct. 22, Oklahoma, 38-0
Oct. 29, Navy (at Philadelphia), 31-7
Nov. 5, Pittsburgh, 40-0
Nov. 12, Duke, 64-0
Nov. 19, Michigan State, 10-10
Nov. 26, USC, 51-0
Record: 9-0-1

1967
Sept. 23, California, 41-8
Sept. 30, Purdue, 21-28
Oct. 7, Iowa, 56-6
Oct. 14, USC, 7-24
Oct. 21, Illinois, 47-7
Oct. 28, Michigan State, 24-12
Nov. 4, Navy, 43-14
Nov. 11, Pittsburgh, 38-0
Nov. 18, Georgia Tech, 36-3
Nov. 24, Miami (Fla.), 24-22
Record: 8-2-0

1968
Sept. 21, Oklahoma, 45-21
Sept. 28, Purdue, 22-37
Oct. 5, Iowa, 51-28
Oct. 12, Northwestern, 27-7
Oct. 19, Illinois, 58-8
Oct. 26, Michigan State, 17-21
Nov. 2, Navy (at Philadelphia), 45-14
Nov. 9, Pittsburgh, 56-7
Nov. 16, Georgia Tech, 34-6
Nov. 30, USC, 21-21
Record: 7-2-1

1969
Sept. 20, Northwestern, 35-10
Sept. 27, Purdue, 14-28
Oct. 4, Michigan State, 42-28
Oct. 11, Army (at Yankee Stadium), 45-0

Oct. 18, USC, 14-14
Oct. 25, Tulane, 37-0
Nov. 1, Navy, 47-0
Nov. 8, Pittsburgh, 49-7
Nov. 15, Georgia Tech, 38-20
Nov. 22, Air Force, 13-6
Record: 8-1-1

1970
Sept. 19, Northwestern, 35-14
Sept. 26, Purdue, 48-0
Oct. 3, Michigan State, 29-0
Oct. 10, Army, 51-10
Oct. 17, Missouri, 24-7
Oct. 31, Navy (at Philadelphia), 56-7
Nov. 7, Pittsburgh, 46-14
Nov. 14, Georgia Tech, 10-7
Nov. 21, LSU, 3-0
Nov. 28, USC, 28-38
Record: 10-1-0

1971
Sept. 18, Northwestern, 37-0
Sept. 25, Purdue, 8-7
Oct. 2, Michigan State, 14-2
Oct. 9, Miami (Fla.), 17-0
Oct. 16, North Carolina, 16-0
Oct. 23, USC, 14-28
Oct. 30, Navy, 21-0
Nov. 6, Pittsburgh, 56-7
Nov. 13, Tulane, 21-7
Nov. 20, LSU, 8-28
Record: 8-2-0

1972
Sept. 23, Northwestern, 37-0
Sept. 30, Purdue, 35-14
Oct. 7, Michigan State, 16-0
Oct. 14, Pittsburgh, 42-16
Oct. 21, Missouri, 26-30
Oct. 28, TCU, 21-0
Nov. 4, Navy (at Philadelphia), 42-23
Nov. 11, Air Force, 21-7
Nov. 18, Miami (Fla.), 20-17
Dec. 2, USC, 23-45
Orange Bowl
Jan. 1, Nebraska (at Miami, Florida), 6-40
Record: 8-3-0

1973
Sept. 22, Northwestern, 44-0
Sept. 29, Purdue, 20-7
Oct. 6, Michigan State, 14-10

Oct. 13, Rice, 28-0
Oct. 20, Army, 62-3
Oct. 27, USC, 23-14
Nov. 3, Navy, 44-7
Nov. 10, Pittsburgh, 31-10
Nov. 22, Air Force, 48-15
Dec. 1, Miami (Fla.), 44-0
Sugar Bowl
Dec. 31, Alabama (at New Orleans), 24-23
Record: 11-0-0

1974
Sept. 9, Georgia Tech, 31-7
Sept. 21, Northwestern, 49-3
Sept. 28, Purdue, 20-31
Oct. 5, Michigan State, 19-14
Oct. 12, Rice, 10-3
Oct. 19, Army, 48-0
Oct. 26, Miami (Fla.), 38-7
Nov. 2, Navy (at Philadelphia), 14-6
Nov. 16, Pitt, 14-10
Nov. 23, Air Force, 38-0
Nov. 30, USC, 24-55
Orange Bowl
Jan. 1, Alabama (at Miami, Fla.), 13-11
Record: 10-2-0

1975
Sept. 15, Boston College (at Foxboro), 17-3
Sept. 20, Purdue, 17-0
Sept. 27, Northwestern, 31-7
Oct. 4, Michigan State, 3-10
Oct. 11, North Carolina, 21-14
Oct. 18, Air Force, 31-30
Oct. 25, USC, 17-24
Nov. 1, Navy, 31-10
Nov. 8, Georgia Tech, 24-3
Nov. 15, Pittsburgh, 20-34
Nov. 22, Miami (Fla.), 32-9
Record: 8-3-0

1976
Sept. 11, Pittsburgh, 10-31
Sept. 18, Purdue, 23-0
Sept. 25, Northwestern, 48-0
Oct. 2, Michigan State, 24-6
Oct. 16, Oregon, 41-0
Oct. 23, South Carolina, 13-6
Oct. 30, Navy (at Cleveland), 27-21
Nov. 6, Georgia Tech, 14-23
Nov. 13, Alabama, 21-18
Nov. 20, Miami (Fla.), 40-27

Nov. 27, USC, 13-17
Gator Bowl
Dec. 27, Penn State (at Jacksonville), 20-9
Record: 9-3-0

1977
Sept. 10, Pittsburgh, 19-9
Sept. 17, Mississippi (at Jackson), 13-20
Sept. 24, Purdue, 31-24
Oct. 1, Michigan State, 16-6
Oct. 15, Army (at Giants Stadium, N.J.), 24-0
Oct. 22, USC, 49-19
Oct. 29, Navy, 43-10
Nov. 5, Georgia Tech, 69-14
Nov. 12, Clemson, 21-17
Nov. 19, Air Force, 49-0
Dec. 3, Miami (Fla.), 48-10
Cotton Bowl
Jan. 2, Texas (at Dallas, Tex.), 38-10
Record: 11-1-0

1978
Sept. 9, Missouri, 0-3
Sept. 23, Michigan, 14-28
Sept. 30, Purdue, 10-6
Oct. 7, Michigan State, 29-25
Oct. 14, Pittsburgh, 26-17
Oct. 21, Air Force, 38-15
Oct. 28, Miami (Fla.), 20-0
Nov. 4, Navy (at Cleveland), 27-7
Nov. 11, Tennessee, 31-14
Nov. 18, Georgia Tech, 38-21
Nov. 25, USC, 25-27
Record: 9-3-0

1979
Sept. 15, Michigan, 12-10
Sept. 22, Purdue, 22-28
Sept. 29, Michigan State, 27-3
Oct. 6, Georgia Tech, 21-13
Oct. 13, Air Force, 38-13
Oct. 20, USC, 23-42
Oct. 27, South Carolina, 18-17
Nov. 3, Navy, 14-0
Nov. 10, Tennessee, 18-40
Nov. 17, Clemson, 10-16
Nov. 24, Miami (Fla.), 40-15
Record: 7-4-0

1980
Sept. 6, Purdue, 31-10
Sept. 20, Michigan, 29-27
Oct. 4, Michigan State, 26-21

Oct. 11, Miami, 32-14
Oct. 18, Army, 30-3
Oct. 25, Arizona, 20-3
Nov. 1, Navy (at Giants Stadium), 33-0
Nov. 8, Georgia Tech, 3-3
Nov. 15, Alabama, 7-0
Nov. 22, Air Force, 24-10
Dec. 6, USC, 3-20
Sugar Bowl
Jan. 1, Georgia (at New Orleans), 10-17
Record: 9-2-1

1981
Sept. 12, LSU, 27-9
Sept. 19, Michigan, 7-25
Sept. 26, Purdue, 14-15
Oct. 3, Michigan State, 20-7
Oct. 10, Florida State, 13-19
Oct. 24, USC, 7-14
Oct. 31, Navy, 38-0
Nov. 7, Georgia Tech, 35-3
Nov. 14, Air Force, 35-7
Nov. 21, Penn State, 21-24
Nov. 27, Miami, 15-37
Record: 5-6-0

1982
Sept. 18, Michigan, 23-17
Sept. 25, Purdue, 28-14
Oct. 2, Michigan State, 11-3
Oct. 9, Miami, 16-14
Oct. 16, Arizona, 13-16
Oct. 23, Oregon, 13-13
Oct. 30, Navy (at Giants Stadium), 27-10
Nov. 6, Pittsburgh, 31-16
Nov. 13, Penn State, 14-24
Nov. 20, Air Force, 17-30
Nov. 27, USC, 13-17
Record: 6-4-1

1983
Sept. 10, Purdue, 52-6
Sept. 17, Michigan State, 23-28
Sept. 24, Miami, 0-20
Oct. 1, Colorado, 27-3
Oct. 8, South Carolina, 30-6
Oct. 15, Army (at Giants Stadium), 42-0
Oct. 22, USC, 27-6
Oct. 29, Navy, 28-12
Nov. 5, Pittsburgh, 16-21
Nov. 12, Penn State, 30-34
Nov. 19, Air Force, 22-23

Liberty Bowl
Dec. 29, Boston College (at Memphis, Tenn.), 19-18
Record: 7-5-0

1984
Sept. 8, Purdue (at Hoosier Dome, Indianapolis), 21-23
Sept. 15, Michigan State, 24-20
Sept. 22, Colorado, 55-14
Sept. 29, Missouri, 16-14
Oct. 6, Miami, 13-31
Oct. 13, Air Force, 7-21
Oct. 20, South Carolina, 32-36
Oct. 27, LSU, 30-22
Nov. 3, Navy (at Giants Stadium), 18-17
Nov. 17, Penn State, 44-7
Nov. 24, USC, 19-7
Aloha Bowl
Dec. 29, SMU (at Honolulu), 20-27
Record: 7-5-0

1985
Sept. 14, Michigan, 12-20
Sept. 21, Michigan State, 27-10
Sept. 28, Purdue, 17-35
Oct. 5, Air Force, 15-21
Oct. 19, Army, 24-10
Oct. 26, USC, 37-3
Nov. 2, Navy, 41-17
Nov. 9, Mississippi, 37-14
Nov. 16, Penn State, 6-36
Nov. 23, LSU, 7-10
Nov. 30, Miami, 7-58
Record: 5-6-0

1986
Sept. 13, Michigan, 23-24
Sept. 20, Michigan State, 15-20
Sept. 27, Purdue, 41-9
Oct. 4, Alabama, 10-28
Oct. 11, Pittsburgh, 9-10
Oct. 18, Air Force, 31-3
Nov. 1, Navy (at Memorial Stadium, Baltimore), 33-14
Nov. 8, SMU, 61-29
Nov. 15, Penn State, 19-24
Nov. 22, LSU, 19-21
Nov. 29, USC, 38-37
Record: 5-6-0

1987
Sept. 12, Michigan, 26-7
Sept. 19, Michigan State, 31-8

Sept. 26, Purdue, 44-20
Oct. 10, Pittsburgh, 22-30
Oct. 17, Air Force, 35-14
Oct. 24, USC, 26-15
Oct. 31, Navy, 56-13
Nov. 7, Boston College, 32-25
Nov. 14, Alabama, 37-6
Nov. 21, Penn State, 20-21
Nov. 28, Miami, 0-24
Cotton Bowl
Jan. 1, Texas A&M (at Dallas, Tex.), 10-35
Record: 8-4-0

1988
Sept. 10, Michigan, 19-17
Sept. 17, Michigan State, 20-3
Sept. 24, Purdue, 52-7
Oct. 1, Stanford, 42-14
Oct. 8, Pittsburgh, 30-20
Oct. 15, Miami, 31-30
Oct. 22, Air Force, 41-13
Oct. 29, Navy (at Memorial Stadium, Baltimore),
    22-7
Nov. 5, Rice, 54-11
Nov. 19, Penn State, 21-3
Nov. 26, USC, 27-10
Fiesta Bowl
Jan. 2, West Virginia (at Tempe, Ariz.), 34-21
Record: 12-0-0

1989
Aug. 31, Virginia (at Giants Stadium), 36-13
Sept. 16, Michigan, 24-19
Sept. 23, Michigan State, 21-3
Sept. 30, Purdue, 40-7
Oct. 7, Stanford, 27-17
Oct. 14, Air Force, 41-27
Oct. 21, USC, 28-24
Oct. 28, Pittsburgh, 45-7
Nov. 4, Navy, 41-0
Nov. 11, SMU, 59-6
Nov. 18, Penn State, 34-23
Nov. 25, Miami, 10-27
Orange Bowl
Jan. 1, Colorado (at Miami, Fla.), 21-6
Record: 12-1-0

1990
Sept. 15, Michigan, 28-24
Sept. 22, Michigan State, 20-19
Sept. 29, Purdue, 37-11
Oct. 6, Stanford, 31-36

Oct. 13, Air Force, 57-27
Oct. 20, Miami, 29-20
Oct. 27, Pittsburgh, 31-22
Nov. 3, Navy (at Giants Stadium), 52-31
Nov. 10, Tennessee, 34-29
Nov. 17, Penn State, 21-24
Nov. 24, USC, 10-6
Orange Bowl
Jan. 1, Colorado (at Miami, Fla.), 9-10
Record: 9-3-0

1991
Sept. 7, Indiana, 49-27
Sept. 14, Michigan, 14-24
Sept. 21, Michigan State, 49-10
Sept. 28, Purdue, 45-20
Oct. 5, Stanford, 42-26
Oct. 12, Pittsburgh, 42-7
Oct. 19, Air Force, 28-15
Oct. 26, USC, 24-20
Nov. 2, Navy, 38-0
Nov. 9, Tennessee, 34-35
Nov. 16, Penn State, 13-35
Nov. 30, Hawaii, 48-42
Sugar Bowl
Jan. 1, Florida (at New Orleans), 39-28

1992
Sept. 5, Northwestern (at Soldier Field), 42-7
Sept. 12, Michigan, 17-17
Sept. 19, Michigan State, 52-31
Sept. 26, Purdue, 48-0
Oct. 3, Stanford, 16-33
Oct. 10, Pittsburgh, 52-21
Oct. 24, Brigham Young, 42-16
Oct. 31, Navy (at Giants Stadium), 38-7
Nov. 7, Boston College, 54-7
Nov. 14, Penn State, 17-16
Nov. 28, USC, 31-23
Cotton Bowl
Jan. 1, Texas A&M (at Dallas, Tex.), 28-3
Record: 10-1-1

1993
Sept. 4, Northwestern, 27-12
Sept. 11, Michigan, 27-23
Sept. 18, Michigan State, 36-14
Sept. 25, Purdue, 17-0
Oct. 2, Stanford, 48-20
Oct. 9, Pittsburgh, 44-0
Oct. 16, Brigham Young, 45-20
Oct. 23, USC, 31-13

Oct. 30, Navy (at Veterans Stadium, Philadelphia), 58-27
Nov. 13, Florida State, 31-24
Nov. 20, Boston College, 39-41
Cotton Bowl
Jan. 1, Texas A&M (at Dallas, Tex.), 24-21
Record: 11-1-0

1994
Sept. 3, Northwestern (at Soldier Field), 42-15
Sept. 10, Michigan, 24-26
Sept. 17, Michigan State, 21-20
Sept. 24, Purdue, 39-21
Oct. 1, Stanford, 34-15
Oct. 8, Boston College, 11-30
Oct. 15, BYU, 14-21
Oct. 29, Navy, 58-21
Nov. 12, Florida State (at Citrus Bowl, Orlando), 16-23
Nov. 19, Air Force, 42-30

Nov. 26, USC, 17-17
Fiesta Bowl
Jan. 2, Colorado (at Tempe, Ariz.), 24-41
Record: 6-5-1

1995
Sept. 2, Northwestern, 15-17
Sept. 9, Purdue, 35-28
Sept. 16, Vanderbilt, 41-0
Sept. 23, Texas, 55-27
Sept. 30, Ohio State, 26-45
Oct. 7, Washington, 29-21
Oct. 14, Army (at Giants Stadium), 28-27
Oct. 21, USC, 38-10
Oct. 28, Boston College, 20-10
Nov. 4, Navy, 35-17
Nov. 18, Air Force, 44-14
Orange Bowl
Jan. 1, Florida State (at Miami, Fla.), 26-31
Record: 9-3-0